POLITY, FEDERALISM AND GENDER

About the Editors

Prof. (Dr.) M.R. Biju, currently working as Dean, School of Social Sciences and Professor of Public Administration and Policy Studies, Central University of Kerala, Kasaragod. He has served the full term as Dean, School of Social Sciences (2017-2020), School of Legal Studies (2019-2022) and also a short span as Dean, Academic (2020). Prof. M.R. Biju is one of the widely cited writers in the field of Social Sciences with 161 citations and H-index of 6 and i10 index of 3.

Prof. Biju is the Editor of *South Asian Journal of Socio-Political Studies* (*SAJOSPS*), a UGC Listed Journal (No. 34425, dated 11.01.2017 with an impact factor of 3.1028). He is also serving as Editor-in-Chief of *International Journal of Political Science* (*IJOPS*). He is a prolific writer on socio-political and developmental issues.

He has published Thirty Three (33) books, One hundred and Seventy-Five (175) research papers, Seventeen (17) book chapters and 11 (Eleven) Seminar Proceedings. All the books were published by leading publishing houses in New Dehi. He has delivered 78 (Seventy-Eight) Invited Lectures,16 (Sixteen) Key note addresses and reviewed over Nine Hundred books for *South Asian Journal of Socio-Political Studies.*

His teaching and research experience, spanning over three decades, includes several achievements such as completion of three major research projects funded by Ministry of Panchayati Raj, Government of India and University Grants Commission, New Delhi and the post-doctoral fellowship awarded by the UGC in 2004-07. He has also successfully guided doctoral students of the University of Kerala. Seven students are currently pursuing their doctoral studies under his supervision at CUK. He is consistently making professional academic contributions in the capacity of an Associate Board Member of *Economics and Management*, a prestigious journal published by the Technical University of Liberce, Czech Republic; as the Director and Member Secretary of the Asian Institute of Development Research (AIDR); and as a life Member of several Academic and Professional Bodies.

M.R.B. Anantha Padmanabha is currently serving as Deputy Editor of *South Asian Journal of Socio-Political Studies.* He has to his credit a sizeable number of publications in reputed research journals and he has presented papers in National Seminars and Conferences. He is a Doctoral Student in International Relations and Politics of Central University of Kerala, Kasaragod.

POLITY, FEDERALISM AND GENDER

New Narratives

Edited by

M.R. Biju

M.R.B. Anantha Padmanabha

CONCEPT PUBLISHING COMPANY PVT. LTD.
NEW DELHI - 110059

ISBN: 978-93-5594-704-8

First Published 2025

Published and Printed by

Concept Since 1974

Concept Publishing Company Pvt. Ltd.
A/15-16, Commercial Block, Mohan Garden
New Delhi-110059 (India)
T: +91-11-41101460
E: publishing@conceptpub.com, *W*: www.conceptpub.com

Cataloging in Publication--Courtesy: D.K. Agencies (P) Ltd. <docinfo@dkagencies.com>

Polity, federalism and gender : new narratives / edited by M.R. Biju, M.R.B. Anantha Padmanabha.
pages cm
Contributed articles.
Includes bibliographical references and index.
ISBN 9789355947048

1. India--Politics and government. 2. Identity politics--India. 3. Federal government--India. I. Biju, M. R., 1965- editor. II. Anantha Padmanabha, M. R. B., editor.

LCC DS480.84.P65 2025 | DDC 954 23

Preface and Acknowledgements

The Indian polity, with its diverse population and complex socio-cultural fabric, has been a subject of numerous narratives concerning its political structure, federalism, and gender dynamics. These narratives reflect the evolving understanding and interpretation of India's democratic framework and its relationship with federalism and gender equality. The narratives surrounding the Indian polity revolve around its democratic ideals, governance structure, and the role of political institutions. One narrative emphasizes the strength of India's democracy, highlighting its multi-party system, periodic elections, and constitutional safeguards. Proponents argue that despite challenges, Indian democracy has ensured political representation, protected civil liberties, and fostered a culture of political participation. However, critics present an alternative narrative, pointing to issues such as corruption, criminalization of politics, and weak institutional mechanisms. They argue that these challenges hamper the effective functioning of Indian polity, hindering the realization of democratic principles and ideals.

Federalism in India is a critical aspect of the country's governance, as power is shared between the central government and the states. Narratives on Indian federalism often revolve around the balance of power, fiscal autonomy, and regional disparities. Proponents of a strong central government argue that it ensures national integration, uniformity, and effective policy implementation. They stress the need for a centralized approach to maintain national unity in a diverse country like India. On the other hand, proponents of a more decentralized approach emphasize the importance of state autonomy, cultural diversity, and regional development. They argue that a robust federal structure fosters cooperative federalism, enabling states to address their unique challenges and effectively represent local interests.

Narratives on gender dynamics in Indian polity highlight the struggles and progress of women in achieving political representation and gender equality. Historically, women have been underrepresented in politics, and narratives have emerged to address this disparity. Advocates for gender equality argue for increased women's political participation, reservation of seats for women in legislatures, and policy reforms to empower women economically and socially.

However, these narratives also intersect with other factors such as caste, religion, and socio-economic status. Intersectional narratives shed light on the diverse experiences and challenges faced by women belonging to marginalized communities, emphasizing the need for inclusive policies and targeted interventions.

The narratives surrounding Indian polity, federalism, and gender reflect the diverse perspectives and debates within the country's socio-political landscape. These narratives shape public discourse, policy formulation, and societal progress. While some narratives emphasize the achievements and strengths of Indian democracy, federalism, and gender equality, others highlight the existing challenges and areas for improvement. Understanding and engaging with these narratives is essential for fostering an inclusive and equitable society. By acknowledging the complexities and nuances within each domain, policymakers and stakeholders can work towards strengthening democratic institutions, balancing power dynamics, and promoting gender equality in India's polity.

Keeping this in background, this volume presents two dozen studies on wide range of issues which are broadly categorized under four parts. The introductory part presents seven chapters focusing on neo-liberal instrumentality, identity politics, subaltern resistance, women's subjectivity, the right to offend, sedition culture and Citizen's Amendment Act. It is followed by Part II, captioned contemporary political discourses. The topics of discussion in this part include new narratives on contemporary Indian polity, constitution for the masses, democracy and insurrection and developmental gap and statehood formation. Part III focuses on issues confronted with federalism which include cooperative federalism, fiscal federalism, finances of southern states and financial self-reliance of common people. Part IV is titled democracy and governance in practice which include studies on the first five years of Modi regime, personalized foreign policy, maritime security, nuclear policy, strategic matter, electoral politics etc.

Before concluding, the volume editors, would like to add that through these research papers and articles from the academics and researchers, they have tried to examine the varied aspects of Indian polity, economy and society. Apart from the academic enquiries, the researchers have tried to put forward practical and pragmatic suggestions to recast the system, which may be useful for the students, researchers, practitioners and policymakers in the field. These prefatory remarks remain incomplete without expressing our gratitude to those who have been kind enough to help us in the preparation of this volume. First of all, we would like to thank our esteemed contributors to this anthology of articles. Similarly, we are extremely thankful to Sri Ashok Kumar Mittal, Managing Director of Concept Publishing Company Pvt. Ltd., New Delhi, who brought out the volume in an elegant form.

M.R. Biju
M.R.B. Anantha Padmanabha

Introduction

The Indian polity, with its diverse population and complex socio-cultural fabric, has been a subject of numerous narratives concerning its political structure, federalism, and gender dynamics. These narratives reflect the evolving understanding and interpretation of India's democratic framework and its relationship with federalism and gender equality. The narratives surrounding the Indian polity revolve around its democratic ideals, governance structure, and the role of political institutions. One narrative emphasizes the strength of India's democracy, highlighting its multi-party system, periodic elections, and constitutional safeguards. Proponents argue that despite challenges, Indian democracy has ensured political representation, protected civil liberties, and fostered a culture of political participation. However, critics present an alternative narrative, pointing to issues such as corruption, criminalization of politics, and weak institutional mechanisms. They argue that these challenges hamper the effective functioning of Indian polity, hindering the realization of democratic principles and ideals.

Federalism in India: Federalism in India is a critical aspect of the country's governance, as power is shared between the central government and the states. Narratives on Indian federalism often revolve around the balance of power, fiscal autonomy, and regional disparities. Proponents of a strong central government argue that it ensures national integration, uniformity, and effective policy implementation. They stress the need for a centralized approach to maintain national unity in a diverse country like India. On the other hand, proponents of a more decentralized approach emphasize the importance of state autonomy, cultural diversity, and regional development. They argue that a robust federal structure fosters cooperative federalism, enabling states to address their unique challenges and effectively represent local interests.

Gender Dynamics: Narratives on gender dynamics in Indian polity highlight the struggles and progress of women in achieving political representation and gender equality. Historically, women have been underrepresented in politics, and narratives have emerged to address this disparity. Advocates for gender equality argue for increased women's political participation, reservation of seats for women in legislatures, and policy reforms to empower women economically and socially. However, these narratives also intersect with other factors such as caste, religion, and socio-economic status. Intersectional narratives shed light on the diverse experiences and challenges faced by women belonging to marginalized communities, emphasizing the need for inclusive policies and targeted interventions.

The narratives surrounding Indian polity, federalism, and gender reflect the diverse perspectives and debates within the country's socio-political landscape. These narratives shape public discourse, policy formulation, and societal progress. While some narratives emphasize the achievements and strengths of Indian democracy, federalism, and gender equality, others highlight the existing challenges and areas for improvement. Understanding and engaging with these narratives is essential for fostering an inclusive and equitable society. By acknowledging the complexities and nuances within each domain, policymakers and stakeholders can work towards strengthening democratic institutions, balancing power dynamics, and promoting gender equality in India's polity.

Content of the Volume

Keeping this in background, this volume presents two dozen studies on wide range of issues which are broadly categorized under four parts. The introductory part presents seven chapters focusing on neo-liberal instrumentality, identity politics, subaltern resistance, women's subjectivity, the right to offend, sedition culture and Citizen's Amendment Act. It is followed by Part II, captioned contemporary political discourses. The topics of discussion in this part include new narratives on contemporary Indian polity, constitution for the masses, democracy and insurrection and developmental gap and statehood formation. Part III focusses on issues confronted with federalism which include cooperative federalism, fiscal federalism, finances of southern states and financial self-reliance of common people. Part IV is titled democracy and governance in practice which include studies on the first five years of Modi regime, personalized foreign policy, maritime security, nuclear policy, strategic matter, electoral politics etc.

In the **inaugural chapter of Part I**, **Arindam Roy** presents a study on exploring neo-liberal instrumentality in the governance. According to Arindam, unlike most of the literatures which primarily concentrate on what is governance, how better it can be conceptualized/managed, and what are the parameters of it; the present chapter moots a rather unsettling existential question as to why governance came into being in the first place. In course of analysis the chapter argues that the concept of governance, especially the way it is understood by the donee countries, is a neoliberal construction of furthering its dream of unification of global markets by downsizing state on the one hand, and establishing mechanism for ensuring the repayment of loan amounts from the regions suffering the 'failed state syndrome' on the other, without strengthening the structure or institution of state. In short, this study views that the origin, maturation, trepidation and ramifications of the concept of governance is inherently associated with neoliberalism. Hence, the time has come to demystify the concept of governance and interrogate the neoliberal motives before adopting it.

In **Chapter 2, Monika Tiwari** and **Vinod Khobragade** examines the intersection of identity with politics. The study is based on refugees in India. According to the authors, the world is witnessing a wide range of wars, causing increase in displacements globally. Each year, the number of refugees is rising rapidly, making it a serious socio-political and humanitarian crisis. In this lieu of the events, India has been hosting refugees since independence. India, over the years, has faced more refugees than ever due to instability and socio-political persecutions in neighbouring countries, such as Bangladesh, Tibet, Afghanistan, Myanmar and Sri Lanka. Yet, India has not developed any national policy or law for dealing with the refugee influx. The absence of law has made stand of government more situational and political rather uniform and consistent, which has increased uncertainty over the refugee rights and refoulement under customary International law. The recent Citizenship Amendment Bill has also increased the fault lines in dealing with the refugee crisis. In short, this study is an attempt to assess the current situation of refugee influx in India and to analyze the stand of Indian government over the years towards the refugee crisis. It suggests for framing National Refugee policy to address the gravity of the matter.

In **Chapter 3**, **Phulmoni Das** has made a critical appraisal of the subaltern resistance in India. It is a case study of the identity movement of the Tea Garden Community of Assam. According to Das, Subaltern resistance led by the subaltern groups is not new phenomenon to Indian history as it has been deeply marked in a long historical time. But the struggles of the subaltern groups have not been added to the mainstream discourses of history writing for quite some time. It was the initiative of the Subaltern Studies Group who first tried to make a serious attempt to trace the missing linkages of Subaltern struggle and to bring it to the mainstream discourses. Indian politics is marked by the influence of different subaltern movements led by different subaltern groups such as *dalits*, *adivasis*, rural landless, tribals, minorities etc. This study is an attempt to trace out the theoretical understanding of the subaltern resistances in India since colonial period. India also has been witnessing the proliferation of subaltern movements in post-Independent period. In her study, the author also tries to highlight, the quest for identity movement of the tea garden community of Assam, as this community has been recognized as the one of the most marginal and depressed groups of section. Based on their marginality and subalternity this community is referred as subaltern. Deprivation of this identity has led to another phase of movement among the tea garden community of Assam. Ever since India became independent these people lost their Scheduled Tribe status in Assam and thus they were deprived of their educational, economic and political privileges guaranteed by the Constitution of India.

Interrogating women's subjectivity in the political discourses is the central theme of discussion in **Chapter 4**, which is contributed by

Nisha Jain. The focus of this study is to probe how the construction of a women subject takes place who accepts her femininity as natural. That way she not only makes it possible to be dominated more easily but she actually becomes an agency of her own oppression. According to the author, Social and Political theory has addressed itself to the question of subjectivity, complex formation of self and the exercise of power through the process of internalization of dominant cultural values. The subjectivity of women cannot be explained with reference to oppression perpetuated by few or many misogynists in the modern societies. The subjectivity is not a function of an external disciplinary power. There is no individual formally empowered to wield disciplinary power charged with the production of a properly embodied femininity—it is much more dispersed and anonymous. Psychological oppression is institutionalized and systematic. It is invested in everyone and no one in particular; women and men alike are ideologically mystified by the dominant pattern. It breaks the spirit of dominated and by rendering them incapable of understanding the nature of those agencies responsible for their subjugation and oppression. This way it serves to make the work of domination easier. In fact, the gendered relations are internalized and are incorporated into the structure of the self. Social structure, cultural norms, and value systems based on the concept of patriarchy influence social expectation regarding the behaviour of both men and women and determine the women's role and position in the society. It is maintained that the subject is a product of institutions, practices and value systems. The question of subjectivity has formed the focus of many social and cultural theorists. Gramsci, Allthusser, and Foucault specifically have contributed to the understanding of the concept.

In **Chapter 5**, **Santhosh Mathew** has made an academic enquiry on the sedition culture and consecutive press freedom index in South Asia. The chapter aims to address one of the most Polarising concepts in India today "Right to Offend". To the author, two events have fuelled this question. Firstly, the Supreme Court attempts in aligning with the collective conscience to remove the sedition law. Secondly, the fall of India and consecutively South Asia's ranking in World Press Freedom Index 2022. Along with increasing number of sedition which is often connotated in a security dimension and used as a weapon by governments to suppress dissent, it also becomes imperative to take note of the rise in ideological and religious extremism in South Asia caused simply by "offensive activities". This poses a question, that should a person have the right to offend anyone as an extension to their own freedom ? or should there be restrictions to speech for promoting harmony and democracy?

In **Chapter 6, Deepak Kumar Pandey** examines state assembly resolutions against the Citizenship Amendment Act. In this study, CAA is taken as a reference case to testify the theoretical nuances of federal theory prevailing in India. According to Pandey, during the CAA protests at Delhi, the idea of citizenship and power of union regarding legislation about citizenship and its applicability across pan India, especially in non-BJP ruling states, brought some serious issues into the debate of Indian polity. The federal structure with assigned subjects, as designed by the constitution makers and which further evolved is being challenged by political actors from those political parties which are in opposition of centre. Though the number of opposing states is comparatively less in number, but it brings some serious questions to think over. In the backdrop of the Citizenship Amendment Act and protests against it in certain areas, this chapter attempts to look into the wider issue of centre-state relationship and its implications on the Indian Polity.

Part II of this book commences with two studies. The first one is titled, 'New Narratives in Contemporary India' and the second one is captioned 'Constitution for the Masses'. Both chapters were contributed by **G. Palanithurai**. In **Chapter 7**, the author states that rural life and livelihood conditions are stressful and they have to struggle for their survival. At the same time, they are being exploited by industrial and market forces. By exploiting the rural masses, the urban centres are enriching and achieving prosperity. On the other hand, pastoral communities are facing severe problems because of vagaries of monsoon. Farming communitites are in debt trap and committing suicides. Craft communities also lost their livelihood. Tribal communities are driven from the forest by the market and state forces to exploit minerals. Fishing communities are also facing severe crisis. Villages are moving towards extinction. He further adds that political parties have miserably failed in democratising society and as a result Indian democracy still in political democracy, that too, at a minimal level, leaving the social democracy unattended by the political parties. They have failed miserably in mitigating the anti-thetical forces to democracy and instead they fuelled the forces to remain active as they used caste and religion as fundamental factors for both political mobilisation and electoral gains.

The author further adds that, all the failures of the left and centrist wing political parties enabled the right wing parties to take politics to a new arena called development politics. In order to achieve the electoral success, market approach was adopted and thereby they have weakened the parties which were in power by accusing them on the issue of large scale corruption. The new middle class which hugely benefited out of globalization of economy joined in the right wing group by seeing the emergence of the right wing parties in the world and worked for the success of the party in the election in India.

According to Palanithurai, Values which had been in active usage for political mobilization during the freedom struggle and at the dawn of Independence have been adopted to create a new consciousness called "Nation First" by the right wing party. It gives a signal message that the country is not safe and enemies are within and outside to weaken the Nation and this party is taking steps to safeguard the nation by building a new consciousness among the people. Corruption has dismantled the fundamentals of the nation and it is to be rooted out from this country. In such a way a new consciousness has been created. It is presumed that it is an alternative. It is only a political alternative. India needs to move from party politics to people's politics. For this alternative politics M.K. Gandhi has much to contribute. To perpetuate people's politics, the cost of politics has to be reduced and the political parties have to reorient their parties from market oriented approach to people-centric approach. The author concludes his study by stating that the slowdown of political socialization has kept the youth away from ideological orientation without perspective. Hence, there is huge perception gap in terms of politics between generations. A new political culture has to be created to enable the people to participate in the process of development, governance and democracy.

As cited earlier, in **Chapter 8**, **Palanithurai** presented another study titled, Constitution for the Masses. According to the author, "a constitution is an approved document created by a human group living in a defined territory in the Modern State system to regulate, modernize and develop the society through a process of governance by the state apparatus. It works in accordance with its capacity to cope up with the requirements and expectations of the society. To handle the Constitution, the state machinery and its operators should have the needed capacity and thereby the expected outcome could be achieved. In the same way, the people or the citizens should have capacity to get best advantage of the constitution."

He further adds that India through its freedom struggle, has shown to the world that through a non-violent peaceful struggle, liberation could be achieved. By following India within 20 years, 45 countries have liberated themselves without much bloodshed. The leaders who led the freedom struggle and who laid foundation for the new nation with a clearcut foresight and forethought created a vibrant rigid and flexible constitution with a resilience to respond to any pressure. Beyond the Institutions they have created the value system to be followed to run the system of governance and administration. A constitution in a country like India sustaining for 70 years in the backdrop of unimaginable differences, diversities, disparities and discriminations, is not a small achievement. It keeps India together, makes the people to have faith in the democratic system. It provides opportunity for the people to raise questions and challenge government when they face problem and through a process of dialogue and negotiation problems could be solved. As generations have passed, the degeneration sets in politics and as a result the constitutional values have been abrogated and abdicated. Governing the vast country of this size with wide variations, diversities, differences, disparities, discriminations is a very big challenge. Many of the occasions, violations of the constitutional values and provisions have been done only by the state authorities and not by ordinary people. The political parties instead of perpetuating development politics to bring unity among the collectivities, they use caste and religion to mobilize people for election and thereby cleavages among the social groups have been created and widened. As a result, Indian democracy could not move beyond a minimal point in a scale of democracy.

The seasoned researcher further states that continuously people are demanding the state to achieve social and economic democracy to make the political democracy meaningful. In the seventy years of democratic governance enabling provisions have been made through enacting legislations and amending the constitutions to help and protect the poor, marginalized and minorities. Development has been made as rights and a bundle of rights have been granted with schemes for development with huge outlays. To empower the people a new governance arrangement has been made through the historic Amendments (73rd and 74th) nearer to the community and through which people could claim their legitimate entitlements in a dignified way. Yet while assessing the impact of all those initiatives, one could see only a minimum outcome and identify a wide variety of barriers to achieve maximum outcome. It needs an alternative path in governance and development. It needs an alternative politics to party politics. A new kind of democratic practice has to be developed negating the party politics. It could be done at the grassroots and wherefrom clearing of polity could be done.

In **Chapter 9**, **Nayakara Veeresha** presents a study on Democracy and Insurrection based on Sukma District of Chhattisgarh state. To her, insurrections are consequences, but not the causes. The causes of the insurrection are multidimensional. Among all the causative factors democracy and governance are critical though other aspects play an influential role in bringing the historical moments of insurrection. Indian democracy is facing the insurrection popularly known as Left Wing Extremism or Maoism. The failure of parliamentary politics and the Indian States have laid the platform for insurrections in Central India. With the help of electoral data on voter participation in three-tiers of governance of Konta Tahsil in Sukma district of Chhattisgarh State, this chapter finds that although there is an electoral legitimacy at State and National levels; it has not been able to transform the ideals of democracy at grassroots politics. The resilience of Indian democracy has the potential to accommodate the insurrection of Central India within the ambit of the legitimate demands of rights and justice of her own citizens in particularly the *adivasis*.

In **Chapter 10**, **K. Vidyasagar Reddy** presents a debate on the developmental gap and its impact on the statehood formation. This chapter is about debating the developmental strategies that would help the new states to achieve the promised development. According to Reddy, debates over developmental notions assume significance when regional disparities exist in various states in India. Different regions of states cannot look alike, geographically and development-wise, so similar pattern of development is unanticipated, nor it is feasible. Based on the local resources and needs, the developmental strategies have to be formulated and implemented. Whenever the state and governments assume the responsibility of balancing the interests of different regions, both advanced and backward, then there cannot be scope for regional inequality. But in the name of democratic governance, usually the numerically dominant regions would seek better development than the others and even at the cost of the latter. Obviously, the interests of both regions would become conflicting at times. In a way, it is about developmental gap that leads to the rise of statehood movements as it happened in more than a dozen states in India. While four such movements got materialised into the formation of new states in the last two decades, many more are anxious about their fate. Of all the factors that contributed for the rise of statehood movements, development gap as part of intra-state differences had become the main bone of contention and that paved the way for organising the mass movements in some states.

In **Chapter 11**, **Naviya Antony K.** and **A. Shahin Sultana** explored about psychological well-being and perceived social support among young adults. According to the authors, the psychological well-being (PWB) and Perceived Social Support (PSS) of 219 (male= 102, female=117) young adults (age between 20 and 28) were examined. Young adults completed the Ryff's scale of Psychological well-being (Ryff, 1989,1995) and the Multidimensional scale of perceived social support (Zimet *et al.*, 1988). The relationship between the study variables and their domains were also investigated using Pearson's Correlation. The independent t-test has been used to see the gender differences in the domains of psychological well-being and perceived social support. To test the moderation effect of gender on the relationship between the dependent variable PWB and the independent variable PSS, hierarchical regression analysis has been used by forming the product term gender × perceived social support. The independent t-test showed significant mean difference in the domain of Environmental mastery (PWB) and perceived social support from friends (PSS). Moderation analysis showed significant moderation effect of gender on the relationship between PSS and PWB.

Part III of the volume opens with a study on the role of Governor in cooperative federalism, which is presented by **Sandeep Inampudi**. He has made an innovative enquiry which examines the changing nature of the Governor's role in independent India and its relevance and challenges in contemporary times. To Sandeep, the office of the governor carries the legacy of colonial administration in India where power structures were centred around the office of the Governor-General. Though the makers of the constitution retained the office of the governor, its powers were reduced significantly and was converted into the nominal head of the state. To meet the political exigencies of the newly independent state and to uphold the spirit of democracy, the office of the governor was given an inferior position compared to that of the democratically "elected council of ministers" of the state. According to the constitution, the governor's office serves as a channel of communication between the "central government and the state", an agent of the central government in the state, and the state is equivalent of India's President. In his study, the author adds that the powers and duties of the governor were not questioned or challenged during the first two decades following independence because of the political predominance of the Indian National Congress and one-party rule in both the central government and in the states. Since a single party ruled the centre and almost all the states, the country functioned as a unitary state in practice. However, after the death of Nehru, the dominance of the Indian National Congress (INC) diminished gradually and regional parties started showing their presence in the national scene heralding the arrival of an era of coalition politics in the country. In this changed premises, the states started perceiving the office of the governor as centre's encroachment into state administration and they began to question the intervention of the governor in the affairs of the state. The mode of appointment of the governor, his power to reserve state bills for presidential consideration, his role in the declaration of a state emergency and his discretion in the appointment of vice-chancellors of state universities all became bones of contention and the political tug of war reached even the Supreme Court leading to long fought legal battles. Despite these political controversies, the "Sarkaria Commission (1988) and the Punchhi Commission (2010)" made recommendations on strengthening the position of the Governor. But from 2014 onwards, the political dynamics of the country has changed significantly with a strong one-party dominated coalition government at the Union, the States ruled by regional parties and a weak opposition. With the states demanding equal opportunities, resources and policy prioritisation in their favour, it has led to a post-cooperative federalist scenario where political debates surrounding the office of the governor is getting intensified.

The impact of pandemic on fiscal federalism is the central theme of discussion in **Chapter 13** which is contributed by **Biju Lekshmanan**. According to the author, the outbreak of COVID-19 pandemic severely affected the already damaged fiscal relations between the Centre and the States in India. Centre's apathy to take proactive initiatives to address the challenges posed by the pandemic created a significant loss of trust towards the Union Government by the states. The Centre's expressed unwillingness to face the financial consequences of its own strategic decisions damaged the political and moral foundations of the federalism. Demand for more fiscal autonomy to states by redefining India's fiscal federalism and strengthening of local governments with sufficient fiscal capacity is highlighted as the solution to address the unique socio-economic challenges in the post-pandemic India.

After presenting two studies on cooperative federalism and fiscal federalism, **Jerry Alwin**, in **Chapter 14** presents an analytical enquiry on the finances of southern States in India. In this study, Jerry tried to examine the finances of Andhra Pradesh, Karnataka, Kerala, Tamil Nadu and Telangana during the period 2009-10 to 2019-20. According to the author, in the southern States, there is considerable difference in the fiscal situation in terms of fiscal indicators, social sector expenditure and development expenditure. The factors influencing the growth rate of revenue receipts are issues related to implementation of GST, issues related to collection of non-tax revenue and devolution of taxes and grants according to recommendations of the UFCs. Persistent high level of revenue deficit forces the states such as Andhra Pradesh, Kerala and Tamil Nadu to rely on borrowings to meet revenue expenditure. This has weakened the fiscal capacity for spending on capital items, development and social sectors and has pushed these states to fiscal crisis.

In **Chapter 15**, **Arindam Gupta** examines the issues connected with financial self-reliance of the common mass. The study is based on the clarion call in the name of *Atmanirbhar Bharat Abhiyan*. According to Arindam, *Atmanirbhar* is no new term if introspected but it matters when and how a term is getting used. Moreover, in the backdrop of a gloomy environment particularly encompassing the economy and health during the peak of the COVID-19 wave, the main objective of the Prime Minister must have been to deliver a vision for turning around the gloominess. It imbibes to a great extent the country's urgent need of self-reliance based on its own unused capacity and a little support from the fellow citizens who are capable of providing so. Later, in course of time, it turns into a concept which is extended to education with the announcement of National Education Policy, 2020 in July 2020 and also with announcements in the banking sector adding features to the existing schemes with attempts to make the people financially more stable. A country's self-reliance cannot be achieved if internally the people of the country suffer from poverty and if the common people remain financially excluded. The following sections of the chapter deal with two distinguished government schemes, *Pradhan Mantri Jan Dhan Yojana* (PMJDY) as announced on 15th August, 2014 and *Pradhan Mantri Mudra Yojana* (PMMY) as announced on 8th April, 2015, to examine to what extent those schemes help the people of the country to become financially "self-reliant". Also digital financial inclusion in the country and issue of entrepreneurship to promote self-employment is discussed.

Part IV of the volume, starts with a study by **Sartik Bagh** (**Chapter 16**). It is an analytical enquiry on the performance of Narendra Modi government from 2014-2019. According to Sartik, the NDA came to power in a time of crisis plagued by corruption and mis-governance of the UPA. During the electoral campaign Modi presented a grand vision for the country. The mandate Modi got in 2014 Lok Sabha elections was impressive. Though a strong, stable and decisive government emerged at the Centre, the performance and functioning of government remained short of the lofty promises Modi made during the elections. Rather his regime witnessed an environment of intolerance, hatred and intimidation leading to many far-reaching consequences for a country which swears in the name of democracy.

In **Chapter 17**, **Vinod Khobragade** made an academic enquiry on the personalized foreign policy of India. According to Vinod, after J.N. Nehru and Indira Gandhi as Prime Ministers of India, Narendra Modi earned great appreciation in the realm of India's foreign affairs. His foreign policy transformations have invited both praise and criticisms domestically and globally as well. Like Nehru and Gandhi, Modi also applied personal calibres in reshaping India's foreign policy. Through this study, attempts are made in mapping the reflection of Modi's personality factor in India's foreign policy such as his 'militaristic approach' against hostile Pakistan. This study also critically looks into India's neighbourhood first policy, India's multilateralism and India's engagement with the major powers especially Russia, the US and China.

Ramesh Kumar in **Chapter 18**, evaluates the issues and challenges pertaining to India's maritime security. This study also examines how these developments and difficulties have influenced India's assessment of maritime security in the Indian Ocean section, as well as how India has developed its strategy to address them? According to the researcher, the Indian Ocean Region handles the majority of India's trade and energy supplies (IOR). The ocean is said to carry the majority of India's trade. As a result, safeguarding the marine region is unavoidable. Apart from this, India's location makes marine security a major worry for policymakers in the country. India has a 7,517-kilometre coastline. Within the continent, there are 5,422 kilometres. Andaman and Nicobar have a coastline of 1962 kilometres, whereas Lakshadweep has a shoreline of 132 kilometers. Piracy, illegal landing of guns and explosives, infiltration, use of the sea and off-shore islands for criminal activity, drug and human trafficking and smuggling are just some of the threats that this extensive coastline poses. The lack of physical barriers along the coast, as well as the presence of critical businesses such as ports and critical defence facilities like as RADARs and nuclear reactors, increases the danger and the necessity to secure its coastal territory. Furthermore, the author adds that there is a need to safeguard the ocean's resources in a long-term way. Traded products and services are delivered to land *via* ports located around the country and along the coastline.

Dipanker Dey in **Chapter 19** made an academic journey through India's maritime connectivity linked with Bay of Bengal. To Dipankar, maritime connectivity has increasingly grown across the Ocean, especially to make it easier to boost economic transit, strategic interdependency, and logistic support. In this context, the Bay of Bengal remained significant for connecting entire South Asia to Southeast Asian countries. In detail, the Bay of Bengal lies at the core of the Indo-Pacific, and its subsidiary, the Andaman Sea, acts as India's Geo-strategic gateway pass in the region. India has referred to the Indo-Pacific as a free, open, inclusive and rule-based order to respect all nations' sovereignty and territorial integrity. The strategic capability and capacity significantly influence to the maritime connectivity. Therefore, this study presents the different dimensions of India's maritime connectivity and security implication for regional integration. Moreover, it also critically analyses that how India's maritime connectivity and security initiatives primarily benefited the Bay of Bengal to enhance India's partnership towards both immediate and extended neighbours.

India's nuclear policy and its strategic implications for regional security in South Asia is the theme of discussion in **Chapter 20**, which is presented by **Pavithran, K.S.** According to the author, nuclear weapons are the most crucial factor which influenced the course of international politics and diplomacy in the last few decades. Since the advent of nuclear weapons, they have become a symbol of power and prestige among the nations of the world. Nuclear power, according to the author, gives the nation that has it, prestige in world politics and psychological leverage in dealing with both friends and foes. However, India's attitude to nuclear weapons has been marked by ambivalence. There was a gap of 24 years in between India's first test of nuclear weapons at Pokhran in 1974 and the second set of tests in 1998. Pakistan also conducted nuclear detonations in 1998. The nuclear capabilities of both India and Pakistan are factors of importance in determining the regional security in South Asia.

In **Chapter 21**, **Lawrence Prabhakar Williams**, **Pooja Raghavan** and **Trishna Rai** present a study on India's strategic interest in SAARC countries. South Asia, according to the researchers, is an eccentric region defaced by inter-state provocation, various disputes and several absurdities.The study has been arranged in the following sequence—an overview of the conceptual framework of soft power, transition of power in India's foreign policy towards other South Asian countries, assess India's foreign policy towards South Asia before the formation of SAARC and focuses on India's stand after the establishment of SAARC. The concluding part presents the future prospects of the regional organisation.

The concluding part is titled 'Democracy in Practice', which contains three studies. The first one is contributed by **Phulmoni Das** and **Robin Hazarika**. It is an analysis of the Assembly Elections, 2021 in the state of Assam. It is an attempt to understand BJP's return to power to the state politics of Assam and also evaluates the major factors, which helped the party for its victory. According to the authors, electoral politics of Assam has been witnessing different dimensions since its independence. It was the Congress which dominated the electoral politics of late British and the early post-Independence period. Till 1996, the party had suffered defeat only in 1978 and 1985 assembly elections. But the electoral politics of the state since 1985 became a turning point in Assam politics. It was the period which seen the debacle of Congress and it also coincided with the emergence of community based smaller parties often called regional parties. The one party dominant system was giving way to a multi-party system in which political parties of various ethnic groups or smaller cultural communities began to play a significant role. This period also showed the emergence of Bharatiya Janata Party (BJP) which is also gradually playing a significant electoral force in the politics of the state. It is in this context the rise of BJP in the politics of the state can be contextualised.

Chapter 23 is also an analysis on the assembly election 2021 in the state of Kerala, which is contributed by the volume editors. According to the authors, "The assembly polls to Kerala" has generally treated as an indicative of a new social compact that is taking place in the state and it could also mark as a realignment of Kerala's political landscape.

The Congress led United Democratic Front (UDF), the CPI(M) led Left Democratic Front (LDF) and the BJP led National Democratic Alliance (NDA) were all betting on an outsize impact by putting their respective political ideals and agendas. The BJP, long seen as a North Indian Political Party has made significant inroads in Kerala in the recent past and hoping to emerge as a third alternative through social engineering that includes wooing a section of the Christians. But the CPI(M) led LDF was experimenting with daring political moves to win a second term which is quite unusual in the state. After presenting a detailed study on the theme, the authors concluded their study with the following observations:

- The overall poll analysis undoubtedly shows that a mix of policies in which development and welfare measures were added in the right proportion and executed over the last 60 months paved the way for the spectacular victory of the LDF. It is a new experience in the state politics after 1977. In other words, the present victory of the LDF can be described as a well thought out political strategy coupled with political pragmatism and social engineering which helped the LDF to capture power. Certainly, the entry of Loktantrik Janata Dal (LJD) and Kerala Congress (Mani), the formal induction of Indian National League (INL), the popularity of Pinarayi Vijayan in handling the governance in times of crisis and calamities and the goodwill generated through social security measures especially welfare pension scheme, distribution of food kits through ration shops have helped the Left in an enormous way. Further right from the implementation of Nava Kerala Mission Projects to bring remarkable changes in the education and health sectors and to provide housing for the poor under Life Mission Project which also paid rich dividends for the Left. Over and above Pinarayi also made some daring moves in social engineering.
- Yet another reason for the spectacular return of the LDF was that after the humiliating defeat in the Lok Sabha Poll 2019, the LDF took a strategic retreat in the Sabarimala Women's Entry Issue. The civic polls held in November 2020 was the testing ground for this strategy and the Left made huge gains

out of it. The more accommodative stand cured the hurt feeling of majority communities and the reading of the assembly poll results makes it clear that the LDF could win the sizeable number of Hindu votes along with minority votes that had mobilized through strong stands taken during issues such as beef ban and Citizen's Amendment Act etc.

- Though the BJP projected themselves as a challenge to the state's bipolar polity, the party miserably failed even to retain its lone seat. Despite working out a Nair-Ezhava binary and securing confidence of a section of Christian community, the party could not hold on. Multiple factors led to poor performance of the party. Generally, the BJP or NDA was unable to match the social base of either the CPI (M) or the Congress. The poll results were nothing but a total washout of the BJP and NDA from the state of Kerala.
- The NDA's vote share in the state had climbed from 6.6 per cent in 2011 Assembly polls to 14.96 per cent in 2016 after BDJS joined its fold. However, its vote share declined to 12.04 per cent in 2021. The vote share of BDJS declined from 3.93 per cent in 2016 to 1 per cent in 2021. It seems that a sizable section of Ezhava voters who were with the Left parties before the formation of BDJS have now returned to their mother fold.
- This electoral predict can also be treated as a reply to the critics of the CM within the party and Left Front who were baiting for his blood after the 2019 Lok Sabha poll setback. It has come as a major morale booster for both CPM and CPI which have been reduced to a mere patch in the national political scenario, but also gives hopes of a re-emergence.

In conclusion it can be stated that Pinarayi Vijayan broke a long term jinx that prevented any incumbent from retaining power beyond a single term in the state. The state-wise picture shows that the LDF was triumphant in both southern and central regions of the state but came a bit short in the northern region. Before conclude it can be added that no doubt the second Pinarayi government will have to deal with a series of challenges from the day of its entry. The worsening COVID situation, the unpleasant fiscal position of the state and above all the group rivalry within the CPI (M) will certainly pose threat to the Chief Minister.

The determinants of voting behaviour of the electorate is the focus of enquiry in the concluding chapter which is contributed by **Manjunatha, K.V.** According to him, voting is the life blood of democracy due to citizens elect their representatives through the elections for forming a better government. People uses voting as a mode of interacting their acceptance or rejection to governmental policies. Voting behaviour denotes to the responses of citizens related to participating in the elections that take place for electing members or their representatives of their local, regional, or national government. Voting behaviour, according to the author, is determined by different forces such as gender, race and pressure groups, religions and communities, the influence of money or charismatic personality of a leader etc.

Before conclude, the volume editors would like to add that through these two dozen research papers and articles, the respective authors tried to explore and examine the fundamental issues confronted by Indian polity, society and economy. No doubt, the contributors, apart from, presenting the issues and concerns, tried to present solid suggestions to revitalise the whole system, which may be useful for the students, researchers and practitioners in the field.

M.R. Biju
M.R.B. Anantha Padmanabha

Contents

Part IV
Democracy and Governance in Practice

List of Contributors

A. Shahin Sultana (Dr.), Professor, Department of Social Work, Social Sciences and International Studies, Pondicherry University, Puducherry. **Email:** shahin.samaroh@gmail.com

Arindam Gupta (Dr.), Professor of Commerce, Vidyasagar University, Midnapur, West Bengal. **Email:** arindamgupta69@gmail.com

Arindam Roy (Dr.), Associate Professor of Political Science, The University of Burdwan, Burdwan, West Bengal. **Email:** arindambu.du@gmail.com

Biju Lekshmanan (Dr.), Professor, Department of Gandhian Studies, Mahatma Gandhi University, Kottayam, Kerala. **Email:** bijulekshmanan@gmail.com

Deepak Kumar Pandey (Dr.), Associate Professor, Legal Cell, Regional Office, Directorate of Higher Education, Dehradun. **Email:** deepakbanti@gmail.com

Dipankar Dey (Dr.), Assistant Professor, Department of Political Science, Central University of Andhra Pradesh, Ananthapur, Andhra Pradesh. **Email:** dipankar833@gmail.com

G. Palanithurai (Dr.), Professor (Retd.), Rajiv Gandhi Chair, The Gandhigram Rural Institute, Gandhigram. **Email:** gpalanithurai@gmail.com

Jerry Alwin (Dr.), Assistant Professor, Department of Economics, Sree Narayana College, Varkala. **Email:** jerryalwin@gmail.com

K.V. Manjunatha, Assistant Professor & Principal, Department of Political Science, Government First Grade College, Srinivaspur. **Email:** kvmanjulekshmi@gmail.com

K. Vidyasagar Reddy (Dr.), Department of Political Science, Mizoram University, Aizawl. **Email:** kvidyasagarr@gmail.com

K.S. Pavithran (Dr.), Formerly, Professor and Head, Department of Political Science, University of Calicut, Kerala. **Email:** drkspavithran@gmail.com

Lawrence Prabhakar Williams (Dr.), Associate Professor, Department of Political Science, Madras Christian College, University of Madras, Chennai. **Email:** lawrence.prabhakar@gmail.com

M.R. Biju (Dr.), Dean, School of Social Sciences, Department of Public Administration and Policy Studies, Central University of Kerala, Kasargode, Kerala.

M.R.B. Anantha Padmanabha, Deputy Editor, South Asian Journal of Socio-Political Studies.

Monika Tiwari (Dr.), Assistant Professor, Department of Sociology & Political Science, Dayalbagh Educational Institute (Deemed University), Agra, Uttar Pradesh. **Email:** vinod_d2003@yahoo.com

Naviya Antony K. (Dr.), Ph.D. Scholar, Department of Social Work, Social Sciences and International Studies, Pondicherry University, Puducherry. **Email:** navyaantony47@gmail.com

Nayakara Veeresha, Ph.D. Scholar, Centre for Political Institution, Governance and Development, Institute for Social and Economic Change (ISEC), Bengaluru. **Email:** nayakaraveeresha@gmail.com

Nisha Jain (Dr.), Assistant Professor of Political Science, Panjab University Regional Centre, Sri Muktsar Sahib, Punjab. **Email:** nishajain14@gmail.com

Phulmoni Das (Dr.), Assistant Professor, Department of Political Science, Dibrugarh University, Dibrugarh, Assam. **Email:** phulmoni2508.das@gmail.com

Pooja Raghav (Dr.), Doctoral Fellow, Department of Political Science, Madras University/Madras Christian College, Tambaram, Chennai, Tamil Nadu.
Email: trishnarai73@gmail.com

Ramesh Kumar (Dr.), Associate Professor & Head, Department of Political Science, Central University of Haryana, Mahendergarh, Haryana. **Email:** dr.rameshkumar@cuh.ac.in

Robin Hazarika (Dr.), Assistant Professor, Department of Political Science, Kamargaon College, Golaghat, Assam.
Email: phulmoni2508.das@gmail.com

Sandeep Inampudi (Dr.), Assistant Professor, Department of Public Administration, Central University of Karnataka, Gulberga, Karnataka. **Email:** sandeepinampudi@cuk.ac.in

Santhosh Mathew (Dr.), Associate Professor, Centre for South Asian Studies, Pondicherry University, Kalapet, Puducherry.
Email: santhoshveranani@gmail.com

Sartik Bagh (Dr.), Department of Political Science, Babasaheb Bhimrao Ambedkar University, (A Central University), Raibareli Road, Lucknow, Uttar Pradesh.
Email: sartkboi@yahoo.co.in

Trishna Rai (Dr.), Doctoral Fellow, Madras University/Madras Christian College, Tambaram, Chennai, Tamil Nadu.
Email: trishnarai73@gmail.com

Vinod Khobragade (Dr.), Professor Dept of Political Science, BR Ambedkar Central University, Lucknow, UP.
Email: vinod_d2003@yahoo.com

PART I

Identity Politics, Subaltern Resistance, Citizen's Charter and Gender Diversity

1
Why Governance? Exploring Neoliberal Instrumentality behind the Birth of Governance

Arindam Roy

I

Governance has become a popular catch-all phrase. From politician to administrator, to a man on street everybody is taking recluse under this capacious term for his/her possible act of commission and omission. The present chapter unpacks a rather critical discourse on governance. Unlike the much talked about narrative of governance which presents World Bank touted checklist of sound administrative/development management as sacrosanct and to be treated as necessary precondition for availing developmental loans, it talks about the inside story of the birth of governance. If one cares to go through a burgeoning literature on governance, he/she may stumble upon as many as four different connotations of governance: governance as a structure, as a process, as a mechanism; and last but not least as a strategy. Interestingly, there has been a perceptible trade-off between structure and processes in the literature of governance. The importance of structure in defining governance was deliberately downplayed in the Fund-Bank prescriptions to facilitate neoliberal dream of unification of global markets. For, any attempt to strengthen the structure in the conceptualization of governance would derail the project of unification of global markets. Hence, process was foregrounded as the basis of governance in the Bank documents. The present chapter is basically concentrating on the fourth connotation of governance, i.e. it views governance as a strategy for the neoliberals to salvage ailing capitalism from the blues of Keynesianism. It views that the very popularization and maturation of the concept of governance is intrinsically associated with neoliberalism. The chapter has the following sections: Section I deals with concept of governance, especially the way it is presented in the World Bank documents; Section II interrogates the conceptualization of governance by bringing in the correlations between governance and neoliberalism; Section III, finally, winds up the chapter with a concluding observation.

This Section deals with concept of governance, especially the way it is represented in the World Bank documents. Topicality notwithstanding, it can hardly claim to have a coherent definition. In fact, the concept is notoriously imprecise as it has multiple connotations. Despite a literal mushrooming of literature on the subject, it remains an elusive enterprise. The opening remark of *The Oxford Handbook of Governance* has endorsed the above conceptual confusions. It reads "governance is an interdisciplinary research agenda on order and disorder, efficiency and legitimacy all in the context of hybridization of modes of control that allow the production of fragmented and multidimensional order within the state, by the state, without the state and beyond the state" (Levi-Faur, 2012). The above statement has identified that the basic puzzle of conceptualizing governance lies in the problem of locating order in the era of increasing hybridization of modes of control. The global interconnectedness has further accentuated the problem of defining governance as the state is often lost in the labyrinth of order marked by a host of national and international non-governmental and civil society organizations operational at the micro, meso and macro levels. The value-loaded slippery adjective 'good', especially its mention in several Fund Bank documents has further confounded the concept. Every government—be it autocratic, democratic or theocratic has been engaged, at least visibly, in this seemingly endless search. Notionally speaking, the concept has always been there with civilized humanity. The etymological root of the term is said to have stemmed from the

Greek word *kybernan*, which signifies the act of piloting or steering, that is subsequently translated into the Latin word *gobernare*. Hence, the steering metaphor approximates the essence of governance in the contemporary world.

The term secures a permanent berth in the policy discourses since the end of cold war. In the 1950s and 1960s, the topic of governance was very much present, but did not get adequate attention in social science and humanities. The publication of an article by Oliver Williamson, entitled "Transaction Costs Economics: Governance of Contractual Relations" in 1979 had literally captivated the academic interest in the concept of governance for the first time. Though the focus of the paper was basically the 'law and economics of corporate governance', it received a huge response in terms of citations (Levi-Faur, David, 2012). However, the World Bank publications have catapulted the concept from a narrow specialized area of economics and law to a truly public discourse. With an objective of bringing about economic and political reforms in the recipient countries, donor agencies like World Bank, IMF have brought in a series of prescriptions under the rubric of governance. The World Bank had drawn to the issue of governance for the first time in 1989 when a *Long Term Perspective Study on Sub-Saharan Africa,* entitled *Sub-Saharan Africa: From Crisis to Sustainable Growth: A Long-Term Perspective Study* (World Bank, 1989) had identified poor governance was at the heart of African crisis. The report had accounted for the crisis of governance with the mounting crisis of population growth, surpassing the GDP growth along with weak agricultural growth, drooping industrial output, deteriorating social indicators and so on. In fact, the said report was instrumental in motivating the Bank's General Council to draft a *Legal Memorandum to its Board of Directors* in December 1990, indicating a future roadmap for further analysis on governance (Lateef, 2016). Subsequently, the World Bank had come up with a discussion paper entitled "Managing Development—the Governance Dimension" in 1991, originally meant for the consumption of its Board of Directors. It was the first ever formal policy statement, issued by the Bank management to lay out the detailed analytical frame for lending work and governance. In 1992, the Bank had set-up a task force for spelling out the nuances of governance under the leadership of Sarwar Lateef, which was later published by the Bank as a booklet entitled, *Governance and Development* (1992). Since then there has been a virtual mushrooming of literature on governance. In fact, the World Bank has been grappling with this concept in its several publications. If one starts browsing through those literatures, he/she would have ended up with a discovery of a prescriptive checklist for sound administrative management, which includes among others, participation, consensus-orientedness, accountability, transparency, responsiveness, effectiveness, equity, inclusiveness, and rule of law. It was projected in such a way that if a country religiously follows that checklist in its administrative deliberations, that country would be considered as 'fit' for availing developmental loans. Otherwise, a country would have been promptly termed as 'failed state' or 'rogue state'. A neoliberal string is said to have been attached with the so-called parameters of governance. Hence, the uncritical compliance of said checklist by the developing countries would sustain the twin objectives of the neoliberalism: on the one hand the compliance to the said checklist would ensure neoliberals with much needed assurance/ guarantee of repayment of loan amount disbursed to the developing countries as developmental loan; and on the other hand it facilitates neoliberal dreams of unification of global markets by substantially displacing government/state from the social sector. Hence, governance agenda is brought into being by the neoliberals as a necessary precondition for better administrative management.

II

This Section intends to understand the supposed correlation between neoliberalism and governance. Before we move into the nuances of this correlation, a brief discussion on the concept of neoliberalism deserves some space here. Neoliberalism, as defined by David Harvey, "is a theory of political economic practices proposing that human well-being can best be advanced by maximization of entrepreneurial freedoms within an institutional framework characterized by private property, individual liberty, unencumbered markets and free trade" (Harvey, 2005). Further, neoliberalism wants state to create an institutional framework conducive for the above practices. ...It believes that market dynamism has the potential of realizing individual well-being by unlocking the individual entrepreneurial spirit. Briefly speaking, neoliberalism stands for four fundamental changes, first, trust in small government; secondly, deregulation of the domestic financial systems; thirdly, deregulation of labour market; and the last but not the least facilitating the entry of international capital (Anthony O'Hara, Philip, 2010). However, the adoption of neoliberalism as policy and as populist culture is not spontaneous either. Hence, neoliberalization calls for a thorough construction of consent *via* microfinance, delegating ownership to the community, poverty alleviation, development, health etc.

The said correlation can be better understood if we put the liberalism into evolutionary matrix. In fact, neoliberalism is an attempt to bail out ailing capitalism which had limped back to life in late 1960s after a brief stint of Keynesianism emerged in the wake of Great Depression of late 1920s. The 'sleight of hand' (invisible hand), howsoever convincing the logic might be, failed to carry forward the project of governance further. The worldwide economic recession or the great depression in 1930s proved the inadequacies of the market model of governance and reiterated the importance of interventionist state in governance *via* Keynesian macroeconomic remedy of more states. Hence, government or state is brought back in the governance discourse over and over again. However, the danger of a stifling Leviathan with its all encompassing legal formal paraphernalia is often proved to be cumbrous and demotivating. Hence, jettisoning of the spectra of Kenyensian overstatism was necessary. The birth of neoliberalism in 1970 was, therefore, a natural outcome. However, neoliberalism did not enjoy a smooth tenure. In fact, since its emergence in 1970s till date it has to undergo several ups and downs to stay afloat. In the initial stage (from late 1970s to mid-1980s), neoliberalism was primarily 'structure-dependent', putting a lot of emphasis on strict monetarism and *laissez faire* and asks for rigorous restructuring of policies which include among others cut in social spending, cut in subsidies, introduction of anti-union laws in order to attract investment and so on. The second phase (from mid-1980s to mid-1990s) was more or less a phase of consolidation for neoliberalism as it has gone past the period of market fundamentalism. The Washington Consensus, a neoliberal 'reform package' gives much more coherence to the policies of neoliberalism. John Willamson has enumerated ten policy prescriptions of the Washington Consensus which was shared by Washington-based institutions like World Bank and IMF along with US Congress. They were, viz. "(1) fiscal discipline; (2) redirecting public expenditure; (3) tax reform; (4) financial liberalization; (5) adoption of a single, competitive exchange rate; (6) trade liberalization; (7) elimination of barriers to foreign direct investment; (8) privatization of state owned enterprises; (9) deregulation of market entry and competition; and (10) secure property rights" (Lopes, Carlos, 2011). Governance, a well thought out project was born at the second phase of periodization as the ten policy prescriptions of the said consensus have presumably necessitated the birth of it. Consequently, the governing process had transcended the boundaries of government to incorporate a host of agencies and associations involved in the act of governing. For, any amount of Keynesianism was counter-productive for the neoliberal dream of unification of global markets. The third phase of the periodization, also known as the 'post-Washington consensus phase' (from mid-1990s to present) has brought certain modifications in the conceptualization of governance by bringing about humane face in governance with its emphasis on redistribution, social safety net, the targeted poverty reduction, selective health intervention and so on.

The neoliberal policy of moving beyond government/state by manufacturing the concept of governance is also marked by an exponential rise of the third sector along with market. For the rise of third sector was necessary to reclaim the social space, left vacant by the departure of state from the social sector as a part of neoliberal conditionality. Hence, by allowing third sector to grow, neoliberals have supplemented the withdrawal of state from the social sector and paved the way for governance framework. If one tracks the trajectories of governance, he/she may find several changes in the model of governance, primarily brought into being to suit the overarching interest of the neoliberals. The revival of the third sector should not be treated uncritically as a spontaneous growth. In fact, they are the policy artifacts, acted as a conduit of global capital by harnessing community. Moreover, due to "continuous relocation of authority structures both outward towards supranational entities and inward towards sub-national groups" (Rosenau and Czempiel, 2009), governance model as a neoliberal instrumentality also gets relocated/graduated from global to local *via* national policy. Interestingly, the neoliberals (as an outcome of Post-Washington Consensus) have gone past the phase of financial orthodoxy and its attendant precondition of rampant deinstitutionalization and seemed to have adopted selective institutionalization (institutional reform) in the field of social sector like health, rural development/poverty alleviation etc. In the next section, an attempt will be made to navigate the continuous graduation of governance models across the globe. The varying connotations of the concept of governance from a schematic prescription of sound administrative management by the donor agencies in the early 1990s to its wide spread orchestration in different Fund Bank publications as the panacea for administrative malfunctioning in the late 1990s, to its present modified form of selective re-institutionalization, is indicative of the shifting fortunes of the capital. The neoliberals in a bid to salvaging capital from crises kept on modifying the notion of governance. Hence, it would not be totally out of place to relate the recent renewal of interest in decentralization with neoliberal form of governance.

The emphasis on local governance or call for decentralization/decentralized governance is not an indigenous model of empowering local, rather it is a well thought out neoliberal design of 'spatial fixation of capital'. With an objective of spatializing capital, neoliberals have adopted a couple of policies: first is empowerment of the institutions and processes of local governing by encouraging decentralization and rural development: and second is the creation of exclusive enclaves or Special Economic Zones (SEZs). Depending upon the nature of capitalist development, neoliberals have adopted policies of furthering the reach of capital. For example, the model adopted in a few early liberalized countries in South East Asia, like Thailand, Indonesia is markedly different from the rest of Asia. Neoliberals in this part of the world have actively encouraged the creation of SEZ/EPZ for the fixation of FDIs. But they have customized their policy in case of the post-colonial countries like India, where the development of capital is by and large uneven. The neoliberal experimentation in India has taken a different route considering its contextuality. The Indian society has had a long independent tradition of local level governance nestling at the margin for centuries together. The vicissitude of power equations at the centre had rarely touched this pristine traditions of governance, as from Metcalfe to Gandhi all have been very appreciative of these tiny village republics. Neoliberals in India have seized upon this opportunity of capitalizing the tradition of local governance by actively advocating decentralization schemes. For, such attempt would not only stabilize the worldwide crisis of market debacle, but also offer alternative virgin rural market to tap. Hence, the rural development projects received huge patronage from the neoliberals and a flurry of rural development schemes including small scale industries have been introduced in the rural hinterland. Even, the neoliberal modalities have also changed over the years. The modalities of neoliberalism during its consolidation phase (Washington Consensus in 1990s), was primarily based on 'investment-growth equations', which believes investment begets growth. The Structural Adjustment Programme (SAP) was introduced as the guiding principle to stabilize the growth of capital. The state is induced to shed off its responsibility by structurally readjusting itself with a host of other institutions. This phase had a definite deinstitutionalizing focus as processes of governing got utmost priority at the cost of Institution (state). However, within a very short span of time a realization sets in that investment alone cannot ensure growth. In fact, strong institutional structure is equally important to bring about growth. Hence, the importance of institutional reforms was the outcome of the failure of Washington Consensus. The institution building which was almost discouraged at the early phase of neoliberalism, has become mainstay of this phase. Institution building had got a tremendous fillip during this phase as it was encouraged in three different tiers—at the micro level, at the meso level and at the macro level. At the micro level, local communities were encouraged to take part in development. Community ownership was also offered to the local and marginal communities. The birth of people's plan, decentralized planning, participatory local resource management were a few such efforts of inducing capital by empowering local communities and giving them a sense of ownership. This is how governance is relocated at the micro level. In the post-1995 onwards, a consensus was reached or what is popularly known as post-Washington

Consensus that growth without distribution will not be sustainable in nature. Consequently, the neoliberals (as an outcome of Post-Washington consensus) have gone past the phase of financial orthodoxy and its attendant precondition of rampant deinstitutionalization and seemed to have adopted selective institutionalization in the garb of institutional reform in the field of social sector like health, rural development/poverty alleviation etc. However, such shift in governance is not spontaneous either. Neoliberals adopted the so-called humane face of governance for at least two reasons: first, such pro-people, community centric governance approach would act as shock absorber for neoliberals as this bit of providential intervention has mystified the people about the real intention of the neoliberals and bestows much coveted legitimacy to neoliberals and its crony state/government. Secondly, the said 'humane turn' of governance paradigm, especially its venture in the form of public health initiatives or poverty alleviation programme has a benign political economic dimension. For, allowing concessions to the state to intervene in the health sector or poverty alleviation was anything but the replication of Keynesian paradigm of social welfare. In fact, health and poverty proved to be a huge market opportunity for the neoliberals. For, example, selective marketization of health sector by introducing health insurance scheme for the poor without dismantling public health infrastructure may be mentioned. This, selective collaboration between market and state intervention has a legitimizing impact for both the state and market; on the one hand, it legitimizes market intervention in social sector; and on the other hand, it also brings back a little bit of legitimacy he states in terms of its commitment towards its citizens. Hence, neoliberals allow crony state to facilitate market expansion. The enamoring of C.K. Prahalad's new innovative book by the neoliberals for example has demonstrated how poverty can best be fought with profitability. "The Fortune at the Bottom of the Pyramid" (2005) could have been an interesting reference point. If one browsing through this book one would invariably stumble upon the rich adulation showered on it. The wide acceptance and readership of the book especially by the chieftain of the industry and market is indicative of the dominant neoliberal perspective towards poverty. Drawing on several cross-country case studies, Prahalad has demonstrated the financial viability of the poverty or what he called BOP market for capital accumulation. Unlike the traditional welfare principle of philanthrophy and providential(ism), a whopping 4/5 billion people at the BOP, as Prahalad viewed, may revolutionize business practices. Hence, the need of the hour is to get out of old prejudices regarding poor. In fact, Prahalad has shown that poor or the BOP could have been a huge market had we customize the market in accordance with the needs of the BOP. Citing the case study of shampoo market, Prahalad had shown that sachetization had multiplied the sale of shampoo as BOP people have choices, demands and brand consciousness. Interestingly by new governance paradigm, the millions of marginal people have been roped in the process governing.

III

Concluding Observations

In the foregoing analysis an attempt has been made to unearth the inside story of the birth of governance. There is no denying that governance has liberated the notion of governing from the clutches of institutionalization. However, considering governance as a panacea for all kinds administrative evil is a grossly overstatement. In fact, there is a serious neoliberal instrumentality behind the birth of the concept of governance. The neoliberals in a bid to salvaging capitalism from severe economic recession in early 1970s has brought the concept of governance. Hence, the origin, maturation and the ramifications of the concept is intrinsically tied up with neoliberal interest. Hence, the modification of the concept, no matter howsoever delicately constructed smacks of typical capitalist design of manufacturing consent/ legitimacy. The occasional tinkering with some eternal normative values, like equity, justice, inclusivity etc. should be read as various modes. Despite heralding of the triumph of capitalism in the 'End of History' thesis, the above desperation of the part of the neoliberals to project governance indicates a perennial anxiety of capitalism. Hence, the time has come to demystify the concept of governance and interrogate the neoliberal motives before uncritically embracing it as 'the' trusted antidote to any type of administrative malfunctioning.

REFERENCES

De Angelis, Massimo (2005). "The Political Economy of Global Neoliberal Governance", *Review (Fernand Braudel Center)*, Vol. 28, No. 3.

Hervey, David (2005). *A Brief History of Neoliberalism*, Oxford: Oxford University Press.

Lateef, K. Sarwa (2016). *Background Paper: Governance and Law, Evolution of The World Bank's thinking on Governance*, Washington DC, The International Bank for Reconstruction and Development.

Levi-Faur, David (ed.) (2012). *The Oxford Handbook of Governance*, Oxford: Oxford University Press.

Lopes, Carlos (2012). "Economic Growth and Inequality: The New Post-Washington Consensus", *RCCS Annual Review*, 4, October.

O'Hara, Philip Anthony (2010). "After Neoliberalism: A Social Structure of Accumulation or Mode of Regulation for Global or Regional Performance?" *Journal of Economic Issues*, Vol. 44, No. 2.

Prahalad, C.K. (2005). *The Fortune at the Bottom of the Pyramid*, New Jersey: Wharton School Publishing, Wharton University.

Rosenau, James N. and Ernst-Otto Czempiel (2009). *Governing Without Government: Order and Challenge in World Politics*, Cambridge: Cambridge University Press.

World Bank (1989). *Sub-Saharan Africa: From Crisis to Sustainable Growth*, Washington DC, The International Bank for Reconstruction and Development.

World Bank (1992). *Governance and Development*, Washington DC, The International Bank for Reconstruction and Development.

2
On the Intersection of Identity and Politics
A Study of Refugees in India

Monika Tiwari and *Vinod Khobragade*

Introduction

The C-17 craft of U.S. evacuation flight witnessed a birth of a baby in a flight. The flight had Afghan nationals and all of a sudden an Afghan origin woman gave birth to a girl in an aircraft which landed at Ramstein Air Base in Germany in August 2021. Now, the question arises that what would be her nationality? As she was a child of an Afghan origin refugee, in U.S. headed aircraft, landed on the Germany air base. This question to ascertain her nation is actually to ensure her future, education, livelihood and her home and all this will be ensured by her State of origin. Thus, state is a cardinal institution for human development. In this regard, Aristotle believed that state is an outcome of a fundamental need of humans, i.e. an Association.[1] Association with other humans forms community and provides a sense of belonging to each member of the commune. It not only satisfies human's psyche but also extends the material benefits of associations. The most common assertion of this associative tendency is state. The state supplies mental and physical security to all associates. Thus, each human agrees to be a part of a larger whole to ascertain the fulfilment of his or her needs. Taking into consideration the hitherto theories of obligation towards state, it manifests this utilitarian aspect of its existence. Though today, state machinery appears to be a spyware machinery or what we sense a 'Surveillance State', it still exists for sake of the benefits of its citizens. The word citizens, here, is of greater importance as it bestows an identity on a person. It helps a person to locate himself/herself in a larger socio-political matrix. Here we ponder on what if we lose our political identity? Does it make any difference to our existence or how far we would sustain not being a citizen but just a human being?

Unsurprisingly, there are people in millions, who, being humans are not citizens, they are refugees. The internal disturbances and wars in Yemen, Syria, Afghanistan, South Sudan, Myanmar, Ukraine[2], Sri Lanka[3] etc. have caused millions of people to leave everything they had. In the passage of moving towards peace, world is witnessing more wars than ever before and consequently, the problem of displacement and rehabilitation has become a global crisis. Unfortunately, devoid of any political identity, they are living unsettled life. In fact, they all need political umbrella to exist, to avail rights, to live, and to develop. Hence, this chapter tries to identify the current crisis of refugees and their citizenship, as the war driven displacements and statelessness has become one of the greatest cry of our times.

Who are Refugees?

Refugees can be described as a group of people who are forced to leave their country and take refuge in other countries. Thus, they are forcefully dislocated population who are looked upon as temporary settler on foreign land. For a sound definition of refugees, UN defines them as:

> Owing to well-founded fear of being persecuted for reasons of race, religion, nationality, membership of a particular social group or political opinion, is outside the country of his nationality and is unable or, owing to such fear, is unwilling to avail himself of the protection of that country; or who, not having a nationality and being outside the country of his former habitual residence, is unable or, owing to such fear, is unwilling to return to it.[4]

Amnesty International not only defines refugees but also distinguishes between migrants, asylum seekers and refugees. According to the Amnesty International, refugees are the people who leave their country because their state seems to be a failure in protecting their lives. Similarly, asylum seekers are defined as the people who are also unprotected by their respective authorities but they are not yet fully accepted as an authorized settler on foreign land. They are in process of claiming their refuge or they have already claimed but their claim has not been legitimized. Therefore, they are considered seekers, not full-fledged refugees. Migrants, on the other hand, are entirely different from above two as the reasons for migrating can be "...Work, study or joint family, for example. Others feel that they must leave because of poverty, political unrest, gang violence, natural disasters or other serious circumstances that exist there."[5]

Apart from the reasons mentioned by United Nations Higher Commission for Refugees (UNHCR), now-a-days, ecological crisis have become a very strong cause of internal dislocation as well as refuge. The climate change, such as forest fires, desertification, tsunamis, cyclones have ruined people's properties and lives.[6] The UNHCR has expressed concerns that approximately 20 million people move from their place to another due to extreme climate conditions or natural hazards each year. In this regard, UN High Commissioner for Refugees, Filippo Grandi, said, "We need to invest now in preparedness to mitigate future protection needs and prevent further climate caused displacement. Waiting for disaster to strike is not an option."[7] However, with respect to the above concern, UNHCR has developed a strategic framework on climate action, where thorough policies and operations, issues regarding 'climate refugees' is being dealt. Under the Framework of Environmental Refugee Protection Fund, strategic operation on Climate Resilience and Environmental Sustainability (CRES) 2022-2025, the UN is working to address the issue of climate refugees. The CRES 2022-2025 aims to "Incorporate climate and environmental considerations into sectoral operational responses, work with refugees, internally displaced people and communities in the most climate vulnerable countries, and develop innovative sustainable energy and reforestation programmes for refugee-hosting areas."[8]

The prevailing Ukraine-Russia war has caused global crisis in terms of food, fuel and economy. The Russian President Putin's threat of using nuclear weapons also has further triggered the panic. However, besides this, war has intensified the debate over the issue of displacement due to war and what can be the role of the community of states in overcoming the wrongs of wars? In fact, at present, the total number of refugees is rising rapidly especially because of the Ukraine crisis. According to Amnesty International, the total count has reached to 26 million.[9] Above all, the worst fact is that the half of the refugee population is of children and from 2018 to 2020; 1 million children were born as a refugee having no political identity. In 2019, it was reported that two-third of the total refugees were from Syria, Venezuela, Afghanistan, South Sudan and Myanmar.[10] Syria stands as the major country for the origin of refugees since 2014 due to lasting internal turmoil and instability.[11] The total number of the 'forcibly displaced' population at the end of 2020 according to UNHCR was 82.4 million. The current statistics have revealed that 1 out of each 95 people is now a displaced person which was 1 out of 159 in 2010. Hence, the crisis of displacement is not only a concern for the single country but it has wider implications for the entire world.[12]

Identity and Politics Driven Displacement

In context of refugees, the real crisis is not only material but also psychological where their identity and existence are at stake. The non-recognition causes undermining sense of self, sufferings of family members, loss of perspectives towards life, their immediate needs surpasses their higher aims of life, and the most disheartening fact is the future of their children and their coming generations. Would these children be able to be citizens ever and what would be their future in case they are not recognized as a citizen for their whole life? When we talk of displacement of people, we cannot forget the identities they carry. Many cases of dislocation are outcome of hate towards ethnic or religious identity of particular group. Such as exodus of Muslims from India and Hindus from Pakistan in 1947, the forceful displacement of Rohingyas from Myanmar, Bangladesh riots of 1992, shows the role of identity as a valid cause of displacement. In recent years, this trend has become fatal for Muslim community, which is often treated with suspicion in the West and other parts of the non-Muslim world. In certain countries, Muslim refugees are treated as a threat to internal security more than any other refugee community. The hate crime against Muslim community had increased within one year (2000-01) from 28 to 481 in United States just after 9/11 attacks.[13] The recent incidents of hate crimes towards Muslims are the result of the stereotypical representation of this community which triggered in post-9/11 era. The Muslim refugees are mostly hit by these islamophobic perceptions.[14]

During the Presidential election campaign of the US in 2021, Mr. Donald Trump openly claimed banning of all Muslim immigrants as suspects of criminal activities. He stated:

> Without looking at the various polling data, it is obvious to anybody the hatred is beyond comprehension. Where this hatred comes from and why we will have to determine. Until we are able to determine and understand this problem and the dangerous threat it poses, our country cannot be the victims of horrendous attacks by people that believe only in *Jihad*, and have no sense of reason or respect for human life. If I win the election for President, we are going to make America Great Again.[15]

The issue of refugees is politicized to the extent that Mr. Trump tried to develop a binary of US insider *versus* outsiders. This self and other image was to boost up the nationalist sentiments amongst the citizens for political gains. The politicians have been posing refugees as potential threats over their demography, jobs and culture and which also heightens the hurdles for refugees in overcoming exclusion. Thus, prejudices against refugees have made resettlement a far cry.

Refugees in India

India has always been a hospitable land for foreigners and intellectuals. The cultural fabric of this country is interwoven with distinct identities; referring to 'guests as God'. Similarly, the Indian stance on refugees and asylum seekers has been liberal since Independence. The first ever refugee influx we faced was the day we got independence. It was the first scar, first emergency, first influx or first massacre of

Independent India, where millions of Hindus and Muslims were uprooted from their original habitats. Also, it was one of the largest displacements of history where approximately 15 million people were displaced. The next case of forceful displacement was witnessed in 1959 when Tibetan spiritual leader the Dalai Lama, along with his hundred thousand followers, had to leave Tibet after Chinese invasion. The Tibetan refugees mainly settled in Dharamshala district of Himachal Pradesh and also are scattered in various parts of India especially in the states of Arunanchal Pradesh, Uttar Pradesh, Odisha, Mysore (Karnataka), Sikkim and West Bengal primarily.[16] In 1964-65, the Chakma and Hajonga community from the then East Pakistan migrated due to social persecution because they were Buddhists and Hindus respectively. The communities were initially provided settlement in Arunanchal Pradesh, and, at present, they are living in Mizoram and southern parts of Tripura.[17] However, in 2015, the Supreme Court ordered Government of India to recognize Chakmas and Hajongas as Indian citizens. The 2011 Census recorded that there are 47,471 Chakmas living in Arunanchal Pradesh.[18]

Furthermore, India saw another influx from Bangladesh again, in 1971, when the latter witnessed internal turmoil due to Pakistan's attack. Consequently, India had to pay a huge cost for this as rows of protest against illegal immigrants rose up in Assam which resulted in Assam accord of 1975. Apart from these, there is large number of Sri Lankan-Tamil people living in India which had fled Sri Lanka after a socio-political persecution by the Sri Lankan government over a separate statehood demands from the Sri Lankan Tamil community. The Sri Lankan-Tamil community is currently residing in the state of Tamil Nadu in almost 117 camps since more than 30 years.[19] The total count in the state is 58,822 refugees in camps and around 30,000 refugees outside the camps.[20] However, the current economic crisis in Sri Lanka has considerably increased the migration in Tamil Nadu once again. Further, adding to India's refugee crisis, recent years have been marked by the influx of Rohingya Muslims from Myanmar and refugees from Afghanistan in huge numbers. The Rohingya community, estimated to be around 40,000, is currently living in various Indian states; Madanpur Khader area of South New Delhi, Jammu, Hyderabad and Nuh in Haryana, primarily.[21] In past few years, there have been new trends and increasing refugee assertion in India for refugee rights. For instance, 29 Sri Lankan Tamil refugees have tried to commit collective suicide twice within a week, against their illegal detention by the Tamil Nadu government. Moreover, the Afghan asylum seekers also had relay of protests against the Indian government for not ensuring ample opportunities for them.[22] The problem of refugee rights is worsened in India due to lack of clarity over the status of people coming to India. For instance, they are simply assumed to be illegal immigrants or trespassers rather refugee or asylum seekers.[23] This creates a grey area for depriving them of their legal rights as per the international customary laws. The UNHCR acknowledges 2,10,991 people, out of which 1,96,960 are refugees and 14,031 are asylum seekers, hosted by India at present. According to UNHCR, in India there are 2,10,991 refugees mainly from Afghanistan (16,724), China (73,407), Sri Lanka (92,691), and Myanmar (23,879) and 4,290 from various other countries.[24]

The above data takes into consideration only recorded and accessed refugees and asylum seekers in India. In an answer to a question in Lok Sabha in 2021, on the issue of refugees, Honourable Home Minister Mr. Amit Shah stated that due to much illegal entry of the refugees and migrants, they have not maintained any centralized data of stateless persons currently residing in India.[25] He said that "Since illegal immigrants enter into the country without valid travel documents in clandestine and surreptitious manner, there is no accurate data regarding number of such migrants living in the country."[26] Moreover, it is often relegated to the state governments to maintain records of the refugees and asylum seekers, where Central Government does not pay enough attention to the growing scale of the refugee influx in India. It is also acknowledged fact by Indian government itself that they have not maintained the data of Rohingyas despite rapid influx in the north-east region. Absence of numbers draws an uncertain image on part of Indian government on one hand and puts question mark over the commitment of the government to the resettlement of refugees on the other.

Provisions Dealing with Refugees in India

After world wars were over, United Nations witnessed one of the largest humanitarian crises ever. The convention on protection of refugees 1951 was adopted to deal with the displaced people. It was then covering only those who were dislocated due to world war prior to 1 January, 1951 within Europe. The UN revised and enlarged this threshold later, when 1967 protocol on status of refugees was adopted. Since then these two documents are supposed to be the patrons of refugees and stateless people worldwide. India, though hosting large numbers of displaced people, is not a member of either of the Conventions nor does it has any formal domestic refugee policy till date. Though, it is not the case that India does not commit to any such conventions. India is a part of the Convention against Torture and other Cruel, Inhuman or Degrading Treatment or Punishment (1997), though, has not ratified it. India acceded to the International Convention on Civil and Political Rights (ICCPR).This includes the Universal Declaration of Human Rights, 1948; the International Convention on Civil and Political Rights, 1966; the International Convention on Economic, Social and Cultural Rights, 1966; the International Convention on the Elimination of all Forms of Racial Discrimination, 1966; the Convention Against Torture and Cruel, Inhuman or Degrading Treatment or Punishment, 1984; and the Convention for the Elimination of all Forms of Discrimination Against Women, 1979. All of these Conventions are observed by Indian authorities and directs them in absence of refugee law. In India, refugees are currently dealt under the Registration of Foreigners Act, 1939, the Foreigners Act , 1946 and the Foreigners Order, 1948. These laws were originally meant for dealing with aliens on Indian land controlling their entry, treatment and deportation. The use of these Acts is now applied to domain of refugees as well. The major concern is that these Acts are unable to differentiate between Migrants; who voluntarily left their country and Refugees; who were forced to do so. This generalization causes grave consequences for refugee rights. They are often mistaken as illegal immigrants causing detentions and suspicion. Indian government framed refugee protection law in 1997, 2006 and 2015 but unable to get them passed over objections on grounds of national security. The absence of national refugee policy undermines the equal treatment to all communities, for instance, Tibetan refugees are the most preferentially treated community as they are provided work permits, better social and political acceptance, were granted land for their programmes, to set up educational institute and office for In-

Exile government of Tibet. However, the Indian government, despite of not being a member of 1951 Geneva Convention, has maintained a good record in terms of treatment of refugees. The Indian judiciary has also played pivotal role in assuring the rights conferred by Constitution to all people living in India; for instance, in Louis De Raedt *versus* Union of India, State of Arunanchal Pradesh *versus* Khudiram Chakma ruled that Article 21, i.e. Right to Life is available for all persons living in India unanimously. In Zothansangpuri *versus* State of Manipur, Supreme Court gave landmark judgment assuring the Right to Non-refoulement, i.e. a person cannot be forced to go back on the land where his or her life is in danger. In consonance with Supreme Court, various NGOs and National Human Rights Commission have assisted in securing refugee rights bestowed by the Constitution of India. As Supreme Court has ruled in various cases time to time, refugees enjoy Right to Equality before Law (Article 14), Protection of life and liberty (Article 21), Right to Practice Freedom of Religion, Right to Leave the Country, Right to Free and Fair Trial and so on.[27] The role of judiciary has been undoubtedly patronizing but a larger proportion of plight is unaddressed due to lack of accessibility, awareness and assistance. The lack of statutory mechanism and definitions, the mounting refugee population is totally a black hole which is always assumed to be big but never measured so far.

India: A 'Refugee Haven'?

In recent years, the rising influx in India has raised a question that why people from neighbourhood countries, after being forcefully displaced from their original country, prefer India? There are several propositions, firstly, the most obvious reason is, the adjacent and porous borders of India. They may find it far convenient to enter India as Indian shares boundary with seven countries. Even, India shares a very thin and informal border with Bangladesh, Bhutan and Nepal, which enables relatively easy trespassing. Secondly, in South Asian region India is one of the major economically and politically stable country. Thirdly, India has always maintained its aura as peaceful country which has never promoted wars unless war is left as the last resort. Fourthly, the vastness of its land and resources also contribute to call on people to believe in India to be refugee haven.

India's Stand over 1951 Convention and National Refugee Policy

India has not been totally devoid of UNHCR presence on its territory. It has taken assistance in some extraordinary situations such as displacement of Tibetan nationals, influx of Chakma refugees from Bangladesh. But in ordinary circumstances, India preferred a distance from UNHCR interventions. The Indian officials stated that both the conventions are highly 'Eurocentric' as originally it focused on European displacement all alone. They are of the view that it does not take into account whole some views of developing countries and their refugee influxes. But is it the only argument from Indian side? Or are there any strategic, administrative arguments to support Indian stance? We can point out certain areas which are the prime concerns of Indian policy-makers.

The common concern for every country is the sharing of already scarce national resources with displaced people. Providing basic amenities to refugees overburdens the government with totally dependent population. This creates pressure over regional and national resources. The heavy influx of the refugees in a country is taken as a threat to national security. Lama explains three types of political security threats due to refugee influx. Strategic-level security; when the refugees are armed, structural level security threat; claiming on scarce resources, regime level security; when refugees start interacting in national and local political processes.[28] Apart from national security at stake, influx of refugees increases socio-cultural insecurities as well. The local politics and regional political parties have converted the issue of influx in to 'Us *versus* Them' binary, emphasizing on limiting refugees and their influences over their culture, resources and demography. They are often posed as outsiders and threat to local culture and resources. There have been cases in which refugee camps are set on fire by local people out of insecurity. A very pragmatic concern is that providing legal safeguards to refugee population as per the formal guidelines might invite more refugee population. Moreover, in an area, where law is silent, authorities take liberty to adjust, to mould and to customize the provisions. It is double edged sword but often it effectively secures national interest. Thus, the absence of authentic Refugee policy has provided a great space for authorities to deal with the refugee cases with particularity and in accordance with the national diplomacy, national tics with the country of origin and the availability of resources.

Indian stance on the issue of refugee explosion is instigated by its national interest and politics which has promoted very strong role of political parties in dealing with the refugee communities particularly. Changing incumbents deal with the cases as per their viewpoints rather than needs of the communities. The case of Tibetan refugees is helpful in explaining the role of political will in dealing with certain refugee communities and provided with better habitat and amenities. Thus, Indian policy for refugee influx is subjected to political and strategic ambiguity rather on defined, uniform standards.

Current Scenario and Citizenship Amendment Bill (CAA)

India's stance over the refugee protection, despite being a non-signatory of UN conventions, has been welcoming so far, but in recent years the government has shown considerable disinterest in the matter and its urgency. The exodus of Rohingyas from Myanmar resulted in millions of asylum seekers into Bangladesh and India, out of which nearly 40,000 headed to India specifically. The Indian government deviating from its hitherto followed approach, tried to pose all of them as simply threat to national security and detained 170 Rohingya refugees in Hiranagar subsidiary jail (Kathua) as illegal immigrants.[29] Being aware of the genocidal war going against the community, government decided to deport nearly 150-160 Rohingyas detained in Jammu to their country of origin under Section 3 of the Foreigners Act citing them as illegally entered foreigners.[30] Where International Court of Justice has acknowledged the Myanmar's situation as a threat to Rohingyas as a community and the principle of Non-refoulement as well, Indian government found an easy escape from the argument. This whole narrative of National Security came into huge question when government came up with Citizenship Amendment Bill, 2019 (CAA), welcoming 6 religious persecuted minorities of three neighbouring countries—Pakistan, Bangladesh and Afghanistan. The Act does not disable anyone to get citizenship of India but certainly favours some refugees over others. It contains provisions that anyone related to above six communities arrived in India on or before 31 December, 2014 will not be deported or detained in absence of sufficient documentation. Moreover, the government also provided with the long term visas to these communities in 2018 itself. The Bill instigated a series of violent protest and criticism across India due to its discriminatory provisions. On one hand, government seeks to raise concerns over national security for Rohingyas and on the other invites only religiously persecuted minority population from the three neighbouring states.[31] Rajeev Dhavan, a senior advocate, considers this Bill as attempt for *"ghar wapasi"* by the BJP-led government. He raises concerns over dual stand of the government over the question of Ahmadiyas and Shias of Pakistan, Uighurs of China, Hazaras of Afghanistan.[32] Thus, CAA is rightfully a concern for those who are concerned with the impartial, unambiguous and uniform treatment of refugees because it clears the stance of the government over issues of influx, citizenship and rehabilitation.

The *adhoc* policy to Indian government was clearly visible in dealing with one of the major displacement crisis of Asia recently, i.e. Afghan refugee crisis after Taliban took the charge in 2021. The prior issued visas were ended and they were asked to apply for E-Visas before entering India in advance.[33] Moreover, the Indian authorities appeared bit skeptic of their stand for Afghan nationals this time as in case of Rohingyas. Thus, the present scenario of refugee policy and protection has been hit by the nationalist agenda and political opinions of the incumbents. The UNHCR has been constantly asking Indian authorities to develop domestic refugee policy to enlarge the humanitarian base for treatment and resettlement.

The Problems of Refugees in India

Being a refugee, in any part of the world, is a prolonged struggle. They face wide range of issues from entering into foreign country to their subsistence, from shelter to security, from economic to education and above all, the resettlement into their own country or citizenship from hosting state. In India, the problems of refugees can be categorized into community specific problems and generic problems, such as the problems of Tibetans are different from that of Sri Lankan Tamils. In case of Sri Lankan Tamils, there has been strong role of political will in addressing their rights such as protection against illegal detentions, educational and professional opportunities.[34] In case of Tibetans, their problem is not the exclusion but better educational and occupational rights, while the issues of Afghans and Rohingyas are of the socio-political exclusion and security primarily.[35] The generic problems of refugees are: their resettlement to their country of origin, the poor condition of refugee camps, *adhoc* policy of Indian government regarding refugee rights, no legal definition and differentiation have been made amongst infiltrators, refugees and migrants, work permits, issuance of visas etc.[36] Thus, the problems of refugees in India cannot be dealt by the opaque legislations. It requires a determined policy to address the persistent issues of refugee rights.

Conclusion

The world is sustained by humanity. At present, the world is going through humanistic catastrophe where governments and politics, are required to reassess their stands over the refugees' plight. In recent years, the issue of refugees have been used as a nationalist agenda on podiums but not taken on forums to have substantive discussions. India, being a neighbour of the two major displaced countries, i.e. Afghanistan and Myanmar, is affected by the regional disturbances. When India locates itself as major stakeholder in South Asian region and Asian politics at large, it is cardinal for India not to escape its responsibilities. Even if India does not sign the 1951 Convention on Refugee safeguards, it is the need of India's foreign as well as the domestic policy makers to manage the refugee influx in its territory. The urgency of India's own refugee policy is underlined by the mounting refugee camps in India as temporary residence of refugees with uncertain future. Moreover, the refugee crises must not be dealt in accordance with the political taste of the state. It must be taken as an integral component of countries' future and image in the world politics. It is an issue which requires much needed attention of the government, failing to which, it can put our national interest at stake.

NOTES

1. Aristotle (2022). *Stanford Encyclopedia of Philosophy*, https://plato.stanford.edu/entries/aristotle/
2. Recent Ukraine and Russia war has forced many natives to leave Ukraine, leaving another country on the edge of a big displacement crisis.
3. Sri Lanka's economic and political breakdown has increased the rate of immigrants in India, in hope of better future.
4. "Refugees", United Nations. Accessed from https://www.un.org/en/global-issues/refugees [Date of accession 11 April, 2022].
5. "Refugees, Asylum-seekers and Migrants", Amnesty International, 2022. Accessed from https://www.amnesty.org/en/what-we-do/refugees-asylum-seekers-and-migrants/[Date of accession 11 April, 2022].
6. The original definition of refugees by UN does not mention climate change and natural hazards as reason for displacement and refugee. But now, UN is taking into account these challenges under refugee crisis as it is not a voluntary migration.
7. "Climate Change and Disaster Displacement", UNHCR, 2022. Accessed from https://www.unhcr.org/climate-change-and-disasters.html [Date of accession 11 April, 2022].
8. "Summary: Operational Strategy on Climate Resilience and Environmental Sustainability 2022-25", UNHCR. Accessed from https://www.unhcr.org/protection/environment/61b85fc84/summary-operational-strategy-climate-resilience-environmental-sustainability.html [Date of accession 11 April, 2022].
9. "Refugees, Asylum-Seekers and Migrants." Amnesty International, 1 June, 2021, https://www.amnesty.org/en/what-we-do/refugees-asylum-seekers-and-migrants/[Date of accession 11 April, 2022].
10. "Refugee Data Finder", UNHCR, 2022. Accessed from https://www.unhcr.org/refugee-statistics/[Date of accession 12 April, 2022].
11. In the end of the 2019, the total count of refugees from Syria reached 6.6 million.
12. "Figures At Glance", UNHCR, 18 June, 2021, https://www.unhcr.org/en-in/figures-at-a-glance.html [Date of accession 11 April, 2022].
13. "Welcoming the Stranger: Combating Anti-Muslim Bigotry Against Afghan Refugees—Interfaith Alliance", 2022 https://interfaithalliance.org/welcoming-the-stranger-combating-anti-muslim-bigotry-against-afghan-refugees/[Date of accession 6 April, 2022].
14. Alagha, S. and Erikat, J. (2021). Opinion: Here's why Muslim refugees don't feel safe in the United States. [online] *San Diego Union-Tribune*. https://www.sandiegouniontribune.com/opinion/commentary/story/2021-09-13/muslim-refugees-safety-united-states[Date of accession 11 April, 2022].

15. Johnson, J. (2015). Trump calls for 'total and complete shutdown of Muslims entering the United States'. *The Washington Post.* Retrieved 11 April, 2022, from https://www.washingtonpost.com/news/post-politics/wp/2015/12/07/donald-trump-calls-for-total-and-complete-shutdown-of-muslims-entering-the-united-states/
16. United States Bureau of Citizenship and Immigration Services, India: Information on Tibetan refugees and settlements, 30 May, 2003, IND03002.ZNY, available at: https://www.refworld.org/docid/3f51f90821.html [accessed 11 April, 2022].
17. "Who are Chakmas", *The Hindu*, 29 November, 2021, https://www.the hindu.com/news/national/who-are-chakmas/article61473775.ece [accessed 11 April, 2022].
18. "Chakma and Hajong refugees—India's new citizens", *Times of India*, 18 September, 2018, https://timesofindia.indiatimes.com/india/chakma-and-hajong-refugees-indias-new-citizens/articleshow/60733409.cms [accessed 11 April, 2022].
19. "With poor conditions in camps, Sri Lankan Tamils remain citizens of no-man's land", *Indian Express,* 22 December, 2019, https://www.newindianexpress.com/states/tamil-nadu/2019/dec/22/with-poor-conditions-in-camps-sri-lankan-tamils-remain-citizens-of-no-mans-land-2079412.html [accessed 11 April, 2022].
20. "Explained: The new refugees from Sri Lanka, driven by hunger, not war", *Indian Express,* 3 April, 2022. https://indianexpress.com/article/explained/tamil-nadu-sri-lankan-refugees-economic-crisis-explained-7834849/ [accessed 11 April, 2022].
21. Aafaq, Z. (22 July, 2021). "Mosque in Indian capital's Rohingya camp bulldozed: Refugees", *Al Jazeera.* Available at: https://www.aljazeera.com/news/2021/7/22/mosque-in-india-capitals-rohingya-camp-bulldozedrefugees#:~:text=An%20estimated%2040%2C000%20Rohingya%20refugees,and%20Nuh%20in%20Haryana%20state [accessed 11 April, 2022].
22. Majumdar, R. (2021). Why Afghan asylum-seekers are protesting in India | DW | 07.09.2021. [online] DW.COM. Available at: < https://www.dw.com/en/why-afghan-asylum-seekers-are-protesting-in-india/a-59108980 > [Accessed 24 March, 2022].
23. There is much difference between a migrant and a refugee, as migrant leaves his country for better opportunities of work and livelihood but a refugee leaves a country under the threat of persecution; leaving the country in much unplanned manner. Thus, putting them into one container exhibits either lack of understanding or deliberate ignorance on the part of authorities.
24. "India", UNHCR, 2022. https://reporting.unhcr.org/india [accessed 6 April, 2022].

25. "Lok Sabha Unstarred Question No. 29", Ministry of Home Affairs, 20 July, 2021, http://164.100.24.220/loksabhaquestions/qhindi/175/AU1318.pdf [accessed 4 April, 2022].
26. "Lok Sabha Unstarred Question No. 296" , Ministry of Home Affairs, 20 July, 2021, https://www.mha.gov.in/MHA1/Par2017/pdfs/par2021-pdfs/LS-20072021/296.pdf [accessed 4 April, 2022].
27. Naik, Y. (2018). "India's Refugee Policy: issues and concerns", *Asian Law & Public Policy Review,* ISSN, 25816551, Vol. 3.
28. Nair, A. (2007). *National Refugee Law for India, Benefits and Roadblocks,* published by: Institute of Peace and Conflict Studies, New Delhi. https://www.ipcs.org/issue_briefs/issue_brief_pdf/51462796IPCS-ResearchPaper11-ArjunNair.pdf
29. Aswani, T. (2021). *Refugee Women From Afghanistan Have a Tough Time Trying to Make India Home.* [online] *The Wire.* https://thewire.in/women/refugee-women-from-afghanistan-have-a-tough-time-trying-to-make-india-home
30. Kumar, A. and Jaiswal, S. (2021). *India's Response to Rohingyas: A Gross Misuse of Defense of National Security and Turning Away from Its International and Constitutional Obligations.* [online] Jurist.org. Available at https://www.jurist.org/commentary/2021/07/jaiswal-kumar-rohingya-muslims-national-security-india/
31. Pradhan, N., Persecuted Refugee and the Citizenship Amendment Act, 2019. [online] Legalserviceindia.com. Available at: < https://www.legalserviceindia.com/legal/article-1436-persecuted-refugee-and-the-citizenship-amendment-act2019.html#:~:text=The%20Ministry%20of%20Home%20affairs,Indian%20citizenship%20through%20registration%2Fnaturalisation> [Accessed 24 March, 2022].
32. Dhavan, R. (2019). India Needs a Proper Refugee Law, Not a CAA Suffused with Discriminatory Intent. [online] *The Wire.* Available at: < https://thewire.in/law/india-needs-a-proper-refugee-law-not-a-caa-suffused-with-discriminatory-intent > [Accessed 24 March, 2022].
33. Ganguly, S. (2021, October 1). Why India won't ease the Afghan refugee crisis. *Foreign Policy.* Retrieved March 23, 2022, https://foreignpolicy.com/2021/10/01/india-refugee-policy-afghanistan-refugees/
34. Radhakrishnan, R.K. (2020). Sri Lankan Tamil refugees in India, the nowhere. https://frontline.thehindu.com/cover-story/article30328790.ece
35. Kaul, A. (2021). Afghan refugees in India highlight need of a domestic Indian refugee law. *Just Security.* https://www.justsecurity.org/78586/afghan-refugees-in-india-highlight-the-need-for-indian-domestic-refugee-law/
36. Bose, N. (2012). *Refugees in India share daily struggles with UNHCR chief.* UNHCR. https://www.unhcr.org/news/latest/2012/12/50d47f056/refugees-india-share-daily-struggles-unhcr-chief.html

3
A Critical Appraisal of the Subaltern Resistance in India

A Study of the Identity Movement of the Tea Garden Community of Assam

Phulmoni Das

Theoretical Understanding of Subaltern Resistance in India

Subaltern struggle led by the subaltern groups is not new to Indian history as it has been deeply marked in a long historical time. But in proposition to it, the struggles of these subaltern groups have not been added to the mainstream discourses of history writing for quite some time. It was the Subaltern Studies Group who first tried to make a serious attempt to trace the missing linkages of Subaltern struggle and to bring it to the mainstream discourses. Broadly speaking, the approach initiated by the Subaltern historians is referred as 'subaltern historiography', which seeks to maintain a balance by highlighting the role of the politics of the people as against elite politics played in Indian history. They asserted how the elite politics has failed to acknowledge the contribution made by the people (masses) on their own way which is independent of the elite politics. "In parallel to the domain of elite politics in colonial period there always existed another form of politics in which the principal actors were not the dominant groups of the society. These actors are the 'subaltern' classes and groups constituting the masses of the labouring population and the intermediate strata in the town and country—the people."[1] Subaltern historiography considers subalternity of the masses as an autonomous domain which neither originates from elite politics nor depends on them. According to Ranajit Guha, the mobilization of the domain of elite politics is achieved vertically but the subaltern politics takes place at the horizontal level. Guha also admitted that due to the diversity of the social composition among the subaltern groups and lack of uniformity in ideological element in terms of quality and density in the subaltern groups has sometimes led to the pursuit of their narrow sectional and economic interest as well as sectarian splits which destabilize the horizontal alliances of the subaltern groups.[2] Therefore, Guha also made the observation that the two domains of politics have not been isolated from each other but most often overlapped with each other. It is mainly the elite domain which always had tried to mobilize and integrate the domain of subaltern into the elite domain of politics to accomplish their own interests. However, the subaltern groups managed to come away from the domination of elite control and able to put their characteristic imprints on the campaigns initiated by the elite domain.[3] The peasant and tribal tenant rebelled against elite domination many times, for example, uprisings of Bhumij, the Kol insurrection, the Santal revolt of 1855 and the indigo disturbances of 1859-1862 and the Deccan riots of 1875 etc. can be referred as some of the subaltern struggles which are accomplished by the masses not with the help of the politics of elite. Thus, the main emphasis of subaltern historiography is to reconstruct the history 'from below' or to reformulate the 'history of the people with the politics of the left out', so it is an attempt to make the history again for those subaltern groups, their politics and movement which has never been given importance and recognized.

People's resistance is a unique phenomenon which takes the form of collective dimensions in complex socio-cultural settings. People's resistance are the collective expressions for survival of their existence which is carried out not on the individual level but as collective venture that take the shape of a 'movement'. The movement is an expression of either one or many interconnected forms of resistance based on specific ideological expression. Therefore, movement, resistance and ideology are the three interrelated factors that can determine the dynamics of social change. The functioning of the state cannot be fully understood without the understanding of the politics of the masses. It is sometimes the perception, beliefs, aspirations and the views of the subaltern classes which come into the conflict with the state apparatus. Most of the time, the collective action of people is often regarded as alienated, estranged, excluded and outside the polity. The movement of the masses has been ignored and neglected for not having their own set of voice or politics and it has been misunderstood that the movement of the masses has been manipulated by the ruling classes. But this is an oversimplification and deviation and stumbling block to the efforts of making a democratic and egalitarian social order. Because masses have their own set of politics and it is independent of elite politics as also referred by Ranajit Guha. Again most of the time social movements are said to be backed by certain objectives, ideology, programmes, leadership and organization which are interdependent influencing each other. But, Ranajit Guha has his own observation of looking into the subaltern struggle, although these components are found in all types of movements or insurgencies, including the so-called 'spontaneous' rebellions, their forms vary from very unstructured to well organized.[4] Guha looked into the different perspectives and the arguments which believe that the peasant insurgencies were spontaneous and lacked political consciousness and organization. Against these contentions, Guha brilliantly offered the study of peasant insurgency in colonial India. The study provides two basic premises:

(a) Subaltern politics was quite different from the elite politics, and
(b) Peasant consciousness had an autonomous domain of its own.

The peasant or tribal insurgency not to be treated merely as the 'objects' of history as Guha believes that they should be rather treated as the 'maker' of their own history bestowed with the transformative consciousness of their own. Guha has extensively discussed both these arguments in his classic, 'Elementary Aspect of Peasant Insurgency in Colonial India'. In this study peasant resistance of nineteenth century has been re-appraised and Guha theorized the incidence of peasant revolts in colonial India which became the landmark effort of the Subaltern historiography to reconstruct 'the other history', i.e.

history of the subaltern people. Subaltern historiography provides useful framework for studying social movements in general and tribal and peasant insurgencies in particular. It also attributed to the complex phenomenon of peasant or ethnic protest movement or at least significant part of it in contemporary India.[5]

Peasant resistance in colonial period were labelled as 'backward looking and unprogressive' and their consciousness as 'pre-political' and 'superstitious' by the colonial historiographers and colonial authorities.[6] To Guha, the term 'pre-political' is misleading. As Eric Hobsbawm in his analysis in the book, 'Primitive Rebels: Studies in Archaic Forms of Social Movement in the 19th and 20th centuries' noted that, the rebel peasants uprisings in colonial period were 'pre-political' in nature, because their uprisings had no 'elaborate blueprint' to replace the existing superstructure.[7] Contesting that, Guha asserted that "the rebel peasant had a clear knowledge of his activity intended principally to destroy the authority of the super ordinate elite".[8] Here the word 'Pre-Political' highlighted the absence of political consciousness or will. 'Pre-political' category according to Hobsbawm included those movements which lacked any organized ideology or consciousness and he even went to observe that social banditry lacked in organization or ideology and he claimed that 'banditry is rather a primitive form of organised social protest'. Though Guha acknowledges that Hobswam's reading may be valid in the historical context he sat out to analyze but the expression 'pre-political' is not made any sense in terms of peasant uprisings of colonial India. Because the peasant and tribal revolt against *sarkari*, *sahukari*, and *zamindari* oppression to which they were subjected and exploited can be looked as the rebellion against the exploited power structure of landlord and *zamindars*. Different uprisings of that time such as Bhumij, the Kol insurrection, the Santal, Deccan riots etc. of nineteenth centuries cannot be termed as pre-political rather they were the subaltern struggle which was an attempt to break the power relationship of the existing structure. However, Guha also admits that the tribal and peasantry movements of twentieth centuries have been different from the earlier nineteenth centuries in terms of maturity, consciousness and organization. But those struggles were essentially political in character and they were significant in history and therefore, those struggles cannot be altogether denied as 'pre-political' phenomenon in history. It was a struggle against the triad nexus of the landlord, moneylender and colonial government. Guha in his book 'Elementary Aspect of Peasant Insurgency in Colonial India' has highlighted six elementary aspects of consciousness of the rebel peasants. These are negation, ambiguity, modality, solidarity, transmission, and territoriality. At the same time, he shows that the peasant consciousness which have been labelled as 'negative consciousness' in the elitist discourses as a hostile power sometimes became manifested at the time of insurrection. Therefore, Guha's framework has the relevance in studying the peasant, tribal or ethnic movement of colonial period. Late colonial India also faced numerous 'transformative' rebellions, particularly in tribal areas. Colonial rule and its commercialization adversely affected the tribal societies and their life which later on became the reason for the various tribal uprisings in colonial period. Because of the oppressive colonial policies, the Adivasis were deprived from their forest rights which led to the rise of fundamental questions of land and forest on which they were traditionally been dependent for their livelihood. The struggles led by the subaltern groups symbolized on how they have been fighting for their existence since historical times. However, the history of the peasant and tribal insurgencies in India were replete with "myths, rituals, rumours, hopes for a Golden Age and fears of an imminent End of World."[9] Conventionally, these factors are rendered as meaningless by the historians by declaring them as manipulative actors to rouse the peasantry. But, it is the attribution of Subaltern historiography which has considered the importance of these elements which not only potentially unite the rebels but also divide them. Subaltern Studies scholars were among the first to acknowledge the role of superstitions and religious beliefs as legitimate causes in understanding rebel consciousness, even when such beliefs defied rational explanations by social scientist.[10] Many of the issues raised by the Subaltern historians such as Shahid Amin's account of rumours and beliefs about colonial India's great personality or symbolic figure, M.K. Gandhi, again Gyanendra Pandey's accounts of sectarian movements related to predominantly agrarian communities in northern India, and in David Hardiman's analysis of tribal uprisings in western India under the apparent command of a local goddess. In his famous essay,

'Gandhi as Mahatma : Gorokhpur District, Eastern U.P., 1921-22', Shaid Amin shows how Mahatma Gandhi's image as great leader, great soul was the factor which empowered the peasant to undertake 'direct action' against the existing order of village society. In fact, sometimes, it evoked the multiple acts of violence which are carried out in the name of Gandhi. For example in Gorakhpur a 'criminal tribe' called *Badhik* looted a market in Gorakhpur and attracted violence to anyone who opposed their immediate goal. Likewise, they attacked the money lenders, judges, local landlords and Englishmen who were the symbols of authority in rural hinterland. At the same time they justified their acts as that it was the command of the Gandhi in their dreams or in miracles to carry out the act of violence as they were also chanting the slogans in the name of Gandhi or 'Gandhi's Swaraj'. Again David Hardiman has discussed a particular tribal movement of South Gujarat during 1922-23 which is known as Devi Movement. Devi according to the Adivasis was a female divinity called Salabai who possessed immense power. It is under 'Devi's command and inspiration which led the Adivasis to agitate against the local liquor and landlords.[11] But according to Hardiman, unfortunately historians have not written much about such tribal movements. It is not always about the limitation of archival information. More importantly these occurrences are not accepted as the standard 'nationalistic or socialistic' historiographies of colonial India. There is no recognition in nationalist history about the fact that peasant and Adivasis fought against colonial domination on their own. Therefore, the subaltern historians were interested in developing a rebel historiography because they believe that conventional studies of Indian nationalism have been shaped by the dictates of colonialist and bourgeois-nationalist elitism.

Subaltern social movements and struggles in India continued to proliferate even after post-colonial period. The conflict becomes acute when it came to the edge of the subaltern questions with the post-colonial state apparatus. "The failings of the modernizing mission of the Nehruvian State" and also the failure of the state to meet the demands and needs of the masses most often led to process of 'struggle and negotiation' between subaltern masses and the state.[12] Again on the other hand the 'elite revolts' of neoliberal restructuring with that of rising trends of Hindu communalism, both of which reflect and are vehicles for the interests and aspirations especially of the middle class and higher caste Indians were noteworthy.[13] Simultaneously, there are other dimensions of multiple forms of 'subaltern politics' which is again representing another long history of struggle of the oppressed against the established existing order. One form of struggle that Corbridge and Harris have mentioned in the book 'Reinventing India' is what they called as 'empowerment from without'. The contentions are for the Dalits and Adivasis of India who are situated at the bottom of the social pile in India, even after the Constitutional provisions for job reservations, reservations of educational places and seats in political assemblies and more generally the extension of the franchise to them, secular education and the laws aimed at the abolition of caste based discrimination for the advancement of the democratic process in India. Such measures according to Corbridge and Harris have not made any change in the lives of these groups in a significant way. But these measures still had a significant impact on "the terms of engagement between India's scheduled and non-scheduled communities by allowing an awareness of potential collection strength among the scheduled communities and improving their bargaining position *vis-a-vis* dominant groups."[14] Corbridge and Harris also mentioned another process, i.e. 'empowerment from within' which is identified with the electoral success of Bahujan Samaj Party (BSP) which is mainly Dalit based party of Uttar Pradesh, although electoral success of the BSP cannot be equated with the improvement of living standards of the poor. But it is an electoral upsurge in which backward caste and class groups are participating more actively in electoral politics and they are able to bypass the politics of local elites which establishes them as a voice to be reckoned with. India with its post-1991 neo-liberalization of economy marked a new shift in the role of state. With the onslaught of globalization, liberalization and privatization, the trend is to roll back the state, and it is with that process marginalized sections became more vulnerable and the legitimacy of the state was questioned. The post-1991 neoliberalization of the Indian political economy has accelerated the process of development which is very much for the interest of the capitalist and corporate sector that has led to the large scale development dislocation, displacement, dispossession and it has also resulted into the frequent resistances and struggle from the subaltern groups such as Adivasis and Dalits for their rights. A large number of subaltern movements in India such as ethnic/tribal movements or the recent farmers, movement, women movements, that have gathered momentum since Independence provides wide spectrum for the rise of subaltern politics in India. However, most of these contemporary movements come fairly close to what T. Di Tella has referred to as 'the revolutions of rising expectations' which are often unleashed by developmental imbalances resulting from the modernization process in the Third World.[15]

Tea Garden Community as Subaltern and their Quest for Identity

Subaltern Resistance is not a new phenomenon in India. It is since colonial period different subaltern social groups have been fighting for their rights. It is in this context even after independence subaltern groups have been struggling for achieving their rights. For the welfare state like India, the presence of the Subaltern groups like Dalits, Adivasis, landless, dispossessed, workers, Scheduled Caste, Scheduled Tribe, rural and urban poor, women and others who are subordinated and excluded from the domain of power have been compelled to accept their inferiority by the dominant social groups and elites of the society. Sumit Sarkar within this standpoint has tried to focus on the tea-garden communities of India as the Subaltern. Reference may be made to the Subaltern Studies project published in *Subaltern Studies,* Volume III where Sumit Sarkar says:

> I am employing the term 'Subaltern' as a convenient short-hand for three social groups—tribal and low caste agricultural labourers and share-croppers; landholding peasants, generally of intermediate-caste status in Bengal (together with their Muslim counterparts) in labour in plantations, mines and industries (along with urban casual labour).[16]

Tea Plantation in India was the outcome of the Colonialism. The process of tea plantation and the recruitment of workers in the plantation of India demonstrate the ways of colonial government's economy of exploitation and also shows the socio-economic backwardness and underdevelopment of the recruited tea garden working community in India. The Colonial Government had created and sustained the hierarchical plantation structure in the tea plantation of India. They have created this hierarchical structure through the indenture labour mobilisation. This hierarchy had been maintained by the colonial plantation authority under the strict disciplinary rule. Strict control through panel laws was exercised to keep the tea garden workers away from desertion and disobedience. Due to the exploitative regime of the plantation authority made against the tea garden workers of India, they had been suffering from diseases, malnutrition and mortality. Tea plantation had achieved a profitable state by putting the tea garden workers in the state of subalternity and marginality, through the coercive recruitment process, very low labour wages and deplorable living and working conditions.

To understand the status of the tea garden community of Assam, one has to keep in mind that because they have been in Assam for more than a century, their identity remains as fluid as it used to be in the colonial era. They have been struggling for their specific identity since colonial days which have pushed the community to the state of subaltern. The Assam tea plantation brought a conglomeration of different ethnic groups mostly from the densely populated neighbouring provinces. The major chunk of workers brought to Assam was drawn mainly from the Chotanagpur and the Santhal Paraganas of colonial India. The recruits in the tea plantations were mainly tribal peasants who were driven out of land and compelled to migrate in search of livelihood through a complex set of colonial policy.[17] Although the community is generally referred to as a single entity but they are the composition of different ethnic groups. Most of the ethnic groups constituting the composite identity are scheduled either as 'tribe' or as 'caste' in the states where they originally belonged. It is observed that there are around 59 ethnic groups belonging to such tribal category and similarly 40 groups to caste category living in Assam which are denied of such status in this state.[18] In Assam, they are officially recognized as Other Backward Community (OBC). Their population in 1971 was found to be around 30 lakh and according to 2011 Census tea garden community constitute about 18 to 20 per cent of the total population.[19] The segregationist attitude of the wider Assamese society towards the tea garden community persisted till the second half of the 20th century, since when a very gradual process of change in public perception regarding them could be observed. It is with the rise of an educated section amongst the tea garden community, along with the changing democratic process and the social movements and political upheavals in the state since the late 1970s have led to the emergence of an inclusive 'tea tribe' identity. It submerged the tribal or caste categories of tea workers, providing the basis for their political attitudes and actions which moved the community to assert for their identity. It is their long standing demand of both the tea garden workers and the ex-tea garden workers community to include them in the list of Scheduled Tribes and Scheduled Castes in Assam like their counterparts in the neighbouring tea growing states of West Bengal and Tripura, who enjoy the status of SC or ST depending upon their actual status on this count in their respective places of origin. Deprivation of this identity has lead to another phase of movement among the tea garden community of Assam. Ever since India became independent these people lost their Scheduled Tribe status in Assam and thus they were deprived of their educational, economic and political privileges guaranteed by the Constitution of India, instead they were classified as OBC.[20] This situation has made the tea garden community increasingly restive in recent years.

In the colonial period, it was specially the tea workers and not the ex-tea garden workers in Assam who were given certain constitutional rights. The issue of rescheduling the tea garden tribes was raised in the 1930s when the Schedules were being prepared. The Reform Officer of that time, in charge of drawing up the list, expressed resentment over the fact that 6,00,000 ex-tea garden coolies have been excluded though the names of most of our coolie castes appear as scheduled in their home province.[21] It is basically done for excluding the ex-tea garden castes from political concession and they had no one to represent their cause. Further, the European lobby did not see much reason to promote their interest in the government.[22] Hence, the removal of ex-tea garden caste from the lists of Scheduled Castes and Scheduled Tribes remained a constitutional mishap, which is not even rectified in the post-Independence period. On the other hand, the reservation of seats for the tea workers' representatives in the provincial legislature was also removed in independent India. It has been observed that many of those claiming to be Scheduled Tribe status in their places of origin say that the ex-tea garden workers are also 'tea tribes'. On the other hand, many who claim to be of non-tribal origin vehemently deny the term as Adivasis. As per an official account around 12 per cent of Indian tribals live in the Northeast, but they do not include the Adivasis who are Munda, Oraon, Santhal and other tribals of Jharkhand origin but are not in the schedule in Assam.[23] The Adivasis are probably 50 to 60 per cent or 30-40 lakh of the 'tea tribes', i.e. present and past plantation labourers who are estimated to be about 60 lakh in Assam.[25] Adivasis can be broadly divided into two communities in Assam, namely the tea garden workers and the ex-tea garden workers who later on after completing their contract term has settled in and around the plantation area after procuring a little land mostly through government schemes. They are forcefully migrated to Assam as indentured workers and of extremely of harsh kind, during colonial period. Poverty, illiteracy, political disenfranchisement and immense socio-economic political problems characterize the conditions of Adivasis in Assam. In the face of misery perpetrated by the colonial state, Adivasis started migrating to Assam and began to work as the tea plantation workers. Their socio-economic conditions were unquestionably in a very pitiable state. The Adivasis, who are aboriginals of this country, are still struggling for the ST status in the State. The demand for Scheduled Tribe status by the Adivasis is not a new phenomenon. The basis of their demand is that, if the communities such as the Santhal, Oraon, Munda, Gor, Kol, Bhil, Tanti, Kurmi etc. could be included in the ST list in other states like West Bengal, Odisha and Jharkhand why should be they deprived this privilege in Assam ? Adivasis are the worst sufferer in BTAD area where they have to face the ethnic cleansing which is again an inhuman treatment meted towards them in post-colonial state. The Bodo Militants in BTAD have separately targeted diverse communities at different points of time. From the history of violence of western Assam, it can be distinctly marked that the Bodo militants perpetually picked up soft targets while going in for massacres. Attacks were unleashed on the communities that included Koch-Rajbanshis, Adivasis, Muslims, Bengali Hindus, Nepalis etc. The worst sufferers among the communities have been the Muslims and Adivasis. Series of incident which can be termed as ethnic cleansing happened against the Adivasis in 1996-98, Beltola incident of 2007 and force eviction of 2010, clashes between Bodos and Adivasis in 2014 are some examples which grossly violated the human rights of Adivasis in Assam. The conflict between the two communities, i.e. Bodos and Adivasis have created a serious havoc in the state which resulted to the large scale of displacement of both the communities. The violence that occurred between the two communities and the consequent displacement brought two pertinent issues to the fore—the non-recognition of Adivasis, including the tea-tribe and ex-tea tribe communities in Assam as S.Ts. and non-granting of land rights under the S.T. and deprivation of other Traditional Forest Dwellers (Recognition of Forest Rights) Act to Adivasi and Bodo forest dwellers in denuded forest areas. According to Forest Rights Act, 2006, the Adivasis are entitled to claim their rights on the forest land which they possess before December 13, 2005. However, the Adivasis of Assam are denied their rights under the Forest Rights Act as well. In fact, Adivasis were not given rights and entitlements on the forest lands which they have been cultivating for decades and it is the reason which makes the Adivasis of these region are highly unsecured.[25] The terror attacks and the subsequent violence triggered the displacement of about 8,000 Adivasis from 26 villages and 1,200 Bodos from nine villages, all of them forest dwellers in the Ultapani reserved forest under the Haltugaon Forest division in Kokrajhar district, within an eight-kilometre radius from Saralpara.[26] The northern bank of Brahmaputra, where Bodos are in majority mostly falls under the tribal belt and block created immediately after independence. This tribal belt and blocks were created to safeguard the tribals from various ways of coercion from other advance communities which is mentioned under the provision of VI Schedule and Article 19(5) of the Constitution of India. One of the most important provisions of the VI Schedule is that in that demarcated belts and blocks, non-tribals have occupied a good portion of land and have legal documents of the same for which today tribals are becoming minority in the tribal belts and block itself.[27] But the said part is that poor implementation of that provision of VI Schedule has further aggravated the violence of the two communities which led to the killing and the lost of innocent lives and property. The ethnic conflict between the two communities left many displaced, homeless and has created a rift between the two communities. These conflicts are seen recurring again in November 24, 2007, when about "5,000 Adivasis comprising men, women and children were attacked in Beltola of Guwahati while they were attending a peaceful procession in demand of Scheduled Tribe Status."[28] They were attacked by the local people of Beltola including shopkeepers. Consequently, "300 Adivasis were brutally wounded, hit by bamboos, iron rods and bricks. More than one dead and a teenage Adivasi girl Laxmi Oraon was stripped, chased and kicked."[29] It was a shameful episode which brought a sharp reaction from the civil society condemning the incident and urged for the sake of maintaining communal harmony not to term the incident as an Assamese-Adivasi community clash.[30] The procession was organized by the All Adivasi Students Association of Assam (AASAA) to press for the inclusion of Santhali Adivasis and the 'Tea Tribes' in the list of Scheduled Tribes (Plains). Adivasi protesters had bows and arrows, bamboo poles with sharpened ends; the odd axe and machete which are according to the protesters are cultural symbols not for attacking or hurting any individuals. In fact, this practice of carrying primitive arms in a political procession has been a recent innovation.[31] The Beltola incident showed the sporadic violent episode which also depicts nature of subaltern movement. The march was a peaceful one for a legitimate cause but it turned violent soon after it started. A section of the protesters resorted to acts of vandalism, and to this invited brutal retaliation from residents of the Beltola locality. The leadership was unable to control the unruly elements and had no influence upon some section of participants in the processions. Procession was infiltrated by some elements which sought trouble and finally, the purpose of the procession was not meted.[32] Because of the failure of the security personnel and police to intervene and control the situation led to the later tragedy. The Adivasis who have been neglected by the state for decades and all this outrage expressed through their movement is the manifestation of their frustration and deprivation. The post-Independence period and in the era of globalization which has placed the region in a state of transition has opened the ethnic communities such as Adivasis, to break free and to cross the delimit of colonial boundaries. The Beltola incident clearly demonstrates the Adivasis' search for an identity through their demand for the ST status and at the same time reflects the failure of the state to grant their demands.

In pursuance of the demand of the Adivasis to secure their identity through granting them as Scheduled Tribe status in Assam has been articulated by the emergence of the leaders of the educated section of the community. The attempt to articulate the socio-political aspirations of the community has started as early as in the decade of 1930s by the leaders such as Chanu Kheria. He was the first matriculate from the community. He submitted a memorandum before Assam Franchise Committee in 1934 to enlist the Tea Garden and Ex-Tea Garden Labourers in the *Dalit* category.[33] Four years later, another highly educated leader P.M. Sarwan, who was also the first post-graduate from the community launched a new platform Assam Chotanagpuri Sabha in 1938, which can be regarded as the first organization originated from the community.[34] The application of the word 'Chotanagpuri' evidently used to evoke the memory of their place of origin and thereby mobilize the support of the community. The first students' organization emerged from the tea garden community was the Assam Chotanagpuri Chatra Sanmilan or Chotanagpuri Students' Association founded in the year of 1947 in Dibrugarh. The main objective of the organization at its initial phase was to bring all the Tea and Ex-Tea Community Students to a common platform and to initiate a socio-political and economic consciousness among them, to drive away the social evils that have deeply entered into their society. The Chotanagpuri Students Association was remained active for a very short period. In 1954, another Students organization was formed under the leadership of Dinanath Choudhury and Chatragopal Karmakar at Golaghat in the name, Assam Chah Bonua Chatra Sanstha and later the name was changed to 'All Assam Tea Garden Community Students Association' by amending the constitution of the organization in 1958. But in 1984, it was again changed into 'Assam Tea Labour Tribes Students Association' and finally, it was converted to 'Assam Tea Tribes Students Association' (ATTSA) and presently it is the largest student organization representing the community. The aim and objectives of the ATTSA is determined to emancipate the tea garden community from exploitation and deprivation. ATTSA has been putting forward number of demands before Central and State

Governments from time to time. The most significant demand among them is the demand for Scheduled Tribe (ST) status for the tea and ex-tea garden community of Assam and they have submitted several memorandums to the Government of India and State Government regarding different issues and demands of the community.

Again in Grahampur, near Gossaigaon another organization called 'All Assam Munda, Oraon and Santhal Association' was floated by Mithius Tudu, a prominent leader of Munda community in the year 1957. This organization was later named as 'Assam Adivasi Council' in 1959. This organization made a serious effort to expedite the process of enlisting the 'Adivasis' as Scheduled Tribe by submitting memorandum before Central Government.

After the Kokrajhar riot between Bodo and the Adivasis in 1996 another student organization called All Adivasi Students Association of Assam (AASAA) emerged around 1997-1998 from Gossaigaon. Presently, AASAA is widening its support base in various parts of Assam mostly in the ex-tea workers. The main demands of AASAA are recognition of Scheduled Tribe status of the Adivasis in Assam and rehabilitation of the victims of Bodo-Adivasi riots in Kokrajhar District.

It has been observed by and large that Adivasis have become conscious of their separate ethnic identity under a separate banner as a means of accelerating their development. Conduction of different groups and bodies such as Adivasi Mahasabha, Adivasi Mahila Mahasabha, Mundari Sahitya Sabha, Adivasi Sahitya Sabha, All Chautal Students Union etc. are some of the organizations where they have been articulating their demand for Scheduled Tribe status as well as different issues of Adivasis encompassing their economic, social, cultural and political issues which gives a new dimension to the Identity movements of tea garden community of Assam. Therefore, the demand of the tea garden community for Scheduled Tribe and Scheduled Caste status can be looked into the larger framework within which the debate is being conducted and which drew the attention of continued reliance on a highly questionable stock of colonial knowledge about Indian society and culture. As noted scholar Sanjib Baruah rightly observed that the "demand of tea garden community of Assam should be a source of embarrassment, as well as cause for serious introspection."[35] Their movement is the clear manifestation of deprivation and is the movement against the betrayal and deception by the privileged and powerful section of the society.

Identity Movement of the Tea Garden Community and Understanding the Autonomy of the Subaltern Movement

If the identity movement of tea garden community of Assam is analysed from the subaltern studies perspective then the question of subaltern autonomy needs to be interpreted. Viewed from the perspective of the subaltern studies, conduction of different Adivasi mahasabhas, different protest march, can be seen as the manifestation of the autonomy of the subaltern agency. Since some of these events happened before the reported fieldwork, and the researcher could not participate in the events, the events are reconstructed through the narratives of the different members of these groups who belonged to the tea garden community. The visual materials such as photographs and pamphlets of those conventions were analysed too. It can be seen that through these movements and celebration of festivals of different ethnic groups of tea garden community, they have tried to reconstruct their identity in cultural and historical terms. By creating an ideological framework for the establishment of an 'alternative counter culture' along with the celebration and adoption of Assamese culture and language a new politics is seen to be developing. So the present study has looked into the question whether the Adiavsis can be analysed as constituting an alternative independent cultural and political domain as observed by noted Subaltern historian Ranajit Guha and whether the subaltern inevitably is an integral part of the dominant discourse and is unable to speak in his/her own words? as pointed by Spivak.[36] According to Ranajit Guha, the colonial Indian State is unable to create an all-inclusive universal hegemonic discourse rather political dominance has been exercised and it created conditions for the emergence of an independent autonomous political and cultural subjectivity of the subaltern.[37] But it is after independence different subaltern groups started to assert their rights and to question the hegemony of the state. Regarding subalterns pertinent discussion on 'autonomy' of the subaltern movement, the arguments put forwarded by Gyan Prakash, a noted historian and Subaltern School proponent aptly describes the changes in the conceptualization of the subaltern:

> Subalternist search for a humanist subject-agent frequently ended up with the discovery of the failure of subaltern agency: the moment of rebellion always contained within it the moment of failure. The desire to recover the subaltern's autonomy was repeatedly frustrated because subalternity, by definition, signified the impossibility of autonomy. Subalterns' resistance did not simply oppose power, but was also constituted by it.[38]

Therefore, the subaltern autonomy cannot be understood in its own. Understanding of the Subaltern cannot come into being its own. The consensus has been arrived on the dependence of the subaltern on the dominant discourse. Arising of the Subaltern started to be visualized not outside but inside the dominant discourse, 'in its interstice' as Gyan Prakash has mentioned. Although, it has been argued that the subaltern has arisen within the dominant discourse, the power of the subaltern clearly reveals their ability to exert pressure on the dominant structures as well. Therefore, the cultural, economic and political assertion of the tea garden community do not happen in vacuum and are not inspired by their own subjectivity. Rather, they emerge as a response to the hegemony of the dominant discourse. Noted subaltern scholar Partha Chatterjee expressed his view on the changes in the conceptualization of the subaltern. Presently, the political activism of the subaltern is no longer manifested the actual confrontational rebellion, as it was in the case of peasant insurgency discussed by Ranajit Guha. In contemporary time, subalterns use bureaucratic and institutional means in fulfilling their objectives. Using of that strategy and tactics resembles the elite politics. As happened with the context of the movement of the tea garden community of Assam where the earlier protest and strike were most often sporadic and although some of the strikes and movement of tea garden community are spontaneous outburst of their anger but most of their movements, such as enhancement of wages, demand for bonus, demand for their land rights and forest rights and assertion of Scheduled Tribe status is guided and articulated by different organizations. The leaders of the different organizations such as ACMS, ATTSA, AASAA, Adivasi Mahasabha, Adivasi Sahitya Sabha etc., have mobilized different issues and grievances of the community and presented in front of the government through memorandum, letters and discussion. Thus, the politics of subaltern and elite shows significant interconnectedness with each other. It is also not true that the political autonomy of the subaltern never existed, rather in post-independence period it has been affected by many elements. Peasant uprisings of colonial time and present social movements reflected the differences in terms of the conceptualization of subaltern. Guha's view on Subaltern as an autonomous political and cultural agent is deconstructed by the Spivak and O'Hanlon as they focused on recent shifts to the interdependency between the subaltern and the dominant culture.[39]

The prevalent discussion on tea garden community's different movement and the celebration of different community festivals and programmes and the formation of different socio-political organization stressed their cultural practices marks their essential differences from the dominant mainstream Assamese society. These movement showed the attempt of the tea garden community as subaltern to unite among themselves as a community against the powerful structure of the society. The community frequently invokes the motives of the suffering, humiliation and other forms of victimhood which act as the factor to unite the subaltern group which they can relate. On the other hand, the identity of the tea garden community as subaltern group is highly fragmented, as the process of acquiring an *Adivasi* identity or tea tribe identity signifies politicization of the subaltern identity of the community. It also depends on the context where it has been used. Because some of the leaders and educated section of the community cannot be termed as subaltern or the subaltern identity can be assumed by non-subaltern groups, as they become elite to their community but on the other hand they might be subaltern in terms of the reference to the other dominant section of the society.

Conclusion

Therefore, the important argument for the analysis of subaltern resistance in today's India, points to the fact that power and resistance are practices which takes place within a set of social relationships.

It is in that context power and resistance of subaltern can be seen where cultural and political symbols and horizons of understandings violate the boundaries between dominant and subaltern groups, and are continually constructed, deconstructed and reconstructed systematically through the exercise of power and resistance.

NOTES

1. Guha Ranajit, "On Some Aspects of the Historiography of Colonial India", in Ranajit Guha (ed.) *Subalten Studies I: Writings on South Asian History and Society*, OUP, Delhi, 1982, pp. 5-6.
2. Guha Ranajit, "Elementary Aspect of Peasant Insurgency in Colonial India", *OUP*, New Delhi, 1983, pp. 3-9.
3. *Ibid.*, pp. 5-6.
4. Shah Ghanshyam, *Social Movement in India*, Sage Publication, New Delhi, http://archive.org >stream>movement.
5. Dhangare, D.N. (Nov. 1988). "Subaltern Consciousness and Populism: Two Approaches in the Study of Social Movements in India", *Social Scientist,* Vol. 16, No. 11, pp. 18-35.
6. *Ibid.*
7. Hobsbawm, Eric (1963). *Primitive Rebels: Studies in Archaic Forms of Social Movement in the 19th and 20th Cencutries,* New York: Praeger.
8. Guha Ranajit (1963). "Elementary Aspect of Peasant Insurgency in Colonial India", *OUP*, New Delhi, pp. 3-9.
9. Guha, Ranajit (1982). "The Pros of Counter Insurgency", in Ranajit Guha (ed.), *Subaltern Studies II*: *Writings on South Asian History and Society*, OUP, Delhi, p. 39.
10. Majumdar, Rochona (2015). "Subaltern Studies as a History of Social Movements in India", *South Asia: Journal of South Asian Studies*, Vol. 38, p. 14.
11. *Ibid.*, p.14.
12. Corridge Stuart, and John Harriss (2000). *Reinventing India: Liberalization, Hindu nationalism and Popular democracy,* Cambridge: Polity Press.
13. Corridge, Stuart, *et al.* (2005). *Seeing the State: Governance and Governability in India,* Cambridge: Cambridge University Press.
14. *Ibid.*, pp. 210-211.
15. Dhangare, D.N. (Nov. 1988). "Subaltern Consciousness and Populism: Two Approaches in the Study of Social Movements in India", *Social Scientist*, Vol. 16, No. 11, pp. 18-35.
16. Sarkar, Sumit (1984). "The Condition and Nature of Subaltern Militancy:

Bengal from Swadeshi to Non-Co-operation, c.1905-22", in Guha, Ranajit (ed.) *Subaltern Studies III, Writing on South Asian History and Society*, OUP, New Delhi, p. 272.

17. Deka, Kangkan (2008). "Colonialism, Migration and the Problemetics of the Making of an Identity: Tea Tribes and 'Adivasis' of Assam", in Srama Chandan Kuamar, (ed.) *Souvenir*, North East History Association, 29th Session, p. 175.
18. Kar, R.K. and Sarma, J.L. in R.K. Bhadra and S.R. Mondol (ed.), *Stratification, Hierarchy and Ethnicity in Nortn East India*, pp. 69-84.
19. Goswami, T.C. *Chah Janagusthi Jivan Charya*, p. 0.10.
20. Kerketta, Robert, "The Adivasis in Assam—Their Past, Present and Future", in Thomas Pullopillil (ed.), *Identity of Adivasis in Assam*, New Delhi, Indian Publishers & Distributors, pp.10-20.
21. J. Dev, Bimal and Lahiri, Dilip, K., *Cosmogony of Caste and Social Mobility in Assam,* Mittal Publications, Delhi.
22. Sharma, Pratim Dhurba, "Demand of Tea Tribes for Scheduled Tribe Status in Assam: A Review", in Goswami Sandhya (ed.), *Troubled Diversity*, OUP, New Delhi, p. 113.
23. Fernandes, Walter, "Assam Adivasi Identity Issues and Liberation", *Vidyajyoti Journal of Theological Reflection*, February 2003.
24. *Ibid.*
25. *Adivasi Struggle in Assam*, www.indiatogether.org 2008.
26. Talukdar, Sushanta, "Tribal Turmoil", *Frontline*, Vol. 24, No. 24, Dec. 8-21, 2007.
27. *Assam*, Hand Book of Govt. Circulation 1981-1990.
28. Nilsen, Gunvald Alf, "Adivasi in and Against the State", *Critical Asian Studies*, 44:2, 251-282, retrived from Jstore.
29. *Ibid.*
30. Mishra, Udayan (December, 2007). "The Adivasi Struggle", *Economic and Political Weekly*, Vol. XLII, No. 51, pp. 22-28.
31. Gohain, Hiren (December 8, 2007). "A Question of Identity: Adivasi Militancy in Assam", *Economic and Political Weekly.*
32. Mishra, Udayan (December, 2007). "The Adivasi Struggle", *Economic and Political Weekly*, Vol. XLII, No. 51, pp. 22-28.
33. Sharma, Debabrata, *Asomia Jatigathan Prakria aru Janagosthigata Anusthan Samuh*, Ekloibya Prakashak, Guwahati, p. 367.
34. *Ibid.*, p. 367.
35. Sanjib Baruah (2007). *Adivasi Politics in Assam*, telegraphindia.com, December 10, 2007.
36. Kristina Garalyte, *Subaltern Autonomy: Dalit Students' Identity Politics in India*, http//ejournals.vdu.it>article.
37. *Ibid.*, p. 57.

38. Prakash, G., "Subaltern Studies as Post-colonial Criticism". *The American Historical Review*, 99(5), 1475-1490, Retrieved from Jstore database.
39. Kristina Garalyte, *Subaltern Autonomy: Dalit Students Identity Politics in India*, http//ejournals.vdu.it>article.

4
Interrogating Women's Subjectivity in Political Discourses

Nisha Jain

Introduction

Feminist political theory has gained wide acceptability in the contemporary political discourses. Feminists question patriarchy, which operates largely through different institutions, processes and practices, which are all controlled by man. This results in women's subordination, which are questioned and challenged by feminists. Feminist political theory has evolved through two different waves. The first wave of feminism can be traced back to the 1840s and 1850s and was associated with the question of legal equality and women's suffrage movement. On the other hand, the question of women's liberation and emancipation from patriarchy forms the basis of second wave of feminism (Heywood, 2004: 62).

Feminist theorists have come to accept that patriarchy is a universal value system, though it exhibits different forms culturally and historically. It does not have the same effect on all women. Some basic features are the same for every woman, others are very different. Still the patriarchy is recognized as a key concept for understanding the oppression of women. The present thinking on patriarchy is much broader and takes into consideration, on the one hand, the importance of the gender as a category for analyzing subordination of women and signifying the value of 'difference' in the category of gender, on the other. Sexual asymmetry presents a universal fact of human social life. Gender is pervasive symbol of power. It is present in the processes, practices, images and ideologies as well as distribution of power in various sectors of social life. Gender processes include overt decisions and procedures that control, segregate, exclude and construct hierarchies. Gendered processes also include the construction of symbol, images and ideologies that justify, explain and give legitimacy to patriarchal structure of power.

The fact that patriarchy persists despite socio-economic and political changes may be explained with reference to the subjectivity of women. This chapter explores how the social and political theory has devoted itself to the question of subjectivity and how the culture intersects with the structure of power and sustains them and how the political struggle takes place in the sphere of culture. In the contemporary studies, culture is analyzed as a site of political struggle. In this chapter, attention is also being drawn to the ways in which culture has helped to reproduce structures as also the ways in which the individual may negotiate such structures through their actions.

At a similar level, we find that the process of modernization, modernity and modernism has led to the impetus for social change on the way we problematize the gender question. The processes of modernity and modernism evoked Scientific Revolution, Industrial Revolution, Renaissance, Enlightenment ideas and theories as well as Reformation. "Modern societies", argues Andrew Heywood, "were seen to be structured by industrialization and class solidarity, social identity being largely determined by one's position within the productive system" (Heywood, 2004: 7).

However, despite modernization, there seems to be no substantial change in the status of women. As a group they remain marginalized, exploited and oppressed. The liberal democratic framework of the Constitution, the whole gamut of progressive laws and the opening of educational and career opportunities, while bringing few urbanized women at par with men, have not contributed much in changing the lot of mass of women. Even for those women who have been exposed to the new opportunities provided by the context of modernization and development, change has not spelled power. Powerlessness remains the lot of women whether modernized or not. Now when the Indian society and the state are grappling with COVID-19 pandemic, it seems that it encouraged the indifference and marginalization of women from the collective consciousness along with the increased apathy in the society. Today the discourse has moved towards facilitating the economic recovery and unfortunately there is no evidence that it includes women and their concerns.

Deprivation and marginalization of women is deep-rooted and lies in the very structure of the society. It is institutionalized in the shape of patriarchy. It is patriarchal structure of the society which while glorifying "Shakti" of women reduces her to hapless creature with no identity, except that of a wife and a mother. While defining different codes of behaviour and morality for males and females and specifying the segregatory role division of both of them, the patriarchal order denotes power men have over women on the one hand and dependence of women upon men on the other. Patriarchy operating through gendered structures, positions men and women in superior and inferior position and grants different values and meaning to them. Gendered institutions indicate the presence of gender in the processes, practices, images and ideologies, and the distribution of power in various sectors of social life. The law, politics, religion and the state all show predominance of men over women and reveal almost an ineffective role of women. Similarly, gendered processes include construction of images, symbols and ideologies which not only reinforce gender division but also legitimize power/powerlessness in the society (Acker, 1988: 473-497).

This chapter has been divided into two sections. The first section probes the question of patriarchy *vis-à-vis* women's subjectivity. In going into this analysis, we have let the subjectivity question as is being looked in the wider political discourses by Foucalt, Althusser and Antonio Gramsci. The second and last section ends with a brief conclusion.

Probing Patriarchy and Women's Subjectivity

Patriarchy represents a system of power exercised over women through institutionalization of gender relations. It characterizes a system by which women are kept subordinated in a number of ways involving discrimination, control, exploitation and violence. The sex differentiation is the pivot around which discrimination of women is institutionalized. There is in the society an ordering of human activities, practices and social structures in terms of differentiation between men and women (Nijjeholt, 1992). Gender, therefore, not only represents the difference of sex but also the difference of power. Similarly, the gender role division not only represents the different roles for men and women, but also the hierarchical relationship between these roles.

So pervasive is the hierarchy governed by the gender division that social processes and social institutions are influenced by such differences. It is because of the operation of gendered processes and institutions that images, symbols and ideologies reinforcing power *versus* powerlessness get legitimized. Segregation, exclusion and construction of power relations on the basis of gender are some of the mechanisms through which patriarchy expresses itself. It is the end product of patriarchy that one can find women being excluded from certain economic and political activities; that their role as 'wife' and 'mother' are associated with fewer powers and prerogatives as compared to those of men; that irrespective of variation in terms of class, religion, ethnicity etc., women are relatively worse off in terms of income and status as compared to the status of men within the same social category (Rosalso & Lamphere, 1974).

Patriarchy is maintained and reinforced as a cultural pattern intersecting with the structures of power. This is the way patriarchal relations and powers are expressed, reinforced and simultaneously reproduced through culture. It is the culture through which patriarchy operates subtly in day-to-day life. The cultural reinforcement and reproduction of patriarchy takes place through embodiment of femininity and masculinity and the construction of the subject in such a manner that the subject accepts her femininity or masculinity as natural.

It is being increasingly recognized that the question of female oppression is quite complex and cannot be explained with reference to merely male domination and repressive exercise of power by men over women. There is no individual formally empowered to wield disciplinary power charged with the production of a properly embodied femininity—rather it is much more dispersed and anonymous. It is invested in everyone and no one in particular; women and men alike are ideologically mystified by the dominant gender pattern. Its understanding involves a profound knowledge of processes and inculcation of patriarchal values in the very personality of men and women. These processes ensure that the patriarchal power operates almost through a self-regulatory mechanism.

The complexity underlying the processes of domination and power over women can be understood from the institutionalized and systematized phenomena of gender relations. There is no individual formally empowered to wield disciplinary power in accordance with the codes of patriarchy. The exercise of power over women is dispersed and anonymous. It operates in a manner which in the words of Foucault has "capillary form of existence" (Seridan, 1980). It is so much internalized that it seeps into their very individual person, "reaches right into their bodies permeates their gestures, their posture..." (Seridan, 1980).

The concept of subjectivity is quite helpful in understanding the subtlety and complexity underlying women's oppression. The argument that the subject is constituted rather than given, can be used to understand how "a subject endowed with a consciousness" who "freely forms or recognizes ideas in which he believe" and "acts in conformity with these ideas", becomes determined by the dominant ideological value patterns (Smith & Cornell, 1984: 80). In other words, the individual who appears to be "a centre of initiatives, author of and responsible for its actions" (Smith & Cornell, 1984: 80) may be perceived as an end product of the process of cultural reproduction. The individual is constituted and constructed as a subject not only accepting the dominant ideas but also reproducing the same.

Lot of theorization that has taken place on the question of subjectivity can be extended to the understanding of domination and oppression of women. Using the concept of subjectivity, one can transcend the simplistic notion that few or many misogynists are mainly responsible for the oppression of women. According to Elizabeth Grosz, acts of discrimination against women can be regarded as notions of structural determination, not simply as random actions committed by the aggressive individuals but an inbuilt feature of the entire social system. "Women's oppression needs not to be seen as a conscious process of oppression perpetuated by few (or many) misogynists because of their irrational hatred of women. It is the result of various social structures unconsciously reproduced by both men and women, independent of their personalities or choices" (Grosz, 1990a: 70).

Almost all the social formations currently operating in the world are patriarchal in nature. Patriarchal ideas are the ruling ideas and have attained a level of, what Gramsci calls 'Hegemony'. Gramscian concept of hegemony makes it possible to understand how ruling ideas, norms and practices have powerful impact over the dominated groups including women. Hegemony is, according to Gramsci, best understood as the process through which the subordinated forms of consciousness are constructed without recourse to violence and coercion (Allum, 1991: 10). The world-view of dominant classes is so thoroughly diffused by its intellectuals that that it becomes the common sense of the whole of the society. Applied to the culture of patriarchy, the process of internalization and diffusion of its values takes place in such a way that ordinary, practical and everyday life is overwhelmingly influenced by such cultural values which appear natural. The ideology of patriarchal values and gendered relations thoroughly penetrates into the society and seeps into the common sense of both men and women.

It is the concept of hegemony which can be helpful in understanding how patriarchal mechanism of power becomes self-regulatory and how women accept their subordination without any manifest resistance. The patriarchal ideas being hegemonical inform day-to-day practices, ritual, lifestyles, patterns of living and thinking processes. These ideas have forceful impression upon both men and women. These ideas create a particular form of consciousness among women that can be defined as a subordinated form of consciousness.

It is the femininity defined by patriarchy which in the process of being produced subjugates women. It is the total process of construction of 'femininity' and 'women subject' because of which much of the oppression against women is passed off as unnoticed. One of the concerns of Althusser was to define how the construction of subject takes place through ideology. According to him, all ideologies have performed the function of continuing concrete individuals as subjects, "Ideology represents the imaginary relationships of individuals to their real conditions of existence" (Barrett, 1991: 84). Individual subjects, according to him, are constructed in the image of dominant ideological subject. Ideologies, in the opinion of Althusser, do not operate principally through the conscious beliefs but are best thought of structures that are imposed on the people (Barrett, 1991: 84).

Althussur believes that every society must ensure a relative continuity through successive generations. Hence, a socially appropriate skill, attitudes and a submission to dominant value system is guaranteed. According to him, certain system of ideas, practices and beliefs are produced and reproduced by various 'Ideological State Apparatuses' like the family, educational system, religion and the media. These 'ideological State Apparatuses' are agencies that are necessary for social and power relations to continue.

It is argued that patriarchy is reproduced in such a manner that it continues in its basic and fundamental form despite the changes in law, the Constitution and even in society. Patriarchy is reproduced subtly as the human being herself/himself becomes an agency of reproduction of patriarchal norms. Here, the concept of subjectivity assumes significance. Gender is considered a fundamental determinant of subjectivity. The concept of subjectivity has been used and developed in sociological, cultural and linguistic theories. It is assumed that the language, institutions, art, literature, popular culture are to a great extent manifestation of the dominant classes and play a significant role in the formation of the unconscious. The exercise of power over women takes place through their subjectivity. Our institutions, popular culture, art, literature all reproduce masculine and feminine subjects. Masculinity and femininity are not naturally given but are socially determined and acquired.

The patriarchal ideology functions in such a manner that women identify themselves with specific ways of given gender relations and assume the same as obvious and natural ones. Sexism permeates the way of general thinking and men and women are both mystified by the dominant gendered ideology. To both of them, the world appears as it should be and men and women appear to be placed in it as they should be (Grosz, 1990b: 149).

Using the Gramscian concept of common sense nature of ideology, we can understand as to how ideology succeeds in getting the overwhelming majority of the population accept certain ideas and certain ideologies as natural. According to Gramsci, every ideology has a common sense nature (Gramsci, 1989: 325). Accordingly, an ideology becomes common sense to the extent that it succeeds in getting overwhelming majority of population to accept certain practices and certain ideas as natural. Explaining the role of ideology and the nature of common sense, Stuart Hall argues, "common sense shapes out ordinary practical, everyday calculation and appears as natural as the air we breathe. It is simply 'taken for granted', in practice and thought, and forms the starting point (never examined or questioned) from which every conversation begins, the premise on which every television programme is predicted" (Hall, 1989: 8).

In understanding the deep-rooted structures of patriarchal domination, the concept of common sense nature of ideology can be useful. The definition of common sense that it is not spontaneous thought of the masses but it is the way in which the subordinate classes live their subordination can well be applied to the understanding of subordination of women (Allum, 1991: 25). The gender question operates through the convention of dresses, playthings, simple do's and don'ts for boys and girls, the commonly used phrases and idioms, the jokes. The folk songs, the folk lores and many more things are expressions of conversion of patriarchal ideology into the common sense (Weedon, 1987: 75-77). The common sensical ideas about men and women, their interrelationships, roles, expected behaviour while representing the power relations also are projected as normal and socially accepted ideas. To quote Hall, "the hope of every ideology is to naturalize itself out of history into nature, and thus to become invisible to operate unconsciously" (Hall, 1989: 8). The gender relations are so naturalized that power operating through these becomes almost invisible. The ideology of patriarchy is culturally reproduced and reinforced as it penetrates into the society and seeps into the common sense of both men and women. It is the common sense which accepts the operative gender relations as natural, which plays an important in maintaining the centrality of gender difference as a focus of power in society. The process of naturalization and diffusion of patriarchal and gender values takes place in such a way that ordinary, patriarchal and everyday life is overwhelmingly influenced by such cultural values which appear natural. Oppressive relations, therefore, do not apparently appear to be oppressive, by being normalized, perception is made imperceptible. The common sense which make women accept the ideas and practices leading to their oppression as natural, render them incapable of understanding either the nature of their oppression or agencies responsible for their subjugation (Weedon, 1987: 79).

Domination becomes easier if those who are dominated accept their domination. This self-regulatory mechanism of domination operates through those ideas and practices which are dominant and which operate as natural. The reason as to why patriarchy persists in spite of the process of modernization may be found in the mechanism of self-imposition of power. The patriarchal power operates in such a manner that a woman herself becomes an agent of her oppression. The patriarchal ideology and patriarchal ideas operate in such a manner that women inculcate the values related to these in their very personalities and they accept their domination of the beliefs emanating from patriarchal ideology and they willingly share the social, cultural and moral values reinforcing male domination. In this way, they themselves enter into the process of their oppression. The production of embodiment of femininity is one such process of internalization of gendered relations and construction of a woman subject who willingly accept her subjugation and domination.

Gramsci related the concept of hegemony with the agency of subject. He made an in-depth analysis of the organization of consent (Barrett, 1991: 55). Following Gramsci, it is being increasingly accepted that the hegemony of ruling ideas is maintained by involving the subjects in the process of obtaining consent to their own subordination. Domination over women becomes easier as they are themselves involved in the process of domination, by willingly accepting their own subordination and thus consenting to their domination and becoming agency of their own oppression. According to Althusser, consent and hegemony are correlated in such a way that the subordinated groups, willingly adopt the subject positions necessary to their participation in the social formation (Belsey, 1985: 49).

Social and political theory has pointed to different ways in understanding how the consent of subject is obtained in its own oppression. In understanding women's agency, attention has been paid to Althusser's concept of 'interpellation'. Althusser was of the view that ideology interpellates concrete individuals as subjects, as a result, people "recognize" (misrecognise) themselves in the ways in which the ideology 'interpellates' them, or in other words, addresses them as subjects calls them by their names and in turn 'recognize' their autonomy (Belsey, 1985: 49). According to him, "the individual is interpellated as a (free) subject in order that he shall submit freely to the commandments of the subjects, i.e. in order that he shall (freely) accepts his subjugation" (Belsey, 1985: 49). Using this concept of interpellation, Himani Bannerjee, has tried to analyze women's relationship to the patriarchal and gendered norms and forms of their own class. Examining the subjugation of women belonging to the propertied classes, she examines how women are simultaneously empowered by their social location and subordinated to the class, patriarchal and gendered organization (Banerjee, 1991).

Gramsci elaborates the process of diffusion of dominant ideology through co-opting intellectuals of subordinated classes. According to Gramsci (1989: 60), "the intellections of the historically progressive class, in the given conditions, exercise such a power of attraction that, in the last analysis, they end up by subjugating the intellectuals of the other social groups; they thereby create a system of solidarity between all the intellectuals, with bonds of a psychological nature and often of a caste character (technico-juridical, corporate etc.)." Thus, the world-view of the dominant classes is so thoroughly diffused by its intellectuals that it becomes the common sense of the whole of society (Gramsci, 1989: 60).

The co-option of women intellectuals into the hegemonic patriarchal nature may be worth examining in understanding the agency and consent of women, in the process of their subordination. Co-option may not be absolute and complete but may operate in such a manner that vocal sanctions provide it an intellectual base, though within the broad social, moral and cultural space within the patriarchal space. Gramscian concept of 'Passive Revolution' may be helpful in understanding how women intellectuals are co-opted by being provided a relatively independent space, yet within the hegemonic space of patriarchy. According to Gramsci, when a hegemony is "weakened in any way and class or a class fraction elaborates an ideological stance in its bid to become morally, culturally and politically a dominant force, than to preserve the hegemony of dominant class, exclude masses from asserting influence over political and economic institutions certain demands are accepted from below, thus limiting the struggle and their accommodation within the current social formation" (Banerjee, 1991). The co-option of women demanding change has been a global process where it is generally observed that whenever a women's movement gained momentum and whenever women asked for more rights, the leadership invariably was mobilized and co-opted. This was done through the process of accepting some of their demands and giving them some incentives while imposing those ideas essential for maintaining the centrality of gender difference as a focus of power in society.

The agency of women in the exercise of power over them operates through much more subtle ways. Foucault brings to our attention the complex work of disciplinary system and prescriptive technologies through which power operates in the modern era. He argues that power does not operate in a global structure, but that which evolves from below. It is induced in the body and produced in every social interaction. Foucault paid much attention to the disciplinary techniques through which docile bodies are constituted. According to him, such power is exercised through the creation of a state of consciousness and permanent visibility which does not rely upon violence and public sanctions nor does it restrain the freedom of body to move from place to place. On the contrary, the body enters a machinery of power that expresses it, breaks it and rearranges it. The feminine subject is thus constructed. A practical and subjugated body is produced, a body on which an inferior status has been inscribed. The *Oxford Concise Dictionary of Politics* elaborates on the notion of 'Discourses' as perceived by Foucault:

> What Foucault's historical research establish, he argues, is the existence of discourses, or discursive formations. These are not structures in the sense employed by structuralist writers such as Levi Strauss or Althusser. In denying rigidly deterministic structures, Foucault creates a space in which political actors can act. This leads us to Foucault's concept of power.
>
> ....Foucault argues that discursive formations are networks of power within which we are all enmeshed. As he claimed on several occasions, power is everywhere and everything, and is therefore 'dangerous'. However, power, he argues, can be positive as well as negative, productive as well as repressive. What is more, he insists that every instance of power brings with it an instance of resistance to power (McLean and MacMillan, 2009: 204).

Foucault uses the term technologies of power to explain the minute and almost invisible structures of power. The technologies of power operate in human bodies to shape organize and inscribe them in particular ways (Barrett, 1991: 134). He talks about the disciplinary power which is exercised on the body and soul of individuals. It increases the power of individuals and at the same time it renders them docile. Foucault gave an in-depth account of the ways in which such disciplinary power operates, which include production of certain forms of knowledge, disciplinary techniques and the use of subject's body. Foucault's concept has been widely used to explain the invisible power exercised over women and the construction of women's subjectivity in such a manner that they neither perceive such power nor resist it (Sawicki, 1991: 221). Applying Foucault's concept, Feminists have documented far-ranging deeply inscribed structures and forms of masculine domination. "The medicalisation of women's bodies, i.e. which made pregnancy a disease and undermined women centred healing institutions, 'the physical and sexual abuse of women', from witch burning to rape; and the mutilation of women's bodies for the sake of 'beauty' are just some of the ways feminists have identified women's bodies as the locus of masculinist power" (Diamond and Quinby, 1988: xv).

Conclusion

Femininity thus represents the universal women subject. This universal subject is an ideal construct representing the womanhood to which each individual woman must conform. This ideal construct is the woman who denies herself and who is willing agent of her own domination. In the Indian context, she is essentially linked with her home and finds her happiness only in a family. Passiveness and powerlessness is her basic character. Patriarchy is a system which systematically evaluates masculinity in positive and femininity in negative terms it is "made up of not only different, unequal treatment of two sexes, but also of the different meanings and values accorded to the two sexes..." (Grosz, 1990a: 49-50). In this hierarchy, the relative power of men over women is institutionalized and legitimized, the discrimination against women is naturalized and thus made invisible and subordination and subjugation of women is internalized.

To conclude, we can argue that we need to appropriate Gramsci in problematizing the gender question. This essentially leads to a conflict between the 'self' and the 'other'. While, the 'self' is the 'man', the 'other' is the 'woman'. Together, the 'self' and the 'other' are supposed to complement and supplement each other. However, the divisive relations between the 'self' and the 'other' rules out any kind of complementary relationship. The only alternative, therefore, is to resort to the Gramscian notion of waging a 'counter-hegemonic struggle' by women against patriarchy, so that every woman can live their lives with self-respect and dignity.

REFERENCES

Acker, J. (1988). "Class, Gender and Relations of Distribution". *Signs*, University of Chicago Press, 13(3), Spring, 473-497.

Allum, P. (1991). "Ideology and Common Sense". *Occasional Paper No. 2, University of Reading,* Department of Politics, February, 10.

Banerjee, H. (1991). "Fashioning a Self: Educational Proposals for and by Women in popular magazines in Colonial Bengal". *Economic and Political Weekly,* 26 (43), October 26.

Barrett, M. (1991). *The Politics of Truth: From Marx to Foucault.* Polity Press.

Belsey, C. (1985). "Constructing the Subject: Deconstructing the text". In J. Newton and D. Rosenfelt (Eds.). *Feminist Criticism and Social Change: Sex Class and Race in Literature and Culture,* pp. 45-64, Methuen.

Diamond, I., and Quinby, L. (Eds.) (1988). *Feminism and Foucault: Reflections on Resistance.* Northeastern University Press.

Gramsci, A. (1989). Edited and translated by Hoare, Q., and Smith, G.N. *Selections from the Prison Notebooks.* International Publishers.

Grosz, E. (1990a). "Contemporary Theories of Power and Subjectivity". In Gunew, S. (ed.). *Feminist Knowledge: Critique and Construct,* pp. 59-120. Routledge.

Grosz, Elizabeth (1990b). "Philosophy". In Gunew, S. (Ed.). *Feminist Knowledge: Critique and Construct,* pp.147-174. Routledge.

Hall, S. (1989). *The Hard Road to Renewal: Thatcherism and the Crisis of the Left.* Verso.

Heywood, A. (2004). *Political Theory: An Introduction, Third Edition.* Palgrave MacMillan.

McLean, I., & McMillan, A. (2009). *Oxford Concise Dictionary of Politics.* Third Edition. Oxford University Press.

Nijjeholt, G.L. (1992). "Women and the meaning of Development: Approaches and Consequences". *Working Paper-Sub Series on Women's History and Development,* 15, 15.

Rosalso, M.Z., & Lamphere, L. (1974). *Women, Culture and Society.* Stanford University Press.

Sawicki, J. (1991). "Foucault and Feminism: Toward a Politics of Difference". In Shanley, M.L., & Pateman, C. (Eds.). *Feminist Interpretation and Political Theory,* pp. 217-231. Polity Press.

Seridan, A. (1980). *Michel Foucault: The Will to Truth.* Tavistock Publications.

Smith, S., & Cornell, B. (1984). *Reading Althusser: An Essay on Structural Marxism.* University Press.

Weedon, C. (1987). *Feminist Practice and Post-Structuralist Theory.* Basil Blackwell.

5
Time for "Right to Offend" in India?
A Study on Sedition Culture and Consecutive Press Freedom Index in South Asia

Santhosh Mathew

Does India Need a "Right To Offend?"

> *"No idea is above scrutiny; no people are below dignity"*
>
> —Majid Nawaz.

In the 2015 *Shreya Singhal* case, Justice Rohinton Fali S. Nariman's judgement on striking down Section 66A of the IT (Information & Technology) Act as unconstitutional owing to lack of clarification of what is "offensive"? is the daunting question that seeks relevance with each passing day in the largest democracy of the world. This question gets a fresh interpretation with the recent Supreme Court judgement aligning with the removal of Sedition in India as also supported by the government marking 'Azadi ka Amrit Mahotsav' or 75 years of Independence. However, implementation is still in questions as governments all-around the world and specifically South Asia has used these tedious laws to either curb dissent or even clamp down on extremism.

So, what exactly can be termed offensive? Racism, misogyny, homophobia? Or can anything one thinks or perceives can be taken as offensive, or can any question asked, or any belief be seen in a kaleidoscopic view of offense? While Nicholas Copernicus did offend the established status quo when he proposed a stationary sun as the centre of the universe, it was Percy Bysshe Shelly's book *"The Necessity of Atheism"*[1] that got him expelled from Oxford University in 1811 as he refused to deny authorship to his belief because many felt offended by the essay.

India from a civilisational perspective has always encouraged the culture *'Tarkshastra'* a treatise dealing with the dialectic process, logic, and debates that took pride in open communications and dialogue. But the recent deluge of arrests under the sedition laws owing to offensiveness highlights a saying that if you have a hammer, everything looks like a nail. This chapter analysis the Indian society as increasingly becoming a group of touch-me not that find the ever-growing need to defend our own country, religion, or community from even the slightest criticisms thrown at it as we become increasingly insecure of our own culture that we feel the need to defend it. Primarily, the right to offend has three separate dimensions and some pre-established legal framework that encourages the right to be offended. *Firstly*, the right to offend the state under which we have section 124-A of IPC as a sedition law to safeguard executive. The number of cases under 124-A has increased by 160 per cent from 2016-2019 and bulk of these cases are filed for criticising political leaders and governments. It is the same Section 124-A which lost its relevance after India adopted a constitution that was used during the colonial rule by British to arrest any dissidents to their atrocious rule. For the judiciary's right to get offended we have the contempt of court and for legislature we have the privilege motions. *Secondly*, the right of a community to get offended that involves 153-A which deals with promoting enmity between communities that is something needed that it refers to clear promotion of enmity or any form of incitement. But 295-A creates questions as it involves insulting a religion in any form to be considered as a violent act and can lead to arrest which is cognizable and non-bailable. *Thirdly*, it is defamation under Sections 499 and 500 IPC involving civil and criminal defamation.

The *Vinod Dua* case in 2021 gives a new interpretation to sedition. The Supreme Court bench tempted to examine the constitutionality of the sedition provisions and a probable strive to define the limits, which gets juxtaposed by frequent and often absurd sedition cases. The Supreme Court's quashing verdict on the case upholding journalistic freedom from sedition cases simply by either criticising the government on their provisions or policy is seen as a huge victory roaring the pledges of press freedom and democracy in the country. The fact that the law's maximum punishment is life imprisonment for something even probably not related to distort the interest of the state as a whole is very concerning. For instance the *1992 Kedarnath Singh* judgement by the Supreme Court circling around IPC section 124-A that previously defined sedition as words or actions that bring "hatred, contempt or dissatisfaction" towards the government. The Supreme Court being fully aware of the implications regarding the bare reading of this provision was keenly aware of the possible ways that could be attempted to silence free speech or quell dissent. Keeping this is mind, the application of sedition by the section was consciously narrowed down to instances having "intention" or "tendencies" to cause any public disorder or endanger the security of the state. But did this anyhow change the prevalent interpretation of sedition cases? What is concerning in this matter and is already discussed is how easy according to law it is to accuse any journalist, artists, academicians or even citizens under sedition with the wording of working against the state's 'interests'.

India, slipping further to 150 in ranking the WPFI 2022 has seen an upsurge of sedition cases in the recent years from 35 in 2016 to 93 in 2019. Sedition charges were brought against the leaders of the Patidar agitation in 2015, protesters against Gurmeet Ram Rahim Singh's conviction in 2017, the Jat unrest in 2017, Pathalgadi movement in 2018 and those opposing the Citizenship (Amendment) Act, 2019. The most controversial instance of what seems to be misuse of this law was the February 14 arrest of 21-year-old Bengaluru-based climate activist Disha Ravi in the "toolkit" case. A very similar fate was shared by many journalists, artists and comedians or protestors. The Delhi police accused Disha Ravi and two other individuals in that very case of collaborating with a pro-Khalistan group—Poetic Justice Foundation—and linked them with the January 26 violence during a farmers' rally in Delhi. While granting bail, the Additional Sessions

Judge, Dharmender Rana, said that the offence of sedition cannot be invoked to minister to the wounded vanity of governments.

On the other hand, the idea of a society with an inherent 'Right to offend' goes against the very grain of Indian culture that believes in the World as one family of *'Vasudhaiva Kutumbakam'* and preaches peaceful coexistence. A right to offend in this setting would mean the right to hurt others by the assertion of our own very rights. This would ideally not only lead to disarray in the administration but is also equivalent to "Right to violence". It is also notable that with the rights also comes the individual responsibilities and accountabilities towards the rights of others. India since its freedom struggles has always talked about rights and duties, for instance Mahatma Gandhi's dissociation from the Chouri Choura movement or any kind of violence came with the essence of harmonious coexistence come what may. The right to offend in India would bring silent undertones of emotional and psychological violence as no individual should have the outright authority to hurt the feelings of others as that would mean an unmindful society deaf of all kinds of sensitivities. These two arguments form the crux of the topic at hand that whether a section of people have a right to be offended by somebody else's freedom of expression.

Sedition (Section 124A IPC)	**National Security Act, 1980**	**Unlawful Activities (Prevention) Act, 1967**
Defines sedition as any words, spoken or written, or signs, visible representations or other communication that can cause 'contempt/ hatred'/'excites/attempts to excite disaffection' towards the government. (Disaffection is defined as feelings of disloyalty or any form of enmity).	This Act provides for 'preventive detention in specific cases and matters connected therewith'. It empowers central and state governments to detain people in order to prevent them from acting in any manner 'prejudicial' to the security of India, for instance: the relations of India, relations with foreign countries or maintenance of public order, maintenance of supplies and essential services to country.	This law is aimed at enabling Central and State Governments to check and prevent terrorist activities threatening the integrity and sovereignty of India.

(Contd.)

Sedition (Section 124A IPC)	National Security Act, 1980	Unlawful Activities (Prevention) Act, 1967
However, any comment that shows disapproval of actions by the government, made with intention to alter the actions of the government are not considered sedition unless they excite or attempt to excite hatred, contempt, or disaffection towards government.		
Tough proviso: It is cognisable, non-bailable and non-compoundable. Those charged under this have to surrender their passports, barred from holding government jobs. Punishment of 3 years to life sentence, a fine or both.	Tough proviso: People can be detained without being charged for up to 12 months. People can be detained for 10 days without informing the reasons for the same. Individuals can file appeals in the High Court advisory board but not allowed lawyer during trial.	Tough Proviso: UAPA permits detention without charges up to 180 days. 2019 amendments gave Union power to notify an individual as a 'terrorist' without any trial. Custody could be extended to 30 days. On February 1, 2021, the Apex Court gave the ruling that bail could be granted to an accused if the right to speedy trial was violated

Sample Size—A demographic division of

- 16-25
- 26-40
- 41-60
- 61-82
- Above

Responses-104

Age

104 responses

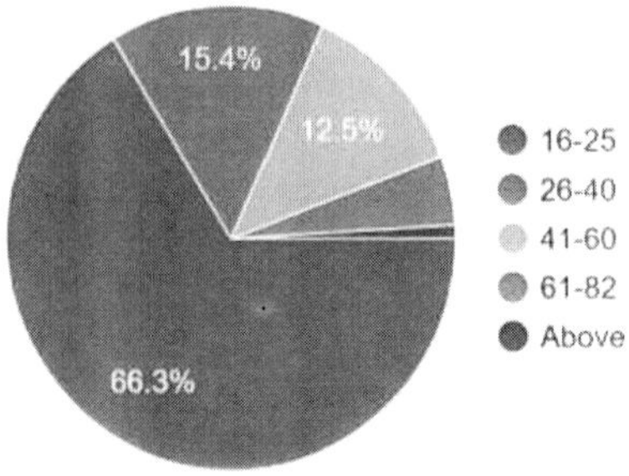

Do you think that freedom of speech should automatically involve the right to offend?

102 responses

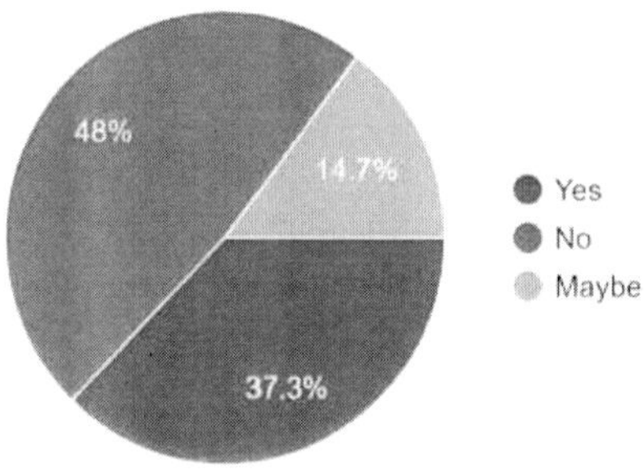

If someone says something racist, misogynistic or tries to denigrate a particular religion or community

101 responses

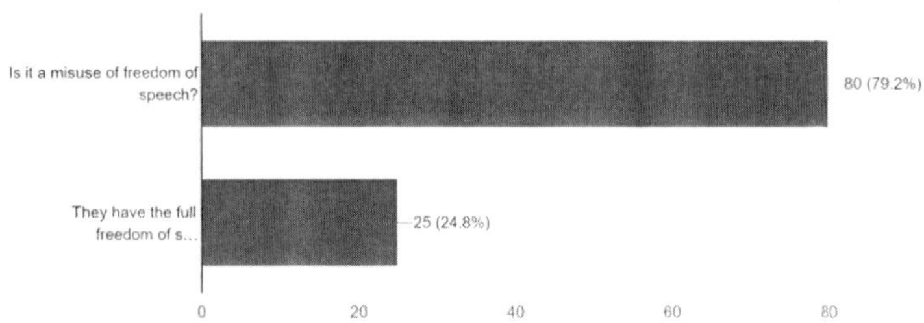

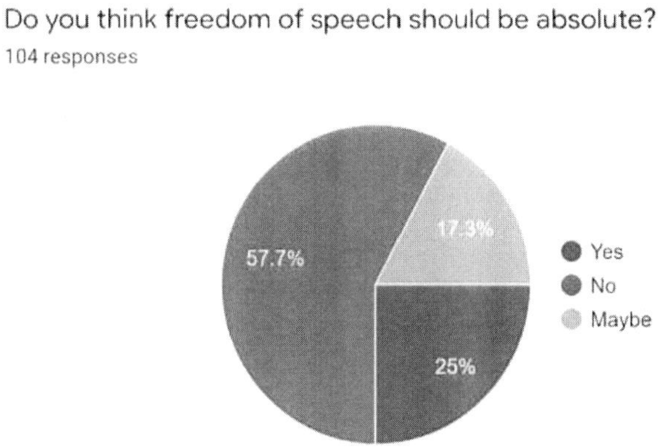

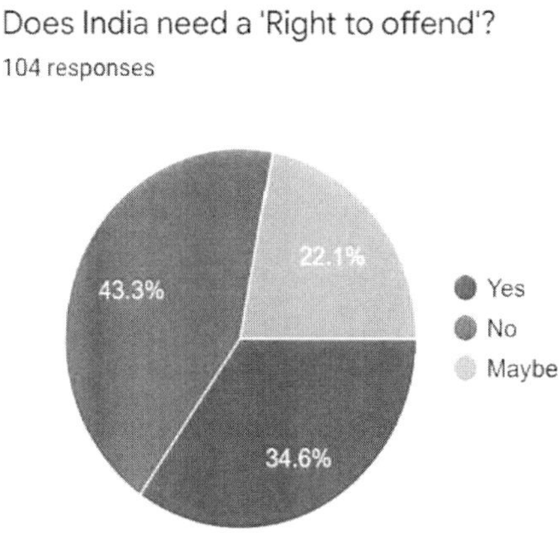

1. But, before we deeply delve into the topic, let us look at some of the "offensive" cases from South Asia and inversely relation to the declining Press Freedom Index 2022.

Bangladesh 

Sedition in Bangladesh is primarily dealt under the 2018 Bangladesh Digital Security Act (BDSA) which succeeded the Information and Communication Technology Act of 2006 in governing cyberspace and laying out framework for determining penalties. In the last few years a number of activists, journalists and poets have been arrested by the governing authorities under the Act. A prime example of the same would be the arrest of a 15 year old boy for defaming Islam simply by liking a Facebook post that seemed blasphemous. Additionally, Bangladesh is also under United States sanctions due to the alleged use of Rapid Action Battalion (RAB) for curbing dissent against the government and accused of several human rights violations. According to the Special Prosecutor in the Cyber tribunal, 65-70 per cent cases under Section 57 of previous ICT Act does not stand a change of legality in any court and is simply used to harass individuals. The current 162 ranking of Bangladesh can be owed to the Bangladesh Government's history of prosecuting citizens based on online crimes. On the other side hate crimes has also been on rise in Bangladesh, the long array of Durga Puja Violence followed by vandalism and countrywide strike after alleged blasphemy felt by the majority of Muslims is an exemplary case and often questions the propagation of secularism in the country. The underlying question again being the debate between freedom and security.

Pakistan 

The controversy over the ranking of Afghanistan and an even worse ranking of Pakistan in the World Press Freedom Index comes as a shocker to many analysists as to how can a government run overtly by Taliban leaders with open assassination of journalists be better that a "supposed" democracy in Pakistan. While throwing an objective light on the press report that inherently is criticised for the vagueness of the questionnaire, inherent bias and lack of transparency, Pakistan does shoulder a significant amount of the blame put on it. Here we can see a significant parallel of rising intolerance based on "offensive" blasphemy and sedition cases with political motive at the core. Similar to India, Pakistani courts are still tied with the colonial 124-A sedition law[2] in Pakistan Penal Code. While on one hand we have the burring of the Sri Lankan national on open street for religious bigotry, on the other we have stricter restrictions on Press freedom like the formation of Pakistan Media Development Authority (PMDA) under Imran Khan's government that denied journalists the constitutional right to peaceful protests and censored journalistic freedom as well in the name of peacekeeping. Extending sedition to political activists, human rights groups and defenders or individuals in a proactive role, the definition for offense and the absolute lack of clarity for the same paves a leeway for the governments to interpret sedition.

Bhutan 

As the best performer in the 2022 World's Press Freedom Index from South Asia, ranking at the 33rd position, Bhutan stands at a juncture of critical analysis to understand sedition. The scrapping of sedition charges against businessman Penjore who actively criticised the government and called it a "lawless nation" came as a welcome relief to the citizens as it reiterated the importance of freedom of speech and the rule of law. On the very other hand we have the Supreme Court upholding the High Court's judgement and sentencing Khandu Wangmo[3] to 21 years in prison for sedition. She is convicted for issuing hateful statements and insulting the King or the Royal Government of Bhutan. Underlying this one cannot ignore the complete lack of plurality in Bhutan and the constant efforts over time to maintain homogeneity like the Lhotshampa massacre. This lack of plurality and the prevailing hierarchical way of administration and living inherently does not create any differences in opinion or separatism that challenges the government. This could invariably be seen reflected in its press freedom ranking which shows the lack of any difference between the people and the acceptance of Bhutanese isolationism to till date. This type of model is not something that countries like India can replicate as its essence lies in pluralism.

Creative Freedom

As individuals, does believe in something and not in the opposite give us the right to decide which ideas are worthy of expression and which are not? Creativity *via* books, films, comedy, songs, dance, graffiti, or any other forms from time to time has been constantly attacked by diverse beliefs of the people from backgrounds. A shocking example would be a classic like Harry Potter. While these books have claimed a world full of potter heads, it still offends a certain section of the world community that find demonic references in the text.

A similar fate is faced by almost all creative content available in India today. And probably the worst is faced by our jesters. It is not only Munawar Faruqui who got jailed for a joke he could have cracked but also several others who have either chosen to tone down on their jokes or go all in with their creativity no matter what offends whom.

In July comic *Agrima Joshua*[4] was sent various rape and death threats after a joke about Chhatrapati Shivaji Maharaj's upcoming statue which is under construction. She issued an official apology yet, her Instagram read about how comedians are going out of control and one of them needs to be killed for the comedians to understand their "*aukaat*".

The world of ***films*** has seen various degrees of censorship from a decade now. While it is mostly done to remove any kind of objectionable content that does not get well with Indian society it also prevents the influx of new ideas into this very society. In this changing paradigm independent films or unregulated content on the OTT platforms came a ray of hope which are soon to be taken away by the new OTT laws that propose to monitor the content on three rigorous level and been always kept under scrutiny. The question here is that can any faith or any belief of a person be shook by a mere negative representation of the truth or a criticism that the audience finds it difficult to integrate with the freedom of speech of these artists or creative minds?

India, for a long time has been recognised as a hub of liberal society with freedom of expression better than at least middle eastern countries or authoritarian governments. But, even on Pakistani television Banana news network spoofs and mimics corrupt politicians. Similarly, Iranian films issue powerful rebuttals to prevailing political conditions and criticising authoritarianism. Chinese dissident Ai Weiwei [5]continues to fearlessly rile the government *via* films and images based on conditions in Hong Kong. These realities show an increasing mediocrity in creative work in India which simply abides by the rules of society out of sheer fear of reprisal.

Academic Freedom

To discuss academic freedom in India we will be analysing three highly publicized events in India. First, the resignation of Professor Pratap Bhanu Mehta[6] from Ashoka University. Second, refusal by the director of IIM, Ahmedabad, Errol D'souza[7] to allow MoE to review a

Ph.D. thesis approved by the institution. And third, heckling of Vivek Agnihotri's screening of Buddha in a Traffic jam in Jadavpur University.

All these three events might seem dissimilar but collectively illustrate the dances of academic freedom and the consequences of 'offence' towards the state or community.

Professor Mehta was a public intellectual at the Ashoka University, who was voicing a fearless critique of the government on national media and finally, impelled to step down to save the private institution. Similarly, with D'souza, director of a public institution who took a stand for academic principles first and claiming autonomy from the state supported by the IIM's Act had to face government harassment and interference.

These incidents involve, two kinds of academic freedom-engagement in public sphere by academicians and researching on controversial matters within the university. Universities and their constituting teachers, students, and staffs for long has been at the receiving end attacking phase of government reactions directly or indirectly. Faculty and students continue to be targeted for unpopular intellectual opinions, attack on campuses, homes raided, and books and papers seized.

Activists like Shoma Sen of Nagpur University, Anand Teltumbde of the Goa Institute of Management and JNU students like Natasha Narwal, Debangana Kaltika, Umar Khalid and Sharjeel Imam are detained under UAPA as 'urban Naxals'[8] conspiring to overthrow the government by inter-community violence. Sharjeel Imam himself stands accused of being 'radicalized' by merely the books he read for his M.Phil. thesis on violence during partition. The further government outreach in these institutions can be highlighted by an increase in contractual teaching staff. New service rules cancelling the right to free speech.

On the contrary, the education phase has also seen simultaneous polarisation that not only simply denies but also violently attacks the ideology of dislike and it is inclusive of teachers and students in these very institutions. This is also a form of curb on academic freedom. The increasing culture of labelling a person for opposing ideologies is also a stamp for views unwelcomed. Two primary examples for these are: (1) How the evolutionary biologist Richard Dawkins was cancelled after being invited to University of California for his alleged Islamophobia. A charge he denied and justified by saying that he criticised all religions at the same time.

A brief history of student protests in India.

(2) In Jadavpur University, the screening of Vivek Agnihotri's Buddha stuck in a Traffic was cancelled at the last minute. He was heckled and attacked outside Gate No. 8 for alleged murder of Rohith Vemula which he denied and claimed to be a suicide. Universities, today need a self-checked and only autonomously checked free and open space of debates, enquiry, and knowledge acquisition that the current structure that keeps on loosing with each passing day.

Religious Freedom

Adding meaning to how scary and destructive 'offence' can be, all we need to do is add religion. Like when a school teacher in France gets beheaded for offending religious extremists by showing a satirical cartoon previously used by Charlie Hebdo to a group of school children in a cultural democracy like France. In a way, we tend to live in the age of offence. And taking offence is not an explicit right to any particular political or non-secular or cultural cluster. From the most self-acclaimed liberals to Hindu fundamentalist social media to various Muslim fanatics, now-a-days all of them operate on getting offended by something or the other with varying degrees of reaction and its course.

Our nation is not a stranger to individuals getting outraged. From artists like M.F. Hussain getting nagged out of the nation for 'offending' Hindu fundamentalists with his artistic speciality. Author Salman Rushdie cancelling his book signing in Jaipur due to intelligence report of a possible mob attack on him from the Indian citizens hurting their religious sentiments, to different brands like Tanishq[9] and Surf Excel[10] pulling out their meaningful and impactful advertisements due to claims of causing religious disharmony is a piece of everyday Indian life.

Secularism is an inherent constitutional principle prohibiting any religious interference in State affairs. The blasphemy laws do not aid the State to become secular in any way. If anything, it may betray secularism by being partial towards religions for appeasement or vote banks at the expense of non-believers. Several clauses within the Indian Penal Code (IPC) make it punishable upon the person expressing himself or herself not to "hurt sentiments", something that is open to broad interpretation and is subjective. Section 295(A) and 298 criminalizes acts and speech intended to outrage religious feelings, including words, visible representations, or any signs. Who is motivated by deliberate and intended malice is left for the court to decide?

In Ramji Lal Modi *versus* State of UP (1957), the Apex Court upheld the constitutionality of India's blasphemy law. It held that the legislation was a reasonable restriction on free speech in the interest of harmonious public order. It held that blasphemy includes a tendency of bringing about the public disorder. This argument is flawed in two ways. Firstly, it allows for what has been popularly termed as the Heckler's Veto. The fact that people will react to someone's speech violently should not silence the voice of others who want to speak out. Yet, this seems to be the case proposed law in Punjab. The government is reacting vigorously to intense protests against the sacrilege of the *Guru Granth Sahib*. But the intensity of protests should at no cost be a reason to silence unpopular expression and opinion.

The second issue is that the trend for public disorder is not clearly defined. The criterion also fails to recognise that speakers cannot be blatantly held responsible for what other people decide to do or not to do. Blasphemy neither constitutes incitement to violence nor does it constitute lawlessness actions as per Supreme Court standards.

For these reasons, the blasphemy law in India is incompatible with the constitutional right to freedom of speech and expression. Any 'deeper' importance of religion integrated into our regular lives does not give us a good reason for making an exception to our freedom of expression.

(a) *Analysing the Primary Data Collected via Google Forms and Questionnaire*

- 47.6 per cent of the respondents believe that freedom of speech should not involve the right to offend. While 37 per cent believe that freedom of speech should automatically involve right to offend. On very similar grounds, 81 per cent of the respondents believe that if someone says something racist, homophobic, or misogynistic or insinuating any religion or community it is a misuse of freedom of speech and that should be stopped. Similarly, the survey also shows that 57.7 per cent or the majority from a highly diversified sample pool thinks that freedom of speech should not be absolute. Integrating these responses with the response by our anonymous respondent in central administrative services, we see there is a clear contrast. Here, the focus is more on the freedom of speech and propagation of thought. The fact that Piers Morgan always had the journalistic freedom of saying what he wanted to and by, but he said to step down because of how the global audience did not see this as "right to speech". Here the respondent believes that the dominant powers in any society—may be civil societies, influential leaders or widely accepted government—free speech simply means nothing more than "right to speech at the right to time". Similarly, for the government what is beneficial for them is free speech.
- 71.6 per cent of the respondents strongly believe that there is an increasing need for amendment to the sedition law of India to suit the democratic framework instead of having colonial underpinnings. This data collected go hand in hand with a paper published by Law Commission of India in 2018 that it

is time to re-think or may be even repel Section 124-A. The United Kingdom or the origin of the sedition law banned it in 2009. But not everyone in India believes it to be that way like 18.6 per cent of the respondents do not feel the need to amend or repel the laws. Repealing the law can have daisy repercussions in India because that would mean no check on any threat from terrorism or any separatist tendencies.

- The responses get intertwined in the very last question of the interview where 43.3 per cent of the population believe that we do not need a "Right to offend", definitely not as a separate fundamental right but it should be inclusive to freedom of speech. While 34.6 per cent believe we need the "Right to offend" in India. Here, the tipping scale is the remaining 22.1 per cent who are not sure about the right but is a very decisive pool with a slight tilt that can, simply, change the majoritarian voice of the people.
- However, what formed the most important part of the qualitative research is the bulk hesitancy noticed in the respondents to fill up the survey. Almost, 30-40 per cent of the respondents personally enquired about the anonymity of their names and if there is any possibility of the paper coming under the government radar. They were afraid that this might lead to unnecessary harassment to them and their family or their future prospects in case the paper gets public. This clearly highlights, the fear of dissent or simply put fear of even criticizing the government.

(b) *Analysing the Collection of Secondary Data*

- Creative scrutiny is something that India has never been a stranger to. Many people are aware about Salman Rushdie's *Satanic Verses* and how one of his meet and greet in India had to be cancelled because of an intelligence warning that there will be a mass attack on him as he reaches the venue. All this happened because of his interpretation of Islam in his book which was not widely accepted to some parts of the community. What we are not aware is how former Prime Minister Indira Gandhi also found *Midnight's Children* offensive due to claims of excessive use of oppressive powers during emergency and alleged involvement in election fraud as well as Sanjay Gandhi's "cleansing" of the Jama Masjid slum. But what is notable is that the book was never banned for offending the Prime Minister unlike *Satanic Verses*. Even if these tales seem a lifetime ago, they still have immense impact in Indian content made on religious and political affairs. From cartoonists like Aseem Trivedi getting arrested on charges of sedition to defamation charges on Hasmukh series by Vir Das, recent arrest of comedian Munawar Faruqui and FIRs on Tandav series, Bombay Begums and anything that does not belong to mainstream Bollywood entertainment has faced clamp down not only the government or the political parties but also from communities at large. While it is important for civil societies, communities, or governments to regulate content that has the potential to disturbing social security or safeguard public and cultural interests, continuous clamp down on creative content with a different angel of representation will put the full stop to creative liberty and thought. It is also the duty of the general public to demand entertainers and creative artists to create something new and meaningful instead to forcing them to stick to what is safe and conventional. The OTT players have widely opened an array of entertainment that we needed the most. This streaming service industry in India is on a high growth trajectory estimated at revenue around Rs. 4,300 crore in FY 2019. OTT is estimated to reach Rs. 17,400 crore by 2024 making it the golden goose that India should not even think about culling with restrictions. At a time like the global pandemic this sector has created employment opportunities for lakhs of workers in the industry. With Delhi Crime winning 'Best Drama Series' in the Emmy's and international fame and recognition of unconventional and exceptional talents like Radhika Apte, Shefali Shah, Shobita Dhulipala, Pankaj Tripathi and many others for the atypical content they are a part of demands support from Indian audience. If these platforms are subjected to obtaining 1.3 billion, no objection certificates for offending any group of citizens it will simply slow down the process of creativity.

- The arrest of students like Disha Ravi, Safoora Zargar, Umar Khalid for voicing their strong ideological standpoints which seems to offend the popular and acceptable free speech by the government is perhaps the main reason behind this chapter. The worst kind of effect to free speech is the curbs on academic freedom. In 2017 when students of BHU protested against gender discrimination, they faced police batons and were accused by the university chancellor. This is a recurring colour almost every central government universities in JNU and Jamia Millia as well as private universities like Ashoka. What is alarming is in NCRB 2019, most sedition cases were slapped on 18–30-year-olds. But for how long can we continue to see the brightest minds of Indian future behind the bars? Simply sharing online documents or participating in protests or campaigning for environment is seen as offensive and subversive actions. In a highly globalized world, Freedom of Speech and Expression should be inclusive to the right to seek a global audience. As Indians we express various thoughts and opinions on policies by the United States, about the presidential election, our favourite international albums, actions by artists just not in India but elsewhere, they also equally have the right to keep opinions about Indian laws, culture, protests etc. until that infringes the sovereignty of the state. It is by sharing and resharing of different cultures and opinions that we learn from each other and get more connected. If everything is taken as an offense, then that part of the communications gets shut and we are left with no exchange of ideas.
- While talking about religious freedom, the primary question is: does criticism of a religion or the disbelief or unlikability towards a religion be a reason for criminal offence?
- After research done on various case studies in India and international affairs, the plausible answer is that if we are talking about right to offend, we also must acknowledge the right to get offended because of their own liberty and freedom of expression. And those who get offended are welcome to protest peacefully but definitely, not kill or gag offenders like the classic Charlie Hebdo case in France.

> "It's high time religious people realised one basic truth: every religious text and tradition is offensive, blasphemous and heretical to the followers of other sects and religions."
>
> —Feroze Mithiborwala

- In India, it is often considered that free speech does not extend to offensive speech. But the irony is every religion has strong beliefs in its own superiority, and this necessarily offends other religions in the process. Freedom to practice any religion inherently implies freedom to offend others, and tolerance by those offended by it. All freedoms are subjected to reasonable curbs. If someone deliberately incites violence that must certainly be stopped. This comes on the very grounds of the propagation of Love Jihad laws which demean interfaith marriages and see them as taboo. Christianity views people who reject Christ as "heathen" who cannot go to heaven just because they do not believe in Christ and are doomed for hell. This is bound to offend non-Christians. But is that a justifiable ground for burning the *Bible* or killing Christians? it does not. The *Quran* and *Hadith* historically led Muslim conquerors to convert by the sword and kill millions of people but that does not justify banning the *Quran* and *Hadith*. Hindu scriptures hold that bad people inclusive of people from other religions will be reborn as animals like dogs and pigs. This can offend non-Hindus but does not explain the killing of Hindus or banning the scriptures. People of different religions can co-exist only *via* tolerance, not punishment or revenge.

  Having said this, Muslim promotion of secular values has similarities with the anti-CAA protests at Shaheen Bagh. The Shaheen Bagh protesters invoked not the Sharia but freedoms of the Constitution with slogans like 'I love India' and singing the national anthem. This shows that as Indian *Hindutva* needs to develop inclusivity towards Islam, Islam should also not support criminal offences in name of religion may it be in India or France. Developing a faith so strong that feels threatened by criticism or disbelief of others is a sign of one's disbelief or insecurity in the faith. People of different religions in a secular country like India can only co-exist only *via* tolerance of ideas and free propagation. Not, by punishment or revenge.

What will happen if India finally incorporates the "right to offend"? Everyone would have the right to offend others may it be offending the state, individual or community and all we have to do is listen to it and not act upon it in any way. Surely, the right to offend would make criticising the state legal, criticising any faith legal, would give absolute artistic freedom and carter to absolute propagation of any ideals. On the other hand, it would support the right of influential public figures like Ram Dev Baba to openly claim to cure homosexuality by *Ayurveda*, or panchayats banning girls for wearing jeans as they find it offensive or outrageous comments celebrating racism, homophobia, communal disharmony etc. Having said that, absolute freedom of speech and expression means safeguarding the speech of every person irrespective of the popularly accepted opinion.

Taking an example of Piers Morgan steeping down due to the global backlash he received for his comments about not believing anything Megan Markel said on the Oprah Winfrey show, the global audience was quite happy with the step down without an inch of doubt about how that was curbing his journalistic freedom. If, instead of Meghan Markel and Prince Harry, it would have been Prince Charles and Camilla, Duchess of Cornwall, the same global community would have nodded in agreement with Piers Morgan's reaction to the interview. Similarly, as after 9/11 it was the accepted speech that enemy combatants primarily from Afghanistan and Iraq in Guantanamo Bay should be tortured to death and it was widely supported. With the change of time and recognition of basic human rights for these detainees such extremism by state faces strong criticism. These examples show that there is no presence of Free speech in any country. As per the government the narrative it has is the free speech and as per the citizens the popular opinion is the free speech and anything opposing that becomes offensive. The concept of free speech is utopian in anywhere in the world, it is the "right" speech that we as a society accept.

Looking from the most complicated perspective of religion, Author Brian Winston[11] in his book "A right to offend" analyses some very important contemporary cases of "offense" which can help in putting things into perspective. He effortlessly brings up the battle for or against free speech in an evergreen and ceaseless manner regarding the religious dimension with examples like the prohibition of film Noah in various Islamic countries, Iran's former supreme leader Ayatollah Ruhollah Khomeini's *fatwa* on Salman Rushdie for *Satanic Verses*, John Milton's *Areopagitica* and many more. In this book he introduces the concept of *Harm principle* being seized by those who fell wronged, to come up with a plan to control and direct the public opinion and beliefs to fulfil their needs and purpose. It is in this harm principle that a right to offend in India would also mean a guarantee of right to get offended and how those getting offended are rightfully reacting to the offense.

We must accept that we do not live in the ideal world or the ideal democracy. There must be some restrictions to freedom of expression and the right to offend being a definite part of freedom of speech but again not absolute, so as to not spread hatred among communities and to incite violence of any sort. These principles have to be constantly negotiated and renegotiated as the society evolves while ensuring that some perpetrators of hate speech do not use the freedom to serve their venom. The right to offend being a part of the freedom of speech and expression is important for the foundational liberty in a democracy which needs self-assessment and reconsiderations before conducting themselves. While Disha Ravi was released on the grounds that criticising the government is not sedition, in Begusurai case 1953 the S.C. upheld the conviction due to acts that clearly indicated the effect of subverting the government by violent means. The blame of the junk sedition cases cannot only be put on Central and State Governments. Sometimes, it is the aggressive media framing and polarisation or reluctance for implementation of laws like Section 66-A which was struck down but still cases are filed under it. Other times it is the widespread misuse of power by police forces booking people for criticising any political party, promulgation of ordinances like 118-D into Police Act criminalizing online posts for offensive content. It can also be owed to India's slow-moving democracy. The judiciary must jealously guard the personal liberty of the people. By not hearing *habeas corpus* petitions for months and denying bail in genuine cases can further decrease India's partially free status to not at all a free status country.

There is, however, complete unanimity of amending the laws on how they are implemented on the ground. Either the sedition law has to be taken off the statute book or use very sparingly and with possible decrease of criminalisation. In cases like sedition, the process in itself becomes the punishment because of media trails, societal influence, and long waiting line in the courts. Use of this law excessively in the name of security will be a negatively defining factor for freedom of expression. In the long-term perspective what could possible help is regular workshops to train police personnel mainly investigators about the scope of various laws in the country. While the population may seem deep-rooted in only the administration, it is actually well delved inside the Indian diaspora. The collective approaches of social, legal, and administrative approaches will be needed to have an inclusive right to offend and also right to get offended and react on it unless it incites crime or violence.

Given that governments in Indian democracy survive on public mandate, they should be mature enough to handle criticism of various policies and adapt more to correct the course rather than penalise its own people. While national security and integrity of the country are non-negotiable, democratic principles enshrined in the constitution also must never be compromised.

NOTES

1. Andrew Copson (2011). (08.00 BST), *Atheism's aesthetic of enchantment*, https://www.theguardian.com/commentisfree/belief/2011/apr/02/shelley-the-necessity-of-atheism#:~:text=As%20an%20Oxford%20undergraduate,The%20argument%20itself%20is%20simple.
2. Reema Omar (2020), "Sedition and its discontents", *Dawn Newspaper*, https://www.dawn.com/news/1532177
3. Tenzing Lamsang (2021). "The story behind the sedition cases against Khandu Wangmo", *The Bhutanese*. https://thebhutanese.bt/the-story-behind-the-sedition-cases-against-khandu-wangmo/
4. Updated July 13, 2020 11.08 pm: "Gujarat man arrested for threatening to rape stand-up comedian for her remarks about Shivaji statue". https://scroll.in/latest/967318/gujarat-man-arrested-for-issuing-rape-threats-to-stand-up-comedian-for-her-remarks-on-shivaji

5. Vanessa Thorpe (October 2020). “Ai Weiwei on China, free speech and message for London”. https://www.theguardian.com/artanddesign/2020/oct/04/ai-weiwei-on-china-free-speech-and-a-message-for-london
6. Timesofindia.com/Updated: (March 2021). “Pratap Bhanu Mehta resignation: Yale, MIT, Harvard professor writes open letter to Ashoka University.” http://timesofindia.indiatimes.com/articleshow/81600504.cms?utm_source=contentofinterest&utm_medium=text&utm_campaign=cppst
7. DHNS (March 11, 2021) is updated: “Leave institutions, PhD theses alone”. https://www.deccanherald.com/opinion/first-edit/leave-institutions-phd-theses-alone-960567.html
8. Abhiram Ghadyalpatil, Shaswati Das (August 2018). “Maharashtra cops crack down on ‘urban naxals’ in five states.” https://www.livemint.com/Politics/83dgRkXPQhrsgfHuFKkgyJ/Maharashtra-cops-crack-down-on-urban-Naxals-in-five-states.html
9. *Times Now Digital* (October 2020). “After internet backlash, Tanishq pulls plug on latest ad—the controversy around ‘Ekatvam’, explainedhttps://www.timesnownews.com/india/article/after-internet-backlash-tanishq-pulls-plug-on-latest-ad-the-controversy-around-ekatvam-explained/666883
10. *Financial Express* (March 2019). “Surf Excel’s Holi ad promoting Hindu-Muslim Harmony faces backlash on Twitter”. https://www.financialexpress.com/india-news/surf-excels-holi-ad-promoting-hindu-muslim-harmony-faces-backlash-on-twitter/1511886/#:~:text=Soon%20after%20the%20ad%20was,girl%20and%20a%20Muslim%20boy.
11. By Brian Winston. London, UK: Bloomsbury, 2012. 414 p. ISBN 9781849660150.

REFERENCES

Abhiram Ghadyalpatil, Shaswati Das, 29 August, 2018: “Maharashtra cops crack down on ‘urban naxals’ in five states. https://www.livemint.com/Politics/83dgRkXPQhrsgfHuFKkgyJ/Maharashtra-cops-crack-down-on-urban-Naxals-in-five-states.html

A Right to Offend: Free Expression in the Twenty-First Century. By Brian Winston. London, UK: Bloomsbury, 2012. 414 p. ISBN 9781849660150. https://www.google.co.in/books/edition/_/CzF824TavGQC?hl=en&gbpv=1

Case CCT 284/17 [2018] ZACC 29 Hearing Date: 31 May, 2018 Judgement Date: 13 September 2018, Constitutional Court of South Africa. https://www.concourt.org.za/index.php/judgement/259-duncanmec-pty-limited-v-gaylard-no-and-others

DHNS, MAR 11 2021, 01:34 ISTUPDATED: MAR 11 2021, 02:03 IST: “Leave institutions, PhD theses alone”. https://www.deccanherald.com/opinion/first-edit/leave-institutions-phd-theses-alone-960567.html

FACING HISTORY AND OURSELVES: August 28, 2020, "UNDERSTANDING #TAKEAKNEE AND ATHLETE ACTIVISM. How are the Athletes protesting Racial Injustice?" https://www.facinghistory.org/educator-resources/current-events/understanding-takeaknee-athlete-activism#:~:text=Over%20the%20summer%20of%202020,left%20the%2049ers%20in%202017.

Financial Express, March 12, 2019, "Surf Excel's Holi ad promoting Hindu-Muslim Harmony faces backlash on Twitter". https://www.financialexpress.com/india-news/surf-excels-holi-ad-promoting-hindu-muslim-harmony-faces-backlash-on-twitter/1511886/#:~:text=Soon%20after%20the%20ad%20was,girl%20and%20a%20Muslim%20boy.

Global Freedom of Expression Columbia University: https://globalfreedomofexpression.columbia.edu/cases/brandenburg-v-ohio/

Press Trust of India, New Delhi, HT correspondent, April 27, 2020, 11:08 IST: "Vir Das Hasmukh in trouble, plea in Delhi H.C. to take series off Netflix for allegedly maligning lawyers". https://www.hindustantimes.com/tv/vir-das-hasmukh-in-trouble-plea-in-delhi-hc-to-take-series-off-netflix-for-allegedly-maligning-lawyers/story-rl21h1D4yF0fFfEh9PQ2TK.html

Roger J. Kreuz, University of Memphis: September 15, 2020, "Charlie Hebdo shootings served as an extreme example of the history of attacks on satirists". https://theconversation.com/au/topics/charlie-hebdo-attack-14299

Times Now Digital, October 14, 2020 : "After internet backlash, Tanishq pulls plug on latest ad—the controversy around 'Ekatvam', explained https://www.timesnownews.com/india/article/after-internet-backlash-tanishq-pulls-plug-on-latest-ad-the-controversy-around-ekatvam-explained/666883

TIMESOFINDIA.COM/Updated: Mar 20, 2021, 12:25 IST: "Pratap Bhanu Mehta resignation: Yale, MIT, Harvard professor writes open letter to Ashoka University". http://timesofindia.indiatimes.com/articleshow/81600504.cms?utm_source=contentofinterest&utm_medium=text&utm_campaign=cppst

Updated Jul 13, 2020 11.08 pm: "Gujarat man arrested for threatening to rape stand-up comedian for her remarks about Shivaji statue". https://scroll.in/latest/967318/gujarat-man-arrested-for-issuing-rape-threats-to-stand-up-comedian-for-her-remarks-on-shivaji

Vanessa Thorpe, October 4, 2020 : "Ai Weiwei on China, free speech and message for London". https://www.theguardian.com/artanddesign/2020/oct/04/ai-weiwei-on-china-free-speech-and-a-message-for-london

6

State Assembly Resolutions Against Citizenship Amendment Act (CAA) and Federal Structure

Deepak Kumar Pandey

In the backdrop of CAA protests at Delhi, the idea of citizenship and power of Union regarding legislation about citizenship and its applicability across pan India, especially in non-BJP ruling states with the outset of state assembly resolutions against CAA bring some serious issues into the debate of Indian polity. The federal structure as designed by the constitution makers and which further evolved is being challenged by political actors from those political parties which are in opposition of centre. Though the number of opposing states is comparatively less in number, but it brings some serious questions to think over. The Union implement its decisions through the machinery of the state in most of the cases, and if state denies to implement the decisions, as many political actors of different states are proclaiming, it will bring not only embarrassing situation for both centre and state but will also bring some constitutional questions too. Can any political party, because of the ideological difference or any other reason may deny, accepting the legislation passed by the Union. And if this tendency becomes practice on different opposing issues, will it not hamper national interests and federal unity of our nation. Though these resolutions are symbolic and indicative of their ideological difference, will it not affect the federal character of our country in long run? Union may have option to use Article 356 in case of the constitutional failure in these states but if even after presidential rule (if applied in case of constitutional failure), elections held and again same party return to power, what kind of way out be there? There is another option that, judicial interference may decide the fate of legislation and its implementation, but larger question is that what kind of federal union we may want to evolve? If on the subjects of Union, state will take inaction and *vice versa,* Union will do something adverse to subject of state, it will not only problematize the issue, but in long run affect the law and order situation, social harmony and national unity. In the backdrop of the Citizenship Amendment Act and protests against it in certain areas, this chapter attempts to look into the wider issue of centre-state relationship and its implications on the Indian Polity. In this chapter, CAA is taken only as a reference case to testify the theoretical nuances of federal theory in Indian context.

Federalism is a constitutional form that divides law-making and administrative powers between a central government and the constituent local governments. Federalism seems to allow more flexibility and responsiveness at the local level while being incorporated in a Union enshrined with tackling of common and overlapping interests of all units. Since its inception in modern polity, federalism has redesigned and restructured itself as per needs of the time and place. Federal theory incorporates democratic principle in it with a sense of some equal footing in decision making by its central legal entity and its constituent units. Though, in principle it starts and developed as political system with political and legal equality, stringed together with bond of common interests. In the federal structure, Centre and constituent units got assigned tasks as defined subjects, mainly the task of foreign affairs, security, telecommunications etc. being the Centre's realm of affairs. Federal polity in different places has evolved in various dimensions and aspects, having some specific characters of their own as per time and space. This evolution is generally manifested in gradual shifting and tilting of power structure towards Centre in most of the cases. Even the American federal structure gradually evolved as federation having strong Centre. Indian federal structure has also its own kind of federalism having peculiar characters which owes its reason in historical and circumstantial conditions. Though, the word 'federation' is nowhere used in our Constitution, yet it is fit into basic principle of federal polity, in which division of power is in-between Centre and its constituent units that are states.

Our Constitution framers have visualized the federalism as a tool by which heterogeneous multicultural character and quality of our society get accommodated in single political entity having the space still remains available for the growth and development of their own culture, values and ethos. It has been assumed and designed as a kind of flexible tool to accommodate the various heterogeneous differences in a single political legal entity. Constitution framers discussed the issue of federalism, like any other issue in great detail and despite being largely democratic by heart keep some reservations and apprehensions because of the partition issue. The idea of provincial or state autonomy was not new to Indian polity. Even when the large part of India comes under a single empire—Mauryan Empire, Vijaynagar Empire or even Mughal Empire—there was considerable regional autonomy and local self-government. In modern context, it is only in the Act of 1935, that the British introduced the concept of provincial autonomy. The word 'federation' was introduced in the Act to facilitate the federating of the Princely states with the Union. But at the time of transfer of power from British to Indians, conditions were altogether different which necessitates that, our Constitution framers designed some protective measures in federal structure to keep our national unity in tact and at the same time to accommodate the diversities of different states, which were joining the Indian Union, whether of the Princely states or erstwhile British provinces of Indian state. There is no denial of the fact that, Indian federalism has a strong tendency towards centralism which provokes K.C. Whearre to term it as quasi-federal structure. But despite having strong tendency towards centralism, there are larger democratic elements in it too. In fact two different committees were constituted—one that is union constitution committee and other is provincial constitution committee to discuss various aspects and subjects related to centre and states. And perhaps Constitution of India is the only constitution having kept the minutes and detailed discussions in such a detailed manner, which has not been visible elsewhere in the world. This in another sense shows that how transparent and democratic, our constitution makers were. Constitution makers did detailed homework and have deliberate discussions while dividing and allocating different subjects to centre and units. In this division, the subject and power to legislate on citizenship comes under the purview of centre. The decisions reached by the Union Constitution and Union Powers Committees at their joint meetings were incorporated in the second report of the Union Powers Committee submitted to the President of the Constituent Assembly on July 5, 1947. The committee came to the conclusion that *"the soundest framework of our Constitution was a Federation with a strong Centre."*[1] The report was presented by Gopalaswami Ayyangar for the consideration of the Assembly on August 20. In its report as adopted by the constituent assembly in August 1947 subject of Citizenship, naturalization and aliens were kept at serial no. 19 in the List 1 of the Federal Legislative list.[2] The intent of our constitution framers for a federation with strong centre and keeping the matter of citizenship in the List 1 of federal legislative list, it indicates a lot. In India, having no dual citizenship, it has been considered as a subject of Union. Another reason behind it is that, because of partition, it needs ultra sensitivity to deal with it, while addressing the sentiments, emotions and sensitivity at one hand and security on the other. The shadow cast by the partition on the constitution making process resulted in the enactment of the citizenship law being deferred till five years later, with constitutional intentions being repeatedly undermined in the administrative and political domains.[3] Across the twentieth century and traversing all three domains of citizenship aspects—who can be a citizen, on what terms, and what the content of citizenship is—a persistent tension is manifest between the tendencies of inclusion and exclusion. The structural inequalities of Indian society are reflected in the fragility of the constitutional settlement as well as in the official strategies adopted to address exclusions of both a material and symbolic nature.[4]

Citizenship has larger and deeper connotations than its legal-political character. It is also a kind of relationship and belongingness with emotional bondage covering it into politico-legal character. In its most legalistic construction, citizenship is a status that confers rights and imposes obligations.[5] Citizenship is a kind of special relationship between the state and individual with the obligations of individual towards the state and the offering of rights and assurances on the other hand by the state. Particular attention has been paid to the ways in which a secular conception of Indian identity was promoted and the means by which various languages and ethnic groups were accommodated to the idea of India as a nation-state by virtue of federal principles mapped out. In Indian context, our constitution framers offer wide range of rights, which were enshrined in the values of national movement, one of the important rights is the right to freedom of religion and conscience, the backbone of secular character of our nation along with other equally important rights. These rights are important aspects of idea of citizenship in Indian state. The English sociologist, T.H. Marshall wrote that, modern drive towards social equality was the latest phase of an evolution of citizenship which had been in continuous progress for some 250 years. He proposed to divide citizenship into three elements: civil, political and social. The 'social element' of citizenship was defined as encompassing the "whole range, from the right to a modicum of economic welfare and security, to the right to share fully in the social heritage and to live the life of a civilized being according to the standards prevailing in the society".[6] The Constitution of India provides this scope of *'whole range'* to its citizens ranging from socio-economic and political dimensions to sharing of social heritage at one hand and maintaining their distinct identity on the other hand. In order to decide the criteria and conditions of citizenship in India, Indian parliament passed the Citizenship Act, 1955 on 30th December, 1955 for the first time in free India to provide for the acquisition and determination of Indian Citizenship. Since December 1955, this Citizenship Act went through many amendments as—the Citizenship (Amendment) Act, 1986, the Citizenship (Amendment) Act, 1992, the Citizenship (Amendment) Act, 2003, the Citizenship (Amendment) Act, 2005, and the Citizenship (Amendment) Act, 2019. But the most recent amendment termed as Citizenship Amendment Act, 2019 not only leads to debates and discussions amongst the political actors of different ideologies (different political parties) but also encroached into the debates and discussions of common man creating the dividing line between those who are in favour of it and those who are protesting against it. The law offers citizenship to non-Muslims feeling religious persecution from three nearby countries, namely Pakistan, Afghanistan and Bangladesh. It prompted outrage and protests in some sections and pockets of India leading to violent protests and deaths in some cases, Shaheen Bagh of Delhi being the recent example of it.

Though this chapter will not indulge into the debate of CAA, but will take it as reference to test, how far the state resolutions against it will make impact on the federal polity. Here basic question emerges that, if the citizenship is matter of Union subject, why states are passing resolutions against it and how far will it affect the centre-state relationship in Indian context. Before going into analysis of different resolutions of states, it is pertinent to have a view on the resolutions passed by different states in which till now only four states have passed the resolution by its legislative assemblies, two states have passed the resolution through its cabinet and is yet to be passed by their state assemblies.

State Resolutions and Federal Structure

Kerala was the first state to pass the resolution against the CAA by its state assembly on 31st December demanding the scrapping of the Citizenship Amendment Act (CAA). Chief Minister of Kerala Pinarayi Vijayan said that, it is against the 'secular' outlook and fabric of the country. Chief Minister Vijayan said that, "The Act contradicts the basic values and principles of the Constitution. In view of the anxiety among the people of the country, the Centre should take steps to drop the CAA and uphold the secular outlook of the Constitution."[7]

After Kerala, Punjab Assembly became the second one to pass the resolution against CAA demanding its removal. Resolution of Punjab assembly reads as "The CAA enacted by Parliament has caused countrywide anguish and social unrest with widespread protests all over the country. The state of Punjab also witnessed protests against this legislation, which were peaceful and involved all segments of our society." It further says that, "It is divisive and stands for everything opposed to a free and fair democracy, which must enshrine equality for all. Alongside the religion-based discrimination in granting citizenship, it is apprehended that the CAA is also likely to endanger the linguistic and cultural identity of some sections of our people. CAA also envisages cancellation of the registration of Overseas Citizens of

India (OCI) card holders, if they violate any law." It further said the CAA is aimed at distinguishing between illegal migrants on the basis of religion, which is not permissible under the Constitution that guarantees the right to equality and equal protection of the laws to all persons. "In the backdrop of these facts, it is evident that the CAA violates the secular identity of India, which is basic feature of our Constitution; therefore, the House resolves to urge the Government of India to repeal the CAA to avoid any discrimination on the basis of religion in granting citizenship and to ensure equality before law for all religious groups in India. Given the apprehensions about National Register of Citizens and that the National Population Register is a prelude to the NRC designed to deprive a section of persons from citizenship of India and implement CAA, this House further resolves that Central Government should amend the forms/documentation associated with the NPR to allay such apprehension in the minds of the people and only thereafter undertake work of enumeration under NPR", the resolution said.[8]

Rajasthan assembly joins this group in passing of resolution against CAA on 25 January, 2020 urging the centre to repeal the Act. The resolution stated that the "Preamble of the Constitution of our country clearly states that, India is a secular country. In addition, Article 14 of the Constitution clearly stipulates that the state shall not deny to any person equality before the law or equal protection of the laws within the territory of India."

The Citizenship (Amendment) Act, 2019 that has been enacted by Parliament recently is aimed at distinguishing illegal migrants on the basis of religion. Such discrimination of people on the grounds of religion is not in consonance with the secular ideals enshrined in the Constitution and is clearly violative of Article 14. It further stated that it is for the first time in the history of the country since Independence that a law has been enacted which discriminates against people on religious grounds.[9]

West Bengal Legislative Assembly became the next one to follow the path by passing a resolution against CAA urging the Union Government to repeal the Citizenship Amendment Act. The resolution noted that since the CAA was passed there was violence in "almost every state". It further states that, "religion has been used as a yardstick to measure eligibility to apply for Indian citizenship" and "the ruling party in the Centre has been driving a wedge among the people using religion [thus] damaging human rights."

The resolution criticised the Centre for issuing a notice to conduct a National Population Register (NPR) and a nationwide National Register of Citizens (NRC) "without clear guidelines", creating "panic among people". Mamata Banerjee described the CAA as something that was against the spirit of the Constitution and demanded its repeal. "It is not a small Hindu Muslim issue...the issue is of humanity...this law is a shame on humanity."[10]

The state cabinet of Congress-led Chhattisgarh government passed a resolution opposing the Act and urged the Centre to repeal it, citing protests across Chhattisgarh on 30 January, 2020. Chief Minister Bhupesh Baghel wrote a letter to Prime Minister Narendra Modi, making a formal appeal in this regard, "Chhattisgarh is witnessing massive peaceful protests against the Act by different sections of society. Chhattisgarh originally has inhabitants belonging to Scheduled Tribes, Scheduled Castes, OBCs." Baghel further said in his letter to Modi that, "and a huge chunk of the state's population live below poverty line, are landless and illiterate. They will surely face difficulties in fulfilling the formalities required by the Act. The CAA erodes the Constitution's fundamental structure on secularism."[11]

The Madhya Pradesh cabinet passed a resolution against the Citizenship Amendment Act, 2019 on 5th February, 2020 and urged the Union Government to revoke it. Resolution termed the CAA as violative of basic character of Constitution of India. The resolution reads, "India is a secular country and there is a clear mention of this in the Preamble of the Constitution. Also, Article 14 of the Constitution guarantees equality before law and non-discrimination through law. These principles of the Constitution have been violated hence the CAA should be revoked."[12]

Telangana Assembly has become the seventh state legislature to pass such resolution against CAA, NPR and NRC. The resolution passed by Telangana says that, "this is nothing less than an attempt to fundamentally alter and undermine the non-religious nature of Indian citizenship."[13]

The Congress-ruled Puducherry adopted an Assembly resolution against the amended Citizenship Act on 12 February, 2020, becoming the first Union Territory in the country to pass such resolution. The resolution urged the Centre to withdraw the CAA saying it was "totally opposed to the principles of secularism."[14]

Delhi assembly became the latest in the series to pass a resolution to withdraw NRC and NPR. The resolution appealed to the Centre to withdraw and not carry out the whole exercise of NRC and NPR "in the interest of the nation, particularly when the economy is witnessing the worst-ever downslide and unemployment is witnessing a terrifying growth, and with the threat of the corona pandemic looming large."[15]

These different state resolutions have been passed with certain political motive and to send some political massage symbolically. In legal terms, these resolutions do not have any impact in realization of this Act, because subject being in the Union list, Centre has the power to legislate on that matter. As per the constitutional arrangements, states cannot deny, to accept and implement the Act. States in their resolutions, only urge the Union to repeal it, but nowhere said that, they would not implement it. If, in any case, state denies implementing the Act, it would be violation of constitutional norms which would attract the other measures to ensure it, including the use of Art. 356. But these resolutions, though used as political tool to put pressure on the Centre as per political suitability of the political parties, this kind of practice is now emerging as one of the issue of contention in Centre-State relationship of Indian federalism. Federal order is not just a particular set of institutions but also the institutionalization of particular relationships among the participants in political life.[16] Institutionalization of relationship among the participants is important aspect in the relationship of Centre and State which demands that, both Centre and State should work in their defined domain without interfering in the subjects of others. State resolutions against any Act, which has been passed by the both houses of parliament is kind of interference, though symbolically in the matter of Union subject, which harms the institutionalization of relationship between Centre and State. Rather than adopting the way of passing resolutions against any Act by any legislature, the judicial way-out to decide the legality and constitutionality is better way. Our Constitution framers have provided the mechanism of judiciary, Supreme Court being the supreme custodian and interpreter of any constitutional matter. If any law or part of it is against the constitutional norms, it could be declared null and void by Court and CAA could also be challenged, which has been done by Kerala and Rajasthan. Rather adopting resolutions, it would be better to find the judicial way out in matter of any difference. In fact, the Supreme Court is also one of the important part of our federal polity which is meant to adjudicate between Centre and State or between State and State.

Another extreme possibility is that, though states nowhere said in their resolutions that, they will not implement the Act, but still if any state denies implementing the Act as reported in media, this condition will be awkward for the federal polity. And even after presidential rule in the state, the same political party gets reelected in the next election and denies implementing Act again, what would be the next step? Here again the constitutional question will emerge, that whether again the democratically elected government be removed by democratically elected government of Centre or will matter go to judicial domain to decide. If such situation emerges, the democratic polity will come under challenge and threat. These resolutions are in themselves an effort and intent to encroach into the legislative domain of democratically elected government. Issues in democratic polity can be resolved through process of democracy and should take that way only. If any Act has to be repealed, it could be done only after getting people's mandate through defined democratic process and institutions. The principle of democratic theory also demands that, Union and its constituent units should also behave and uphold the democratic values. Centre should also take decisions on sensitive political issues by taking the constituent units in confidence or at least by informing them. Those systems could not develop the underlying social and political structures of cohesion, where federalism has been merely a disguise for unitarian party dictatorship, it was pseudo-federalism; it is no wonder that it faltered and gave place to a surge of exclusionary politics fostering centrifugal tendencies.[17] The task of striking a balance among the prevailing forces accompanies not merely the formation of a federal state; it persists to place its stamp on future developments. The reasons why the American federal state was founded are one thing, while the concrete pattern of the relative strength of federation and its member-states is another matter altogether.[18] The strength of federal structure and its constituent units are complemented by each other and if any of the structure disrupts this institutional mechanism, it may hamper not only its relationship amongst the units and centre but also may lead to the weakening of whole structure. There has been a kind of role reversal in the Rudolphian idea of command politics after a short interval of time. Rudolph & Rudolph in their book *In Pursuit of Lakshmi: The Political Economy of Indian State* discusses the Indian state and its different paradoxical elements, which were supposed to be sustained in the Indian polity in surprising manner. They said that, "the paradox of India's weak-strong state arises from the juxtaposition of the Congress Party's durable command of a centrist ideological and foreign policy consensus, social pluralism, permanent government and a dynamic charisma on the one hand with highly mobilized albeit fragmented social forces that threaten governability, political stability and a national purpose on the other."[19] The Congress regime has been replaced by the Bharatiya Janata Party and dynamic charisma of Modi has filled the vacuum of leadership in Indian polity, despite having the presence of fragmented social forces regularly threatening the governability and nation's purpose. The values of social pluralism have been intermixed with market driven capitalist economy, the paradox of Indian polity. Even the development of some demand politics is still governed and dictated by the command politics. Many of the political decisions taken by the Modi regime, including the CAA are reflective of the tendency of this command politics which needs to be democratized little bit.

Our Constitution framers have visualized the idea of cooperative federalism with strong centre. The provision of Inter-State Council (Art. 263) is best example in this regard. The Inter-State Council should be given effective mandate to realise the idea of cooperative federalism in effective manner. Inter-State Council should be given effective mandate to review the actions of Centre to discuss the issues of national interests and to maintain the cultural uniqueness and solidarity amongst the different sections through giving autonomy to State, to keep the states informed about sensitive issues of national salience, about defence, diplomatic issues, foreign policy, Centre-

State relations, about any prospective policy change that may affect the Centre-State or State-State relationship and national economy to take not only into confidence the constituent units of Union but as a way to build trust amongst Union and States and also between the different states. Federalism in India should evolve in kind of cooperative federalism. Granville Austin commented optimistically in 1966 that, this kind of federalism (cooperative federalism) should produce a strong Central Government, yet it does not necessarily result in weak provincial governments.[20]

The institutional relationship of federal polity should be allowed to work in their institutional framework. This practice of passing resolutions is harmful for the institutional relationship of federal polity in long run. So far resolutions remain ideological, symbolic and normative underpinning, it is not matter of big concern having no legal meaning. It only shows the mandate of state wish in some sense, it only creates problem for federal polity and also for national interests, when it get implemented in action.

NOTES

1. Rao, B. Shiva (Chairman of the Project Committee), Menon, V.K., Khosla J.N., Padmanabhan, K.V., Ganesan C. and Krishna Mani, P.N. (Members of the Project Committee), *The Framing of India's Constitution Select Documents,* Vol.II, The Indian Institute of Public Administration, New Delhi, Distributors, N.M. Tripathi Private Ltd., Bombay, 1967, p. 776.
2. *Ibid.*, pp. 803-804.
3. Jayal, Niraja Gopal (2013). *Citizenship and its Discontents: An Indian History*, Permanent Black, Ranikhet, p. 18.
4. *Ibid.*, p. 17.
5. Zolov, Terri Gordon and Rogers Robin, 'Citizenship', *Women's Studies Quartterly,* Vol. 38, No. ½ (Spring/Summer 2010), p. 13.
6. Marshall, T.H. (1964). *Class, Citizenship and Social Development*, Cambridge University Press, Cambridge, pp. 71-72.
7. https://www.indiatoday.in/india/story/kerala-cm-tables-anti-caa-resolution-in-assembly-1632845-2019-12-31
8. https://www.indiatoday.in/india/story/resolution-against-caa-moved-in-punjab-assembly-1637704-2020-01-17
9. https://www.indiatoday.in/india/story/rajasthan-assembly-passes-resolution-against-caa-1640111-2020-01-25

10. https://www.thehindu.com/news/national/other-states/west-bengal-govt-tables-anti-caa-resolution-in-assembly/article30664646.ece
11. https://timesofindia.indiatimes.com/city/raipur/chhattisgarh-cabinet-passes-anti-caa-resolution-may-bring-motion-in-assembly/articleshow/73776311.cms
12. https://www.indiatoday.in/india/story/madhya-pradesh-anti-caa-resolution-1643512-2020-02-05
13. https://www.thehindu.com/news/national/telangana/telangana-assembly-passes-resolution-opposing-caa-npr-and-nrc/article31081955.ece
14. https://www.ndtv.com/india-news/puducherry-assembly-passes-resolution-against-caa-npr-nrc-2179357
15. https://www.indiatoday.in/india/story/delhi-assembly-passes-resolution-against-ncr-npr-1655332-2020-03-13
16. Gress Franz (1998). "What is Federalism?" in *Federalism and Decentralisation: Centre-State Relations in India and Germany*, edited by Gert W. Kueck, Sudhir Chandra Mathur and Klaus Schindler, Konrad Adenauer Foundation, New Delhi, Max Mueller Bhavan, Chennai and Satyamurti Centre for Democratic Studies, Chennai in collaboration with Mudrit Publications, New Delhi, p. 6.
17. *Ibid.*, p. 8.
18. *Ibid.*, p. 17.
19. Rudolph Lloyd I. and Rudolph Sussane Hoeber (1987). *In Pursuit of Lakshmi: The Political Economy of Indian State*, The University of Chicago Press, Chicago, p. 6.
20. c.f. Guhan S. (1998). "Federalism in India and Germany" in *Federalism and Decentralisation: Centre-State Relations in India and Germany*, edited by Gert W. Kueck, Sudhir Chandra Mathur and Klaus Schindler, Konrad Adenauer Foundation, New Delhi, Max Muller Bhavan, Chennai and Satyamurti Centre for Democratic Studies, Chennai in collaboration with Mudrit Publications, New Delhi, pp. 253-254.

PART II
Contemporary Political Discourses

7
New Narratives in Contemporary India

G. Palanithurai

Introduction

India is basically a civic nation known for its civilizational values which has got the characteristics of unity internally and integration externally[1]. Its richness lies in accommodating its extreme diversities. It has got a philosophical connotation popularly termed as "Unity in Diversity". Basically its greatness is in civilizational values and not in the material values. The cultural and civilizational values have kept the Indian society to practice tolerance, patience, endurance, benevolence, compassion and non-violence which became the causes for its subjugation by the materialistic forces called Western civilization. It is always a question, how a civilized society will exploit and subjugate others. Is exploitation a value of civilization? It is an irony that the British colonial administration gave a justification that their stay in the colonized societies was with an aim of transforming the traditional societies into modernized and civilized communities. There is no difference between the West and the East in terms of civilizational values, till West started using industrialization for material advancement through establishing colonies and subjugating colonized societies. Western civilization is basically an exploitative after it became an Industrial society.[2] It evolved strategies to exploit and subjugate people who live with nature. Indian society had been exploited for a long time by various forces and it was deeply exploited and subjugated by the British. To free the society from subjugation and exploitation, a civilizational value "non-violence" rooted in Indian soil has been used as a powerful weapon by preparing the masses in the spiritual path and the external liberation has been achieved under the leadership of M.K. Gandhi. It is to be understood that liberation is complete only when people liberate themselves internally as envisioned by M.K. Gandhi. It is being explained by Vinoba Bhave in his "Swaraj Sastra."[3] M.K. Gandhi dispelled the cloud over the path to be pursued and followed for literating India that violence never be the path and value for the society in India to achieve any progress and non-violence is the base of India to human advancement. From 1915 to 1947, M.K. Gandhi played a decisive role in shaping the freedom movement by laying the path to be followed for liberation understandable to the common man and women in India. The whole process of liberation demonstrated to the world that without violence and weapons, society can be liberated by invoking the power of the people which is popularly called "soul force".[4] M.K. Gandhi's role lies in massification of the people's movement to liberate in India and evolving ways and means to involve people in the liberation struggle. Further, M.K. Gandhi enabled the people to evolve themselves by following the value framework created by M.K. Gandhi by using the values embedded in the cultural practices of the people. Thus, M.K. Gandhi prepared the people internally by using the soul force. He created a new consciousness among the ordinary people of the Indian society to perform the task of liberating India by sacrifice.[5]

After liberation it was promised to the people that through a Democratic process of governance, inequalities in socio-economic sphere would be addressed and equally the discriminative practices would be wiped out. Here it is to be remembered that M.K. Gandhi was a mass leader and was in the centre stage to lead the freedom struggle in an innovative way.[6] He never made a promise that the struggle will be over after India gets independence. He unequivocally made it clear that all the social reformatory process could be achieved only through a struggle not by mere intervention of the state. In such a way masses have been prepared not only for liberation from the colonial administration but also from the internal colonialism.

The moment India got Independence, the leaders who were with M.K. Gandhi decisively took a decision to create a strong state to maintain order and peace and to transform Indian society. To achieve the above, a rule book has been created in the name of the constitution. The rule book has given more space for state and its institutions to work for transformation instead of providing space for people and their institutions for their transformative activities[7]. It is a fundamental text to be followed by all to regulate themselves and to get advantage of the state. This was the perception of the founding fathers and mothers of Indian state and not M.K. Gandhi. While doing so, it was an assumption that the state will perform the duty of an equalizer to bring equality and equity to enable the people to lead a civilized life in India. Essentially, the path chosen for transforming India by the founding fathers and mothers of India barring M.K. Gandhi are Western in thought as they are influenced by the liberal education.[8] They reposed confidence and faith in the Western model of governance and development as the whole world believed in big state for big achievements. Since material advancement is the basic aspect of development and hence everyone was tempted to follow the Western mode of development. This model has some records to show that it delivered public goods to the people in an effective way. It was unfortunate that they did not have a clue that it will be an exploitative one.[9]

Even at that point of time there was an alternative approach of development, democracy, and governance evolved by M.K. Gandhi through his intensive experimentation analysis who spearheaded the freedom struggle with an alternative approach of non-violence to liberate India, *Satyagragh* to oppose oppressive steps of colonial administration, *Sarvodaya* a new social order and *Gram Swaraj* for governance and development.[10] Indian masses had been prepared by M.K. Gandhi for liberating India and reconstruct Indian society by following the alternative path.[11] The slow departure of the British from the Indian soil marked with implanting of their systems of governance, and economy. While leaving the Indian soil, the British created an unending internal war in Bharat between two religious communities with a hope that people would fight against each other and the elites will have to rely on the power of the state in order to maintain unity.

The British left India with the belief that Indians did not have proven alternative and hence they will rely on the Western system and model for governance, administration, economy and democracy. The leaders who had been trained and groomed by M.K. Gandhi promised the masses that the Indian state takes the responsibility of alleviating poverty, ending discriminatory practices against the oppressed and achieve prosperity speedily.[12] Thus fastly the state institutions had been built up and state soveignity had been recognized with the hope that all promises would be realized as the leaders were dedicated for the cause of the nation and the people and they were known for their integrity. Here it is to be noted that the masses prepared for social reconstruction involved in freedom struggle had been in wait list because the state took the whole responsibilities of transformation by building its own development army. While the constitution was prepared for India, the backdrop was the partition and its implication in the Indian and Pakistani societies and care was taken to build a strong Indian state to maintain its unity and integrity rather than attending the diverse requirements and needs of the people living in India with extreme inequalities in socio-economic conditions. Within a short span of time administrative thinkers from the US has cautioned that the whole process of state building and development activities without the involvement of the people will lead to exploitation of the masses in general and particular the poor in the long run.

The much debated alternative disappeared as M.K. Gandhi disappeared from the scene as he was assacinated within a short span of time after India got independence. State activities continued and promised the people that state is the responsible authority for the development and peace of the society.[13] Till the middle of 1980s, state responded the needs of the society. Yet the needs and aspirations of the people had not been fulfilled as the increasing aspiration of the people could not be met by the state authorities as the capacity of the state could not match with the increasing aspirations of the people. Yet the state *versus* society praxis continued as state declared its failure giving way to Market to join with state to deliver public goods and the new state Market-led activities continued for three decades.[14] The globalization of economy has intensified the market activities which continued the exploitative process.[15] Finally, Market also declared that the increasing aspirations of the people could not be met by mere state and Market alone.[16] What is the alternative for the development process is the next question. Unless the community, namely people are involved in the development and governance process, no force or strategy can solve the problems of the people more specifically the poor in India.[17] In this context one has to ponder over what will be the need of the hour to redeem the conditions of the poor in India, as it faces unprecedented crises[18]. What we need to India, what new arrangement needs to be in place for governance and development in India have to be debated.

Where We are in India Today?

India is in a new consciousness and it is called "development consciousness". Growth, development, profit, business, reform, new India, clean India, skill India, fit India, one India, one Nation, one language, patriotism, and new nationalism are in discourse. The new consciousness has not taken into account the problems of the farming community (which constitutes 58% of the total population), tribal community (which constitute 11% of the total population), pastoral and nomadic community (which constitute 2% of the population), fishing community (which constitute 2% of the total population) and craft communities (which constitute 4% of the population). All the above communities are in the rural areas. They are totally disturbed in the development process. It is to be noted that the Government of India has introduced Mahatma Gandhi National Rural Employment Scheme with a view to arrest the distress migration from the rural areas. Knowing fully well the growing discontent in the rural areas, the Government of India and the states have introduced 2000 development schemes and programmes to improve the conditions of the poor as stated by the World Bank Report. Yet the conditions of the poor in the rural areas have not been improved as expected. As an alternative the Government of India made development as a right. Thus all development schemes have been given in the form of rights with huge outlays. Hence, a bundle of rights have been given to the poor. From the above one can conclude easily that the conditions of the poor who live in the rural areas face plethora of problems and hence they need such a kind of assistance from the state.

To understand the conditions of the above segments of the people and general conditions of Indian governance and society, a few global reports have to be perused. They are: the world inequality report, the world environment report, the world ecology report, the world governance report, the human development report, the world hunger report, the world wealth report, the world human rights report, the report of democracy in the world, and the world corruption report. All the reports have brought the status of the people in Indian society. 82 per cent of the rural households lack basic amenities to lead a decent dignified human life. 50 per cent of the Indian farmers are indebted. 85 per cent of the rural female workforce are either illiterate or educated up to primary level only.[19] The above data are enough to prove that the contemporary rural India is in deep distress. While comparing the living conditions of the people with some of the poor countries in the world, the performance of the Indian government is dismal even though it has higher level of economic growth. This has brought an argument in the public discourse that the development efforts of the government have not helped the deprived, poor and marginalized substantially. It is to be noted here that exponents on democracy, development and governance argued that governance failure is attributed for all the failures in the domain of development.[20] This condition has enabled the market to come to the rescue of the state.

The market demanded reforms for its free movement and functions without much restrictions. In the name of reforms, powers of the state governments have been taken away.[21] In order to ease the tension and frustration of the people over the poor performance of the government, state governments have been asked to devolve powers to the grassroots institutions by amending the Constitution of India.[22] This has also enabled the Market to carry out its activities without much interference of the state government by getting consent from the local government. Decentralization of powers came only to enable the poor to empower themselves and achieve economic prosperity. But it has been used effectively by the market and not by the poor segments of the society. In the whole process of market dominated activities in the globalised economic world, people have been oriented to look at every aspect of human life as a tradable commodity. As a result, much of the values and ethics of the society, politics and economics have been given a goby. At this juncture a new consciousness has been created for new India.

On the other hand, social reforms and political change or reformation activities have not been taken forward with the initiative of the state as promised by the founding fathers of India through the constitution of India.[23] Indian society struggled hard to achieve freedom from the British yet it had not put up such an effort to democratize the Indian communities and thereby it failed to achieve social democracy.[24] The Parliamentary democracy established in India did not move beyond the minimal democracy. As a result, our democracy revolves around elections.[25] Hence, it is electoral democracy which could achieve only institutional democracy and not the behaviour democracy. The continued political mobilization of the people by the political parties for the electoral democracy used only the caste and the religion, culture, region and language as factors. This kind of mobilization has kept the communities to be grounded only in primordial loyalties. Hence, it has kept the society in the caste hierarchy which works against deepening of democracy.[26] Thus Indian society has witnessed a new paradox of economic growth and democratic deficit. Poor political engagement of the people by the political parties kept the people away from the government. The gap between the people and the government is increased and as a result poor has developed a fear over the power of the state. Poor people have been made to live as they lived during colonial administration in the state of mind. Though services have been provided to the poor, their dignity is at stake. Market forces have engaged the government and the political parties and as a result, character of the market influenced with the political parties.[27] Thus political parties have acquired the corporate culture for their functioning. As a result, politics becomes costlier as political activities are done by the professionals and not by the party workers. Votes for electoral victory is determined by its price and thereby it becomes a commodity.

Democracy has been reduced only to election leaving the core values such as equality, fairness, justice, liberty, are unattended to. The proud citizens have been reduced as voters to the political parties, as beneficiaries to the ruling regime, as petitioners to the officials working in the government and as consumer to the market forces. Honorable citizens have been reduced as voters, beneficiaries and petitioners. Dignity of the majority of the people is at stake. Majority of the people are living in sub-human living conditions which are not in the new consciousness of India.

The "New consciousness" has been created around 2013 and 2014 by a group of technocrats by using the anticorruption movement. From there the group intensified their activities among the unoriented youth with a sense that India is entering into a new era. The new era is meant for decisiveness, leadership pride, strong nation, patriotism, national values, unity of the nation, and nation first. Since the party was known for the above values (the Indian National Congress) has abandoned, and all these values have been snatched away and used them for the success of the party (the BJP) which created new consciousness in the general election in 2014. The parties both national and regional who were in power and the parties who supported the parties in power have given up the political socialization process to orient new youth in their ideological tenet in the last three decades. But they involved in managing the parties and carried out the activities with the money drawn from market and the money drawn from rent seeking activities when they were in power.

Since Independence gap between the promises and performance of the parties in power has increased and it was exposed by the media in an organized way. As a result, major segments of the people who were with the ruling party left the party and joined with regional and casteist outfits. People have been lured by the regional political parties by citing the failure of the national governments. Basically, the space left out by the national forces has been occupied by the regional political parties. It is interesting to note that the regional political parties had adopted a different approach borrowed from the market. By following the client pattern model, the regional political parties have strongly established their parties as institutions with full promises to the party cadres. The regional political parties have drawn financial support from the market and run the party. If they come to power, the ruling party indulged in corruption as transaction cost while delivering services to the people. As a result, the regional political parties emerged as business institutions to make money through its political marketing to face the elections.

Market forces in the globalised economy have corrupted the political establishments. As a result, all the national parties which had been in power and the regional parties which had been in power for a long have been facing the charges of corruption. It is not only politicians but also the bureaucrats involved in corrupt practices. Individuals, groups, parties, business houses joined together and worked for market and market enabled everyone to make profit out of their transactions. As a result, all the national and regional political parties which were in power have been exposed at a point of time by the right wing parties.

The new capitalist groups mostly crony have supported the campaign to malign the ruling regime by brining allegation of corruption. It is to be noted here that the parties which had faced the charges of corruption as they were in governance for a long had a history of both achievements and corruption. As the propaganda machinery under the newly emerged public relation companies intensified their social media propaganda with a back-up of the new market forces which faced problems because of policy paralysis, the achievements of the party in power could not reach the people. Both the regional and national parties had their own achievements record but their achievements have not reached the people. In this context, the regional political parties and smaller national political parties wanted to use this opportunity to maximize their tally in the general election without forecasting the emerging political force with new promises to the people. But, the campaign for clean India, corruption free India, new India gained currency as there was no unified contest against the emergence of the right wing party.

Here yet another factor has to be taken note of. It is the major failure of the Indian political parties both national and regional instead of engaging development politics, involved in communal politics by using the caste and religion for electoral gain. As a result, masses have been oriented in communal politics rather than in development politics. There is a slight change in the behaviour of the people that they have shifted their science from caste to religion. Communization continued with new vigour. Since the electoral verdict in 2014 enabled the right wing alliance to form the government with a strong footing, the ruling front started yet another campaign to discredit the path through which governance took place in this country and the process adopted for achieving development. It has given a sense that the approach of the previous regimes has weakened the country and it enabled a few to amass wealth. This campaign continued despite the poor performance of the government.

The opposition parties both national and regional who opposed the ruling party have not united themselves with a clear-cut programme and agenda to oppose the continuation of the right wing ruling party in power from 2014. Further, the image created against the previous ruling parties and the other regional parties by the right wing parties sustained in the memory of the people in the next election also because of the campaign approach adopted by the ruling party and its leaders when they are in power to keep the opposition parties in defence. Hence, the present regime got a thumping majority to form the government even in 2019 election. After it became a ruling party, it has removed the special status of the Jammu & Kashmir by making Article 370 of the Constitution of India null and void. The new middle class has supported the Central government for its stand on Kashmir. Even this created a division in the opposition parties. The mainstream parties in Jammu & Kashmir which were in power have not been with the people. They were with Delhi to carry out their political careerism and ignoring the consciousness of the people of Jammu & Kashmir. This kind of politics in Jammu & Kashmir created a perception that it is a thorn in the Indian government and politics. Everyone felt that there had been anarchy and that anarchy had been continued with the support of Federal government. The dominant right wing party with its organizational back-up and technocrats support ganged the public mood and acted in a direction which gives rich dividends. Thus, the opposition parties have been driven to periphery through action against corruption and propaganda initiated that they are working with divisive forces.

These are all political strategies to keep the opposition voiceless. At present all the opposition parties have lost their moral base and lost their ideological roots and as a result the failure of governance, policies, programmes of the ruling party could not be effectively addressed through their parties. There is yet another phenomenon in Indian politics in the recent years that too after the introduction of globalization of economy. Political parties are not initiating any struggle on the crises of the people. In the last thirty years India has not witnessed a single pan India peoples movement against the state as political parties have moved away from the politics of struggle.

At present all the political parties barring a few have become political companies or mutts and they have increased their asset base locked up with families. The wealth of the party has been increased beyond their imagination and expectation and it drew substantial income from the market. For the market expansion, the companies have extended financial support to political parties who are active in the political systems in order to create a conducive eco-system for their market activities. As a result, the political parties moved from agitational politics to demonstration politics. In this kind of agitational political activities, the participants are not the party men and women but they are paid for their political labour.

In this market era, political meetings in the form of conferences are done with much fanfare to attract the participants by investing huge money drawn from the market. Now political activities are time passing activities and not serious political discourses and debates aiming for transformation. Since they are paid political labourers, they are not interested in listening to the meaningful debates or discourses. There have been active participants in all political activities of the parties with the hope that if their party comes to power they can get a lions share in the spoils. This is the new methodology borrowed from the market and adopted it for their success in the party politics.

Many of the occasions in India, it has been seen in the past the rule of law is replaced by ruling party law. There is yet another phenomenon one would observe in the new context. There are individuals playing key role in the party have their own institutions to retain the funds for party activities of the party with high risk and they are inevitable for the party. In the fifty years political history of this country India has witnessed a degeneration of politics by corrupting the party politics, electoral politics, governance and administration and finally, citizenry in a phased manner. As a result, corruption as regularized phenomenon. Till the arrival of the right wing party with a new mass leader to lead the masses corruption was not an issue in the public discourse. It was the right wing party with new leadership with a persuasive tone propagated among the Indian mass about the menace of the corruption and its ramification. This propaganda gained currency among the public, as there had been a movement meant for ending corruption in the backdrop.

At this juncture, a new middle class found out this opportunity and sided with the right wing establishment as it highlighted, nation patriotism, sacrifice, service, following national ethos and development of all. When a leader with an alternative approach, programme, activities came in the political scene, people have jumped into the bandwagon to support this new arrival as national alternative. The new leader with his scheme of things has taken the politics discourse at a different level keeping the opposition far away from him and his political establishment. The opposition parties both national and regional did not have a clue as where is our politics and they could not reposition themselves and understood the realities. They have underestimated the power of the new leader and his organizational ability. Every party was in its old track with old belief of managing the election through electoral chemistry and alliance formulae. They could not realize the fact that change is imminent and bound to come. As a result, they are all reduced as spent thrift forces and not vibrant alternative political force.

Yet the problems of the farmers and farm workers, tribals, fisher folk, artisans, have not been solved and they are further intensified because of the intensified market activities. It is interesting to note the fact that the ruling establishment is accusing the previous regimes who were in power for the longer period have done a huge damage and it will take time for the present regime to repair the damages and hence it takes time to reach the new place. It has been communicated powerfully to the people by the leader of the new regime.

Reaching out to the masses through the powerful communication, nobody has come nearer to the new leader who is in power and command of the party. The opposition parties neither have such leadership to change the narrative or to counter the arguments of the ruling establishment. They look like organizations without force and clue to what to do to counter this. In fact, all those parties who oppose the present ruling arrangement at the centre face the problem of trust deficit.

To face the problem arise out of the economic crises and its own mismanagement of the economy, the ruling establishment find new narratives and equally it saw to it that opposition parties could not come together to oppose the government. Further it weakens the opposition parties by framing corruption charges against the leaders who were active in taking on the ruling party in the political discourse.

Parties who were raising voices seriously in three or four decades ago on the people's issues, state's rights, language purity, cultural and regional identity, now they are mere passive spectator, react to the actions of the Federal government only through release of statements and not through political struggles. 'Political struggle' as a word disappeared from the practice of the political parties in India today. But people are in political struggle to save farming, natural resources, environment, ecology and to fight against the repressive policies of the government. But these people's struggles are being supported by the political parties they are not struggling. It is the new phenomenon in Indian politics. It gives a sense that our political parties are acting without the soul force. There is no national leader of masses like M.K. Gandhi, and Jayaprakash Narayan. People are looking for alternative politics, alternative development paradigm, and alternative governance mechanism. But our leaders are performing the role of mere managers. It is time to revisit Gandhi and reread Gandhi in the present backdrop, Gandhi has much to offer to evolve a new politics, new development paradigm, new governance.

Need of the hour is revisiting M.K. Gandhi. Instead of glorifying Gandhi, deifying M.K. Gandhi which he never liked, he can be reread and contextualize the Gandhian framework and that will guide us to re-correct ourselves in politics, governance, democracy and development.

Emerging New Postulates

Many political parties in India have moved away from the people and losing their relevance in the context. Political parties who enjoyed power for a longer period faced the trust deficit. They have lost their original constituents. They failed to contextualize themselves and reconnect themselves with their original constituents. These parties have failed miserably to harmonise the relationship between the society and the market.

Political parties have changed the character of the parties into corporate companies by the Market forces. By adopting market friendly approach and filled their coffer through liberal donations from the market and run the parties by adopting the market approach of "win win". "Votes" have been converted into tradeable commodity.

The leaders of the National and Regional political parties who were in power have lived in old perception without ganging the expectations of the youth and the new middle class. They relied on the power of castes and money.

The values of the National political parties who were in power or in support of the regime have been powerfully used by the right wing party for its electoral success. The parties which were in power could not reach out to the masses with their achievements as the right wing party outwitted others in reaching out the masses with its agenda and programme which are attractive and achievable.

The major achievements of the present ruling regime from 2014 to 2019 for the benefit of the poor, namely gas connection to the poor households, free housing scheme for the poor, toilets for the poor, have influenced the poor.

The original constituents of the old ruling regime at the centre have moved away from the party as they were disillusioned by the performance of the party in power. They joined with new regionalistic political forces. The remaining joined with the right wing party.

Politics has gone into the hands of the Market. Hence, the Market men and women have played their role effectively in deciding matters in election. Market nuances have been used to decide matters in the electoral process. As a result, every aspect of election is commodified and made it into a profit making venture which excluded the ideology.

As political leaders have given up the struggle mode, politics have been reduced to election and activities are intense only during election and normal course of politics is in the form of political shows to demonstrate their existence. Political parties have given up the practice of agitational politics. Equally, the political parties have not continued the practice of socialization process among the youth. As a result in the past three decades there is no political struggle.

Middle class which played a predominant role in the process of social change and political transformation through political struggle aligned with market forces leaving the problems of the poor unattended to. As a result, a new middle class emerged from techno market strategy group to create a new consciousness.

Conclusion

Basically still India is in the villages as 68 per cent of the people are in the rural areas. Pastoral communities, craft communities, farming communities, fishing communities and tribal communities are in the rural areas. Their life and livelihood conditions are stressful and they have to struggle for their livelihood. At the same time, they are being exploited by the industrial and market forces. By exploiting the rural masses, the urban centres are enriching and achieving prosperity. Pastoral communities are facing problem because of vagaries of monsoon. Farming communities are in debt trap and committing suicides. Craft communities have lost their livelihood. Tribal communities are driven from the forest by the market and state forces to exploit the minerals. Fishing communities are also facing crisis. Virtually villages are moving towards extinct.

The political parties have failed miserably in democratizing the society and as a result Indian democracy still in political democracy that too at a minimal level leaving the social democracy unattended by the political parties. They have failed miserably in mitigating the antithetical forces to democracy and instead they fuelled the forces to remain active as they used caste and religion as factors for political mobilization for electoral democracy.

All the failures of the left and centrist wing political parties enabled the right wing parties to take politics to a new arena called development politics. In order to achieve the electoral success, market approach was adopted and thereby they have weakened the parties which were in power by accusing them on the issue of large scale corruption. The new middle class which hugely benefited out of globalization of economy joined in the right wing group by seeing the emergence of the right wing parties in the world and worked for the success of the party in the election in India.

Values which had been in active usage for political mobilization during the freedom struggle and at the dawn of Independence have been adopted to create a new consciousness called "Nation First" by the right wing party. It gives a signal message that the country is not safe and enemies are within and outside to weaken the Nation and this party is taking steps to safeguard the nation by building a new consciousness among the people. Corruption has dismantled the fundamentals of the nation and it is to be rooted out from this country. In such a way, a new consciousness have been created. It is presumed that it is an alternative. It is only a political alternative. India needs to move from party politics to people's politics. For this alternative politics M.K. Gandhi has much to contribute. To perpetuate people's politics, the cost of politics has to be reduced and the political parties have to reorient their parties from market oriented approach to people centric approach.

The slowdown of political socialization has kept the youth away from ideological orientation without perspective. Hence, there is huge perception gap in terms of politics between generations.

A new political culture has to be created to enable the people to participate in the process of development, governance and democracy.

NOTES

1. Anthony J. Parel (ed.) (2009). *Gandhi Hind Swaraj and other writings,* New Delhi: Cambridge University Press, p. xv.
2. M.K. Gandhi, *Hind Swaraj,* Ahmedabad: Navajivan Publications.
3. Vinoba Bhave (1955). *Swaraj Sastra: The Principles of a Non-violent Political Order,* Wardha: Sarva-Seva-Sangh Publication.
4. Suzanne Franco (2018). *Soul Force,* Chennai: Notion Press.
5. S. Radhakrishnan (ed.) (1949). *Mahatma Gandhi: Essays and Reflections on his Life and Work,* London: Cambridge University Press.
6. B.M. Bass and P. Steidlmeier, "Ethics, Character and authentic transformational leadership", *Leadership Quarterly.*
7. P. Bandhu (ed.) (2011). *Back to Basics: J.C. Kumarappa A Reader,* Ooty: Odyssey.
8. Prem Shankar Jha (2006). *The Twilight of the Nation State,* New Delhi: Vistaar Publications.
9. Lala Lajpat Raj (1917). *England's Deft to India: A Historical Narrative of Britain's Fiscal Policy in India,* New York: B.W. Huebsch.

10. G. Palanithurai (2018). "Will J.C. Kumarappa Guide Another Village Movement?" *Gandhi Marg,* Vol. 40, No. 3 & 4, p. 207.
11. Dharampal (2003). *Understanding Gandhi,* Goa: Other India Press.
12. Mani Shankar Aiyar (2014). "A vision for India", *Frontline* (Nehru's Legacy), Vol. 31, No. 24, Nov. 29-Dec., 12, pp. 35-39.
13. Baldev Raj Nayar (2009). *The Myth of the Shrinking State,* New Delhi: Oxford University Press.
14. Sirpa Tenhuneu and Minna Saavala (2013). *An Introduction to changing India: Culture, Politics and Development,* London: Anthem Press.
15. Arvind Veermani (1st June, 2002). "A New Development Paradigm". *Economic and Political Weekly,* Vol. 37, No. 22, pp. 2151-2160.
16. Raguram Rajan (2019). *Third Pillar,* New Delhi: Penguin Press.
17. G. Palanithurai (2018). *New Rural Higher Education: Need of the Hour to Transform Rural India,* New Delhi: Concept Publishing Company Pvt. Ltd.
18. K. Swaminathan (1998). *Relevance of Gandhi and Other Essays,* Gandhism: Gandhigram Trust.
19. National Institute of Rural Development and Panchayati Raj, *Rural Development Statistics 2015-2016,* Hyderabad, NIRD & PR, 2018.
20. Daron Acemoglu and James A. Robinson (2013). *Why Nations Fail: The origins of power, prosperity and poverty,* London: Profile Books.
21. Prashanthi Mallela (2017). "Centralization through Decentralization: A Bureaucratic perspective" in A.V. Satish Chandra (ed) *From Centralised Government to Decentralized Governance,* New Delhi: Viva Books.
22. G. Palanithurai (April-June, 2016). "Decentralization: Unused Potentials". *Gandhi Marg,* Vol. 38: No.1, pp. 95-114.
23. Rajni Kothari (2005). *Rethinking Democracy,* New Delhi: Orient Longman, p. 55.
24. G. Palanithurai (1998). "Parliamentary Reforms in India" in Sundar Ram (ed) *Parliamentary Institutions in India: Development or Decay,* New Delhi: National Publishing House, p. 279.
25. G. Palanithurai (January-June, 2019). "Democracy: Changing Nature and Dimensions". *South Asian Journal of Socio Political Studies,* Vol. XIX, No. 2.
26. Rajni Kothari (2004). "Issues before Indian Democracy: An Overview" in Rajendra Vora and Suhas Palshikar (eds.), *Indian Democracy: Meaning and Practices,* New Delhi: Sage Publications, pp. 45-54.
27. Atul Kohli (1997). "Crisis of Governability" in Sudipta Kaviraj (ed.) *Politics in India.* Delhi: Oxford University Press.

8
Constitution for the Masses

G. Palanithurai

Introduction

A constitution is an approved document created by a human group living in a defined territory in the Modern State system to regulate, modernize and develop the society through a process of governance by the state apparatus. It works in accordance with its capacity to cope up with the requirements and expectations of the society. To handle the constitution, the state machinery and its operators should have the needed capacity and thereby the expected outcome could be achieved. In the same way, the people or the citizens should have capacity to get best advantage of the constitution.

Health of the constitution is determined based on its longevity. Constitution is a dynamic document responding to the needs of the society through the governance instrument called 'government'. Impact of the constitution could be gauged through a process of utilization of the document by the people living in the defined territory of a country. Thus enabling the people or citizens of the country to make use of the constitution for the betterment of the society is a fundamental task to be performed by the Government and other political agencies who are in constant interaction with the government and the people. Thus, a variety of factors are responsible for increasing the longevity of a constitution and in the same way the impact of the constitution in a society.

Constitutions are assessed, reviewed and evaluated periodically, and reorient and update the same by amending the constitutions. Value of the constitutions depends on the faith of the people on the constitutions. Utility of the constitution is determined by the socialization process of the citizens on the constitution. Likewise, the impact of the constitution is based on the implementation of the provisions of the constitution by the ruling class and the political class of the country. If a constitution is lengthy and detailed, one should not presume that it has covered all the aspects of the human activities and thereby all segments of the society would get advantage out of it. In the same way, one should not consider that if a constitution has got a longer life that it would have served the society better than the shorter constitutions. It all depends on the utilization of the provisions of the constitution by the citizens. Against this background, one should look at the Constitution of India and its impact on the society.

Context

Every year public institutions more specifically higher education institutions are celebrating the Constitution Day on 26th November as that was the day our Constitution was ratified. Constitution Day signifies two things. They are: (a) essentially awareness has to be created among the citizens of India on the constitution; and (b) while doing so that the thoughts of Ambedkar should also be taken to the people as they were all essential to understand the importance of our constitution and its implication in the life of the ordinary persons. Primarily, it is a task assigned to public institutions to take the constitution to the people through such a kind of activities. It is to be noted here that the circular issued by the authorities to the higher learning institutions is only a reminder every year to carry out the activities pertinent to taking the constitution to the masses continuously. By spending a day on creation of awareness among the people about the constitution will not fulfil the objectives of the event unless the institutions involved themselves in carrying out such a kind of activities in the society throughout the year through the outreach programmes of the higher learning institutions.

As institutions receive communication from the UGC, the funding and regulating agency the academic institutions organize Constitution

Day function and deliberate on the functioning of the Constitution of India by inviting a guest from other higher learning institution. In this context, a realistic evaluation of the impact created in the society by the Constitution of India is also being done. Against this background, a small exercise is being done in this chapter as part of the celebration of the Constitution Day at Karaikudi Alagappa University where I was invited as a guest to speak on that day. Before coming into the evaluation exercise it is necessary to project the historical context in which the Constitution was prepared and approved.

Historical Background

To prepare a constitution for India, a Constituent Assembly was constituted on 6th December, 1946. It took near about three years to complete the task. Totally 11 sessions have been conducted in 165 days. First session began on 9th December, 1946. The whole document as 'Constitution of India' was adopted on 26th November, 1949 with the approval of 284 members of the Constituent Assembly. The draft constitution was sent to different public fora to get the feedback from the opinion makers and the public. The Constituent Assembly received huge response and many of them were considered and rest of them had been responded by the Constituent Assembly through writing reply to the questions. Several amendments had been moved and of which 103 Amendments had been adopted. As a result, a constitution was created with 22 parts, 395 Articles and 8 Schedules. It came into practice on 26th January, 1950. The Constituent Assembly was chaired by Dr. Rajendra Prasad and a Drafting Committee was constituted for preparing the document with Dr. B.R. Ambedkar as chairperson along with seven members. Dr. B.R. Ambedkar had discharged his role and responsibilities deligently to meet the requirements of the diverse population in India. To perform the task effectively and efficiently he had gone through 60 constitutions of the world single handedly with a view to get the best parts of the constitution of many countries. Even though there was a committee for drafting the constitution, the single handed work of Dr. B.R. Ambedkar was appreciated by both Dr.Rajendra Prasad and Jawaharlal Nehru in their concluding remarks in the Constituent Assembly's final session.[1]

Background

To understand the real tasks and achievements of our constitutional pundits one has to go through the conditions of the Indian society at the dawn of Independence.

Never we had a unified territory ever before as we see today. It was done only at the dawn of Independence. Even the British Administration had only the part of what we have in India today. The British established an unified administration in some of the territories in India. But 600 princely, states were not under the British Administration. Only after Independence our leaders have integrated 600 princely states with India with great difficulty. India got independence through a non-violent struggle but when it was born the new India had to face a horror as more than million people had been butchered and more than 18 million people migrated due to creation of Pakistan. So in a turbulent environment nation building exercise was initiated and of which one is the preparation of the constitution. It is to be understood that despite the holocaust and massive displacement of people from Pakistan, the excitement of mass on the creation of independent nation has not diminished. People had enthusiasm and excitement to participate in the nation building process.[2] With this backdrop the constitution making exercise started.

Challenges before the Makers of the Constitution

When British left India, they left India with extreme poverty, extreme inequality and equally ignorant masses.[3] But M.K. Gandhi through his leadership the masses have been mobilized not only to liberate India but also to reconstruct India.[4] The mobilized masses had been waiting for the call of the political pundits to bring a radical change in the society through a new nation with their participation. To bring a radical transformation in the society, to alleviate poverty and establish equality a governance system has to be created. At the same time India as a nation, to be kept together massive exercise is needed as all variations have to be accommodated. The biggest challenge is to manage the antithetical forces of democracy through democratic form of governance. The existing social and economic conditions were against the practice of democracy.[5] But it has been declared that India will have to follow the representative democracy. Making a constitution is not very difficult. But making a workable constitution for a long period is a big challenge.[6]

Accommodating regional, lingual, cultural variations in the governance system requires lot of flexibilities and yet the divisive forces were on the rise during that period. Fear of the minorities due to massive killings during Pakistan creation, has to be dealt with by giving assurance to them for a peaceful life in Indian soil is yet another challenge. Basically Indian society is communitarian in nature. They led life with community practices. They were under the control of the British Administration in British India and were under the chieftains and kings of the native India. Never they led life with responsibility, dignity as Independent citizens but they led life as subjects of the chieftains and the colonial masters.[7]

Preparation of the masses to the newly created Independent democratic nation is a tough task and more difficult than preparing them for the struggle to liberate the society from the colonial yoke. The social capital created during the freedom struggle is the only asset India had at the dawn of Independence. The nation is big and vast, the problems it faced at the dawn of Independence were insurmountable. Against this condition the constitution was drafted.

Fundamentals

Unequivocally it has been declared that India will follow a democratic form of government. It should be through a representative system of governance. The representatives will be selected through a process of election by providing opportunity to all the citizens of the country through adult franchise. It should have republican character with peoples' sovereignty. Fundamental rights are guaranteed. In order to ensure democracy, checks and balance has been maintained by creating independent agencies in the governing process. Accountability has been ensured through installation of an independent institution. Government took responsibility for the development of the people. Welfare of the people is the prime responsibility of the state. Under Directive Principles of state policy direction has been given to the states to initiate activities to administer development. All the above features have been incorporated in the Constitution of India.[8] Thus, a detailed, elaborate and lengthy document has been placed before the people.

The Constitution enables the state to control, regulate and reform the Indian society. Basically a system has been designed through the Constitution in such a way to bring a radical transformation in the Indian society as it has got all negative elements to democratic practice in the society. It is designed to create a strong centre with a democratic institutional set up. At the same time in order to accommodate the regional units in the state system, they are not federated but they are linked with the Union as units with unique features to work with the Central Government to deliver services and administer development to the people. Deliberately it has been called as a union of states not as federal structure. The machineries created through the Constitution have to work to practice the provisions of the Constitution to enable people to lead a decent dignified human life by following the rule of law and scientific and technological knowhow. Practicing democracy, transforming radically the Indian society and achieving inclusive development are the goals enshrined in the Constitution of India. Contrary to the wishes of Mahatma Gandhi, enormous powers have been given to the state to regulate, reform and develop the Indian society. It is a major argument that the Constitution of India has given enormous space for government machineries to act in the society without giving adequate space for the communities to reconstruct the Indian society by involving themselves in the transformative process. This argument has been projected by J.C. Kumarappa, a Gandhian economist. He emphatically argued that M.K. Gandhi prepared the masses more for reconstruction rather than freedom struggle. In the whole freedom struggle systematically M.K. Gandhi indicated the path to be pursued for transforming India. He laid down institutional structures for the transformative process. But unfortunately the framers of the Constitution and the political pundits had closed a different path as west had followed by creating a strong state with enormous powers.

Indian Society

In India 80 per cent of the population were in the rural areas at the dawn of Independence. They were pastoral, farming, craft, tribal, fishing, and trading communities. The rural communities follow the traditional caste system maintaining the caste hierarchy[9]. Since it was an agrarian society, the feudal mindset and practice were in the rural areas. It was coupled with patriarchy.[10] Dr. B.R. Ambedkar aptly described the Indian village as "a sink of localism, a den of ignorance, (and) narrow mindedness". The Constitution has to work for total transformation of the villages in India. M.K. Gandhi wanted to create villages a "little republics" not as little kingdoms. The last man voice has to be heard and responded to make that man to feel that he is also the citizen of the country. To achieve the goal, M.K. Gandhi has evolved a paradigm and a framework of governance and development contrary to the vision of the liberal thinkers who were managing the country as leaders at the dawn of Independence. But attempts have been made to work for the poor through a different strategy and framework. The leaders who led the country wanted to move in the path of Industrialization and state led development. To remove the aberrations what has been described by B.R. Ambedkar about the rural villages and to achieve the dream of M.K. Gandhi, the Constitution has to be used. Constitution of India grants status to the people but community rejects what constitution grants. Constitution has not reached the masses.[11] The masses have followed the practices of the community. As a result one will find more of violations of the provisions of the Constitution. When social practices are looked at from the perspective of the constitution of India, one will find violation as culture and not adherence of the rights granted to individuals by the constitution.[12]

Once the constitution making work was completed, the chairman of the drafting committee Dr. B.R. Ambedkar observed that a best document has been prepared for this country to find solution to many of the ills afflicted the Indian society. It is up to the leaders who implement the provisions of the Constitution to achieve the goals of the Constitution. If anything wrong comes out one should not blame the people who prepared the constitution but blame the people who are in the positions to operate the provisions of the Constitution. He made this observation as the chairman of the drafting committee. Dr. Rajendra Prasad, the Chairman of the Constituent Assembly observed that if good people are in position, even a bad law and Constitution would deliver good things to the citizens and suppose if bad are elected, even a good constitution will fail the people. Now arguments have been projected that moral degeneration sets in Indian politics as self-centric individuals create into the political system through political parties. It is also argued that cleansing of politics is the need of the hour and for which mass mobilization is the need of the hour.

Evaluation

We tend to look at the Constitution after seven decades of experience and in-between three generations have gone. The document was prepared by men of high calibre and integrity with a sense of dedication and a vision to transform the Indian society. No doubt it was the product of the elites. It moved in the track of the West both for governance and economic development as the founding fathers found that it is the best way to reduce poverty and transform the society radically through the state machineries. It is true that there is no space for people in the Constitution. The constitutional pundits had agreed with the worldview that the big states would do all such transformations what they wanted to see in India and what they promised to the people during the freedom struggle. The partition of India and its related events were in the back of their minds while drafting the Constitution of India. Keeping the provinces together in one nation was the biggest challenge which they have confronted while preparing the Constitution. Once the constitution was drafted and adopted opinions, observations and comments started pouring in.

Ivor Jennings, a legal and constitutional luminary, advised many countries while they prepared constitutions for their countries, observed that Indian constitution will not last long as it is a very detailed one without having much flexibility. He made this observation once the constitution came into being after its ratification. His observations had been seriously viewed by constitutional experts and comments have been passed on his observation. It had been an academic tradition in the world to look at issues of the society in the backdrop of the Western theories with the premise that West is developed and it is civilized and it is a model for development. Many argued that India cannot keep the democracy for a long as anti-democratic elements are in operation in Indian society.[13] In India all the theoretical insights based on the Western theories proved wrong. Thus, the Indian Constitution has crossed 69 years. It is not a mean achievement. But the question is whether the Constitution has delivered what it ought to deliver?[14] All the scholars have raised their doubts about the longevity of the Indian Constitution. It is a fact to be noted here that the same Ivor Jennings acted as a consultant for the preparation of the constitution for the Sri Lanka. But that constitution lived only for a few years. All Western scholars looked at India from the experience of the West and made observations about India and its practices. Indian Government had attempted to review the Constitution of India when it reached the fiftieth year of Independence. But Grenville Austin made a plea that Indian Constitution need not be reviewed as it is a well-conceived comprehensive document. But its functioning has to be reviewed as many of the provisions in the Constitution have not been put into practice. Based on his plea, the Government of India has modified the proposal and initiated action to review the functioning of the Indian Constitution. Report has been prepared and submitted to the Government of India by Justice Dr. Venkata Chellaiah. Before coming to the evaluation of the Indian Constitution, it is necessary to look at the history of the constitutions of many of the countries in the world.

History of the Constitutions

When Dr. Ambedkar started the drafting the exercise to prepare a constitution for India as chairman of the drafting committee, he had glanced through nearly 60 constitutions of the world singlehandedly. Without any technological and research advisory bodies, he took pain to read and take notes from the constitutions to take the best parts and provisions to incorporate into the draft constitution meant for India. But now constitutions have been comprehensively and comparatively analysed. There are institutions with liberal funding of several agencies to undertake research studies on the constitutions of the countries in the world. Studies have been carried out on the impact of the constitutions in the societies.

Recent study, "Life span of written constitutions" by Thomas Ginsburg, Zachary Elkins and James Melton covered a period from 1789 to 2006 made a comprehensive analysis of the functioning of the constitutions of many of the countries in the world. The study has analysed 792 constitutions. Of them 518 have been replaced.

192 are still in force. 82 constitutions have been formally suspended. The mean life span of the constitutions of the countries since 1789 is mere 17 years. Only 19 per cent of the constitutions in the world remain 50 years old. 7 per cent of the constitutions did not see the second birthday. Durability of the constitution depends on the inclusion of public both at the drafting as well as approval stage. Longer constitutions are more durable than shorter ones. Longevity and impact of the constitutions are determined by an array of factors. Our constitution withstood pressures for seventy years and amended to contextualize itself. This is not a mean achievement.[15]

When our constitution was drafted, the country had got a band of dedicated leaders with high moral stature and intellectual background. A culture of public morality was very high at the dawn of Independence as it was cultivated in the freedom movement by the transformational leadership of M.K. Gandhi. But now both are absent and yet the institutions created by the founding Fathers and Mothers are in operation. At this point of time, we are looking at our constitution and its implications.

Elections are taking place regularly in Independent India with a brief gap of two years (Emergency). Electoral participation of people and political parties are always very high compared to even the Western democracies. Victorious parties assumed the responsibilities and run the government. People have faith in the state machinery, however, weak it is. Thus our democracy survives with minimal attributes of democracy. It raises a question even after 70 years why the Indian society could not move beyond minimal democracy.

Over a period of time people have picked up the art of changing the regimes and thereby people have established their supremacy. Constitutional machineries in India continue to function, however, weak they are in discharging their roles and responsibilities. People have reposed faith in those bodies since Independence. Though power was with the traditional elites, at the dawn of Independence much of the established procedures and practices were in tact. There was no serious violations of the provisions of the constitution for about three decades in India. In the same way, there was no financial corruption at large scale neither in Central Government nor in State Governments up to a point of time.

After 1967, the state governments have started abusing the powers and involved in corrupt practices. Many of the regional political parties in the name of welfare of the people many of the established procedures have been violated and even financial corrupt practices have been followed in governance and administration. The administrative system created with an aim of maintaining unity and achieving development had been stabilized under unity of command has been dismantled now. The political class which determined to continue in power by adopting any means started running administration by nurturing a committed bureaucracy. As a result, the steel frame bureaucracy forms rusts and it is also a part of the corrupt political class. Thus, the nexus between the political class and bureaucratic class became stronger. Slowly the intellectual and honest politicians have moved away from the political system and enabled the criminals to move into the political organizations and indulged in nefarious activities. This kind of practice entrenched in state politics since 1967. Later it entered into Central Government also. All established administrative and ethical norms had been violated from below to top and rent seeking became order of the day. This kind of governance and administrative culture has sidelined the honest officials in the administrative system. The next phase of degeneration of governance and administration started during the period of economic globalization since 1991.[16] In the name of simplifying governance, many of the regulatory norms and rules have been removed from the process of governance and administration. It is meant for market and yet they are being misused. Corruption was rampant in both Central and State governments during the entire period. Political class made money by favouring and facilitating crony capitalist activities. Corruption has loomed large to the extent ordinary citizens understand how political class makes money. In such a way corruption has deepened and regularised.

However, the Government has done enormous pro-poor activities.[17] Development has been made as right. Series of development rights have been given in the form of Acts. The Acts have been coupled with schemes with huge outlays. Plethora of schemes have been implemented over a period of time to reduce poverty and vulnerability. Despite the implementation of all the schemes in the rural areas, the rustic folk in the rural areas are in deep crises.[18] The farming community, pastoral community, tribal community, fishing community, and craft community are in deep trouble in the rural areas.[19] The self-reliance and self-dignity of the poor are essential for the survival of democracy. But they become a problem in India.[20]

Reform initiatives have helped the market and enabled the market forces to exploit the natural resources beyond the level of replenishment.[21] But such a kind of reform initiatives have not taken place for empowering the poor.[22] Decentralization was one such a measure was not taken seriously either by the State governments or by the Central Government. Democratization is yet another opportunity to enable the poor and the marginalized to empower themselves to claim their entitlements rightfully and in a dignified way.[23] The political institutions in the democratic political system have not worked for democratization and instead they conducted themselves in a feudal mode.[24] Hence, it is necessary to reform the political institutions and insist the institutions to democratize themselves.

In India democracy has been saved by the poor in participating in the electoral process continuously. Secondly, despite the difficult conditions with which the poor lead life, they continue to adopt legal, peaceful and non-violent means to settle their issues. In the name of development poor are disturbed directly and indirectly continuously as environment is being disturbed, the poor never resort into violence. Seeing the plight of the poor and the non-performance of the state, extremist elements have disturbed peace not the majority poor. They still patient enough to wait for the state to look after their plights. If one wants to find out the reason for the poor implementation of the Constitution of India it is pertinent to remember the last speech delivered by the chairperson of the Constituent Assembly, Dr. Rajendra Prasad, on 26th November, 1994. "If the people who are elected are capable and men of character and integrity, they would be able to make the best even of a defective constitution. If they are lacking in these, the Constitution cannot help the country.... India needs today nothing more than a set of honest men who will have the interest of the country before them."

While celebrating the success of the unity maintained in India with functional democracy there is a darker side and it has to be understood properly and perspectively. It has been described aptly by a report.

It observed that "several distortions had crept into it (our polity) including those in the structure and functioning of legislative bodies, the growing role of money and muscle power in elections, increasing religious and caste conflicts, imbalance in the federal structure, inadequate attention to local self-government and inability to stem the population explosion and failure to provide universal primary education. Taken together, the list added up to serious challenges to the very basis of democracy in India."

There are certain important provisions of the Constitution of India not operationalised. There are certain provisions which have been misused. They are being misused by the Central Government. The Union Government and the Governors have misused Artide 356 many times in India. It is being criticized not only by political parties but also the intellectuals of the tall order in India and abroad.

The amending procedures of the Constitution of India clearly indicate the mixture of both rigid and flexible characteristics. This has been used and misused. As a result, the Supreme Court has outlined the basic structure of the Constitution which cannot be altered or mutilated. They are: (a) Supremacy of the constitution; (b) Republican and democratic form of government; (c) Secular character of the constitution; (d) Separation of powers, and (e) Federal character of the constitution. Thus, the basic structure has been codified and made it clear that nobody has the authority to alter the basic structure of the Constitution of India.

At present it has been noticed that the political and bureaucratic class instead of adhering to the values of the Constitution, they have violated all the established values. Instead of integrating and unifying the divisive forces, the political class act as merchants to buy votes by dividing the people by caste and religion for their vested interests capturing with an objective of and holding on to power. Yet Indian polity has vitality to withstand the pressures. A living organism will have always problems as it evolves. Likewise Indian Democracy is a living democracy it has its own problems. To overcome the problems, we have to evaluate ourselves and initiate remedial actions through the constitutional means.[25]

Conclusion

India, through its freedom struggle, has shown to the world that through a non-violent peaceful struggle, liberation could be achieved. By following India within 20 years, 45 countries have liberated themselves without much bloodshed. The leaders who led the freedom struggle and who laid foundation for the new nation with a clear-cut foresight and forethought created a vibrant rigid and flexible constitution with a resilience to respond to any pressure. Beyond the Institutions they have created the value system to be followed to run the system of governance and administration. A constitution in a country like India sustaining for 70 years in the backdrop of unimaginable differences, diversities, disparities and discriminations, is not a small achievement. It keeps India together, makes the people to have faith in the democratic system. It provides opportunity for the people to raise questions and challenge government when they face problem and through a process of dialogue and negotiation problems could be solved. As generations have passed, the degeneration sets in politics and as a result the constitutional values have been abrogated and abdicated. Governing the vast country of this size with wide variations, diversities, differences, disparities, discriminations is a very big challenge. Many of the occasions violations of the constitutional values and provisions have been done only by the state authorities and not by ordinary people. The political parties instead of perpetuating development politics to bring unity among the collectivities, they use caste and religion to mobilize people for election and thereby cleavages among the social groups have been created and widened. As a result, Indian democracy could not move beyond a minimal point in a scale of democracy.

Continuously people are demanding the state to achieve social and economic democracy to make the political democracy meaningful. In the seventy years of democratic governance enabling provisions have been made through enacting legislations and amending the constitution to help and protect the poor, marginalized and minorities. Development has been made as rights and a bundle of rights have been granted with schemes for development with huge outlays. To empower the people a new governance, arrangement has been made through the historic Amendments (73rd and 74th) nearer to the community and through which people could claim their legitimate entitlements in a dignified way. Yet while assessing the impact of all those initiatives, one could see only a minimum outcome and identify a wide variety of barriers to achieve maximum outcome. It needs an alternative path in governance and development. It needs an alternative politics to party politics. A new kind of democratic practice has to be developed negating the party politics. It could be done at the grassroots and wherefrom clearing of polity could be done.

NOTES

1. Subhash C. Kashyap (1998). "Working of the constitution of India" in V.A. Pai Panandiku (ed.). *Fifty years of Swaraj: Highlights and Shadows.* New Delhi: Konark Publishers, pp. 118-177.
2. Christophe Jaffrelot (ed.) (2012). *India Since 1950: Society, Politics, Economic and Culture.* New Delhi: Yatra Books.
3. Lala Lajpat Rai (1917). *England's deft to India.* New York: B.W. Herebsch.
4. P. Bandhu, (ed.) (2011). *Back to Basics: A.J.C. Kumarappa Reader,* Ooty: Odyssey.
5. Suhas Palshikar (2004). "Whose Democracy are we Talking About? Hegemony and Democracy in India" in Rajendra Vora and Suhas Palshikar (eds.). *Indian Democracy: Meanings and Practices.* New Delhi: Sage Publications, pp. 127-164.
6. N.L. Raja (2019). "India's Enduring Document of Governance." *The Hindu,* 26th November.
7. V.A. Pai Panandikar (ed.) (1998). *Fifty years of Swaraj: Highlights and Shadows,* New Delhi: Kanark Publishers.
8. Granville Austin (2012). *Working a Democratic Constitution: A History of the Indian Experience,* New Delhi: Oxford University Press.
9. B.B. Kumar (2016). *India: Caste, Culture and Traditions,* New Delhi: Concept Publishing Company.
10. Jasbir Jain (ed.) (2006). *Narrative of the Village: Centre of the Periphery,* New Delhi: Rawat Publications.
11. T. Scarlelt Epstein, A.P. Suryanarayana and T. Thirmmegowda (1998). *Village Voices: Forty Years of Rural Transformation in South India,* New Delhi: Sage Publications.
12. Madhu Purnima Kishwar (2005). *Deepening Democracy: Challenges of Governance and Globalization in India,* New Delhi: Oxford University Press.
13. Atul Kohli (2009). *Democracy and Development in India: From Socialism to Pro-Business,* New Delhi: Oxford University Press.

14. Vinod Rai and Amitendu Palit (eds.) (2018). *Seven Decades of Independent India,* New Delhi: Penguin.
15. N.L. Raja, *Ibid.*
16. N.N. Vohra (1998). "Fifty Years of National Governance" in V.A. Pai Panandikar (ed.). *Fifty Years of Swaraj: Highlights and Shadows,* New Delhi: Konark Publishers, pp. 178-197.
17. Jos Mooij (ed.) (2005). *The Politics of Economic Reforms in India,* New Delhi: Sage Publications.
18. Alternative Survey Group (2006). *Alternative Economic Survey, India 2005-06: Disempowering Masses,* Delhi: Daanish Books.
19. Kanchan Chopra and C.H. Hanumantha Rao (ed.) (2007). *Growth, Equity, Environment and Population: Economic and Sociological Perspective,* New Delhi: Sage Publications.
20. Amitabh Behar, John Samuel, Jagadananda and Yogesh Kumar (2006). *Social Watch India: Citizens Report on Governance and Development,* Delhi: Pearson Education.
21. Amita Singh (ed.) (2005). *Administrative Reforms Towards Sustainable Practices,* New Delhi: Sage Publications.
22. S. Parasuraman, Gomathy, Kuruvan Raj and Bina Fernandez (2003). *Listening to people living in Poverty,* Bangalore: Books for Change.
23. Swami Ranganathananda (2006). *Democratic Administration: In the light of Practical Vedanta,* Chennai: Sri Ramakrishan Math.
24. S. Viswanathan (2005). *Dalits in Dravidian Land,* Chennai: Navayana Publishing.
25. Ramashray Roy (1985). *Self and Society: A Study in Gandhian Thought,* New Delhi: Sage Publications.

9
Democracy and Insurrection

Evidences from Konta Tahsil, Sukma District, Chhattisgarh State, India

Nayakara Veeresha

Indian democracy, especially the State in India is facing insurrection in Central and Eastern states what is popularly known as Left Wing Extremism (here after LWE) in official term and 'Maoism' in an informal discourse. The insurrection is intense in the States of Chhattisgarh, Jharkhand and Odisha. The ongoing discourses related to insurrection have dealt the issue at hand from security, law and order, underdevelopment, political ideology, social movements and state building perspectives. However, there is little in the ongoing discourse about the functioning of Indian democracy and its limitations especially in the context of insurrection in Central India. Set in this context, why do insurrection/s occur in a democracy? Is there any relationship between democracy and insurrection? If yes, what is the nature of relationship, i.e. symbiotic or rivalry? How to contextualise democracy in insurrectionary situations? The chapter attempts to answer these research questions with the help of voter turnout data in Panchayat (2015) and Assembly elections (2013) in the State of Chhattisgarh. It explores the relationship between electoral democracy and insurrection with respect to Konta Tahsil in Sukma District of Chhattisgarh State, one of the districts severely affected by insurrection as per the classification of Ministry of Home Affairs, Government of India.

Why the term Insurrection?

The use of term 'insurrection' to describe the ongoing socio-political conflict in the central India in place of other popular constructs such as civil war, extremism, insurgency, maoism, naxalism, social movement, rebellion and revolution is based upon theoretical, philosophical, empirical and policy premises. Max Stirner's work (2005) *The Ego and His Own* and Etienne Balibar's *Writings of Citizenship* (2015), *Equaliberty: Political Essays* (2014) and *Violence and Civility: On the limits of Political Philosophy* (2015) constitute theoretical and philosophical context for the insurrection.

> "Revolution and insurrection must not be looked upon as synonymous. The former consists in an overturning of conditions, of the established condition or status, the State or society, and is accordingly a political or social act; the latter has indeed for its unavoidable consequence a transformation of circumstances, yet does not start from it but from men's discontent with themselves, is not an armed rising, but a rising of individuals, a getting up, without regard to the arrangements that spring from it." (Stirner, 2005: 316)
>
> "Insurrection, in its different forms, is the active modality of citizenship: the modality that it brings into action." (Balibar, 2015: 131)
>
> "Democratic citizenship in a stable state is supposed to be a system that has abolished the need for insurrection by allowing for the ordered participation of citizens. But it is precisely because the inclusion into the sphere of citizenship is never total, that there is always the potential for a return of insurrection." (Ulbricht, 2017: 116-19)

Set in this theoretical and philosophical context, insurrection is a rising of individuals who are discontent with the system of governance. The insurrectionary zeal of the *adivasis* has been tapped by the CPI (Maoist) party to achieve their political goal of "New Democratic

Revolution" through "protracted people's war". The participants of insurrection are not depending upon the existing institutions to bring in the social and political change and operate through extra constitutional means. The interactions[1] held with the surrendered youth has revealed that the local youth mostly consist of *adivasis* in the state of Chhattisgarh has become part of the CPI (Maoist) party for their personal reasons rather than wholly on the basis of political ideology of Marx-Lenin-Mao (MLM). Newman (2016: 3) supplements the use of insurrection by arguing that:

> "the Marxist-Leninist project of revolution—that is, the attempt to transform the field of social relations through the seizure of state power—is no longer operative today, and that we need a new 'non-strategic' paradigm of political action that, at the same time, contests and transcends the current neoliberal order in which politics has for the past decades been trapped."

This empirical reality of the participants of insurrection is absent in the above mentioned popular and dominant constructs. Understanding and appreciating the individual subjective reasons for participating in the insurrection is critical for developing appropriate policy responses going beyond the current security and law and order approach.

Democracy in Insurrectionary Situation: A Theoretical Understanding

Democracy is not a fixed category of political system to share the power. It is one of the ways to gain legitimacy in a given society to exercise power and authority. Despite its shortcomings, it is one of the most favoured forms of government which the nation-states are striving to establish especially in the post-cold war period. The consensus theories of democracy have ascertained the role of democratic institutions in mitigating conflict situations to enable a stable socio-political order. This is important for heterogeneous, ethnically divided societies more specifically to Global South and South Asian countries. In democratic states, the sharing of power between various organs of the government, devolution of powers to the local governments, necessary checks and balances to restrain the state power and authority are critical both for development, peace and order in society.

In the context of democracy and conflict it is expected that "if human security is understood more broadly, in terms of internal conflict and inter-state war as well, it is a commonly held belief that democratic states generate an important "peace dividend" at home and abroad" (Norris, 2012: 26). If this theoretical assumption goes correct then India should not have been seen some of the worst of mass killings with high levels of violence (communal and non-communal) in post-Independence period. Electoral democracy is one of the indicators of democratic governance. Electoral systems give legitimacy to the political parties to govern the nation in progressive direction. An armed uprising in a democracy is a consequence and indicates that "some elements of the social system which are dedicated to the integration of political institutions are not doing their jobs properly" (Johnston, 2011:138). So which are the entities of social system and political institutions that are not doing their jobs properly in the context of insurrection in Central India?

Contextualising Indian Democracy in Insurrectionary Zone

The birth of parliamentary democracy in India has intrinsically linked with the State violence through the repressive apparatus such as Military and Police. Massive killings have taken place in military operation known as 'Operation Polo' in Telangana region as documented in Pandit Sundarlal Committee Report on the Massacres in Hyderabad (1948). Currently, Indian democracy is experiencing various uprisings in the regions of Central and Eastern India, Jammu & Kashmir and North-Eastern regions. However, the nature and causative factors of these uprisings are different. The insurrection in Central India is popularly known as "largest internal security threat" that the country is facing as described by former Prime Minister of India Manmohan Singh in 2010. The insurrections of Jammu & Kashmir and North-Eastern regions have strong identity base and assumed the form of insurgencies.

Why and how the insurrection in Central India does become "largest internal security threat" concern for the governing class of people? In this context, Sundar (2016: 14) argues that:

> "My narrative is really about Indian democracy when it reduces what are essentially political contests over rights, distributive justice and alternative visions of the good to law and order problems, and when it would rather fight against its poorest citizens than talk to them."

This means that the government, media and the ongoing discourses on insurrection in Central India have deduced the issues of rights over natural resources, tensions between self *versus* state led governance systems, distribution of economic prosperity to the local communities, coercive land acquisition and faulty development model imposed by State on *adivasis* communities to a *security and law and order problem*. The discourse has become sanitised to an extent that if anyone questions or raises voice against the State actions they will be labelled as anti-national and anti-development.

In her recent work entitled '*The Burning Forest: India's War in Bastar*', Sundar observes that "not only have India's democratic institutions failed to respond adequately to serious human rights violations" (Sundar, 2016: 256) in the name of fighting Maoist insurgents and providing security to the local people in the chapter on 'The Amnesias of Democracy'. To what extent it is true that the democratic failures of Indian State have given rise to insurrection in Central India? The answer to this question is plausible yet. It is argued that the "current Maoist upheaval needs to be understood as a part of the general phenomenon of democratic deficit" (Mukherji, 2013: 73). In order to explain how exactly the deficits of Indian democracy have contributed to the rise of insurrection in Central India, here an effort has been made to understand the democracy with the help of electoral politics.

Status of Democracy in Insurrectionary Zones: Case of Konta Tahsil, Sukma District

Sukma district is one of the worst affected districts by Left-Wing Extremism as classified by the Ministry of Home Affairs. The district was newly carved out from Dantewada district in 2012. It has attracted the attention of the national media when the insurgents abducted Alex Paul Menon, the first District Collector in April 2012. It has three Tahsils, namely Chindgarh, Konta and Sukma. Almost 80 per cent of the area in Konta Tahsil is not in the reach of government. In this context, it is interesting to see the extent of electoral democracy and political legitimacy of the government in insurrectionary zones. A crucial element in insurrection is fight for the territorial control thereby establishing the political legitimacy in the given territory or locality. Electoral system and voters' participation in the elections is an indicator of the extent of the territorial control of the State and insurgents.

Data Sources and Methodology

To analyse the status of democracy in Konta Tahsil two sets of data has been used:

1. Per cent of voter participation in Panchayat elections of 2015 with a view to understand the people's participation in local politics and governance, and
2. Voter turnout in Assembly elections of 2013.

These two data sets were extrapolated with the data of voter participation in the recent general elections of 2014 for the analytical purpose. The exercise was done in order to understand the functioning of the electoral system in our democracy, challenges in holding elections in conflict zones and broadly to extract insights about the present status of constitutional governance as we explore the trends and political behaviour of the citizens in three-tiers of governance (Union, State and Local governments). Most importantly it provides crucial inputs on the functioning of different democratic institutions, i.e. Parliament, Assembly and Panchayats.

The rationale for assessing the voter turnout in elections as an indicator of democracy is electoral incentives and median voter theory advocated by Meltzer and Richard. This theory was developed "within the context of long-established democracies, and thus rests on assumptions about the existence of a broader framework of political rights and civil liberties" (Norris, 2012: 28). A plethora of political rights to the individuals was embedded in the Constitution of India, including the liberty, especially to the politically alienated communities such as *Adivasis*, Scheduled Castes, Women and Other

Backward Classes in the form of affirmative actions. Besides reservation in political seats in three-tiers of governance, there are numerous independent commissions to oversee the protection of civic and political rights to these communities. Central and Chhattisgarh State governments derive electoral legitimacy to implement these provisions of welfare and development. The two data sets were corroborated with the opinion/views of local and state elected representatives (4), political party associates (1), *adivasis* association members (4), government officials (6), members of judiciary (1), media representatives (1) and the members of civil society (2) elicited through informal discussions.

The strength of democracy lies in accommodating multiple voices, especially from opposition groups and to engage them in the decision-making process to enrich the spirit of democracy. Replacing the existing socio-political order may not be the short term goals of ideologues of CPI (Maoist) party. The Maoist party argues that it is fighting with the deficiencies of Indian Democracy, particularly with the structures of inequality in economic, political and social institutions. It is observed that,

> "Though elections have been held several times and several governments had changed in the past 65 years of 'independent' rule, it is a fact that even to this day the basic needs of the people like food, clothing, shelter, education and health care remained out of reach. The oppressed masses who constitute 95 per cent of the population are confronting poverty, illiteracy, unemployment, price rises, diseases, starvation deaths, corruption etc. on a daily basis (Collected Statements of Central Committee, CPI" (Maoist) Party, 2014: 302).

The view of the CPI (Maoist) party is that, Indian democracy is working only for the big industrialists, landlords and not improving the lives of mass people. It is perpetuating the social and economic inequalities in the social fabric and is the growing cause of social and political unrest. The issues raised by the CPI (Maoist) party are definitely serious aspects of our social and economic development. The question is not just about the democracy, but its deliverables in terms of public goods and services. In the following paragraphs, an attempt

Table 9.1: Brief Profile of Local Governance in Sukma

S.No.	District	Name of the Development Block	No. of Sarpanch in GP	No. of Elected Members in JP	No. of Elected Members in ZP	Total No. of Voting Centres	Nagar Palika		Nagar Panchayat	
							No. of Wards	No. of Voting Centres	No. of Wards	No. of Voting Centres
1	Sukma	Chindgarh	46	13	4	129				
2		Dornapal	–	–	–	–	–	–	15	15
3		Konta	57	19	4	122	–	–	–	–
4		Sukma	32	10	2	81	15	15	–	–
Total			**135**	**42**	**10**	**332**	**15**	**15**	**15**	**15**

Source: District Electoral Office, Office of the District Collector, Sukma (2016).

has been made to understand and analyse this critique by looking at the functioning of democracy with particular reference to the local governance and its legitimacy.

Voter Participation in Panchayat Elections of 2015 in Konta Tahsil

The introduction of 73rd and 74th Amendments to the Constitution in 1992-93 has provided Panchayats a legitimate and institutional space in the democratic governance framework of the country. India has the largest representative democracy with 32 lakh of elected representatives in 2.5 lakh Panchayats of all the three-tiers. Out of this 32 lakh, nearly half, constitutes women representatives in local governance.

Table 9.2: Voter turnout in 2015 Panchayat Elections—Tahsil-wise

S.No.	Tahsil	Voter turnout in %
1.	Chindgarh	61.30
2.	Konta	22.06
3.	Sukma	44.79
Total		**42.71**

Source: District Electoral Office, Office of the District Collector, Sukma (2016).

Table 9.2 indicates that, the voter turnout is least in Konta Tahsil and more in Chindgarh Tahsil. A question arises here, why Konta Tahsil has witnessed low voter turnout in the Panchayat elections of 2015? How do we explain the low voter's participation in the local elections especially in Konta Tahsil? To answer these questions, an attempt has been made to analyse the voting patterns in each Panchayats. Konta Tahsil is the biggest Tahsil in the district with 57 Gram Panchayat. Voter participation in each of the Panchayats have been analysed to understand the extent of territorial control of the State and the CPI (Maoist) party. A detailed analysis of the voter turnout in Panchayat elections may give rise to five different sets of Gram Panchayats in the Tahsil and district. A typology has been developed on the basis of 'legitimacy' of electoral system and 'functionality' of the formal institutions of governance, i.e. Panchayats.

The analysis of voter turnout in Panchayat elections of 2015 are summarised in Table 9.3. On the basis of the voter turnout per cent, all the Panchayats of Konta Tahsil are classified in five categories.

Table 9.3: Typology of Patterns for Electoral Democracy in Insurrectionary Zones

	Category I	**Category II**	**Category III**	**Category IV**	**Category V**	**Total**
Extent of Voter Turnout in Percentage	>40	>20-<40	>10-<20	>1-<10	>0-<1	
No. of Panchayats	9	16	5	22	5	57
Variations in Democratic Patterns	Functional Democracy	Moderate Democracy	Least Democracy	Democracy in Transition	Alternative Democracy	
Local Governance	Yes	Yes	Partially yes	Contestation	Insurgent's Model of Governance	

Source: Author's construction.

The first category of Gram Panchayats has witnessed more than 40 per cent of the voter turnout in Panchayat elections. In these Panchayats, the 'writ of the state' is working as per the statutory rules which means the social and functional legitimacy of the existing institutions of governance. The government can implement welfare programmes and schemes in the Panchayats falling under Category-I. In the second category of Panchayats, the voter turnout is moderately good and falls within the range of 20-40 per cent. In these Panchayats the government can reach most of the areas and can enforce the rule of law of the country.

A close observation of Table 9.3 reveals some of the interesting points for discussion. 25 Panchayats of both Category I and II out of 57 have witnessed voter turnout in the range of >20-40 per cent. These 25 Panchayats mostly lie on the main road side of state and national highways. It means that the electoral system is not pervasive in most of the periphery areas of the Tahsil. Sundar (2016: 240-43) describes "elections as battleground and polls as a form of counter-insurgency".

Conducting elections in the interiors of Panchayats are taken as a challenge by both the State government and the insurgents. The State deploys heavy paramilitary forces in order to conduct the elections and so by the insurgents call for the boycott of the elections to the democratic institutions, be it to the local governments, Assembly or Parliament.

The third category of Panchayats has seen voter turnout between 10-20 per cent. These Panchayats may be categorised as least democratic local bodies. In this category of Panchayats, the legitimacy of formal institutions of governance is present; however, the 'functionality' aspects are not seen as insurgents are influencing the Panchayat elections by deciding the contesting candidates in the local elections. This kind of capturing of functional aspects of the democracy by the insurgents is the most common and can be observed in other insurrectionary States[2] also. In other words here a dual position of local authority can be seen. This may be attributed to the existence of 'parallel administrative structures' of the insurgents in these localities commonly known as *Janathana Sarkar* (people's government). The *Janathana Sarkar* consists of following departments: (1) Financial, (2) Defence, (3) Agriculture, (4) Judicial, (5) Education-Culture, (6) Health, (7) Forest protection, and (8) Public relations.

Democracy in *transitory phase* can be seen in the fourth category of Panchayats and this process of democratization is known as *transitory democracy*. The Panchayats are still in an evolutionary phase gradually developing from traditional forms of institutions of governance. In these Panchayats, traditional or informal institutions have strong influence over the formal structures of the State. It is interesting to note here is that, in this category the local affairs are still conducted by traditional headman through old Panchayats. The fourth category of Panchayats is experiencing *contentious politics* in following ways:

1. Contestation between traditional and modern Panchayats. In other words conflict between Self *versus* State led Governance. It is also arguable that why there is low voter turnout even in Panchayats where there is no influence of insurgents. Panchayats (Extension to Scheduled Areas) Act, 1996 (hereafter PESA) legislation recognises the right to self-governance of *adivasis*

with specific reference to the rights over natural resources. In fact, there should not be any or negligible interference by the State in PESA governed Panchayats. An illustration will help in detailing the role of PESA in enabling self-governance of *adivasis*.

Box I: Chhattisgarh Panchayats pass resolution against coal auctions

Twenty gram Panchayats in Chhattisgarh have passed a resolution against the auction of five of the state's 42 coal blocks. The five coal blocks are located in Sarguja, Raigarh and Dharamjaigarh districts of the state and have been in operation since 2010. In their resolution, the villages have stated that while they are not against development in their region, all issues related to land and forest rights of residents must be resolved. They have asked for government reallocation and re-auction of coal blocks in the area to be stopped until such issues are settled. The resolution also states that local indigenous *adivasis* and other traditional forest dwellers should be treated as key stakeholders in any development activity in the region, including mining.

Source: Chakravarthy, A. (2015), *Down to Earth* http://www.downtoearth.org.in/news/chhattisgarh-panchayats-pass-resolution-against-coal-auctions-48270

2. Conflict between State and insurgents to establish territorial control. There is a heavy contestation going on between both parties to get hold of the localities at any cost. The scholars called these kinds of shared localities as "quasi-state" (Kennedy, 2014: 229), "liberated" territories (Johnston, 2011: 138) or even as Para state also.
3. Traditional Panchayats are facing extinction in the wake of superimposed Panchayat System and the insurgents are keen to establish *Janathana Sarkar* (people's government). The endogenous Panchayats in Chhattisgarh especially in Bastar region has been replaced by the modern Panchayats on one side and the *Janathana Sarkar* (people's government) of CPI (Maoist) on the other side. The fact is that both parties, i.e. State and Insurgents are trying to appropriate the traditional

Panchayats[3] (such as *Adimjatiya Panchayats*, *Jati Panchayats*, *Pargania Panchayats* and *Village Panchayats*).

The State is attempting through consent methods, whereas the insurgents are making efforts through the means of coercion and consent depending upon the nature and strength of the local headman. Historical facts suggest that the Panchayats in Chhattisgarh "are of very ancient date" (Agnew, 1820) and have the elements containing "embryonic beginnings of constitutional rule" (Wills, 1920: 256). Precisely on these factors former and late district collector of undivided Bastar and Commissioner for Scheduled Castes and Scheduled Tribes have argued that "tribals have their traditional governance system that the Constitution recognises. Why don't you empower those institutions?" (Mahapatra, 2012).

The voter turnout in the fifth and final category of Panchayats is completely absent or recorded less than one per cent. The democratic functioning of the Panchayats is almost absent and the local affairs are being carried out through insurgent's model of local governance. From the democracy point of view, the fourth and fifth categories are important as they are facing the 'democratic deficit' owing to the factors such as forest terrain, lack of adequate state infrastructure, inability of the State apparatus to persuade in these difficult areas. The capacity of the State to govern is critical; stronger State capacity creates robust institutions to check and regulate the political behaviour of insurgent groups. In the final category of Panchayats, the writ of the state appears to be fully dysfunctional. The CPI (Maoist) party is trying to establish *Janathana Sarkars* in these areas and is envisioning an alternative democratic system through armed revolution and the government formed is known as revolutionary people's government.

A question arises here is that, how far the alternative people's democratic system is functioning in these areas? The CPI (Maoist) party in Dandakaranya is running primary schools, teaching in local languages, engaged in organic farming, establishing village defence committees, organising cultural festivals, fighting for the land and forest rights with the local bureaucracy, traders, providing health volunteers. One of the main factors of people's support of the CPI (Maoist) party is it has come to the rescue of the *adivasis* communities in providing the much needed support when they are in need especially in meeting the day-to-day requirements. To illustrate, the Maoist party has made efforts to negotiate the wage rates paid for *adivasis* for the collection of *tendu* leaves and other minor forest produces with the local contractors. It is observed that,

> "these wages—negotiated by Maoists with private contractors—are higher than those announced by the Chhattisgarh government. Maoists were also able to eliminate traditional social evils such as free first day labour for tilling the land of the village chief. These measures explain why *adivasis* feel indebted to Maoists" (Mukherji, 2012: 118).

By the time Chhattisgarh State has come into existence in 2000, the party has established its social base in the region. In a way, the Maoist party's social legitimacy is relatively better when compared to that of the elected local government in the State. This observation can be corroborated by the fact that,

> "We are implementing the MGNREGS in 25 Panchayats only. Earlier it was only in 16 Panchayats; this year another 9 were added making it to 25. The CPI (Maoist) party has initially resisted; however due to the people's pressure we were able to extend it to another 9 Panchayats in this current financial year."[4]

According to the Ministry of Home Affairs, a total number of 338 *Adalats* (People's Court) have been held throughout the country during 2011-16 by the CPI (Maoist) party. From the above discussion, it may be inferred that the parliamentary democracy of India is facing resistance from the CPI (Maoist) party whose aim is to establish people's democratic government. A competition between democratic politics and the politics of insurrection is seen. The Maoist party led *Janathana Sarkars* or people led governments have established the different departments; however, the delivery of public goods and services to the local people is not known widely. For example,

> "there is no mention of even a single health centre with permanent structure initiated by Maoists. Given the acute conditions of malnutrition among childern and women, what the 'alternative model' of agriculture and other efforts at Maoist 'develoment' has done to the people of Dandakaranya" (Mukherji, 2012: 120-21).

Apart from these deficiencies in delivering the developmental outcomes at the local level, one of the most important critique towards CPI (Maoist) party is its restrictions on the people's mobility and freedom of movement. The CPI (Maoist) party does not hesitate to use coercive means to stop the villagers from voting in particularly the villages located in interior areas. In this context it is worth to recollect the words of a Standing Sarpanch[5] of a Gram Panchayat as follows,

> "Each person who is coming out of the village has to communicate to the local dalam member of the party and their purpose of going out of the village. They have to report after reaching the home in time. If there is a delay proper explanation has to be given otherwise the villagers have to be ready to face the severe consequences."

This indicates that the CPI (Maoist) party is restricting the people's movements and curtailing the liberty in their own vicinities. This is not desirable for a party which is aiming to bring 'New Democratic Revolution' in the country. This kind of restrictions on people's mobility in itself negates the spirit of democracy which insurgents are claiming to establish through insurrection. One of the main limitations in understanding the CPI (Maoist) party's *Janathana Sarkar*'s functioning is the unavailability of the same for an objective and open inquiry. This itself raises many doubts in the minds of the citizens about the claims of CPI (Maoist) party on what the party calls as "liberated zones".

The above analysis of the electoral patterns in Panchayat elections give raise to following relationship between democracy and insurrection in case-specific Konta Tahsil of Sukma district.

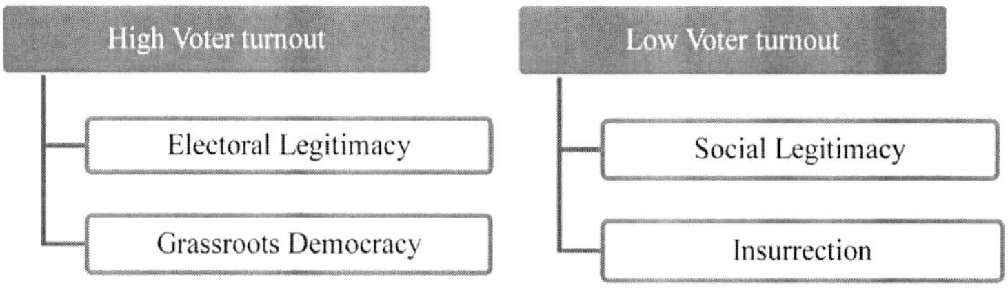

Fig. 9.1: Relationship between Voter turnout in Elections—Democracy and Insurrection.

Fig. 9.1 indicates that there is a link between electoral participation, political legitimacy, democracy and insurrection. Lower voter turnout in local democratic elections gives space to administrative and governance vacuum. The State needs to take efforts to fill these least democratic spaces in order to both strengthen the Panchayats and also to curb the tendencies towards insurrectionary activities. Otherwise there is a danger which "Democracy, at least in the form it has usually taken to date in the societies of the bottom billion, does not seem to enhance the prospects of internal peace. On the contrary, it seems to increase proneness to political violence. Probably related to this failure to secure social peace, democracy has not yet produced accountable and therefore, legitimate government" (Collier, 2009: 49). In the following paragraphs, an attempt has been made to analyse the voter turnout in Assembly and Parliament elections. This will help in providing insights about the complete picture of the parliamentary democratic system and its functioning in the areas of insurrection. Fig. 92 shows the voter turnout in all the three assemblies of representative democracy with particular reference to Konta Tahsil.

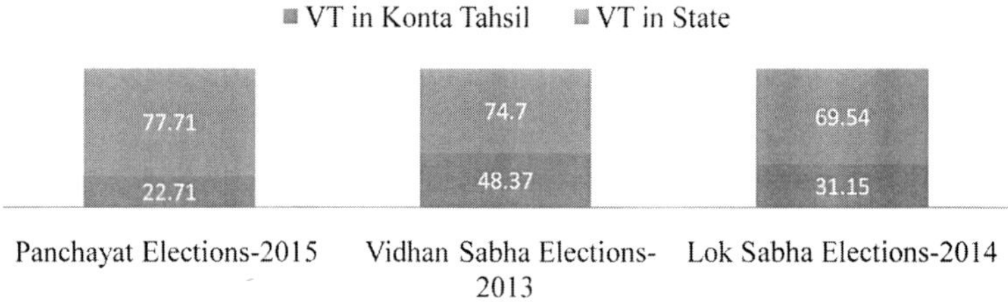

Fig. 9.2: Voter turnout in Konta Tahsil in Democratic Elections to three-tier Governance.

Source: Election Commission of India (2014), Chief Electoral Office, Raipur Chhattisgarh (2013), and District Electoral Office, District Collectorate, Sukma (2016).

The voter turnout in Panchayats, Assembly and General Elections to the Parliament with particular reference to Konta Tahsil shows the electoral pattern and its variations in democratic governance. It also indicates the voting behaviour of citizens in three tiers of governance, i.e. Nation, State and Local. The voter turnout in Assembly elections of 2013 is greater than the voter's turnout in the Parliamentary and Panchayat elections. Panchayats have witnessed low voter turnout in comparison to the Assembly and Parliamentary elections. There is a difference of 50 per cent of votes in Panchayat elections to that of State's average. What does this imply in the context of insurrection? What are its implications to Parliamentary form of democracy and decentralised governance?

From the above tabular form, following observations and implications can be drawn. The low voter turnout in Panchayat elections of 2015 infers that the insurgents have substantial influence on the local democratic politics. However, the influence is transitory in nature. It also indicates the *local specificity of insurrections*. This does not imply insurrections are purely local phenomenons; however, it must be understood that the starting point for insurrections may contain in the local factors which have visible impact on the everyday lives of the people with regional and national attention. Insurrections arise in a democracy when the immediate people's needs are not met by the successive governments. The real challenge for Indian democracy is at *micro politics* though state and national politics may influence the dynamics of local state and governance. This dialectic between micro and macro politics produces a third kind of *meso* level of politics, i.e. State politics which is the potential and powerful instrument to usher positive changes in the local grassroots politics.

When it comes to the Assembly elections, the influence got reduced almost by one-half. Out of 90 Vidhan Sabha Constituencies, Konta Tahsil have witnessed second lowest voter turnout as Bijapur district has witnessed voter turnout of 44.68 per cent which is the lowest in 2013 elections. Both Bijapur and Sukma districts are experiencing insurrection in intense form. Containing deep forest areas have made these districts as safe and strategic place for insurgents to carry out insurrection and guerrilla warfare. The failure of Parliamentary democracy in implementing the provisions of Fifth Schedule is one of the major causative factors for the growth of insurrection. In other words, insurrections are inevitable when the elected governments fail to deliver the rights and justice in day-to-day life of the citizens. Democracy and insurrections are the two sides of the same coin, i.e. political legitimacy. Proper understanding and appreciation of insurrections have the potentiality to strengthen democratic tradition, helpful in improving the quality of local governance.

The whole Bastar region of the Chhattisgarh State has only one Member of Parliament. It consists of seven districts and all of them are experiencing insurrection. There is a need to increase the representation of *adivasis* from this region in Parliament. Since from its inception, the Vidhan Sabha consists of only 90 constituencies. Increase in representation of *adivasis* both in Parliament and Vidhan Sabha through delimitation of seats should be as per the Article 170 of the Constitution. Accordingly, there has to increase the representation of local democratic entities. Along with this the long pending National Policy on Tribals has to be tabled in the coming parliamentary session for its enactment. This is with respect to the representation in parliamentary democracy. The poor representation of *adivasis* is also reflected in executive positions and in judiciary. There are no official estimates about these figures. The following facts provide a grim picture about the representation of *adivasis* in Indian democracy,

> "The one-third strong *adivasi* populace of Chhattisgarh had failed to force the government to give its constitutionally mandated share of jobs, both an indication and an outcome of its marginality in the state's electoral arena" (Sharma, 2012: 21).

> "The *adivasi*, we know, has not been able to participate fully and effectively in this system of representation, because neither numbers nor the liberal concept of minority works in their favour" (Banerjee, 2016: 9-10).

The above analysis reveal that under or poor representation of *adivasis* in legislative, executive and judiciary positions, i.e. organs of government is a clear *indicator of the political 'alienation'* (term borrowed from Marx's writings) in the Indian democracy. In every census there is an increase in the per cent of *adivasis* (from 30 millions in 1961 to 104 millions in 2011) in the country but not the representation in democracy. Ironically *adivasis* are one of the largest sections of the society who has displaced in post-Independent India in the process of pursuit of so-called development.

Concluding Observations

The foregoing analysis and discussion on the electoral legitimacy and the functioning of Indian democracy, the following observations and plausible inferences may be drawn. Insurrections take place in a given society for the reasons of failure of democracy as a political system in ensuring equality and justice. In this case it is observed that even though there is an electoral legitimacy at State and National levels; it has not been able to transform the ideals of democracy at grassroots politics. The failure of parliamentary politics and the Indian State in addressing the specific democratic governance issues have laid the platform for insurrections in Central India. The evidences of voter turnout in Konta Tahsil of Sukma district is a case-specific.

The location of Konta Tahsil is very important for both Chhattisgarh State and the insurgents. For the Chhattisgarh State it is essential to have control over this locality as it helps in coordinating with other States of insurrection such as Telangana, Andhra Pradesh and Odisha in fighting the insurgents. This is important for inter-State coordination to deal with the tactics of CPI (Maoist) party. The insurgents are also trying hard to get hold of this area as it is the place which connects at least three States for their strategies of 'guerilla war'. It is also a good trade centre for the minor forest produces and the CPI (Maoist) party gets their share from local contractors and traders. Due to this condition, the democratisation process in Konta Tahsil is always like walking on a double edge sword. The low voter turnout in Panchayat elections of 2015 may not be entirely due to the insurrectionary situation. It might be because of the low literacy levels among *adivasis*. Konta Tahsil has 90 per cent of *adivasis* with a literacy rate of just 7.5 per cent. Other causative factors are high displacement of local people to the bordering Andhra Pradesh and Telangana States due to the ongoing tensions and violent conflict, especially during Salwa Judum and development induced displacement.

The preceding analysis of electoral politics and voting patterns (Graph I) indicates that there a relationship exists between democracy and insurrection. The nature of relationship is both symbiotic to a larger extent and rivalry to a smaller extent. When the political rulers understand insurrection as part of *democratic building activity and an exercise of active status of citizenship* then it is regarded as symbiotic relationship. If the governing leadership perceives insurrection as state dismantling enterprise and a broken citizenship then the nature of relationship becomes rivalry competing for the same resources, locality and socio-political legitimacy. The current insurrection in Central India is a classic example for the rivalry relationship between democracy and insurrection. In this context, Indian State needs to change her position to see insurrections fall under the category of democratic governance framework. Similarly, the CPI (Maoist) party needs to acknowledge and appreciate the legitimacy of the electoral system functioning through independent Election Commission of India in spite of limitations on the grounds of elements of accountability and transparency.

Having said these, there is no escape for the Indian State from addressing genuine issues raised by the CPI (Maoist) party especially poverty, unemployment, land reforms, rights over resources and most importantly social and political inequality. Insurrections are potential tools to build 'active citizenry'. There is a need to locate insurrections in a broader framework of democracy and its institutions for a stable social order. To sum up the current insurrection is to be seen as an extension of *adivasis* political uprisings in Bastar against the intrusive and exploitative governance regime inherited from the colonial rule. Insurrections are consequences but not the causes. The causes of insurrection are multidimensional. Among all the causative factors democracy and governance are critical though other aspects play an influential role in bringing the historical moments of insurrection.

Indian democracy has the potential to accommodate the insurrection of Central India within the ambit of legitimate demands of rights and justice by her own citizens in particularly the *adivasis* (original inhabitants).

Acknowledgements and Funding

The arguments made in the paper are part of the ongoing doctoral dissertation work of the author. The research is being carried out at the Institute for Social and Economic Change (ISEC), Bengaluru with the financial support of Prof. V.K.R.V. Rao Fellowship in association with Indian Council for Social Science Research (ICSSR). I am grateful to my Supervisor Prof. N. Sivanna for his valuable guidance and support. I would like to express my sincere thanks to the Doctoral Committee members, Panel of Experts in particularly late Prof. B.S. Bhargava for their valuable comments and suggestions during the research progress from time to time. My special thanks to Dr. V. Anil Kumar for his academic inputs during the course work. I would like to convey sincere thanks to Dr. A.V. Satish Chandra for his valuable feedback and insights on the earlier draft of the chapter.

NOTES

1. An interview with the surrendered young people who worked with CPI (Maoist) party conducted on 12.7.2016. Along with this a total of 232 surrendered youth profiles have been analysed to arrive at this inference. This is supplemented by the data of CPI (Maoist) party document naming the list of martyrs who have been killed in the armed struggle.
2. This kind of phenomenon was observed in Panchayat elections of 2015 in Konta Tahsil. I was also observed in States of Bihar, Jharkhand and Odisha during General elections of 2014.
3. Guru and Pandey (2000: 330-31).
4. As expressed by the MGNREGS Sukma District Technical Coordinator during an informal discussion with the author on 25.6.2016 at 8.12 A.M.
5. In an informal and long discussion with the author on 19.7.2016 at 7.48 P.M.

REFERENCES

Agnew, V.P. (1820). *A Report on the Subah or Province of Chhattisgarh,* Nagpur (1920).

Balibar, E. (2014). *Equaliberty: Political essays.* Durham, NC: Duke University Press.

Balibar, E. (2015). *Citizenship*. Cambridge: Polity.

Balibar, E. (2015). *Violence and civility: On the limits of political philosophy*. New York: Columbia University Press.

Banerjee, P. (2016). "Writing the Adivasi: Some historiographical notes", *The Indian Economic and Social History Review*, *53*(1): 1-23.

Chakravartty, A. (2015). "Chhattisgarh panchayats pass resolution against coal auctions", *Down to Earth,* http://www.downtoearth.org.in/news/chhattisgarh-panchayats-pass-resolution-against-coal-auctions-48270

Collier, P. (2009). *Wars, Guns and Votes: Democracy in Dangerous Places*, London: The Bodley Head.

Communist Party of India (Maoist) (2014). CPI (Maoist) 10th Commemorative Volume, Collected Statements, Part 3, http://www.bannedthought.net/India/CPI-Maoist-Docs/Statements-2014/Collection_of_CC_Statements_Part_3__2010-2014__Book.pdf (last accessed on (7.2.2015).

Government of Chhattisgarh (2016). *District Electoral Office in the Office of the Collectorate*, Sukma: DEO.

Government of Chhattisgarh (2013). Office of the Chief Electoral Officer, Voting % AC Wise General Election 2013, Raipur (http://ceochhattisgarh.nic.in/pdf/Voter%20Turn%20Out%20ac2013.pdf) last accessed on 9.12.2016

Government of India (2014). PC wise distribution of Votes Polled (http://eci.nic.in/eci_main/archiveofge2014/13%20%20PC%20wise%20Voters%20Turn%20Out.pdf). New Delhi: Election Commission of India last accessed on 9.12.2016.

Guru, S.D. and Pandey, N.P. (2000). *Madhya Pradesh District Gazetteer: Bastar*, Bhopal: Directorate of Rajbhasha Evam Sanskriti, Department of Culture.

Kennedy, J. (2014). "Gangsters or Gandhians? The Political Sociology of the Maoist Insurgency in India". *India Review*, *13*(3): 212-234.

Mahapatra, R. (2012). "Independent India worse for tribals", *Down to Earth*http://www.downtoearth.org.in/interviews/independent-india-worse-for-tribals-38299

Mukherji, N. (2013). *The Maoists in India: Tribals Under Siege*, New Delhi: Amaryllus.

Newman, S. (2016). "What is Insurrection? Destituent Power and Ontological Anarchy in Agamben and Stirner". *Political Studies*, *65*(2): 1-16.

Norris. P. (2012). *Making Democratic Governance Work: How Regimes Shape Prosperity, Welfare, and Peace*, New York: Cambridge University Press.

Johnston, H. (2011). *States and Social Movements*, Cambridge, United Kingdom: Polity Press.

Sharma, S. (2012). "Adivasi Predicament in Chhattisgarh", *Economic & Political Weekly*, Vol. XLVII (2): 19-22.

Stirner, M. (2005). *The Ego and His Own*, Mineola, New York: Dover.

Sundar, N. (2016). The *Burning Forest: India's War in Bastar*, New Delhi: Juggernaut Books.

Ulbricht, A. (2017). Democratising Democracy, *European Political Science, 16* (1): 116-119.

Wills, C.U. (1919). The Territorial system of the Rajput Kingdoms of Mediaeval Chhattisgarh, *Journal and Proceedings of the Asiatic Society of Bengal*, New Series, XV: 197-262.

10
Developmental Gap and Statehood Formation
Debatable Issues

K. Vidyasagar Reddy

At the outset, in the last few decades some Indian states had witnessed a few socio-political movements that attracted the policymakers and the political parties among others. Those movements were marked by the regional and sub-regional trends. Those regional movements were aimed at achieving statehood in several states.[1] Most of those movements are largely associated with the issues and concerns of underdevelopment, developmental gap, regional disparities and sub-regionalism. Generally, developmental issues get focused whenever statehood movements surface on the political horizon of concerned states. At times, some statehood movements were either withdrawn or converted into regional autonomy movements,[2] depending upon the response of concerned governments. Wherever certain developmental programmes were initiated, the statehood movements had been suspended at once or else, transformed into long-term ones over a period of time. Whereas some of these had become triumphant as new states were created as per the constitutional provisions.[3]

Whether or not development should be undertaken is reliant on the nature of state and its political resolve. What sort of development is appropriate for a region of the state is also to be obvious on the basis of local needs and resources. Of course, availability of the resource base, both human and material, of the state is also imperative in ensuring regional development. States that lacked sufficient resources might find it difficult to develop on its own. Such states may be reliant on the Central Government or other international financial agencies. In any case, mere resource-rich regions alone cannot develop always. The very process of regional development is determined by the existing political leadership that would be at the helm of affairs in the state and at the Centre.

Incidentally, it is both the major national parties, the Congress and BJP that were largely at the controlling position at the Centre and in several states for decades on end. Hence, these parties cannot abdicate their proportional responsibility for not being able to develop such regions as per the local expectations. Apparently, these two parties were so preoccupied with the national issues that the regional development was hardly focused in their governance models. Since local and region-specific issues were neglected, national parties started losing popularity. Obviously, the issue of rapidly increasing regional parties got into public eye in this backdrop. Alternatively, several sub-regional parties were established in the areas that were deprived of development. Once regional backwardness and lack of development were focused as priority issues, regional parties had dominated at the local and state levels. Viewed in this backdrop, both the national parties were compelled to play pillion riding role on the strength of regional parties. Particularly, the issue of developmental gap had posed a grave challenge to the continuation of national parties in several states. This problem arises when only a few regions are developed at the cost of the others. Certainly that would create a developmental gap between the advanced and backward regions in the same state. Since the underdevelopment or developmental gap has been one of the factors responsible for the rise of regionalism and thereby new state formation demands in India, debate over the meaning of 'development' assumes significance.

Developmental Notions

Meanwhile, there are a few studies available in the academic circles on the conceptual understanding of the term 'development'. Unlike the conventional notions of development (economic growth in terms of GNP, GDP/GSDP and per capita income), new yardstick of development (human and social dimensions of development as per the SDGs) for instance, had changed the course of developmental initiatives in recent times. Expectedly, both state and non-state actors have been associated with the process of development. In the name of governance, various stakeholders of development, be they political or non-political, have been drawn into the developmental policy dynamics in the country.

In the wake of globalisation, state and governments have been playing certain functions that were limited and restricted. Unlike before, the state has been faced with several challenges that had undermined its role of developing the people and communities at a time when the process of global transformation was taking place (R.Kothari, 1988). Further, development has been understood as developing collective capacities for long term growth with a view to eradicating poverty and raising the living standards generally and providing a fair measure of distributive justice that would remove gross inequities and injustices and move the country forward to the goal of democratic socialism (A. Bhat, 1989). In a way the notion of development had become more broad-based and aimed at ensuring the welfare of different sections of the society.

Hence, the process of development has been focused in terms of socially desirable outcomes and not merely in terms of material benefits. In other words, social development has become a much sought after concept than the human development index (HDI) over the years. Of late the concept was criticised as more a conventional index, which is 'rough and ready though very useful policy tool'. Responding to the criticism on the notion of HDI, whose author Mahbubul Haq commented that if the HDI was considered crude, then the GNP should be considered 'vulgar and less useful' in the context of measuring the performance of the states. And he observed that the economic growth alone was not sufficient to generate sustained development. Because its impact does not necessarily percolate down to the bottom-most sections of society in the desired way (Shovan Ray, 2010).

Social justice theorist John Rawls proposed that the people's standards of living should be judged by certain objective factors like basic liberties and opportunities and social basis for self-respect.

And, economic and social conditions do not justify the violation of individual rights (P.S. Shekhawat, 2010). But Nobel Laureate Amartya Sen critiques Rawlsian notion on existing inequalities and disadvantages in a diverse society and the need to improving social conditions and structure in favour of deprived communities. In fact, A. Sen's capabilities approach that builds human capacities to be able to choose and fulfil 'valuable goals in terms of both subjective and objective actors and values'. In the context of UNDP's notion of HDI that determined the living standards based on indices of life span, educational opportunities and per capita income, as has been further improved by Amartya Sen's emphatic rejection of a relative definition of development and poverty. He insisted that the definition had included the lack of entitlements/rights essential for the realisation of capabilities shared in common by members of a society.

Political Scientist Atul Kohli observed that the developmental performance of Indian states continues to deviate along several dimensions, including economic growth, distribution and poverty alleviation and quality of governance. Further, he supposed that instead of using state authority and resources to pursue the public good, ruling elites in these settings use their power for personal and sectional gains. Since economic liberalisation and related shift of initiative from the centre to states, a few of India's states like Gujarat and Andhra Pradesh had sought actively to promote business and industry. Besides, he felt that as a large federal polity where states were often ruled by political parties other than those controlling the Centre, India provides a considerable variety of development models within one country (A. Kohli, 2009).

In any case, economic growth with social justice had been the main goal of development strategy in India from the inception of planning age. And, sustainable development is a development strategy that would manage all assets, natural resources and human resources as well as financial and physical assets, for increasing long-term wealth and well-being. Besides, sustainable development has to be people-oriented effort at last. People have to be 'subjects, not just objects' of their development (Surat Singh, 2009). While economic development is a process whereby real GDP of a country increases over a long period of time, development as a long-run increase in the per capita income instead of total GDP, distributive justice is an aspect of development process in another development paradigm.

According to some social activists, the development is not a 'jugglery of numbers of gross national/state product and growth rates'. It is a harsh reality of people's daily existence. It is perceived by people in their daily life as 'denial or shortfall of educational facilities, employment, income and development opportunities' (M.B. Bhushan and N. Venugopal, 2009). And, the development debates based on traditional income indices of per capita and GNP and attendant per capita consumption, per capita expenditure and per capita wealth seem to have moved a long way to overcome the constraints of an average indicator that hides and ignores the stark realities.

As development is a multidimensional process that would be undertaken by the state through its various governance agencies, an individual or two cannot be held accountable for either development or otherwise. Incidentally an individual or political leader might appear as responsible for the developmental achievement or otherwise. But it is the combination of forces and institutions that would matter the most in ensuring the development in the given state. For instance, it is not just governments that would promote development; there are many other institutions, be they political or otherwise, which would contribute for the development. As part of the governance process, state and non-state actors, multiple institutions play the role of development.

Statehood Movements

Although there are several factors responsible for developmental gap in some states, role of state and governments cannot be set aside. Of these factors, specific ethnicity, tribal identity, language or dialect, communitarian lifestyle, common history and intra-regional differences appear predominant. While certain natural and local factors contribute for the regional backwardness as is the case with some North-east Indian states that stem from in the hilly terrain backdrop, state and governments can remedy the regional disparities within the same states. In other words, certain parts of the hilly terrain states are more developed than the others, due to the partisan role of state and governments. In a way it is about intra-regional differences that would lead to either a movement of regional autonomy or of statehood. Suffice it to cite the case of Bodoland in Assam. Despite series of movements being launched for over decades in the Bodoland area of Assam, only regional autonomy[4] was granted as against statehood demands of the Bodo people. Similar attempts were made in the context of Gorkhaland area of the West Bengal state a decade ago. Both the movements seemed to have subsided, but the statehood problem continues to haunt the concerned governments.

More than the inter-regional differences, intra-regional ones are largely responsible for the regional imbalances and thereby statehood movements in several states. As a result of intra-state differences, several statehood movements were organised in the 1980s and 90s. Since some states constitute regionally unequal parts, developmental gap continued to exist.[5] While some advanced regions witnessed better development, other regions remained backward for decades on end. This cannot be justified on the basis of natural factors alone. Man-made factors like the intervention of the state and governments were attributed for the lack of development in the backward regions. Of course, the role of state in any democratic government is depended upon the legislative majority. Unless majority legislators raise the developmental issues and convince the state government, favourable public policies cannot be formulated, leave alone implemented.[6]

While it is true that some regional disparities had been existing in different states for over decades even after Indian independence, state and governance alone cannot be faulted for the same. For, natural factors are attributed for the geographical inequality as a result of which some regions were developed faster than the others within the same state. Hilly terrain and Himalayan range settings are cases in point. North-east India is largely about hilly terrain and thus lacks development. Similarly, in the case of Uttar Pradesh, hill regions of Uttarakhand were less developed due to existence of hilly terrain. Since infrastructural facilities cannot be developed as those in the plain areas, neither agricultural nor industrial development could be undertaken effectively. Obviously, the state governments hardly focused on the development of the region and thus statehood movements were very volatile way back in1980s.

However, there are some other regions that consisted of rich natural and mineral resources, yet remained underdeveloped. For instance, regions like Jharkhand in Bihar, Chhattisgarh in Madhya Pradesh and Telangana in Andhra Pradesh, which were known for rich resources, but hardly developed when compared with their respective parent states. In these cases, more than the natural factors, man-made ones were held responsible for the lack of development. In other words, it is state and government that had to share the blame for the deliberate regional discrimination. In a way, political leadership that controlled the state governments for over decades was accused of prejudiced governance. There is an element of actuality in the accusation that gained legitimacy when the statehood movements were being launched.

Incidentally, most of the states that witnessed statehood movements were those that consisted of regionally minority legislators. Numerically strong legislators since hail from the advanced regions, backward minority legislators hardly had the choice of influencing the concerned state governments. One can cite several such cases wherein, the dominant regions used to undermine the interests of the backward regions. In the case of UP, backward regions like the Uttrakhand and Bundelkhand have always been minority regions that suffered backwardness. Similar is the case with Chhattisgarh in MP, Jharkhand in Bihar, Vidarbha in Maharashtra, Telangana in Andhra Pradesh, Gorkhaland in West Bengal and Bodoland in Assam for instance.

New State Formation

Although there are more than dozen statehood movements in some big states in the country, only four of them got statehood so far. Statehood movements like those of Vidarbha, Bodoland, Gorkhaland among few others are distressed about it. Since the political voice of these minority regions was feeble and numerically weak, majority of regional leaderships had always come in the way of statehood formation. Left to the parent states and their local leaderships, none of the four new states would have become reality so far. Thanks to the Article 3 of the Constitution of India, that the national parties were able to clinch the statehood in the last two decades. Despite strong resistance from the numerically strong regions and dominant political leaderships, the four new states were created by the national parties like the Congress and the BJP in the year 2000 and after in 2014. While the three new states were created peacefully during the A.B. Vajpayee-led NDA regime, with the active support of main opposition party like the Congress, the last new state of Telangana was possible under difficult situation during the Manmohan Singh-led UPA regime.

In any democratic state, numerical strength of the legislators enables it to exert political pressure on the government at different levels. Obviously, public policies and governance of the state are likely to be favouring the numerically majority groups. Failed to evoke any positive response from the national parties on the issue of regional disparities, the local communities would be set to support the regional parties. In a way, let-down of the national parties in ensuring regional equality had resulted in the rise and growth of regional parties. While in the case of some states, the national parties had become attentive and paved the way for new state formation, and in some other states these parties were indifferent towards the underdeveloped regions.

While the three states, viz. Chhattisgarh, Jharkhand and Uttarakhand were created in the year 2000, the state of Telangana was created in 2014. All these four new states were endowed with rich resources both natural and human alike, yet these regions remained underdeveloped within their respective parent states, namely Madhya Pradesh, Bihar, Uttar Pradesh and Andhra Pradesh. In fact, there were statehood movements, marked by violence of different kinds, witnessed for over decades in these states. Despite stiff resistance being presented by the dominant regions of big states, the new ones were carved out of them by the Union Government. In the case of first three states, the BJP-led NDA had taken lead, whereas the Congress-led UPA played a decisive role in the formation of 29th state of Telangana.

Ultimately, both the national parties came to an agreement on the formation of these new states. More than the movements of both violent and silent nature, political strategies of the national parties appeared crucial in the creation of such new states. As part of these political strategies were the developmental agendas that attracted the masses when the statehood movements were very volatile. Following the creation of new states, certain political strategies were implemented whereby the promised developmental agendas got underway. Whether or not such developmental programmes would lead to development of the region and the communities is something that deserves one's attention. Viewed in this backdrop, the issue of developmental strategies is crucial in the study of new state accomplishment and thereby execution of various developmental demands.

Developmental Strategies

What sort of public policies have to be initiated and in what geographical setting is for the political leadership and policymakers to be more concerned with. For, the character of public policy and its bearing is reliant on the political regime that controls the government of the day. Eventually, it is the public choice that would be decisive if any public policy is to be designed in any democratic form of government. Rather, many stakeholders expected to articulate their developmental interests through periodic elections. Obviously, the political parties have to prioritise the needs and demands of different stakeholders, on the basis of available resources and proceed in proper direction.

Whether or not the state government could mobilise the requisite resources *per se* or through other governments/financial institutions, be they national or international is also significant in this context. At times, state governments may generate local resources through taxation policies. At other times, these governments hunt for long-term loans from a variety of institutions. In any case, financial implications of every developmental policy have to be cautiously assessed. Viewed in this perspective, developmental strategies cannot simply be based on populist policies, political or otherwise. Nor can these strategies be formulated instinctively. And, all these strategies may not be pertinent to every state in the same way.

Keeping in view the needs and necessities of the concerned regions and local communities, the developmental strategies would be designed and implemented accordingly. Besides, the availability and accessibility of local resources of both human and natural would be kept in view prior to identifying the basic developmental strategies therein. In other words, both the available resources and anticipated requirements would be correlated so as to avoid the mismatch in setting the developmental agenda. Based on the regional and geographical characteristics, local development can be planned and ensured. In the plain locale, agriculture can be developed better than that in the hilly terrain, for instance. Similarly, educated employment can be enhanced more in the industrial and service sectors than that in the agriculture sector. These are a few indicators to help determining a better strategy in the case of development of the new states.

Conclusion

To conclude it, developmental issues have always been influential in precipitating the regional movements so that the new states could be formed in the country. Besides many issues and problems, uneven development, underdevelopment, development gap among different regions within the same states had become rallying point for the regional leaders to launch regional and sub-regional movements in several states. While the theme of decentralisation and delegated governance was responsible for effecting the change in the case of few big states in India, developmental issues like the regional inequality and underdevelopment had become catalyst in some other states. In consequence, statehood movements were being launched in some big states in India. While some of those movements got successful climax and four new states formed in the last two decades, many others had failed to convince the concerned governments at the Centre so far. In the post-statehood scenario, it is time to study if the promised development was undertaken in the new states so that the development gap could be addressed at once. Ultimately, what sort of developmental strategies would lead to satisfy the people and communities is a question that deserves the attention of policymakers and the political leaderships in the country.

NOTES

1. Big states like Uttar Pradesh, Bihar, Maharashtra, Madhya Pradesh, Andhra Pradesh, West Bengal, Assam, Jammu & Kashmir, Odisha, Karnataka, Tamil Nadu among others are such states which witnessed the statehood movements.
2. Bodoland and Gorkhaland movements are cases in point.

3. Article 3 of the Constitution of India provides for creation of new states like Uttarakhand, Jharkhand, Chhattisgarh and Telangana in the last two decades.
4. As part of providing more regional autonomy, regional administrative unit like the BTAD was created within the state of Assam.
5. States like Maharashtra, Andhra Pradesh were witnessing statehood movements on account of intra-state regional inequalities for long.
6. Hence, the developmental issue has been raised in the form of dominant regions' regional discrimination towards the 'backward regions' in some big states in the country.

REFERENCES

Anil Bhat (1989). *Development and Social Justice*, New Delhi: Sage Publications.

Atul Kohli (2009). *Democracy and Development in India—From Socialism to Pro-Business*, New Delhi: Oxford.

Bhushan, M. Bharat and N.Venugopal (ed.) (2009). *Telangana: The State of Affairs*, AdEd Value Ventures, Hyderabad.

Kothari, Rajani (1988). *Transformation and Survival*. New Delhi: Ajanta Publication.

Pingle, Gautam (2021). *The Formation and History of Telangana: A Collection of Nine Critical Essays,* Hyderabad: Orient BlackSwan.

Ray, Shovan (ed.) (2010). *Backwaters of Development—Six Deprived States of India*, New Delhi: Oxford.

Shekhavat, Prahlad Singh (2010). *Human Development, Wellbeing and Globalisation*, New Delhi: Rawat Publications.

Singh, Surat (ed.) (2003). *Strategies for Sustainable Rural Development*, Delhi: Deep & Deep Publication.

PART III
Issues Related to Federalism

11
Psychological Well-being and Perceived Social Support Among Young Adults
Role of Gender

Naviya Antony, K. and *A. Shahin Sultana*

Introduction

The early years of adulthood are really challenging for individuals as they experience significant physical and psychological development and there will be far changes in their social and economic roles (Hogan & Astone, 1986). The term young adulthood indicates young people have already attained their adulthood, but there is ambiguity in their position being partially dependent, unmarried and still in the educational and career development phase (Arnett, 2000, 2004). Five features exhibited by young adults who have the opportunity to pursue higher level of education and chances of changing their career (Arnett, 2000; Seiter, 2009) are identity exploration, instability, self-focused, feeling in-between and exploring possibilities (Arnett, 2000, 2004, 2006). At this point of life, they are challenged by the expectations of institutions and social norms. The psychological outcome of young adults is much affected by these stressors (Camara *et al.*, 2017) and considerably varies because they are affected by individual characteristics, social constraints, young people's agency and aspirations (Kong *et al.*, 2013). Contemporary young adults are diverse from their parents with better preparedness and with a dissimilar set of values. In a broader sense, adulthood denotes independent decision making. Most of the time the first independent decisions young adult phase covering is their further education, leaving home, working for their career development. Young adults have become more mobile compared to their early generation (Domenech & Salmeron, 2019). The independent life include travel away from family for higher studies, live separately from parents, move to the city, travelling or migrate and exposure to variety of cultures. Young adults in their 20s prefer to live on their own (Rosenfeld, 2010). At the same time independent life away from family sometimes can make people vulnerable, lonely, makes simple problems more complicated and it may adversely affect their psychological well-being (Olds & Richard, 2009).

Psychological well-being as the experiences of happiness and life satisfaction is a state of balance where better quality of life and fewer social problems are found. Subjective well-being composed by cognitive component and affective component, i.e. life satisfaction, presence of positive mood and absence of negative mood (Kahnemann *et al.*, 1999; Diener *et al.*, 1999) and purposeful aspect of psychological well-being consists of self-acceptance, environmental mastery, positive relationships, personal growth, purpose in life and autonomy (Ryff, 1989; Ryff and Keyes,1995). In a simple way, psychological well-being denotes living a good life or with good spirit (Ryan & Deci, 2001; Huppert *et al.*, 2004; Huppert, 2009).

Perceived social support has great influence on psychological well-being. Perceived social support can be explained as the social support perceived by the individual from friends, family members and others at the time of needs in the form of material, psychological and overall support. Perceived social support can be the better predictor of psychological well-being than the actual social support (Cohen *et al.*, 2000; Gallegher & Vella-Brodrick, 2008) and it is always linked to better mental health (Barrera, 1986). The mental health and well-being of youth are influenced by their stressful life (Buchman, 1989) and they are more likely to be depressed than their parents (Seligman, 1988). Young Indians now keep a physical and mental distance from family and society as they chase after their individual ambitions (Rajagopalan, 2019) and develop a sense of individuality and balance in their personal and social relationships (Bansal, 2012). Social support helps in adversity and at the time of intense social change especially in young adulthood (Loneliness, stress and social support in young adulthood). The direct relationship between the social support and psychological well-being reveals greater positive effect for people who have more social support (Rami, 2013). The study among group of nursing students also shows an increase level of psychological well-being in students with increased perceived social support (Aydin *et al.,* 2017). Higher perception of social support contributes to higher psychological well-being (Rani, 2016) and prevent psychological problems in young people (Walen & Lachman, 2000; Whitney, 2010). While few studies reports domains of family and significant others are highly associated with psychological well-being (Lai & Ma, 2016), others reports friends' domain more associated with psychological well-being (Sheets & Mohr, 2009; Faltoba and Bzdzikot, 2015; Hagen *et al.*, 2005, Kong *et al.,* 2013) and it is negatively associated with loneliness (Lee & Goldstein, 2016).

Speaking about gender differences in psychological well-being, most of the studies show no difference between male and female (Ryff & Correy, 1995; Salleh & Mustaffa, 2016, Donovan & Halpern, 2002; Helliwell, 2003). Few studies present gender differences in certain domains of psychological well-being even though no significant gender differences in total psychological well-being (Li *et al.,* 2015). Different from this, most of the studies show gender differences in the case of perceived social support (Ross & Mirowsky, 1989, Cashwell, 1995, Kendler *et al.*, 2005, Sharir *et al.*, 2007). Females score more perceived social support than males especially from their friends (Desousa & Cerqueira-Santos, 2012; Eberhart & Hammen, 2006). The aim of the present study is to investigate the role of gender in psychological well-being, perceived social support and on their relationship.

Theoretical Framework

Gender as the moderating variable on the relationship between perceived social support and psychological well-being has hypothesized with the support of various psycho-social theories.

Feminist and self-in-relation theories (e.g. Belenky *et al.,* 1986; Gilligan, 1982; Josselson, 1987) have claimed that psycho-social development and moral reflection of individuals are inclined to their gender and socialization. Often the label of male or female delivers a structure around which one's behaviour, roles and opportunities are organized (Worrel, 1981). It also influences how male and female retort to psycho-social developmental challenges and resolve moral dilemmas (Gilligan, 1982).

Another theory which leads to the assumption of influences of gender on the relationship of study variables is the psycho-social stages explained by Erickson (1966). The eight stages are: trust *versus* mistrust, autonomy *versus* shame, initiative *versus* guilt, industry *versus* inferiority, identity consolidation *versus* identity diffusion, intimacy *versus* isolation, generativity *versus* self-absorption, and integrity *versus* despair. Among the eight stages, the stages of identity consolidation, intimacy and generativity are dominant in adolescence, young adulthood and middle age. Gilligan (1979) argued that for females, intimacy precedes or go along with stage of identity, differ from the order specified in the theory where identity consolidation comes before intimacy. In this way, females identify themselves through intimacy and close relation with others. For male, identity precedes intimacy and generativity as explained in the theory. This difference in gender development is more obvious during the time of young adulthood as these stages occur during this period of life.

Objectives of the Study

The aim of the study is to investigate gender differences in perceived social support and psychological well-being and to examine the role of gender on the relationship between the independent variable perceived social support and the dependent variable psychological well-being.

Hypothesis

Based on the first objective, expected to find the following gender differences: (1) Among young adults, male would report overall greater psychological well-being than females. (2) Male would report greater psychological well-being in all the six domains than females. (3) Female would report overall greater perceived social support than males. (4) Female would report greater perceived social support from family, friends and significant others than males. (5) Gender would moderate the relationship between psychological well-being and perceived social support.

Methods

Participants

The total of 219 young adults (102 males and 117 females) participated in the survey. The data was collected *via* online using google forms. The participants were unmarried young adults age between 20 and 28. The other inclusion criteria for the study were: (1) all the participants had a college under graduation as their minimum educational qualification, and (2) all the participants belong to the state of Kerala, India who presently reside in different parts of the country, away from their family to pursue their higher education and career. The data was being collected using non-probability convenient sampling method.

Consent

The data for the study has been collected through online survey forms. Before beginning the survey, consent form (voluntary nature of participation, what participation entails, risks) presented to the participants and it was informed that the data will be maintained on password protected computer. Only those who were agreed and were willing to participate have been directed to the research survey questionnaire.

Measures

Multidimensional Perceived Social Support Scale (Zimet, Dahlem, Zimet and Farley, 1988)

To assess the perceived social support of young adults, the multi-dimensional perceived social support scale developed by Zimmet *et al.* (1988) has been used. The multidimensional perceived social support scale is a 12-item, Likert scale. The seven-point scale range from very strongly disagree (1) to very strongly agree (7). The scale assesses perceived social support from family, friends and significant persons (the major sources of social support) using three sub-scales. Each sub-scale consists of 4 items. The minimum possible total score of the scale is 12 and the maximum is 84. The possible minimum and maximum score of each sub-scale are 4 and 28 respectively. High score reflects strong perceived social support. In the pre-test, the scale reported Cronbach's alpha .87 ranged between .85 and .87 and all the three domains yielding value ≥ .84.

The Ryff's Scales of Psychological Well-Being (Ryff 1989, 1995)

The Ryff's scales of psychological well-being (PWB) is a comprehensive instrument to measure the multiple constructs of the psychological well-being. The PWB scales has different versions. For the present study, the 18 items (three items per construct) instrument was selected and the overlap between items in the shorter version is quite low. The scale consists of six sub-scales each comprise three items: Autonomy (independence and self-determination), Environmental Mastery (the ability to manage one's life), Personal Growth (welcoming to new experience), Positive relations with others (quality and satisfying relationships), Purpose in life (believing in meaningfulness of life). Participants rated PWB on a 7-point Likert scale (1= Strongly Agree to 7= Strongly Disagree). Higher scores mean higher Psychological well-being. Cronbach's alpha value of PWB was .71 ranging from .66 to .73. There were some reliability issues with the domains and it can be explained with some factors. Primarily each domain was constituted by three items and it has been claimed that it is almost not possible to get high alphas in measurements which was designed to get broad domains with only few numbers of items per domain (Gosling *et al.*, 2003). It has been also reasoned that alpha values may be to some extent misleading when calculated on scales or sub-scales with small numbers of items (Kline, 2000; Wood & Hampson, 2005).

Analysis

Analysis were conducted using SPSS v. 21. Pearson's correlations (two-tailed) were calculated between Psychological well-being and Perceived social support measures and their domains. Independent samples t-test were figured with gender as the grouping variable and psychological well-being and perceived social support as dependent variables. It was hypothesized that gender could moderate the relationship between Perceived social support and Psychological well-being. To examine this product term gender × perceived social support has been formulated. The potential moderating effect has been examined using hierarchical regression analysis.

Results

Descriptive Statistics

Table 11.1: Descriptive Statistics

	Possible Range	**Mean**	**Standard Deviation**
Psychological well-being (PWB)	18-126	88.78	12.85
PWB Autonomy	3-21	14.16	2.79
PWB Environmental Mastery	3-21	14.17	3.65
PWB Personal Growth	3-21	17.08	3.11
PWB Positive Relationship with Others	3-21	13.89	4.43
PWB Purpose in Life	3-21	14.87	3.27
PWB Self-Acceptance	3-21	14.58	3.86
Perceived social support Total	12-84	61.94	13.20
Perceived social support family	4-28	20.01	5.80
Perceived social support friends	4-28	21.76	4.98
Perceived social support significant others	4-28	20.16	6.46

Descriptive statistics for the variables examined in the study is presented in Table 11.1.

Table 11.2: Results of Independent sample T-Test for gender regarding psychological well-being and perceived social support domains. Shown are means (+SD)

	Male (102)	**Female (117)**	**T-Test**
Psychological well-being	89.35 (13.54)	88.28 (12.25)	1.07
Autonomy	14.11 (2.81)	14.21 (2.78)	-0.08
Environmental mastery	14.67 (3.25)	13.74 (3.93)	0.93*
Personal growth	17.11 (2.92)	17.05 (3.27)	0.06
Positive relationship	14.23 (5.06)	13.58 (3.79)	0.64

(*Contd.*)

	Male (102)	Female (117)	T-Test
Purpose in life	14.47 (3.29)	15.23 (3.24)	-0.76
Self-acceptance	14.73 (3.94)	14.46 (3.80)	0.27
Perceived social support	61.14 (14.38)	62.64 (12.10)	-1.49
PSS Friends	20.88 (5.20)	22.53 (4.68)	-1.65*
PSS Family	19.64 (6.48)	20.33 (5.15)	-.68
PSS Significant	20.61 (6.20)	19.76 (6.69)	.84

*p <.05

Table 11.2 illustrates that there were significant gender differences on one out of the six domains of psychological well-being, i.e., Environmental Mastery and one out of the three domains of Perceived social support, i.e. Perceived social support from friend's domain. Males scored significantly higher in Environmental mastery (t= 0.93; df= 217; p< 0.05) than females, while females reported significantly higher score in Perceived social support from friend's domain (t=-1. 65; df= 217, p< 0.05) than males. The result of independent sample T-Test revealed that there was no significant difference between males and females in terms of the overall scores of Psychological well-being (t= 1.07; df= 217; p= .58) and perceived social support (t=-1.49; df= 217; p= .40).

Table 11.3 demonstrates results of Pearson's correlation between the Psychological well-being total score, Perceived social support total score and the total scores of each of their domains. As reported elsewhere, the psychological well-being and perceived social support have a significant, strong and positive correlation (r=0.51; p< 0.01). Psychological well-being is significantly correlated with all the three domains of perceived social support and also all the domains of psychological well-being except the domain of purpose and meaning in life, are significantly correlated with total perceived social support and its domains. 'Purpose and meaning in life' domain of psychological well-being produces a dissimilar correlation result. The total score of psychological well-being and its domain, personal growth are the two constructs which have a significant and positive correlation with the purpose and meaning of life domain.

Table 11.3: Correlations among young adults' psychological well-being, perceived social support and their domains

		1	2	3	4	5	6	7	8	9	10	11
1	PWB total											
2	Autonomy	.552**										
3	Environmental mastery	.640**	.262**									
4	Personal growth	.607**	.306**	.144*								
5	Positive relationship with others	.694**	.234**	.334**	.254**							
6	Purpose and meaning in life	.285**	.020	.-080	.149*	.027						
7	Self-Acceptance	.796**	.334**	.563**	.438**	.447**	.009					
8	PSS total	0.51**	.209**	.356**	.376**	.481**	-.031	.411**				
9	Friends	0.43**	.161*	.338**	.278**	.437**	-.044	.330**	.778**			
10	Family	0.43**	.204**	.352**	.278**	.241**	.015	.449**	.727**	.396**		
11	Significant others	0.33**	.120	.151*	.304**	.430**	-.043	.182**	.788**	.462**	.282**	

**$p < 0.01$, *$p < 0.05$.

Table 11.4: Moderation Effects of Gender on Perceived Social Support in predicting Psychological Well-being (N = 219), (female-1, male-2)

Step	Variable	r	R^2 change	B	SE	Beta
1.	Perceived social support	.519**	.270***	.092	.183	.523***
2.	Gender	.042	.005	-14.85	7.117	.071
3.	Perceived Social Support × Gender		.019*	.269	.112	
	Constant			80.516	11.646	

***p < .001; **p < .01; *p < .05.

Table 11.4 summarizes key information with four conceptually distinct types of data. First, we have the simple correlations (r) which tell us how each individual predictor variable is related to the criterion variable, ignoring all other variables. We can see that Perceived Social Support is a better predictor of Psychological Well-being. The correlation of the interaction term with the criterion is not easily interpreted, because this correlation is greatly influenced by scaling of the main effects; so, it is omitted from the table. The second information is R^2 change in each step. Perceived Social Support as a better predictor in the model can predict 27 per cent of variation in the dependent variable. Due to the partial overlap with Perceived Social Support, gender adds only .005 R^2 change (not significant) when it is entered after Perceived Social Support in the model. The interaction term adds .019 R^2 change at significant level $p < .05$. However, the interaction term adds significantly beyond the main effects (R^2 change = .019, $p<.05$), indicating that we do have a statistically significant interaction between Gender and Perceived Social Support in predicting Psychological well-being. The modelled difference of male and female in Psychological well-being is –14.850. The slopes of the regression model for male and female are different and the difference is .269. R^2 change measures and tests the effect sizes of components, while controlling for variables that were entered into the model earlier.

This model predicts total 29 per cent of variation in the dependent variable Psychological well-being.

Discussion

The present study investigates the relationship between the psychological well-being and perceived social support among young adults and further to what degree the relationship between the psychological well-being and perceived social support is moderated by the gender among young adults. Study also investigate the gender differences in the study variables.

While comparing the means of perceived social support of three domains, perceived social support from friends shows comparatively high score than the other two domains with minimum standard deviation. The mean of family domain is 20.01 with standard deviation 5.80, while the mean value of friends' domain and significant others' domain are 21.76 and 20.16 with standard deviations 4.98 and 6.46 respectively. In adolescence individual perceive high support from family (Poudel *et al.*, 2020) and it continues in the adulthood (Antonucci, 1994). Different from that the present study shows higher score in the domain of perceived social support from friends comparing to the other two domains. Study of communication with family and friends across life (David-Barrett *et al.*, 2017) report that young adulthood is the time where the gradual shift of communication from parents to friends and then to the romantic partner occurs. This continues contact, emotional closeness, validation and the partnership in leisure activities may be the reasons to make this support more appealing to the individual young adult (Fehr, 1996; Clark & Mills, 1979; Neyer *et al.*, 2011).

The current study provides little support for the gender differences in the psychological well-being. The hypothesis has been stated as male would score better psychological well-being than females in the total well-being and in the domains. However, the results do not show any gender differences in psychological well-being except in the domain of environmental mastery. In the present study, environmental mastery score of males is significantly higher than females ($p < 0.05$). This shows male exhibit more skill to choose or change the surrounding context using physical or mental actions as well as being able to control events (Ryff, 1989). The study conducted by Stafford *et al.* (2016) among women shows that higher environmental mastery is not universally found amongst educated and surprisingly the same study shows association between low education and higher mastery skill. It explains that low socio-economic position in childhood force them to gain the skill to manage different situations. Studies on gender differences in Psychological well-being have not produced consistency in outcomes so far. Most of the time, the results are driven by the situations and it may lead to variety of conclusions which are unable to connect with each other. The study of gender differences among psychological well-being revealed that women had more environmental mastery than men (Li *et al.*, 2015) and their study population was more of general. Various other studies reveal the similarity of environmental mastery among both genders (Ryff and Corey, 1995; Salleh & Mustaffa, 2016). More studies among various populations of socio-economic educational background can bring more light to the differences shown by gender in psychological well-being. Apart from the differences in the domain of Environmental mastery, present study does not show any significant difference between male and female in psychological well-being.

Female score significantly ($p < 0.05$) higher in the independent sample T-test of Perceived social support in the domain of friends while the other two domains are indifferent with gender. This is similar to the studies where female perceive more social support from the friend's circle (DeSousa and Cerqueira-Santos, 2012). Females report more support, especially emotional support from friends and neighbours (Allen & Stoltenberg, 1995; Robinson, 1995; Wohlgemuth & Betz, 1991) and they specified that women are more active than men in giving and accepting social support. The young female adults are more likely to live independently, away from their parents (Rosenfeld, 2010) and more likely to be in contact with their friends than any other social group. Study conducted by DeSousa & Cerqueira-Santos (2012) among young adults shows that male usually specified more male as close friends and the female normally shows more female as their friends. All those results make it clear that being independent from family and as an active giver and receptor of social support, it is highly likeable for young female adults to perceive more social support from their friends' group.

Psychological well-being, the dependent variable of the study and the Perceived social support, independent variable of the study is significantly associated ($r= .51, p< .01$). It is consistent with the result elsewhere (Adyani *et al.*, 2019). This relationship has been explored, tested and proved across time and place. The regression analysis shows that Perceived social support is a good predictor of Psychological well-being and explains 27 per cent of variation in the dependent variable. This strong positive relation constitutes the underlying mechanism for the moderation analysis. The study does not find any significant direct association of gender and psychological well-being. Previous studies also support that there are no consistent findings to prove the gender differences in psychological well-being (Ryff and Corey, 1995; Salleh and Mustaffa, 2016). In the moderation analysis, the moderator variable gender has a significant interaction with the independent variable Perceived Social Support and together they have a strong and significant effect on the dependent variable Psychological well-being, increasing the effect size from 27 per cent to 29 per cent. The analysis shows different slopes for male and female indicating that the effect of Perceived social support on Psychological well-being is different for male and female. Perceived social support leads to more psychological well-being among females than males. This also can be said as gender differences on Psychological well-being varies with the score of Perceived social support. Based on the theories of development patterns of psycho-social and emotional development in females differ from those of males in relation to their respective capacities to achieve mastery over their psycho-social environments (e.g. Belenky *et al.*, 1986; Gilligan, 1982; Josselson, 1987). The finding of gender variance here does, therefore, goes along with the well-developed expectation.

Conclusion

The results emerging from this study highlight the significant moderation effect of gender on the relationship between psychological well-being and perceived social support among young adults. This result is more likely to believe, that the perceived social support in female young adults enhances their psychological well-being more than that do in the case of male young adults. Based on the development theories, the social and emotional development patterns of females are different from males (Steinberg, 2008) and the result is supported by this fact. The univariate analysis shows the gender differences in the domain of Environmental mastery of Psychological well-being and the domain of perceived social support from friends of the scale Perceived social support, where in the former case male scored significantly higher than female and in the latter female score was significantly higher than male. The underlying difference between male and female in their perceived social support and how it makes difference in their well-being will help the professionals in different fields like mental health, psychology, social work, counselling, therapy and in education to develop appropriate models in their field of practice for both genders.

REFERENCES

Adyani, L., Suzanna, E., Safuwan, S., & Muryali, M. (2019). "Perceived Social Support and Psychological Well-Being Among Interstate Students at Malikussaleh University". *Indigenous: Jurnal Ilmiah Psikologi, 3*(2). 98-104 doi: https://doi.org/10.23917/indegenous3i2.6591

Allen, S.F., & Stoltengberg, C.D. (1995). "Psychological separation of older adolescents and young adults from their parents: An investigation of gender differences". *Journal of Consulting and Development, 73*, 542-546.

Antonucci, T.C. (1994). *A life span view of women's social relations: Women growing older, Psychological perspectives*, 239-269, Sage Publications.

Arnett, J. J. (2000). "Emerging adulthood: a theory of development from the late teens through the twenties". *American Psychologist, 55*, 469-80.

Arnett, J.J. (2004). *Emerging Adulthood: The winding road from the late teens through the twenties.* New York: Oxford University Press.

Arnett, J.J. (2006). "Emerging adulthood in Europe: A response to Bynner". *Journal of Youth Studies, 9*, 111-123.

Aydin, A., Kahraman, N., Hicdurmaz, D., (2017). "Determining the perceived social support and Psychological Well-being Levels of Nursing Students", *Journal of Psychiatric Nursing, 8* (1): 40-47, DOI 10.14744/PHD. 2017. 95967.

Bansal, P., (2012). *Youth in contemporary India: Images of Identity and Social Change*, Springer India, ISBN: 9788132207153.

Barrera, M. (1986). "Distinctions between Social Support Concepts, Measures and Models". *American Journal of Community Psychology. 14*(4) 413-445. Doi: 10.1007/bf 00922627

Belenky, M., Clinche, B., Goldberger, N., & Trule, J. (1986). *Women's ways of knowing.* New York: Basic Books.

Buchmann, M. (1989). *The Script of Life in Modern Society.* Chicago: University of Chicago Press.

Camara, M., Bacigalupc, G., Padella, P. (2017). "The role of social support in adolescents: Are you helping me or stressing me out?" *International Journal of Adolescents and Youth, 22* (2) 123-136. http:/dx.doi.org/10.1080/02673843.2013.875480

Cashwell, C.S. (1995). "Family functioning and self-esteem of middle school students: A matter of perspective?" *Journal of Humanistic Education & Development, 34*, 83-91.

Clark, M.S., & Mills, J. (1979). "Interpersonal attraction exchange and communal relationships". *Journal of Personality and Social Psychology, 37*, 12-24.

Cohen, S., Underwood, L., & Gottlieb, B. (2000). *Social Support Measurement and Intervention: A Guide for Health and Social Scientists.* New York: Oxford University Press.

David-Barrett, T., Kertesz, J., Rotkrich, A., Ghosh, A., Bhattacharya, K., Monsivais, D. & Kaski, K. (2017). *Communication with family and friends across life course.*

DeSousa, D.A., & Cerqueira-Santos, E. (2012). "Intimate friendship relationships between young adults". *Paidéia (Ribeirão Preto), 22*(53), 325-333. doi: http://dx.doi.org/10.1590/1982-43272253201304

Diener, E., Suh, E.M., Lucas R.E., & Smith H.L., (1999). "Subjective well-being: The decades of progress". *Psychology Bulletin, 125*, 276-302.

Domenech, J.M., Salmeron, A.M., (2019). *Young adults in the 21st century, a different approach to life?* Caixabankresearch.com

Donovan, N. & Halpern, D. (2002). *Life Satisfaction: the state of knowledge and implications for government.* Cabinet Office analytical paper. London: Cabinet Office.

Eberhart, N.K. & Hammen, C.L., (2006). "Interpersonal predictors of onset of depression during the transition to adulthood". *Personal Relationships, 13*, 195-206. doi:10.1111/j.1475 6811.2006.00113.x

Erikson, E.H. (1966). "Eight ages of man". *International Journal of Psychiatry, 2*, 281-300.

Fehr, B. (1996). *Friendship Processes.* Thousand Oaks, CA: Sage.

Gallegher, N.E. & Vella-Brodrick, A.D. (2008). "Social Support and Emotional Intelligence as predictors of Subjective Well-being". *Personality and Individual Differences 44*(7), 1551-1561.

Gilligan, C. (1979). "Women's place in man's life cycle". *Harvard Educational Review, 49*, 431446.

Gilligan, C. (1982). *In a Different Voice.* Cambridge, MA: Harvard University Press.

Gosling, S.D., Rentfrow, P.J., &. Swann, W.B. (2003). "A Very Brief Measure of the Big Five Personality Domains." *Journal of Research in Personality, 37*: 504–528. doi:10.1016/S00926566(03)00046-1

Helliwell, John, F. (2003). "How's life? Combining individual and national variables to explain subjective well-being". *Economic Modelling, 20*(2), 331-360.

Hogan, D.P. & Astone, N.M. (1986). "The transition to adulthood". *Annual Review of Sociology, 12,* 109-130, doi: 10.1146/annurev.soc.12.1.109

Huppert, F.A. (2009). "Psychological well-being: Evidence regarding its causes and consequences". *Applied Psychology: Health and Well-being, 1,* 137-164.

Huppert, F.A., Marks, N., Clark, A., Siegrist, J., Stutzer, A., Vittersø, J. & Wahrendorf, J. (2009). "Measuring well-being across Europe: Description of the ESS well-being module and preliminary findings". *Social Indicators Research, 91*(3):301-315. doi: 10.1007/s11205008-9346-0

Josselson, R. (1987). *Finding herself: Pathways to identity development in women.* San Francisco: Jossey-Bass.

Kahnemann, D., Diener, E., & Schwarz, N., (1999). *Well-being: The foundation of hedonic psychology.* New York: Russel-Sage.

Kendler, K.S., Myers, J., & Prescott, C.A. (2005). "Sex differences in the relationship between social support and risk for major depression: a longitudinal study of opposite-sex twin pairs". *Am. J. Psychiatry, 162*: 250-256.

Kline, P. (2000). *Handbook of Psychological Testing.* London: Routledge.

Kong, F., Zhavo, J., You, X., (2013). "Self Esteem as mediator and moderator of the relationship between social support and Subjective well-being among Chinese University Students". *Soc Inde Res, 112*(1): 151-161.

Lai, C.C., and Ma, C.M., (2016). "The mediating role of social support in the relationship between psychological well-being and health risk behaviors among Chinese university students". *Health Psychology Open. 3*(2), https://doi.org/10.1177/2055102916678106 retrieved on 10.10.2020.

Lee, C.Y. & Goldstein, S.E. (2016). "Loneliness, stress and social support in young adulthood: Does the sources of support matters". *Journal of Youth and Adolescence, 45*(3), 568-580. https;//doi.org/10.1007/s10964-015-03959

Li, R.H., Kao, C.M. & Wu, Yi-Yang. (2015). "Gender differences in psychological well-being: Test of factorial invariance". *Qual Life Res., 24* (11); 2577-81.

Neyer, F.J., Wrzus, C., Wagner, J. & Lang, F.R. (2011). "Principles of relationship differentiation". *European Psychologist, 16,* 267-277. doi: 10.1027/10169040/a000055

Olds, J. & Richard, S. Schwartz. (2009). *The Lonely American: Drifting Apart in the Twenty-First Century.* Boston: Beacon Press.

Poudel, A., Gurung, B. & Khanal, G.P. (2020). "Perceived Social Support and Psychological well-being among Nepalese adolescents: The Mediating Role of Self-esteem". *BMC Psychol, 43*(8). https://doi/10.1186/S40359-02000409. retrieved on 11.10.2020.

Rajagopalan, N. (2019). *Lonely, under pressure and young: the mental well-being of India's young.* http://Blogs.lse.ac.uk/southasia/2019/09/27/lonely_under_pressure_and_young_the_mental_well-being_of_india's_young retrieved on 11.10.2020.

Rami, S. (2013). *Social support, emotional well-being, and emotion regulation: A mediation model.*

Rani, E.K. (2016) "Perceived Social Support and Psychological Well-being: Testing the Unique Association and Gender Differences among Young Working Adults". *The International Journal of Indian Psychology, 3* (2), 4 DIP: 18.01.066/20160302

Robinson, N.S. (1995). "Evaluating the nature of perceived support and its relation to perceived self-worth in adolescents". *Journal of Research on Adolescence, 5*(2), 253-280.

Rosenfeld, M.J. (2010). "The Independence of Young Adults, in Historical Perspective". *Family Therapy Magazine, 9*(3), 17-19.

Ross, C.E. & Mirowsky, J. (1989). "Explaining the social patterns of depression: Control and problem solving or support and talking". *Journal of Health and Social Behaviour, 30.*

Ryan, R.M. & Deci, E.L. (2001). "On happiness and human potentials: a review of research on hedonic and eudaimonic well-being". *Annual Review of Psychology, 52,* 141-166.

Ryff, C.D. (1989). "Happiness is everything, or is it? Explorations on the meaning of psychological well-being". *Journal of Aging Health, 19* (6), 907-920.

Ryff, C.D. & Correy, L.M.K. (1995). "The structure of psychological well-being revisited". *Journal of Personality and Social Psychology.*

Ryff, C.D. & Keyes, C.L. (1995). "The structure of psychological well-being revisited". *Journal of Personality and Social Psychology, 69*(4), 719-727.

Salleh, N.A.B. & Mustaffa, C.S.B. (2016). *Examining the Differences of Gender on Psychological Well-being.* International Conference on Applied Science and Technology (ICAST), Malaysia.

Seligman, M. (1988). "Boomer Blues". *Psychology Today,* 50-55.

Sharir D., Tanasescu M., Turbow, D. & Maman, Y. (2007). "Social Support and Quality of Life Among Psychiatric Patients in Residential Homes". *International Journal of Psycho-social Rehabilitation, 11*(1), 85.

Sheets, L.R. & Mohr, J.J. (2009). "Perceived Social Support from friends and family and psycho-social functioning in bisexual young adult college students". *Journal Counselling Psychology.*

Stafford, M., Deeg, D. & Kuh, D. (2016). "Educational Attainment and Women's Environmental Mastery in Midlife". *International Journal of Aging and Human Development.* http://doi.org/10.1177/0091415016641687 retrieved on 12.10.2020.

Steinberg, L. (2008). *Adolescence.* 8. New York: McGraw-Hill.

Walen, H.R. & Lachman, M.E. (2000). "Social Support and Strain from Partner, Family, and Friends: Costs and Benefits for Men and Women in Adulthood". *Journal of Social and Personal Relationships, 17*(1), 5-30.

Wohlgemuth, E. & Betz, N.E (1991). "Gender as a moderator of the relationships of stress and social support to health". *Journal of Counselling Psychology*, 38 (3), 367-374.

Wood, S.A. & S.E. Hampson. (2005). "Measuring the Big Five with Single Items Using a Bipolar Response Scale." *European Journal of Personality 19*: 373-390. doi:10.1002/per.542.

Zimet, G.D., Dahlem, N.W., Zimet, S.G. & Farley, G.K. (1988). "The Multidimensional Scale of Perceived Social Support". *Journal of Personality Assessment*, *52*, 30-41.

12
Revitalising the Role of Governor in Co-operative Federalism

With Special Reference to the 75 Years of Journey of India

Sandeep Inampudi

Introduction

India is the single example of a quasi-federal state in the Federal Government and "it is a unitary state with subsidiary federal features". Over the past 75 years, Indian federalism has undergone different stages and altered in reaction to new democratic developments such as coalition politics, the establishment of regional parties, federalisation of the party system, judicial interventions, the emergence of powerful regional *ksatraps* etc. The President appoints the Governor to serve as the executive head of the State, according to the Constitution of India (Anushree, 2022). He plays a key role in resolving political and administrative issues of the state government (Douglas V. Verney, 1997: 365). The governor is not merely a political appointee—he is essential for maintaining the administrative standards of the nation. The Constitution of India has specifically mentioned the role and responsibilities of the Governor (Mohan Singh Saggu, 2021: 7). The "people of the State or their representatives" has no role in the nomination of the Governor, even though he serves as the state's administrative head, is a member of the State Legislature, and is responsible for carrying out its administration. Instead of the President, who is chosen by the people's representatives, i.e. the Members of Parliament and the Members of the State Legislatures, the Union Council of Ministers appoints the Governor (Justice Shri R.S. Sarkaria, 2001: para 6).

Historical Background

Considering the interactions of "nationalist leaders with the Governor in the British Indian provinces following the Government of India Act of 1935, the nature of his office was extensively contested by the Constitution makers" (Anushree, 2022). The idea of a strong executive has deep roots in Indian constitutional history because it emerged following a protracted period of Moghul and British imperial rule (Douglas V. Verney, 1985: 1249). The "Constituent Assembly (CA)" of India was established based on the "Cabinet Mission Plan", which called for a confederal Constitution for India. To create "model constitutions for the union and the provinces", respectively, the CA "constituted a Union Constitution Committee and a Provincial Constitution Committee" on April 30, 1947. As a result, the "model provincial constitution" recommended an "elected Governor" with the authority to stop any severe threat to the province's peace and tranquility, or any part of it, and with the security of tenure (Ashok Pankaj, 2017: 13-14).

Constituent Assembly (1947) expressed that the Governor should be a head of every Province and appointed by the Province and not by the Central Government. The Governor "should be appointed by direct election based on adult franchise through a special electoral college." The emergency powers of the Governor had, however, a chequered career in the Assembly and decisively influenced the provision relating to his appointment (Singh, K.P., 1965: 39-40).

In the past, there was a great deal of public controversy surrounding the removal of numerous "belligerent" state governments "through the Governor's report and the subsequent imposition of the President's rule in the states", with allegations that the Governor was "acting as an agent of the Central Government" to overthrow "democratically elected governments in these places". Presently, the governor's position is little more than a pension plan for ageing "politicians, and political considerations" have taken preference over the "constitutional requirements for an appointed" (rather than "elected") Head of State. The impartiality and transparency of this position have been questioned by the continued practise of routinely replacing governors when the Central Government changes (Agnidipto Tarafder & Avantik Tamta, 2017: 118-119). The function of the State Governors under our Federal Constitution is the subject of a critical constitutional debate that is remarkable in the history of the Indian parliamentary system. This debate is raging throughout the nation. The actions of some State Governors have generated a great deal of confusion. They have been strongly criticised by various groups in society, especially the opposition benches. The press and the public have used terms like "rape of the Constitution", "fraud on the Constitution", and "murder of Democracy" to express their shock and rage at these arbitrary actions (Dalip Singh, 1968: 51). In this context, the present study examines the changing nature of governor's role in Independent India, identifies the challenges and offers suggestions for the effective working of the governor's office in India.

Powers and Authority of the Governor

In a federal government like India, the "powers and functions of the governor" is comparable to that of the President. lieutenant governors played such a role in Union Territories (Aishwarya Sandeep, 2021) and (Advocatespedia, 2022). "The Constitution of India" provides dual responsibility to "the Governor" such as follow the instructions of the state cabinet and to follow his own discretion. Further, the Constitution provides special powers under different articles, which can be exercised without any dependence or consideration of state cabinet (Dalip Singh, 1968: 54). Article 153 stipulates the necessity of "a governor for each state and a person can be appointed as a governor for two or more states". Articles 155 and 156 specify that the importance of the "President of India" in appointing the Governor of a State. The tenure of governor was five years (Ramesh Kumar Arora and

Rajni Goyal, 2005: 191) and (Supreme Court of India, 2010). Except, in the exercise of discretionary powers, "the council of ministers" has to offer support to "the governor" in the discharge of his duties (Art. 163) (Patil, S.H., 2016: 276). He is working as "agent of the Union Government in a few specific areas". In some situations, the governor uses discretionary powers such as when "no party has a clear-cut majority" to frame the government, the existing chief minister dies suddenly, dissolution of state legislative assembly when it cannot prove confidence and if the legislative assembly is dissolved when council of ministers loses its majority (*Journal of India*, 2021).

The fact "that the governor can ask the Council of Ministers to reconsider" any proposal. The governor can reserve a state Bill for presidential assent and can ask the council of ministers to reconsider any proposal made by it. There is no rule the governor must accept every "advice of the Council of Ministers". Similarly, "the Governor" is limited from using his discretionary authority in an autocratic manner since the President of India has the power to impose restrictions on him or, as the last option, remove him (Sudhanshu Tripathi, 2008: 64-65).

Changing Dynamics of the Office of the Governor

Within a short time after Independence, the Government of India has adopted parliamentary system of governance taking lessons from the British legacy. Arguments made in the Constituent Assembly indicated that the Governor's role was first seen to be constrained. However, when the framers emphasised the need for extensive legal authority, they may have been more foresighted. Governors were expected to be knowledgeable about the possibility of "a constitutional crisis and to alert the President (i.e. the Centre) if the state's political situation" appeared to be out of control (Douglas V. Verney, 1985: 1247-1249).

During the Nehruvian era, constitutional proprieties were mostly respected (*The Tribune*, 2016). The political landscape of the nation has experienced a significant change after 1967. Despite a significant fall in support, Congress was able to successfully maintain control of the government. The party also lost control of many states. Non-Congress Coalition Ministries were founded in "West Bengal, Bihar, Uttar Pradesh, Orissa, Kerala, Punjab, Madhya Pradesh, and Haryana".

The Federal pattern on which our Constitution is based underwent its first test as various political governments took power in the states (Sibranjan Chatterjee, 1971: 522).

As a result "of the activity of Coalition Governments in various States", the debates on Governor's office came to the fore. The Governor's actions were openly criticised by several states, and he was forced into politics (Sibranjan Chatterjee, 1971: 523). The number of coalition governments in the provinces increased and decreased quickly, the Congress split, Mrs. Indira Gandhi won remarkably in the mid-term parliamentary elections of 1971, centre-state relations changed, and there was a great deal of debate over the roles of the Governor and the President (Sibranjan Chatterjee, 1971: 522).

When Congress gained control over most of the country, the governor served "as a competitive power centre." The governor was used by the "high command" to control the more popular local leader. Due to the emergence of regional forces, no governor can longer afford to meddle with the structure of the federal government or the autonomy of state governments (Rajesh Ramachandran, 2014).

In 1977, the Janata Party suddenly removed all governors appointed by the Congress government, most of whom had been selected under Indira Gandhi's infamous domestic emergency. It was a more controversial action taken by the Janata Government. Thus, the removal of governors in 1977 was an exceptional circumstance following an exceptional incident (Jagannathan, R., 2014). At the beginning of the 1980s, non-Congress parties aggressively engaged in political mobilisation, and several of these parties made specific requests to reduce the governor's political authority. The "Rajamannar Committee and the Communist Party of India have recommended to abolish Articles 356 and 357 of the Constitution" (Ashok Pankaj, 2017: 33).

The Governor's position and responsibilities are once again a controversial issue in India after around 25 years (1990-2014) of relatively low-key politics. This inevitably takes place concurrently with one party winning a big majority at the Centre. Over the past "few years, the governors of Karnataka, Madhya Pradesh, Kerala, Maharashtra, and of course, West Bengal, have all played their positions in a way that has made them extremely contentious without necessarily raising the status of the position" (Rakhahari Chatterji, 2020).

The Governor's office has recently gained attention, but for the wrong reasons (Snehil Kunwar Singh, 2022). The current disagreements centre on several issues, including selecting the chief minister, determining whether to demonstrate a parliamentary majority, requesting information about daily operations, appearing to take "a long time to assent to" laws or reserve measures "for the President", criticising particular state programmes, and using the "governor's authority as chancellor of state universities" (Rakhahari Chatterji, 2020). The "distrust between the Chief Minister and the Governor" necessitated the Bombay High Court making strong observations about it and emphasising the importance of following constitutional principles. The relationship between the governor and the state administration does not appear to be one where key constitutional officials agree, despite constitutional morality calling for this. The constitutional silence regarding this relationship is much to blame for this. Reform is, therefore, required as a result (Snehil Kunwar Singh, 2022).

Major Debates

Since the period "of the Constituent Assembly, the position of the governor" has faced controversies related to discretionary powers. Even though the Government of India has appointed governors to monitor the performance of states (Sarkaria Commission, 1988: 115-138). It is generally believed that the Centre paid attention for the Governors' recommendations to depose certain Chief Ministers and their administrations. There have been numerous occasions where state administrations have allegedly failed to handle problems with law and order, corruption, or both, dating back to the "first imposition of the President's power in Kerala in 1959 and ending in Bihar in 2005" (Sudhanshu Tripathi, 2008: 67-68). These controversies caused for Dismissal of Governors in many states. The details are presented below:

Major Controversies and Dismissal of State Governors since 1967

Year	Event
1967	In 1967, West Bengal Governor Dharma Vira removed Chief Minister Ajay Mukherjee and replaced him with P.C. Ghose. He convenes the meeting against Mukherjee's wishes.
1977	About 15 governors were removed by the Janata government in 1977.
1980	The removal of the then Tamil Nadu Governor Prabhudas Patwari in October 1980 served as an example of how the Prime Minister might utilise the President's "pleasure" under Article 156 (1) to remove any Governor for political purposes without giving any justification.
1981	The previous governor of Rajasthan, Raghulal Tilak, was also removed from office in 1981. The state High Court ruled that the Presidential pleasure indicated in Article 156 was "not justiciable" when Tilak was dismissed from office.
1984	Congressman Ram Lal overthrew the NT Rama Rao administration in 1984 and appointed Nadendla Bhaskara Rao as Andhra Pradesh's chief minister for 31 days. The position of the governors was not secure when the State government was overthrown.
1988	Regarding the governor's tenure, the 1988 Sarkaria Commission Report on Centre-State Relations made the following observations: "The ever-present possibility of the tenure being terminated before the full term of five years can create considerable insecurity in the mind of the Governor and impair his capacity to withstand pressures, resist extraneous influences, and act impartially in the discharge of his discretionary functions", the 1988 Sarkaria Commission Report on Centre-State Relations noted regarding the Governor's tenure issue.
1989	The S.R. Bommai case was anticipated to result in some modification of the role of state governors. The rules of Article 356 were examined by the Supreme Court of India. The Central Government exploited Article 356 to overthrow the state government. In circumstances where it is clear that there is a stalemate and the state government has collapsed, the Supreme Court ruled that Article 356 is an extraordinary power and should only be employed as a last resort. Similar to the Sarkaria Commission case, the court's opinions in this case were expressed.
1998	Krishna Pal Singh, the governor of Gujarat who had been chosen by the UPA administration, was dismissed by the BJP government.
2001	The NDA removed M. Fathima Beevi, another governor of Tamil Nadu nominated by the UPA, citing her "failure" to carry out her responsibilities.

(*Contd.*)

Year	Event
2004	Four Governors who had been nominated by the NDA government—Kidar Nath Sahni of Goa, Kailashpati Mishra of Gujarat, Babu Parmanand of Haryana, and Vishnu Kant Shastri of Uttar Pradesh—had been removed by the United Progressive Alliance administration.
2014	The President gave the order to remove Kamla Beniwal. "List of additional governors removed throughout Modi's term: (1) The Governor of Puducherry, Virendra Kataria, was dismissed. (2) Vakkom B. Purushothaman, the governor of Mizoram, resigned after objecting to his transfer to Nagaland. (3) The former governor of Gujarat, Kamla Beniwal, who was later transferred to Mizoram, was asked to resign. (4) Uttar Pradesh's B.L. Joshi resigned from his position. (5) In Chhattisgarh, Shekhar Dutt resigned from his position. (6) Ashwani Kumar left his position in Nagaland. (7) In Goa, B.V. Wanchoo submitted his resignation. (8) M.K. Narayan left his position in West Bengal."
2016	When the Governor of Arunachal Pradesh decided to hold the state's assembly elections earlier than scheduled, a political crisis ensued, and President Rule was imposed.

Source: *The Hindu*, 2014, *The Hindu*, 2014a and *Hindustan Times*, 2010, *Journal of India*, 2021.

Any extension of the President's Rule for a period longer than six months requires legislative consent. Despite this, it is clear that governors have been used as "Central Executive agents to impose the Centre's rule on the states. They have temporarily replaced the federal ideal with the Central Government" by doing this (Douglas V. Verney, 1985: 1248).

Judicial Interventions

"S.R. Bommai *versus* the Union of India (1994), a landmark judgement by the Supreme Court", issued as a serious reminder against routinely utilising Article 356 to overturn state governments led by opposition parties. Because of this, the Federal Government was somewhat strengthened. The number of times the President was in-charge reduced dramatically from 63 between 1971 and 1990 to just 27 between 1991 and 2010. It is not guaranteed that similar decisions will be taken on other contentious issues in the future (Rakhahari Chatterji, 2020). In 1997, the Supreme Court declared that the

Governor was "not bound by the support and advice of the Council of Ministers" when fulfilling the functions of a different statutory post (such as the Chancellor) (Rajat Asthana, 2022). The Supreme Court was asked to rule "on the legality of the President's Rule declaration and the dissolution of the Bihar Assembly" in 2005. Rameshwar Prasad Case (2006) stated that the "President's rule was not imposed based on the Governor's" decision opinions (*Journal of India*, 2021). Following the Supreme Court's reinstatement of the Congress-led government in the state, Jyoti Prasad Rajkhowa, the Governor of Arunachal Pradesh, was removed from office on grounds of constitutional violations. "On July 13, 2016, the Supreme Court reinstated the Congress administration in Arunachal Pradesh by rejecting all of Mr. Rajkhowa's decisions that had led to its downfall in January." A five-judge constitutional court held that "the Governor must maintain a distance from any disagreement, quarrel, disharmony, discontent, or discord within certain political parties" (Rahul Shrivastava, 2016).

Governor as the Chancellor of the Universities

In India, the Governor has been considered the university's chancellor for more than a century. Since the establishment of the universities in Bombay, Madras, and Calcutta, the Governor has acted as their chancellor (Dole, N.Y., 1961: 379). The power, protocol, and implements associated with the Governors of British India served to legitimise the position of Chancellor of the Universities (Nawal Kishore Pd. Sinha, 1962: 72-73). This approach continued both during and after British rule (Dole, N.Y., 1961: 379). The Chancellor's duties and authority are *de jure* rather than *de facto* in the University. As per custom, the State legislature's University Acts give the Chancellor-Governor his authority. The State legislature is well within its rights to either expand or contract the Chancellor's authority. Each university has different requirements for his duties under the University Act (Thandavan, R., 1986: 77).

There have been instances where governors and governments have gotten into disagreements over the selection of vice-chancellors. For instance, in 1971, the Governor of Orissa appointed Dr. Chaudhary Nismani Nanda as Vice-Chancellor in defiance of Mr. Biswanath Das, the Chief Minister of Orissa, and Mr. S.S. Ansari. Dr. A.V. Verghese was appointed Vice-Chancellor of Kerala University in 1981 by Mrs. Jothi Venkatachalam, the Governor of Kerala, without the consent of the Chief Minister of Kerala (Thandavan, R., 1986: 78). Since 1980, the Governor-Chancellor position has become more controversial. His *ex-officio* Chancellor status has been questioned in many Indian states. The episodes in West Bengal, Bihar, Maharashtra, Andhra Pradesh, Haryana, and Tamil Nadu are reflective of this issue. The Governor-Chancellor conflicts with the State Government have got worse. Undoubtedly, both the Governor's and the Chancellor's positions have lost their prior status and respect (Thandavan, R., 1986: 76).

In 2019, the West Bengal Trinamool Congress government restricted the governor's ability to appoint VCs and conduct enforcement action against them. The University Grants Commission and the state of Odisha are engaged in a legal dispute over the Odisha Universities (Amendment) Act at the Orissa High Court. The Act gives the state government power over recruitment at state universities. The state government has disputed and rejected the UGC's claim that the Act violates its rules (Sourav Roy Barman, Shaju Philip, 2021). In 2021, Maharashtra modified the process for choosing the vice-chancellor of state-run public universities. Recently, some states have taken initiatives to reduce the governor's powers over state-run public colleges (Rajat Asthana, 2022). The Tamil Nadu Legislative Assembly passed two laws to that effect in April 2022, namely the "Tamil Nadu Universities Laws (Amendment) Bill, 2022, and the Madras (Chennai) University Amendment Act, 2022 for restrict the governor of the authority to choose and appoint vice-chancellors of the state's 13 state-run universities", which resulted in the Governor losing his or her jurisdiction to designate vice-chancellors (at public universities). As of June 8, 2022, these Bills have not yet received the governor's approval (Rajat Asthana, 2022) and (Venkatesh, M.R., 2002). The West Bengal Assembly approved a Bill on June 13, 2022, which would have removed the Governor from the role of chancellor and replaced him or her with the chief minister. The action "by the Mamata Banerjee administration has once again brought to light similar conflicts taking place in opposition-ruled states like Tamil Nadu and Maharashtra, which have also reduced the authority possessed by Governors in their capacity as Chancellors" (Sourav Roy Barman, 2022) and (Rajat Asthana, 2022).

Major Controversies on Governor in Contemporary Times

In West Bengal, the Governor Dhankhar has been charged with delaying elections for the local government by refusing to sign the Howrah Municipal Corporation (Amendment) Bill, 2021. He has alleged wrongdoing in welfare programmes and disputed government assertions regarding investments in the State. In Maharashtra, the election for Speaker has been delayed by Governor Bhagat Singh Koshyari ever since the position became vacant in February 2021. The governor's claim that the State Assembly cannot establish its own rules is rejected by the ruling coalition. Until the case reached the High Court, he had rejected to accept the "Council of Ministers' advice about the nomination of 12 members to the Legislative Council". The Tamil Nadu Admission to Undergraduate Medical Degree Courses Bill, which was approved by the Assembly in September 2021, was not implemented in Tamil Nadu by Governor R.N. Ravi (*Journal of India*, 2022). Discussions about the constitution, politics, and law have long centred on the role, power, and discretion of the governor's office. Political unrest has resulted in Jharkhand from the Governor of Jharkhand's protracted silence regarding Chief Minister Hemant Soren's likely dismissal as an MLA. It is possible to observe a power struggle between the Raj Bhavan and the elected government in a State in the impasse over the National Eligibility Compulsory Entrance Test (NEET) Exemption Bill in Tamil Nadu or in the disagreement over the appointment of bureaucrats between the Delhi government and the Lieutenant Governor appointed by the Centre. Thus, it is important to understand the role that the governor was given with in the Constitution's design as well as the precise authorities that the office of governors and the lieutenant governor have been assigned (Diksha Munjal, 2022).

Need for Reforms

"The Administrative Reforms Commission in 1968, the Rajamannar Committee in 1969, the Committee of Governors in 1971, the Bangalore Seminar of Experts in 1983, and finally, the Sarkaria

Commission in 1988 all made notable and sincere efforts" to acknowledge the role of the governor in our federal democratic system and to offer recommendations on how to make this institution amenable to promoting positive centre-state relations (Rakhahari Chatterji, 2020).

The "Sarkaria Commission (1988) pointed out the three main facets of the Governor's role". They are: "(a) as the constitutional head of the State operating normally under a system of Parliamentary democracy; (b) as a vital link between the Union Government and the State Government; and (c) as an agent of the Union Government in a few specific areas during normal times [e.g. Article 239(2)] and in several areas during abnormal situations [e.g. Article 356(1)]" (Justice Shri R.S. Sarkaria, 2001: para 13).

In terms of the "appointment, this Commission was opposed to the idea of selecting a governor from a shortlist of candidates placed out by the state. Furthermore, it promoted greater involvement from the Chief Minister and the state government." The Centre's current practice of unilaterally selecting Governors in various states is said to have contributed to the growing mistrust between these two constitutional officials (Agnidipto Tarafder & Avantik Tamta, 2017: 133-134). Sarkaria Commission (1988) felt that a candidate for governor must fulfil the following criteria: "(i) He should be eminent in some walk of life; (ii) He should be a person from outside the state; (iii) He should be a detached figure and not too intimately connected with the local politics of the State; and (iv) He should be a person who has not taken too great a part in politics generally, and particularly in the recent past" (Sarkaria Commission, 1988: 135).

The "Sarkaria Commission (1988)" also proposed that "(a) the appointment of the Governor should be entrusted to a committee comprising the Prime Minister of India, Union Minister for Home Affairs, the Speaker of the Lok Sabha and the Chief Minister of the concerned State; (b) the term of office should be fixed to five years; (c) the provision that the Governor holds office "during the pleasure of the President" be deleted; (d) provision be made for the impeachment of the Governor by the State Legislature on the same lines as the impeachment of the President by the Parliament" (Justice Shri R.S. Sarkaria, 2001: para 26).

As if now, "the State Legislature" is not allowed to remove "the Governor" through impeachment. If the Governor behaves improperly or takes actions that, in the State Legislature's opinion, are contrary to the "interests of the people of the State", the only option is to file a complaint with the President (Justice Shri R.S. Sarkaria, 2001: para 6). The "Sarkaria Commission (1988) suggested that governors" only be dismissed in exceptional and convincing situations. This was meant to give Governors some tenure security, allowing them to perform "their duties without fear or favour". The Commission said that the removal process must provide the Governors an opportunity to defend their choices and that the federal government must carefully consider their viewpoints if such extraordinary and powerful circumstances exist (Anviti Chaturvedi, 2014).

The "Punchhi Commission (2010)" proposed abolishing "the term during the pleasure of the President from the Constitution because a governor should be removed by a decision of the state legislature" rather than at the whim of the federal government (Anviti Chaturvedi, 2014). The Commission has proposed "localising emergency provisions" "under Article 356 by suggesting that localised area can be defined as a district or a certain part of a district should be brought under the ambit of the Governor's rule rather than the whole state. They recommended that even such provision should not be of duration of more than three months" (Utkarsh Jain and Bhavya Sharma, 2017).

The Sarkaria and Punchhi Commission also discussed the governor's role in educational institutions. Both Commissions stated that, when performing his or her statutory obligations, the Governor is not contractually obligated to consider the suggestions and guidance of the "Council of Ministers". However, it may be useful for "the Governor" to communicate with the concerned Minister. The Punchhi Commission stated that the Governor's role as Chancellor could lead to arguments or public criticism. As a practical matter, the Constitution should be the only instrument that guarantees the Governor's authority (Rajat Asthana, 2022). The "National Commission to Review the Working of the Constitution (2002)" advised attempting to make the governor's term, which is "five years, a fixed tenure" and removing the phrase "during the pleasure of the president" from the "governor's term of office". The NCRWC also recommended introducing a provision in the Constitution allowing the state legislature to dismiss the governor, as much as how parliament eliminates the president (Venkatesan, V., 2021).

Even though the initial text of the "constitution provided for either direct election or appointment of the governor (Article 131 of the document, which would later become Article 155), the Constituent Assembly chose a third option for the appointment of the governor by the president to avoid a dispute with the elected government". Snehil Kunwar Singh (2022) states that the Governor's office was purposefully chosen by the Constitution's framers and in this respect, it carries much political significance. Even if this has changed over the past 75 years as a result of the evolution of regional political parties, coalition governments and due to their changing legislative experience, certain checks on the legislature are still necessary too. This is because the legislature occasionally tends to adopt legislation that may not be in the state's best interests causing difference of opinion between the state government and the governor.

In the context of the current constitutional environment, the Governor is required to act by constitutional morality by imbibing the spirit of "federalism" and "democracy", which are "the basic features of the Constitution. In Government of NCT of Delhi *versus* Union of India (2018), then-Chief Justice of India Dipak Misra highlighted that democracy requires the continuous acceptance of constitutional morality. He also clearly stated that democracy and federalism are deeply rooted in India's constitutional ideology" (Anmolam, 2019).

The function of Governors and Lieutenant Governors has grown in importance as the country focuses "on cooperative and competitive federalism for national progress. The function of the Governor is not confined to the safeguarding and maintenance of the Constitution, but he is committed to maintaining consistency in the service and welfare of the people of their states". Using the constitutional authority granted to them, governors can provide the necessary direction to these populations, who have lagged behind in development (The Hans India, 2019).

Conclusion

The office of the Governor was specifically chosen by the Constitution's framers considering its significance as a channel of communication between the centre and the states. Though the post was constitutionally conceived to make the centre-state relations cooperative and cordial, it became a reason for rising hostility "between the central and state governments". Controversies and debates on the mode of appointment and powers of governors are as old as the republic itself. States often consider the "exercise of discretionary powers" by the governors as an encroachment into their administrative jurisdiction. In reality, disagreements between the governor and the state government frequently arise because there are no clear rules or laws specifying how the governor should behave. When the parties in "power in the state and at the centre" are political rivals, there is an especially strong feeling that the governor is a political appointee and is committed to follow the central government. In recent past, especially after the NDA came into power in 2014, the political debates and controversies surrounding the office of governor got intensified. The general mistrust and difference of opinion between central government and the state governments ruled by opposition or regional parties also got reflected in the relationship between the governors and respective "state governments: West Bengal, Maharashtra, Tamil Nadu and Telangana" have questioned the role of the governor in appointing the Vice-chancellors in state universities. Recently, West Bengal Chief Minister appointed Vice-Chancellor at State Universities according to the state enactments. All these events points to the immediate need to redefine the role of the governor in accordance with the changing circumstances.

None of the central governments including the current one has made any efforts to implement the recommendations made by "the committees and commissions" for redefining the office of the governor to suit the dynamics and requirements of the federal polity. The NDA is reluctant to initiate any steps in this regard despite enjoying majority in both the houses of the parliament and though it had vehemently demanded the implementation of these recommendations when it was in the opposition. Governments may be showing hesitation to enforce the suggestions knowing the fact that any change in the powers of the governor will result in a shift in the power "balance between the centre and the states". Whatever the case, it is undeniably true that the astute and responsible recommendations made by the committees and commissions looking into centre-state relations have raised public awareness of the various wrong doings of the centre through the "office of the governor" and shaped public opinion regarding them, which has proven detrimental for India's essential federal structure. In the long run, it is better for the nation to accept "such public opinion and allow the governor act on his wisdom and sound judgement rather than using the governor's office as a tool to control state politics by capitalising on his tenurial insecurity, party loyalty, or convincing to his ambition. It remains to be seen if informed public opinion would be able to organise itself to have a desirable impact" on the current political situation.

REFERENCES

Abhilash, M.R. (2022). "The office of the Governor". *The Hindu*. 9th March. https://www.thehindu.com/thread/law/the-office-of-the-governor/article65204517.ece

Administrative Reforms Commission (1968). *Report of the study team: Centre state relationships*. Delhi, India: Manager of Publications.

Advocatespedia, (2022). *Critical Overview on the role of Governor in India*. 21st June. https://advocatespedia.com/Critical_Overview_on_the_role_of_Governor_In_India#cite_note-1

Agnidipto Tarafder & Avantik Tamta (2017). Reassessing the Role of the Rajpramukh: An analysis of the continuing relevance of the Governor's position. NUJS Law Review.http://nujslawreview.org/wp-content/uploads/2017/06/10-2-Agnidipto-Tarafder-Avantik-Tamta-%E2%80%93-Reassessing-the-Role-of-the-Rajpramukh_-An-Analysis-of-the-Continuing-Relevance-of-the-Governors-Position.pdf

Aishwarya Sandeep (2021). *Role of Governor in Federal Structure*. 1st July. https://aishwaryasandeep.com/2021/07/01/role-of-governor/

Anmolam (2019). "Gubernatorial impropriety". *The Hindu*. 11th April. https://www.thehindu.com/opinion/op-ed/gubernatorial-impropriety/article26798817.ece

Anushree (2022). "Cooperative Federalism. Governing the Governors". *Frontline*. 25th August. https://frontline.thehindu.com/cover-story/article24440645.ece

Ashok Pankaj (2017). "Governor in Indian Federalism—II: Hiatus between Constitutional Intents and Practices". *Indian Journal of Public Administration, 63* (1), pp. 13-40. https://journals.sagepub.com/doi/full/10.1177/0019556117689850. https://doi.org/10.1177/0019556117689850

Anviti Chaturvedi, (2014). "Removal of Governors: What does the law say?" *PRS*. 19th June. https://prsindia.org/theprsblog/removal-of-governors-what-does-the-law-say

Dalip Singh (1968). "The Role of the Governor under the Constitution and the Working of Coalition Governments". *The Indian Journal of Political Science, 29*(1), 51-61. doi:10.2307/41854247

Diksha Munjal (2022). "Explained | The office of the Governor: its origins, powers, and controversies". *The Hindu*. 21st September. https://www.thehindu.com/news/national/federalism-the-office-of-the-governor-in-india/article65882166.ece

Dole, N.Y. (1961). "The Position of the Chancellor-Governor in India". *The Indian Journal of Political Science, 22*(4), 377-382. doi:10.2307/41853904 , https://www.jstor.org/stable/41853904

Douglas, V. Verney (1985). "Role of Governor in India's "Administrative Federalism": A Comparative Perspective". *Indian Journal of Public Administration, 31* (4). https://journals.sagepub.com/doi/pdf/10.1177/0019556119850405

Douglas, V. Verney (1997). "Role of Governor in India's "Administrative Federalism: A Comparative Perspective". In Verinder Grover (Ed). *Political Process, Government Structure and Administration*. New Delhi: Deep and Deep Publications, p. 365.

Hindustan Times (2010). Practice of dismissing Governors started in 1977. 7th May. https://www.hindustantimes.com/delhi/practice-of-dismissing-governors-started-in-1977/story-OWzv1wYOmQxTKmgHPVOZqL.html

Jagannathan, R. (2014). Changing UPA's governors: Why Tharoor is only half-right. First Post, 18th June. https://www.firstpost.com/politics/changing-upas-governors-tharoor-half-right-1576401.html

Jayaprakash Narayan (2017). Reimagining Governor's Institution and Federalism. *Indian Journal of Public Administration, 63*(3), 418-430. doi:10.1177/0019556117720612

Journals of India (2021). "Governor's Role, Controversies and Reforms". 21st June. https://journalsofindia.com/governors-role-controversies-and-reforms/

Journal of India (2022). "Tussle over role of the Governor in recent times". 23rd June. https://journalsofindia.com/tussle-over-role-of-the-governor-in-recent-times/

Justice Shri R.S. Sarkaria (2001). A Consultation Paper on "The Institution of Governor under the Constitution". *National Commission to Review the Working of The Constitution*. https://legalaffairs.gov.in/sites/default/files/The%20Institution%20of%20Governor%20under%20the%20Constitution.pdf

Mamata Sawakar (2019). "The Role of Governor: Constitutional Position and Functions". *JETIR,* November 2019, 6 (11). https://www.jetir.org/papers/JETIR1907P05.pdf

Mohan Singh Saggu (2021). *Dynamics of the Institution of Governor in India.* New Delhi: K.K. Publications.

Mansi Jaiswal (2018). Here's a timeline of controversial decisions by 'Honourable Governors'. *Business Standard,* 21st May, https://www.business-standard.com/article/politics/here-s-a-timeline-of-controversial-decisions-by-honourable-governors-118052100857_1.html

Nawal Kishore Pd. Sinha (1962). "Governors' Functions as the Chancellor of the Universities: A Case Study in Bihar during the Period 1952-60". *The Indian Journal of Political Science, 23* (1/4). January-December, https://ur.booksc.me/book/28658771/83964e

Patil, S.H. (2016). *The Governor. The Constitution, Government and Politics in India.* New Delhi: Vikas Publishing House, p. 276.

Rahul Shrivastava (2016). Arunachal Pradesh Governor Jyoti Prasad Rajkhowa Sacked. *NDTV.* 12th September. https://www.ndtv.com/india-news/jyoti-prasad-rajkhowa-removed-as-arunachal-pradesh-governor-report-1457717

Rajat Asthana (2022). "Explained: Role of Governor in Public Universities. States and State Legislatures". *PRS.* 13th June. https://prsindia.org/theprsblog/removal-of-governors-what-does-the-law-say

Rajeev Dhawan (1989). "Power without Responsibility". *Express Magazine,* New Delhi, 15th January.

Rajesh Ramachandran (2014). "Why the post of governors should be abolished". *The Economic Times,* 19th June. https://economictimes.indiatimes.com/news/politics-and-nation/why-the-post-of-governors-should-be-abolished/articleshow/36787130.cms

Rakhahari Chatterji (2020). "Recurring controversy about Governor's role in state politics". *ORF.* https://www.orfonline.org/expert-speak/recurring-controversy-governor-role-state-politics-67433/

Ramesh Kumar Arora and Rajni Goyal (2005). "The Governor: Constitutional Position and Political Reality". *Indian Public Administration: Institutions and Issues.* New Delhi: Wishwa Prakashan, p. 191.

Sarkaria Commission (1988). *Report of the Commission on Centre-state Relations,* part I. Nasik, India: Government of India Press.

Snehil Kunwar Singh (2022). "Reforming the Office of the Governor". *Deccan Herald,* 24th March. https://www.deccanherald.com/opinion/in-perspective/reforming-the-office-of-the-governor-1094068.html

Sibranjan Chatterjee (1971). "The Role of Governor in Indian Politics Since 1967". *The Indian Journal of Political Science, 32*(4). https://www.jstor.org/stable/41854471

Singh, K.P. (1965). "The Governor in the Constituent Assembly". *The Indian Journal of Political Science, 26* (4). October-December, pp. 39-40. https://www.jstor.org/stable/41854120

Sourav Roy Barman, Shaju Philip (2021). "Kerala row and beyond: Governor's role in state, central universities". *The Indian Express.* 13th December. https://indianexpress.com/article/explained/explained-kerala-row-governors-role-in-universities-7669572/

Sourav Roy Barman (2022). "Explained: Bengal passes Bill replacing Governor with CM as State University Chancellor. What are the constitutional and political issues here?" *The Indian Express.* 14th June. https://indianexpress.com/article/explained/explained-bengal-bill-governor-cm-state-university-chancellor-constitutional-political-issues-7969628/

Sudhanshu Tripathi (2008). "Indian Federalism at Work: Role of Governor". *Indian Journal of Public Administration, 54*(1). https://doi.org/10.1177/0019556120080105

Supreme Court of India (2010). "B.P. Singhal *vs.* Union of India and Another". *Casemine.* 7th May. https://www.casemine.com/judgement/in/5609aeede4b01497114152e5

Thandavan, R. (1986). "Governor-Chancellor: Trends and Issues". *The Indian Journal of Political Science, 47*(1), 76-86. doi:10.2307/41855218 , https://www.jstor.org/stable/41855218

The Hans India, (2019). *Role of Governors important in cooperative federalism: President Ram Nath Kovind.* 24th November. https://www.thehansindia.com/news/national/role-of-governors-important-in-cooperative-federalism-president-ram-nath-kovind-583966

The Hindu (2014). "The story behind Kamla Beniwal's dismissal". 8th August. https://www.thehindu.com/news/national/The-story-behind-Kamla-Beniwal%E2%80%99s-dismissal/article60385221.ece

The Hindu (2014a). "Timeline: Dismissal of State Governors since 1967". 8th August, https://www.thehindu.com/news/national/Timeline-Dismissal-of-State-Governors-since-1967/article60385227.ecehttps://www.thehindu.com/news/national/Timeline-Dismissal-of-State-Governors-since-1967/article60385227.ece

The Tribune (2016). "Revisiting Past Elections". October 30, 2016, https://www.tribuneindia.com/news/archive/features/revisiting-past-elections-316070

Utkarsh Jain and Bhavya Sharma, (2017). *Article 356: Emergency Or Tyranny?* The Law Brigade Publishers. 21st April, https://thelawbrigade.com/constitutional-law/article-356-emergency-or-tyranny/

Venkatesan, V. (2021). "Kiran Bedi's Sudden Removal as Lieutenant Governor Smacks of Arbitrariness". *The Wire.* 17th February. https://thewire.in/law/kiran-bedi-sudden-removal-puducherry-lieutenant-governor-arbitrariness-centre

Venkatesh, M.R. (2002). "Tamil Nadu government seeks right to pick vice-chancellors". *The Telegraph Online*, 27th April. https://www.telegraphindia.com/india/tamil-nadu-assembly-passes-two-bills-to-take-away-governors-powers-to-pick-vcs/cid/1862428

13

Trust Deficit in Centre-State Relations

Impact of Pandemic on Fiscal Federalism in India

Biju Lekshmanan

Fiscal Federalism and its Crisis in India

Fiscal federalism is the "economic counterpart of political federalism" (Rangarajan, 2018). It is concerned with appropriate assignment of functions and fiscal instruments to different levels of government in a way to enable them to carry out their functions. Maintaining appropriate balance between the Centre and the states in a federation is a difficult task (Bagchi, 2003). India being a quasi-federal State has centralizing tendency is imminent in the political administration. This tendency of political centralization has spillover effects on its economic counterpart. However, the call for more autonomy to states in administrative and economic fronts has been creating tensions in the Centre-State relations. Creation of NITI Aayog replacing Planning Commission, introduction of Goods and Services Tax (GST) and the proposal for increasing devolution to states by 14th Finance Commission were three important landmarks in redefining fiscal federalism in India. These reforms aimed to ensure increased states' participation in decision making in fiscal matters and give more fiscal autonomy to states. However, these developments were also criticized for creating imbalances in fiscal capacity of states and even termed as encroachment of federal government to the fiscal spaces of its units.

Coalition politics and changing political nature of federalism in India have been creating a trust deficit in federalism as a whole, especially in administrative, developmental and political matters between the Centre and the states where opposition parties are in power. These events have spillover effects on fiscal federalism. Some states even accuse Union Government over uneven allocation of disaster relief fund. The most visible point of tension in fiscal federalism is in the matter of devolution of divisible funds to states. Former Karnataka Minister Krishna Byra Gowda argued that the actual devolution was 14 per cent less than the increased projection of 14th Finance Commission (Gowda, 2020). He also criticized the GST regime for constraining states' ability to expand revenue. Union's repeated imposition of cessses and surcharges instead of taxes is unfavourable to states' fiscal capability as it reduces their divisible pools (Gowda, 2020). Prescription of some unprecedented Terms of References (ToR) for 15th Finance Commission also criticized as Centre's onslaught to the fiscal spaces of the states (Ghosh, 2020). The ToR 5 on the examination of revenue deficit grants to the states and ToR 7 on the control of populist measures of state governments created significant concerns over the fiscal federalism in India (XV Finance Commission, 2019). States' increasing major expenditure responsibilities coupled with the lack of fiscal autonomy on par with the new social responsibilities made federal relations in peril.

Ideological and political questions on issues of parameters of economic development was also a point of cleavage between the Centre and states on fiscal matters. There are people who wish that any public investment in health and education to be counted exclusively as capital expenditure on the ground that it contributes to the human resource development. But it cannot be fitted into a uniform national accounting. Hence, some people argue for autonomy of states as self-sustaining economies in which parallel ideas of economic development have reasonable space. Fiscal Responsibility and Budget Management Act shrinks scope for such parallel ideas on economic development.

However, some scholarships has led many observers skeptical about the decentralized fiscal powers to sub-national units (Sinha, 2005). They argue that a centralized economy rather than fragmented sub-national economy is better equipped with the potential capabilities for economic growth in a globalized world. Rangarajan (2018) also alludes to the other perspectives on the debate on fiscal federalism in India. He writes:

> It is true that centrally sponsored schemes which have ballooned in recent years and may have 'encroached' on the territory of states. But over years, the performance of central government is judged not only on the basis of actions taken which fall strictly in its jurisdiction, but also no initiative undertaken in areas which fall in concurrent and even state lists. (pp. vi-vii)

It is important to make sure that the demand for more fiscal autonomy should not end up in fragmenting economies into parochial units. Landmark developments such as NITI Aayog and GST helped to leverage the idea of cooperative and competitive federalism. Attracting Foreign Direct Investments, ease of doing business, unified, simple and rational tax system etc. demand tinge of centralization in fiscal matters. However, these are not sufficient conditions to monopolize fiscal matters in favour of the Union Government.

Pandemic and Trust Deficit in Centre-State Relations

Disasters helped to scientise states (Visvanathan, 2020). Events of emergencies, even in a democracy justify the concentration of power in the hands of a decision maker who is obliged to immediately respond to the crisis. Visvanathan (2020) writes, "The Bengal famine helped internalize the logic of planning, the scientisation of governance. Even later, in the case of emergency at the Bhopal disaster, science added to the legitimacy of state" (p. 31). Hence, the disaster itself provides rationale for monopolizing decision making power in a single authority for efficient management of the crisis. Centralized decision making helps for swift response in a state of exception. A quasi-federal State like India is constitutionally flexible for centralized administration while responding to unforeseen events. Centralized instruction has some basis of law in India (Biswas & Mohanka, 2020). Article 256 of the Constitution of India mandates states to act in conformity with the Centre's direction to implement laws made by the Parliament. The Central Government also recourse to Epidemic Act of 1897 and

Disaster Management Act of 2005 during the pandemic. Hence in a state of exception federal units in India are legally subordinate to the Union Government. Crisis of COVID-19 in its initial phase created no obstacle to this legal subordination as the states voluntarily cooperated with the Centre despite political differences. However, Centre's apathy to take proactive initiatives to manage the consequences of its own strategic decision to contain the pandemic has created tussle with states. The effects of pandemic were visible on legislative, executive and financial federalism in India (Agrawal, 2020). This was more evident in tensions in fiscal relations between the Centre and the States particularly during the debate on GST compensation.

The fiscal crisis in federal relations during the pandemic is not an exclusive issue in India. A study on Organization for Economic Cooperation and Development (OECD) countries shows that the outbreak of COVID-19 made the sub-national governments vulnerable (OECD, 2020). The OECD study (2020) was based on the Forman, Dougherty and Blochliger framework formulated from the experiences of economic crisis in 2008-09. The following figure linking the pandemic to typical policy recommendations on fiscal federalism in OECD countries alludes to the asymmetric impacts, costs and losses on the federal units.

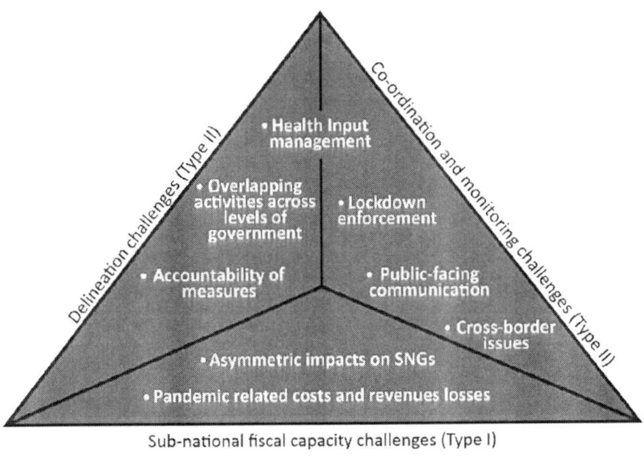

Source: https://www.oecd.org/coronavirus/policy-responses/covid-19-and-fiscal-relations-across-levels-of-government-ab438b9f/

The burden of essential services were imposed upon the states since the outbreak of COVID-19 in India as well. Health, social protection, safety, welfare of vulnerable sections, public order etc. became the immediate responsibilities of the states. The horizontal imbalances in the fiscal and social capabilities of states reflected in outcomes of their responses to the pandemic. But the vertical imbalances in the fiscal capacity of governments of different level led to the serious debates on fiscal autonomy of sub-national units. But the crisis of fiscal federalism was not a creation of the pandemic. But the social and economic challenges posed by the pandemic created severe trust deficit in the federal relations.

The trust deficit in federal relation between the Centre and States became apparent when the issue of GST compensation became a matter of tussle. Fiscal burden arose out of the tax shortfall was passed on to the states (Aiyer, 2020). The Centre expressed unwillingness to comply with its constitutional duty to compensate the revenue loss of states during the pandemic crisis created gap in a viable fiscal relation between the two. The "act of God" arguments were not sufficient to address the deficit in trust by the fiscally damaged states towards the Union Government. It may seem paradoxical that while residuary powers are constitutionally given to the Union Government, state governments disproportionately bear the residuary liabilities arise out of unforeseen events. The "act of God" argument is not on par with the political and fiscal privileges of the Union Government in the pre-COVID world. Centre has the moral as well as legal obligations towards the states to compensate their revenue deficit (Guru, 2020). Centre's unilateral decision to suspend MPLAD scheme for two years also made states suspicious about the Centre's apathy to take proactive fiscal responsibilities to respond to the unforeseen crisis.

Some states also complain that they were not properly consulted before the national lockdown is declared and therefore, they could not prepare to address the severe fiscal crisis immediately resulted from the pandemic and lockdown. Some accused that the celebrated federal body of NITI Aayog—the GST Council was sidelined when important decisions on matters affecting the fiscal federalism were taken. The matters affecting the fiscal federalism were arbitrarily decided by the Centre outside the Council. Country's lack of preparedness to manage the crisis of reverse migration was another matter which created trust deficit in the Centre-States relation. Lack of unified national strategy to address the issue of migrants during COVID-19 crisis and the reverse migration made states further vulnerable.

States like Kerala, Punjab, Rajasthan etc. were raising concerns over the crisis of economic federalism in a post-pandemic India. Kerala's Finance Minister Thomas Isaac accused the Centre for its arbitrariness in decision making (Jigeesh, 2020). Isaac also highlighted the need for an alternative approach when annual budgets become irrelevant. The state of Kerala is also critical of the present state of fiscal federalism in India. Fiscal Responsibility and Budget Management (FRBM) Act is another point of tussle. They argue that "FRBM severely curtails the states' fiscal space" (Jigeesh, 2020). Similarly, "Centre has veto power in GST Council" (Jigeesh, 2020). Horizontally diversified challenges of states is also a justification for fiscal federalism in favour of state economies. For instance, Kerala has the unique challenge of accommodating repatriates from Middle Eastern countries coupled with the contraction of economy which may severely affect the fiscal capacity of the state in the post-COVID period.

Pandemic also raises some future concerns for those who demand fiscal autonomy to federal units in India. Biswas and Mohanka (2020) argue that the coming danger of food security crisis and unemployment rates coupled with severe contraction of economy demands a paradigm shift in fiscal federalism. An outcome oriented approach is also need of the time. Some argue that in order to address the social and welfare needs of the economy states need to be self-sustaining economies (Khosla, 2020). They need justiciable Directive Principles of State Policies as precondition to address the social and welfare needs. Khosla (2020) writes, "Our macro-economy needs to be reassembled into a federal cluster of 28 independent and state economies." Learning from EU model also suggests that federal governments should confine its role into mere facilitator in economic matters. Union's repeated imposition of cessses and surcharges instead of taxes and the possibility of decline in Central grants are also a matter of serious concern in a post-pandemic India (Gowda, 2020).

States also fear a debt crisis in future if Union Government refuse to take responsible initiative to meet unforeseen socio-economic and welfare requirements in the post-pandemic world. Gowda (2020) writes, "The systemic weakening of states saves neither federalism nor national interest." Hence, the redefining of fiscal relations between the Centre and the State governments and enhancing the fiscal autonomy of states are the necessary strategies to address the unprecedented socio-economic needs of the post-pandemic world. Building of trust between the Union Government and its units is the necessary precondition for the redefinition of fiscal federalism in India.

Beyond Fiscal Federalism

Can fiscally autonomous states address the socio-economic crisis in the post-pandemic India alone? The immediate responsibilities to address the pandemic crisis at the ground level was vested upon the local governments. Sanitation, contact tracing, community kitchen, awareness generation etc. were the duties of the local governments. This made visible the fiscal vulnerabilities of institutions of local governance to meet the unforeseen necessities. States like Kerala where the grassroots governance system is strong succeeded in effectively managing the local social and welfare needs. But there too fiscal vulnerabilities were hurdle for the effective working of the local governments. Decentralization of fiscal capacity to the grassroots is highlighted as a viable solution to the future challenges in the post-pandemic India. However, the demand for decentralization of fiscal capacities to local level also was not the creation of pandemic.

"One of the major shortcomings of Indian federalism is that failure to decentralize below the state level" (Rao, 2018: 13). Everyone wants power devolution and decentralization up to their level. Inability to decentralize sub-state level is a serious concern in debates on Indian federalism (Rao, 2018). Hence demand for financial autonomy to local governments (Biswas & Mohanka, 2020). Khosla (2020) has come to the forefront again. The emerging challenges in the management of disasters in India raises debate on the necessity of strengthening the capacity of local government institutions. Risks associated with climate change, urban floods, droughts, waste management, deteriorating water quality, air pollution etc. are serious matters of concern which demand the capacity building, and building the physical and social infrastructure at local level. These future threats also substantiate the rationale for more fiscal autonomy to the local level governments.

The experience of Kerala where the local governments played a robust role in the fight against the pandemic alludes to the necessary and efficient role of grassroots governance and physical and social capacities at local level in facing the unprecedented challenges during the sudden outbreak of unforeseen events. From this experience, Kerala's Chief Minister Pinarayi Vijayan (2020) suggested that the empowered states and local governments can be equal partners with the Union Government in a cooperative federal set up. Only they together can ensure the social security in the future (Vijayan, 2020). Hence, the Union, states and local governments need to cooperate to address the socio-economic needs in the post-pandemic India. Horizontal as well as vertical distribution of fiscal capacities at different levels of governments is the precondition for the robust cooperation.

Conclusion

The pandemic had severely damaged the fiscal capacity of both the Union and State governments. Already existing vertical imbalances in fiscal capacities at different levels of governments made the fiscal autonomy of states in peril, though the crisis of fiscal federalism is not a creation of the pandemic. Centre's refusal to compensate revenue deficit, temporary suspension of MPLAD scheme, crisis of reverse migration, lack of consultation with states on fiscal matters etc. created platform for tussle between the Centre and States and consequently resulted in a trust deficit in fiscal federalism in India. Centre's refusal to face the financial consequences of its own strategic decisions challenged the moral and political foundations of federalism. However, pandemic gives more rationale for enhancing the fiscal autonomy to states. It also gives a unique opportunity to states to consolidate and raise their call to redefine fiscal federal relationship in favour of the federal units. Moreover, the decentralized fiscal capacities and strengthening of social and physical capabilities of local government institutions can be the long term strategy to address the challenges posed by unforeseen events in the future.

REFERENCES

Agrawal, P. (2020, June 27-July 4). "COVID-19 and Dwindling Indian Federalism". *Economic and Political Weekly, LV*(26 & 27), 16-19.

Aiyer, Y. (2020, July 23). "COVID: The State-citizen Trust Deficit". *Hindustan Times*. Retrieved November 4, 2020, from https://m.hindustantimes.com/columns/covid-the-state-citizen-trust-deficit/story-uAmoX3ZXtnJPsbChEjNcIN_amp.html

Bagchi, A. (2003). "Rethinking Federalism: Changing Power Relations between the Centre and the States". *The Journal of Federalism*, 21-42.

Biswas, R.R. & Mohanka, M. (2020, July 03). "Lockdown: How We Pay for Centre-States Trust Deficit". *Rediff News*. Retrieved October 30, 2020, from http://m.rediff.com/amp/news/colum/lockdown-on-how-we-pay-for-centre-states-trust-deficit-/20200703.htm

Ghosh, K.S. (2020, May 25). "Erosion of Fiscal Federalism in the Times of Covid-19". *The Hindu Business Line*. Retrieved November 3, 2020, from https://www.thehindubusinessline.com/opinion/erosion-of-fiscal-federalism-in-the-times-of-covid-19/article31670568.ece/amp/

Gowda, K.B. (2020, Novemeber 5). "The Financial Capacity of States is being Weakened". *The Hindu*.

Guru, G. (2020, September 19). "The Impasse over GST Compensation" (Editorial). *Economic and Political Weekly, LV*(38), 8.

Jigeesh, A. (2020, April 28). "Fiscal Federalism has collapsed: Centres Decision Arbitrary". *The Hindu Business Line*. Retrieved November 1, 2020, from https://www.thehindubusinessline.com/news/national/fiscal-federalism-has-collapsed-centres-decisions-arbitrary/article31456483.ece/amp/

Khosla, R. (2020, May 16). "In a Post-COVID-19 World, the Only Way Ahead is Economic Federalism". *The Wire*. Retrieved November 1, 2020, from https://m.thewire.in/article/political/covid-19-economic-federalism/amp

OECD (2020, July 31). "COVID-19 and Fiscal Relation across Levels of Government". *OECD*. Retrieved November 4, 2020, from https://www.oecd.org/coronavirus/policy-responses/covid-19-and-fiscal-relations-across-levels-of-government-ab438b9f/

Rangarajan, C. (2018). *Foreword*. In N.A. Khan, *Challenges and Issues in Fiscal Federalism* (pp. v-vii). Singapore: Springer.

Rao, G. (2018). "Making Federalism Work for India's Development". In N.A. Khan, *Challenges and Issues in Indian Fiscal Federalism*, pp. 9-14. Singapore: Springer.

Sinha, A. (2005). "Political Foundtions of Market-Enhancing Federalism: Theoretical Lessons from India and China". *Comparative Politics*, 337-356. Retrieved October 30, 2020, from httpps://www.jstor.org/stable/20072893

Vijayan, P. (2020, June 13). "Challeneges in the midst of the COVID-19 Pandemic". *Economic and Political Weekly, LV*(24), 11-13.

Visvanathan, S. (2020, October 17). "The COVID-19 Pandemic and Crisis of Social Science". *Economic and Political Weekly, LV*(42), 29-33.

XV Finance Commission (2019). *Report for the Year 2020-21.* Finance Commission of India. Retrieved October 27, 2020, from https://fincomindia.nic.in/showContent.aspx?uid1=3&uid2=0&uid3=0&uid4=0

14

Finances of Southern States in India

An Analysis

Jerry Alwin

Introduction

Fiscal situation of states in India is not sound. Reserve Bank of India (RBI) review on state finances indicates that during the period 2014-2019, there is a strong drive towards fiscal consolidation. Over the period the combined gross fiscal deficit (GFD) of states averaged 2.5 per cent of gross domestic product (GDP), which is in striking range of the recommendations of fiscal responsibility and budget management (FRBM) review committee. But this has been achieved by sharp retrenchment in expenditure, mainly capital expenditure which has adverse implications for economic development (RBI, 2019). In southern states there is considerable difference in the fiscal situation in terms of fiscal indicators such as revenue deficit, GFD and debt GSDP ratio. Social sector expenditure and development expenditure shows considerable variations. In this context, an attempt is made to study the finances of Southern States. Our analysis is confined to pre-pandemic period and have not examined the impact of COVID-19 on state finances. It is likely that pandemic related spending particularly on health and other support measures for households and firms are likely to keep the expenditures of the State governments high. State governments may have to face the difficult choice of putting investment projects on hold which will have adverse implications for development of Southern States.

In this chapter an attempt is made to study the finances of southern states in India such as Andhra Pradesh, Karnataka, Kerala, Tamil Nadu and Telangana during the period 2009-10 to 2019-20. The objectives of the study are: (1) to examine the fiscal performance of southern states, (2) to analyse the trends in revenue receipts, (3) to discuss the trends in revenue expenditure, and (4) to examine the trends in development and social sector expenditure. The study is based on secondary data from RBI study on state finances, other studies on state finances, budget documents of state governments etc. The study is presented in five sections, viz. a review of studies on finances of southern states, trends in fiscal performance, trends in revenue receipts, trends in revenue expenditure and expenditure on development and social sectors.

Hypothesis

To explain finances of the southern states of India, we present the following hypothesis. "Persistent high level of revenue deficit forces the states to rely heavily on borrowing to meet non-development revenue expenditure, which in turn weaken the fiscal capacity for spending on capital items, development and social sector and push the states to a fiscal crisis. Among southern states in India, Kerala, Andhra Pradesh and Tamil Nadu have been experiencing such a transition."

Review of Studies

In this section, a review of studies on the finances of southern states is attempted. In a study which evaluated the finances of Andhra Pradesh during the period 2002-2012, found that during the period 2007-2012, there was a fall in growth rate of own tax and non-tax revenues, fall in the growth rate of share in central taxes, huge increase in debt and non-debt components of capital receipts and relatively lower economic growth rate (Sreedevi, 2013). Another study evaluated fiscal management of Andhra Pradesh during the period 2014-2019. The study found that during the period revenue expenditure continued to rise unabated and borrowed funds were used to finance revenue expenditure. This substantially reduced the resource availability for capital investment and resulted in poor spending on social services (Government of Andhra Pradesh, 2019). Another study came to the conclusion that since the bifurcation of Andhra Pradesh in 2014 there is a deterioration in States finances (Sreedevi, 2019).

A study on Karnataka finances came to the conclusion that Karnataka's fiscal front changed from one of severe fiscal stress in the decade of 1990s to that of fiscal prudence following a series of fiscal reforms during the period 2002-03 to 2013-14. The state has been able to adhere to the fiscal and revenue deficit targets and also has been in a position to enhance the outlays on social sector and capital account (Gayithri, 2014). Another study came to the finding that the state of Karnataka was able to attain revenue deficit to zero by 2005 and has been able to maintain it throughout from 2011-12 to 2019-20. While maintaining fiscal prudence, the state has curtailed on capital expenditure and expenditure on social sector which has serious implications on development [National Institute of Public Finance and Policy (NIPFP)] 2020.

The important studies which examine the finances of Kerala are the following. The White Paper of 2011 on state finances presented the acute fiscal situation that prevailed in the state and the rapid rise in public debt, making Kerala a debt stressed state (GoK, 2011). Kerala Public Expenditure Review Committee (KPERC) reviewed the state finances and submitted reports for the financial years from 2004-05 to 2017-18. The Committee had examined the issues in state finances and given a number of recommendations on tax and non-tax revenue, capital and revenue expenditure, plan expenditure and debt management. The Committee had also stressed the need for curtailing non-plan revenue expenditure (KPERC). The White Paper of 2016 gives a clear picture about nature and magnitude of fiscal crisis of Kerala (GoK, 2016). The other notable studies on state finances are that of Sen (2012) and Issac Thomas and Mohan (2016). A recent study found that slump in research mobilisation, lack of periodical revision of rate of taxes and non-taxes, fall in growth of tax revenue, under performance of commercial taxes department in the collection of Sales Tax and Value Added Tax (VAT), non-realisation of additional resource mobilisation targeted in the budget, inflated plan outlays, fall in dividend and profit and inefficient and poor collection of taxes and non-tax items contributed to the fiscal crisis of Kerala on revenue side. Excessive and uncontrolled growth of non-plan revenue expenditure is the root cause of fiscal crisis on the expenditure side (Prakash and Jerry Alwin, 2018).

In a study which examines Tamil Nadu finances during the period 2002-03 to 2014-15 came to the conclusion that state fared better in the resource mobilisation. Own tax revenues of the state were high among the major states in the country. But non-tax revenues were fairly low, while the central transfers showed a decline (Shanmugan *et al.*, 2014). Another study is of the view that Tamil Nadu finances have been well managed since 2005-06. The fiscal parameters such as revenue deficit, fiscal deficit and public debt relative to gross state domestic product (GSDP) have been kept as per norms of FRBM legislations. But during last two years revenue deficit exceeded one per cent of GSDP and this is a concern since borrowed funds will be used to finance revenue expenditure (Shanmugan, 2018).

A study on Telangana state finances during the period 2014-15 to 2017-18 came to the following conclusions. The state has a high average growth rate of revenue receipts. States own tax revenue and tax collections through state goods and services tax (GST) has been highest nationwide. But growth of non-tax revenue is dismal. Committed expenditure of Telangana accounted for about 52 per cent of total revenue receipts during 2016-17 thereby restraining considerable resources for capital expenditure (Bharati Institute of Public Policy, 2018). Though Telangana is a revenue surplus state, the state has higher public debt due to ambitious capital projects. The public debt strategy of Telangana is to go for elongation of maturity structure of outstanding debt, to over 40 years which can mitigate roll over risks and debt servicing costs (NIPFP, 2019).

Trends in Fiscal Performance

This section examines the fiscal performance of southern states with the help of fiscal indicators such as revenue deficit Gross State Domestic Product (GSDP) ratio, Gross Fiscal Deficit (GFD)-GSDP ratio, primary deficit GSDP ratio, total outstanding liabilities as percentage of GSDP etc. When we examine the Revenue deficit/

surplus of southern states, we can infer that States such as Karnataka and Telengana are revenue surplus States while Andhra Pradesh, Kerala and Tamil Nadu have revenue deficit. Revenue deficit denoting the gap between revenue receipts and revenue expenditure indicates the borrowing to meet revenue deficit. High revenue deficit is an indicator of poor fiscal performance. GFD denoting the gap between total receipts (excluding borrowing) and total expenditure in the consolidated fund indicates the borrowing required to meet the deficit. States such as Andhra Pradesh and Tamil Nadu recorded higher growth of GFD during years 2018-19 to 2019-20 (Table 14.1). GFD if incurred for development or capital expenditure is a sound thing but if it is incurred for financing revenue deficit it will lead to deterioration of State finances. Persistent efforts to increase the own source revenue, *viz.* own tax revenue and non-tax revenue is also a prerequisite for improving the finances.

Table 14.1: Revenue Deficit/Surplus and Gross Fiscal Deficit of Southern States of India

Year	Andhra Pradesh	Karnataka	Kerala	Tamil Nadu	Telangana	All States
Revenue Deficit/Surplus						
2009-10	-1230	-1620	5020	3530	–	31020
2014-15	24190	-530	13800	6410	-370	45700
2019-20 (RE)	26647	-285	17474	25072	-104	136702
Gross Fiscal Deficit						
2009-10	14010	10870	7870	11810	–	188820
2014-15	31750	19580	18640	27160	9410	327190
2019-20 (RE)	40494	38752	26186	55058	21913	652375

Negative (-) sign indicates surplus.

Source: RBI, State Finances: A Study of Budgets, 2009-10 to 2020-21.

According to the fiscal rules proposed by the 14th Union Finance Commission (UFC), revenue deficit GSDP ratio should be zero per cent. Of the southern states, Kerala and Andhra Pradesh are the states with higher revenue deficit GSDP ratio exceeding 2 per cent for the years 2016-17, 2017-18 and 2019-20 (Table 14.2). One of the major reasons for the increase in revenue deficit is the underperformance of state governments in the collection of tax revenues. For the state of Andhra Pradesh owing to policy lacunae and insufficient tax effort by state government, tax buoyancy and tax collection have remained suboptimal (Government of Andhra Pradesh, 2019). Transitional changes in the implementation of GST especially the application of GST rules and rates, associated confusion and frequent changes in the design in GST by GST council have impacted revenue collection in Kerala (KPERC, 2019). The states of Andhra Pradesh and Kerala also recorded a poor collection of non-tax revenue. Tamil Nadu is another state which has revenue deficit GSDP ratio of more than one per cent since 2015-16. The reason for the rise in the revenue deficit of the State is decrease in tax revenue due to introduction of GST and impact of global slow down on regional economy. Another reason for fall in revenue receipts in the recent past is the decrease in state excise duties due to abolition of vend fees (Shanmugan, 2018). Lower growth rate of non-tax revenues in Tamil Nadu also contributed to revenue deficit.

Table 14.2: Revenue Deficit GSDP ratio of Southern States in India

Year	Andhra Pradesh	Karnataka	Kerala	Tamil Nadu	Telangana	All States
2009-10	-0.3	-0.5	2.2	0.7	–	0.5
2010-11	-0.4	-1.1	1.3	0.5	–	-0.0
2011-12	-0.5	-1.0	2.5	-0.2	–	-0.3
2012-13	-0.1	-0.4	2.7	-0.2	–	-0.2
2013-14	0.0	-0.1	2.9	0.2	–	0.1
2014-15	4.6	-0.1	2.6	0.6	-0.1	0.4
2015-16	1.2	-0.2	1.7	1.0	0.0	0.0
2016-17	2.5	-0.1	2.4	1.0	-0.2	0.2
2017-18	2.0	-0.3	2.4	1.5	-0.5	0.1
2018-19	1.6	0.0	2.2	1.4	-0.5	0.1
2019-20 (RE)	2.7	0.0	2.0	1.4	0.0	0.7

Note: GSDP (Gross State Domestic Product).
Negative (-) sign indicates surplus.
Source: Same as Table 14.1.

Another reason for high revenue deficits in these Southern States is due to higher revenue expenditure due to floods in different States, expenditure on social security and welfare, energy, interest on market loans and urban development. Factors such as farm loan waivers and pay revision also contributed to high revenue deficit GSDP ratios (RBI, 2019).

According to the targets laid down by 14th UFC GFD-GSDP ratio should be less than 3 per cent of GSDP. Andhra Pradesh had GFD-GSDP ratio of above 4 per cent since 2016-17, indicating a high rate of borrowing (Table 14.3). The Andhra Pradesh government used the borrowed funds for financing the revenue expenditure which substantially reduced the resource availability for capital investment and resulted in the abysmal state of education, health care and nutritional services (Government of Andhra Pradesh, 2019). The state of Kerala had high GFD-GSDP ratio of above 3 per cent for all years since 2011-12. This can be attributed to the use of borrowing to finance revenue expenditure on wages, salaries, pension payments and interest payments. Tamil Nadu and Karnataka are the states which have relatively lower GFD-GSDP ratio. The state of Telangana, a revenue surplus state had a very high GFD-GSDP ratio since 2015-16. But high rate of borrowings were used for schemes like Vaddi Leni Runalu (interest free loans), Rythubandhu (income support scheme for farmers), Mission Bhagiratha (comprehensive drinking water programme) and capital infrastructure projects for public irrigation (Ghosh Anindita and Lekha Chakraborty, 2019). Another reason for higher GFD-GSDP ratio for Southern States except Kerala is largely due to Ujwal Discom Assurance Yojana (UDAY). Under UDAY, 75 per cent of the outstanding debt of State owned discoms (about Rs. 2.1 lakh crore) was taken over by 15 State governments between 2015-16 and 2016-17. UDAY also required these States to fund a portion of losses of Discoms until 2019-20 (RBI, 2019). This has also led to a rise in contingent liabilities of States.

Table 14.3: Gross Fiscal Deficit GSDP ratio of Southern States in India

Year	Andhra Pradesh	Karna-taka	Kerala	Tamil Nadu	Telangana	All States
2009-10	2.9	3.2	3.4	2.5	–	2.9
2010-11	2.0	2.8	2.8	3.2	–	2.1
2011-12	2.4	2.7	4.1	2.6	–	1.9
2012-13	2.3	2.8	4.3	2.2	–	2.0
2013-14	2.1	2.8	4.3	2.4	–	2.2
2014-15	6.0	2.1	3.5	2.5	1.8	2.6
2015-16	3.6	1.9	3.2	2.8	3.3	3.1
2016-17	4.4	2.4	4.2	4.3	5.3	3.5
2017-18	4.0	2.3	3.8	2.7	3.5	2.4
2018-19	4.1	2.5	3.4	2.9	3.1	2.4
2019-20 (RE)	4.2	2.3	3.0	3.0	2.3	3.2

Note: GSDP (Gross State Domestic Product).
Source: Same as Table 14.1.

Primary deficit refers to the difference between current year's fiscal deficit and interest payment on previous borrowings. It indicates the borrowing requirements of the government excluding interest. Primary deficit GSDP ratio of Andhra Pradesh is higher than 2 per cent since 2014-15 (Table 14.4). Other Southern States have Primary Deficit GSDP between 0.8 to 1.5 per cent in the recent years.

Table 14.4: Primary Deficit GSDP ratio of Southern States in India

Year	Andhra Pradesh	Karna-taka	Kerala	Tamil Nadu	Telangana	All States
2009-10	1.1	1.6	1.1	1.1	–	1.2
2010-11	0.4	1.3	0.7	1.7	–	0.5
2011-12	0.7	1.4	2.1	1.3	–	0.4
2012-13	0.8	1.5	2.2	0.8	–	0.5
2013-14	0.6	1.5	2.2	1.0	–	0.7
2014-15	4.1	1.1	1.7	1.2	0.8	1.1
2015-16	2.0	0.8	1.2	1.3	1.9	1.5
2016-17	2.7	1.5	2.3	2.7	4.1	1.9

(*Contd.*)

Year	Andhra Pradesh	Karna-taka	Kerala	Tamil Nadu	Telangana	All States
2017-18	2.3	1.3	1.7	0.9	2.1	0.7
2018-19	2.3	1.5	1.3	1.1	1.7	0.8
2019-20 (RE)	2.5	1.2	0.9	1.3	0.8	1.5

Note: GSDP (Gross State Domestic Product).
Source: Same as Table 14.1.

Table 14.5: Decomposition of Gross Fiscal Deficit in Southern States

States	2009-10 (Accounts)				GFD
	Revenue Deficit	Capital Outlay	Net Lending	Non-Debt Capital Receipts	
Andhra Pradesh	-8.8	98.4	10.3	–	100
Karnataka	-14.9	111.7	3.96	0.64	100
Kerala	63.8	26.2	10.67	0.64	100
Tamil Nadu	29.9	72.6	-0.3	–	100
Telangana	–	–	–	–	–
All States	**16.4**	**79.02**	**4.9**	**0.43**	**100**
2018-19 (Accounts)					
Andhra Pradesh	39.22	56.4	4.42	–	100
Karnataka	-1.8	90.1	11.6	0.02	100
Kerala	64.8	27.6	7.8	0.1	100
Tamil Nadu	49.6	51.4	-0.91	–	100
Telangana	-16.1	84.03	32.1	–	100
All States	**3.8**	**95.1**	**1.2**	**0.2**	**100**

Source: Same as Table 14.1.

The decomposition of GFD gives an idea about the utilisation of borrowing for revenue and capital expenditure. In the year 2009-10, states such as Andhra Pradesh and Karnataka spent 100 per cent of their borrowing for capital expenditure while Tamil Nadu spent 73 per cent (Table 14.5). The state of Kerala performed poorly in this respect spending only 26 per cent of borrowed funds for capital expenditure. But in the year 2018-19 states such as Karnataka and

Telangana spent more than 80 per cent of the borrowed funds for capital expenditure. States such as Tamil Nadu, Kerala and Andhra Pradesh spent 51 per cent, 28 per cent and 56 per cent of borrowed funds for capital expenditure. It should be noted that Kerala spent 64 per cent of borrowing in 2009-10 and 65 per cent of borrowing in 2018-19 to finance revenue expenditure leading to meagre capital expenditure. There exists an inverse relationship between high revenue deficit and low capital expenditure. The States with high revenue deficits are forced to divert the borrowed funds for financing revenue expenditure leading to low capital expenditure.

Table 14.6: Total Outstanding Liabilities of Southern States (Rs. in Crores)

Year	Andhra Pradesh	Karna-taka	Kerala	Tamil Nadu	Telangana	All States
2009-10	123678 (25.9)	84534 (25.0)	75453 (32.5)	75453 (21.2)	–	1648648 (25.5)
2010-11	139506 (23.9)	93447 (22.8)	83963 (31.8)	83963 (19.6)	–	1828976 (23.5)
2011-12	150553 (39.7)	106089 (17.5)	94817 (26.0)	94817 (17.4)	–	1993916 (22.8)
2012-13	174259 (42.4)	112667 (16.2)	109966 (26.7)	109966 (17.9)	–	2210246 (22.2)
2013-14	196202 (42.3)	138976 (17.0)	125678 (27.0)	125678 (18.5)	–	2471263 (22.0)
2014-15	122606 (23.9)	158370 (17.4)	143557 (28.0)	143557 (17.3)	72658	2703760 (21.7)
2015-16	147935 (24.5)	185698 (17.8)	162271 (28.9)	162271 (19.4)	90523 (15.7)	3218126 (23.4)
2016-17	254283 (36.5)	211169 (17.5)	191623 (30.2)	191623 (21.8)	81821 (12.4)	3809357 (25.1)
2017-18	229334 (28.3)	245951 (18.2)	216499 (30.9)	216499 (22.3)	160296 (21.3)	4292495 (25.1)
2018-19	264451 (30.6)	286329 (18.5)	243746 (31.2)	401504 (24.6)	190203 (22.1)	4786770 (25.2)
2019-20 (RE)	309144 (31.8)	326737 (19.2)	266185 (30.5)	452845 (24.5)	219346 (22.6)	5343022 (26.3)

Figures in bracket represent total outstanding liabilities as percentage of GSDP.
Source: Same as Table 14.1.

Another indicator of fiscal performance is the total outstanding liabilities GSDP ratio or debt GSDP ratio (Table 14.6). As per the fiscal rules proposed by the 14th UFC total outstanding liabilities GSDP ratio should be below 31.34 per cent in 2015-16, 30.84 per cent in 2016-17 and 30.4 per cent in 2017-18. The state of Andhra Pradesh could not achieve the target in 2016-17. The state of Kerala also had debt GSDP ratio of 30.9 per cent in 2017-18 exceeding the targets set by 14th UFC. The states of Karnataka, Tamil Nadu and Telangana were able to achieve debt GSDP targets of 14th UFC. Outstanding liabilities of States are growing at double digits, except 2014-15. The issuance of UDAY bonds in 2016 and 2017 led to higher debt GSDP ratio. There is deterioration in deficit indicators despite the discontinuation of UDAY scheme. This is mainly due to farm loan waivers and pay revisions and also due to shortfall in revenue receipts (RBI, 2019). The share of market borrowings in the debt of States is rising and now higher than 75 per cent, while loans from banks and financial institutions stagnated, share of National Small Savings Fund (NSSF) declined, loans from centre and public account are declining and replaced by market loans. The shift in debt towards market borrowings arise due to the recommendations of 14th UFC to exclude States from NSSF financing facility. Increased financing of fiscal deficits with market borrowings has pushed up debt levels which may lead to higher debt servicing costs.

Trends in Revenue Receipts

States revenue prospects are confronted with low tax buoyancies, shrinking revenue autonomy under GST framework and unpredictability associated with transfers of IGST and grants (RBI, 2020). There was a decline in the revenue receipts GSDP ratio of Andhra Pradesh from 17.2 per cent in 2014-15 to 11.4 per cent in 2019-20 (Table 14.7). The bifurcation of Andhra Pradesh and subsequent loss of revenue and poor tax collection have contributed to this trend. We can also witness fluctuations in revenue receipts GSDP ratio of Karnataka due to decline in own tax revenue. There was a decline in revenue receipts GSDP ratio of Kerala and Tamil Nadu during 2016-17 to 2019-20. Tamil Nadu recorded lower growth of revenue receipts GSDP ratio of less than 11 per cent of GSDP from 2016-17 to 2019-20 mainly due to introduction of GST and decrease in the share of devolution. The revenue receipts GSDP ratio of Telangana was nearly 12 per cent since 2016-17, which is due to robustness of tax collection and higher devolution from the 14th UFC.

Table 14.7: Revenue Receipts of Southern States (Rs. in Crores)

Year	Andhra Pradesh	Karnataka	Kerala	Tamil Nadu	Telangana	All States
2009-10	64680 (13.6)	49160 (14.3)	26110 (11.3)	55840 (11.8)	–	768140 (11.9)
2010-11	81000 (13.8)	58210 (15.3)	30990 (11.2)	70190 (13.5)	–	935350 (12.2)
2011-12	93550 (14.3)	69810 (15.2)	38010 (12.1)	85202 (12.8)	–	1098530 (12.2)
2012-13	103830 (13.7)	78180 (15.1)	44140 (12.7)	98830 (13.3)	–	1252020 (12.5)
2013-14	110720 (12.9)	89540 (14.6)	49180 (12.4)	108040 (12.6)	–	1369190 (12.1)
2014-15	90670 (17.2)	104140 (11.3)	57950 (11.0)	122420 (11.2)	51040 (10.0)	1591580 (12.8)
2015-16	88650 (14.5)	118820 (11.7)	69030 (12.4)	129010 (11.1)	76130 (13.4)	1832880 (13.3)
2016-17	98980 (14.2)	133210 (11.8)	75610 (12.3)	140230 (10.8)	82820 (12.8)	2046400 (13.4)
2017-18	105062 (13.0)	146999 (10.9)	83020 (11.9)	146279 (10.0)	88824 (11.8)	2321241 (13.6)
2018-19	114671 (13.3)	164979 (10.7)	92855 (11.9)	173741 (10.7)	101420 (11.8)	2620353 (13.8)
2019-20 (RE)	110871 (11.4)	177256 (10.4)	99043 (11.4)	191861 (10.4)	110928 (11.4)	2939693 (14.5)

Figures in bracket represent revenue Receipts GSDP ratio.
Source: Same as Table 14.1.

The decline in tax revenues of these States is essentially associated with pending accounting issues related to GST implementation, which was partly offset by transfers from the Centre (RBI, 2019).

Table 14.8: Percentage share of taxes to States according to 13th and 14th Union Finance Commission (UFC)

States	13th UFC	14th UFC
Andhra Pradesh	6.937	4.305
Karnataka	4.328	4.713
Kerala	2.341	2.500
Tamil Nadu	4.969	4.023
Telangana	-	2.437

Source: Reports of 13th and 14th UFC.

The transfers from the Central Government for the states such as Central tax transfer and grant-in-aid plays an important role in finances of state governments. These transfers are determined by the recommendations of successive finance commissions. As per the recommendations of 14th UFC, the state's share in net proceeds of Union tax revenues would be 42 per cent when compared to 32 per cent as recommended by 13th UFC. An attempt is made to examine the percentage share of taxes to states according to 13th UFC and 14th UFC (Table 14.8). From the table we can infer that the percentage share of states such as Karnataka and Kerala rose during 14th UFC when compared to 13th UFC.

A State-wise Analysis of Revenue Receipts

In this section an attempt is made to examine state-wise analysis of revenue receipts.

Table 14.9: Growth Rate of Revenue Receipts of Andhra Pradesh (%)

Year	Own taxes	Non-tax revenue	Central tax transfer	Grant-in-aid	Total revenue receipts
2009-10	–	–	–	–	–
2010-11	28.33	37.38	25.49	3.59	25.23
2011-12	18.04	9.09	16.49	9.34	15.49
2012-13	12.37	36.81	14.19	29.01	10.99
2013-14	7.09	-3.29	9.19	16.99	6.64
2014-15	-33.53	-29.06	-30.87	142.23	-18.11

(*Contd.*)

Year	Own taxes	Non-tax revenue	Central tax transfer	Grant-in-aid	Total revenue receipts
2015-16	-6.36	-55.17	43.11	0.68	-2.23
2016-17	10.71	5.53	20.10	6.47	11.65
2017-18	18.64	-26.5	-0.72	-2.51	6.14
2018-19	11.94	15.26	23.27	-14.52	9.15
2019-20 (RE)	-2.13	-24.39	-12.13	12.43	-3.31

Source: Computed from "State Finances: A Study of Budgets, 2009-10 to 2020-21".

Revenue receipts GSDP of Andhra Pradesh which was more than 14 per cent till 2016-17 declined in the later years (Table 14.9). The growth rate of revenue receipts was negative during the years 2014-15 and 2015-16 due to revenue loss following bifurcation of Andhra Pradesh (Table 14.9). During the year 2019-20, the growth rate of own taxes was negative. This may be due to issues related to implementation of GST. Another item of revenue receipts, own non-tax revenue GSDP ratio of Andhra Pradesh declined from 2.1 per cent in 2014-15 to 0.3 per cent in 2019-20. This is due to poor collection of non-tax revenue. The states collection of non-tax revenue on per capita basis is also one of the lowest for the country (Government of Andhra Pradesh, 2019). Due to bifurcation of Andhra Pradesh, the percentage share of taxes devolved declined from 6.937 during 13th UFC to 4.305 in 14th UFC. This has led to reduction in the Central transfers and grant-in-aid and these two items recorded negative growth rate in 2017-18 (Table 14.9).

Table 14.10: Growth Rate of Revenue Receipts of Karnataka (%)

Year	Own taxes	Non-tax revenue	Central tax transfer	Grant-in-aid	Total revenue receipts
2009-10	–	–	–	–	–
2010-11	25.82	0.72	29.16	-12.86	18.41
2011-12	20.81	21.71	16.51	18.91	19.93
2012-13	15.66	-2.96	14.19	-4.39	11.99

(*Contd.*)

Year	Own taxes	Non-tax revenue	Central tax transfer	Grant-in-aid	Total revenue receipts
2013-14	16.85	1.66	9.18	16.52	14.53
2014-15	12.10	16.27	6.12	60.67	16.31
2015-16	7.65	14.23	63.66	-4.72	14.09
2016-17	9.80	8.22	19.92	12.74	12.11
2017-18	8.89	11.75	-1.05	37.81	10.35
2018-19	7.97	4.59	23.26	17.74	12.23
2019-20 (RE)	4.31	10.84	-12.13	45.55	7.44

Source: Same as Table 14.9.

An examination of the growth rate of total revenue receipts of Karnataka indicates that revenue receipts was higher than 12 per cent for most of the years. But the growth rate of own revenue was less than 10 per cent for the period 2015-16 to 2019-20. The decline in own tax revenue during this period can be attributed to tax reforms brought in through the implementation of GST and tax collection is expected to increase once GST system streamlines. The low growth rate in own tax revenue was compensated to a great deal by higher tax devolution owing to 14th UFCs recommendations. The 14th UFC recommended an increase in tax devolution from the centre to states from 32 per cent to 42 per cent of the divisible pool of taxes. The percentage share of taxes to Karnataka increased from 4.328 per cent in 13th UFC to 4.713 per cent in 14th UFC. This is evident from Central tax transfers recording a growth rate of 63.66 per cent in 2015-16 (Table 14.10). The share of own non-tax revenue GSDP ratio declined from 1 per cent of GSDP in 2009-10 to 0.4 per cent in 2019-20. One study pointed out that state may have to resort ways to increase user charges wherever possible to diversify the means to enhance non-tax revenue to augment revenue receipts (Farida, Jacob Jannet and Lekha Chakraborthy, 2020). During the period of our study, the growth rate of grant-in-aid was very high (above 37%) for the years 2014-15, 2017-18 and 2019-20 and this is another factor which created a better fiscal situation for the state (Table 14.10).

Table 14.11: Growth Rate of Revenue Receipts of Kerala (%)

Year	Own taxes	Non-tax revenue	Central tax transfer	Grant-in-aid	Total revenue receipts
2009-10	–	–	–	–	–
2010-11	23.25	4.27	16.89	-1.61	18.69
2011-12	18.40	34.23	16.49	68.82	22.65
2012-13	16.94	61.96	14.21	-18.55	16.13
2013-14	6.38	33.28	9.18	36.97	11.42
2014-15	10.12	30.65	6.12	81.44	17.83
2015-16	10.68	15.66	60.12	18.82	19.11
2016-17	8.16	15.13	19.97	-4.61	9.53
2017-18	14.19	15.45	-0.60	0.21	9.80
2018-19	5.94	5.22	23.32	33.54	11.85
2019-20 (RE)	9.31	12.39	1.27	-2.28	6.66

Source: Same as Table 14.9.

The growth rate of total revenue receipts of Kerala shows that the growth rate is less than 12 per cent for the period 2016-17 to 2019-20 (Table 14.11). This is due to poor growth in own tax revenue due to implementation of GST. It should be noted that during 2015-16 and 2018-19, the low growth rate in own-tax revenues were partly offset by high growth rate in share of taxes from Central Government. The years 2011-12, 2014-15 and 2018-19 recorded a very high growth rate in grant-in-aid from the Government of India. It should also be noted that during the 14th UFC period, the percentage share of taxes to states increased to 2.5 per cent from 2.34 per cent in 13th UFC. This indicates a structural shift in revenue receipts witnessing a fall in the share of state resources on the one hand and a rise in the Central funds on the other.

Kerala is one of the states which have higher non-tax revenue and the growth rates of non-tax revenue is higher when compared to tax revenue (Table 14.11). This is due to income from lotteries, which is the major source of non-tax revenue. In the case of income from lotteries, the net income is only about 18 to 22 per cent of the total earnings after deducting the cost of conducting lotteries (Prakash and Jerry Alwin, 2018). There is negative growth rate of collection of all other items of non-tax revenue except lotteries in 2017 (KPERC, 2019). The fiscal policy pursued by the successive governments in the state generally does not favour timely upward revision of taxes, fees and user charges due to political factors. The revision of taxes invite strong protests and agitation from opposition political parties. So the governments used to give very low priority for periodical revision of taxes and non-taxes. Another issue is the underperformance of the tax collection machinery, lack of sincere effort by government to mobilize tax revenue and inefficient and poor collection of tax.

Table 14.12: Growth Rate of Revenue Receipts of Tamil Nadu (%)

Year	Own taxes	Non-tax revenue	Central tax transfer	Grant-in-aid	Total revenue receipts
2009-10	–	–	–	–	–
2010-11	30.74	-7.48	24.62	24.05	25.70
2011-12	24.56	22.20	16.52	5.94	19.45
2012-13	19.72	15.31	14.20	-10.80	17.88
2013-14	3.46	42.55	9.18	40.36	9.32
2014-15	6.69	-10.62	6.13	103.79	13.31
2015-16	2.31	6.79	20.98	3.60	5.38
2016-17	6.45	11.17	20.56	3.01	8.70
2017-18	12.25	8.88	-0.17	-26.01	4.31
2018-19	10.19	31.92	23.28	59.19	18.77
2019-20 (RE)	13.82	-0.04	-12.13	30.36	10.43

Source: Same as Table 14.9.

The revenue receipts GSDP ratio of Tamil Nadu decreased from 12.6 in 2013-14 to 10.4 per cent in 2019-20 (Table 14.7). During the years 2013-14, 2015-16, 2016-17 and 2017-18, the growth rate of total revenue receipts was below 10 per cent (Table 14.12). One of the reasons is due to poor resource mobilization efforts as can be seen from poor growth rates of own tax revenue and non-tax revenues. Though Tamil Nadu has a record of better resource mobilization, during the recent years the growth rates of own taxes and non-taxes were poor particularly due to factors such as implementation of GST and the impact of global slowdown on regional economy of Tamil Nadu etc. A study points out that the share of state excise in total own tax revenue declined from 14.4 per cent in 2006-07 to 6 per cent in 2018-19 due to abolition of vend fees and additional vend fees for malt liquor, foreign liquor and spirit (Shanmugan, 2018). The study also points out that though the state is endowed with low coastal areas but the contribution from the fisheries sector is low. Similarly, forestry and tourism bring very low revenue to state exchequer. There is potential to increase non-tax revenues from these sources. Another issue faced by Tamil Nadu on the revenue side is that Tamil Nadu's share in tax devolution is declining during the recent years. The share in tax devolution declined from 4.969 per cent in13th UFC to 4.023 (Table 14.8). This is evident from the negative growth rate of Central tax transfers in 2017-18 and 2019-20. The growth rate of grant-in-aid also recorded lower growth rates from 2015-16 to 2017-18.

Table 14.13: Growth Rate of Revenue Receipts of Telangana (%)

Year	Own taxes	Non-tax revenue	Central tax transfer	Grant-in-aid	Total revenue receipts
2014-15	–	–	–	–	–
2015-16	36.49	123.58	50.82	31.98	49.16
2016-17	21.09	-32.14	20.45	3.81	8.79
2017-18	20.18	-20.01	-0.77	-17.36	7.25
2018-19	11.80	27.88	23.25	1.48	14.18
2019-20 (RE)	9.67	22.66	12.13	38.64	9.37

Source: Same as Table 14.9.

Telengana is one of the states which fared better in the mobilisation of own taxes and its high growth rates (Table 14.13). One study has pointed out that Telangana's average state own tax revenue growth rate of 17.2 per cent which is the highest nationwide for the financial years 2014-15 to 2017-18 (Bharati Institute of Public Policy, 2018). Though state recorded a high growth rate of own revenue, it also observed that states own tax revenue GSDP ratio has remained within the range of 5 per cent to 9 per cent and never touched double digit mark during the period of study. The state also registered higher growth rates of Central tax transfers and grant-in-aid from the Central Government (Table 14.13). The 14th UFC allotted a 2.437 per cent share of taxes to Telengana state. Another study which examined the finances of Telangana found that co-efficient of own tax revenue receipt is 1.24 per cent. The study found that the co-efficient of Central transfer is 1.6, which is more than that of tax buoyancy. This implies that a single percentage increase in GSDP keeps more impact on Central transfers (Ghosh Aninditha and Lekha Chakraborthy, 2019). Regarding the growth rate in own non-tax revenue, Telengana recorded negative growth rates in 2015-16 and 2016-17.

From the above analysis of revenue receipts of southern states we come to the conclusion that for states such as Karnataka, Kerala and Telangana the lower growth rates of revenue receipts was offset to a great extent by higher growth rates of Central tax transfer and grant-in-aid given to states as per recommendations of the 14th UFC. On the other hand, the states such as Andhra Pradesh and Tamil Nadu witnessed reduction in share of taxes in 14th UFC when compared to 13th UFC. The major reason for poor growth rate of own tax revenue during the recent years for states such as Andhra Pradesh, Karnataka, Kerala and Tamil Nadu are the issues related to implementation of GST. Telangana is the only state which witnessed better growth rate in own tax revenue. All the southern states have more potential to tap non-tax revenue.

In the future perspective, sustained efforts towards mobilizing own revenue need to be combined with strategies to maximize efficiency gains rather than increase in tax rates which involve expanding the tax base using IT infrastructure, data analytics, and reduction in the cost of tax compliance. Charging of breakeven user charges and better cost recovery mechanism also improves scope for State's revenue. Reprioritising Central transfers towards productive expenditures should also form part of the policies of State governments.

Trends in Revenue Expenditure

Fiscal consolidation and pressures to increase current spending have led to an overall decline in capital spending to the tune of about 0.3 to 0.5 per cent of GDP during 2017-19. Arresting this trend is crucial to avoid adverse effects of long term growth and welfare (RBI, 2020). In this context, we may examine the revenue expenditure and revenue expenditure GSDP ratio of southern states (Table 14.14). Andhra Pradesh and Kerala recorded higher revenue expenditure GSDP ratio of around 14 per cent. One of the important reasons for high growth rate of revenue expenditure is the higher growth rate of wages, salary and interest payments. Kerala witnessed a very high growth rate of revenue expenditure of 33 per cent in 2011-12 due to pay revision commitments. It should be noted that in Kerala, salaries and pensions of government employees are revised once in five years which is one of the major reason for the growth of revenue expenditure. On the other hand, states of Karnataka and Telangana have a comparatively lower revenue expenditure GSDP ratio. The main reason for the high revenue expenditure is the expenditure on wages and salaries. Of the southern states, Kerala spends about one-third of its revenue expenditure on wages and salaries (Table 14.15). States such as Andhra Pradesh and Tamil Nadu spends more than one-fourth of its revenue expenditure on wages and salaries. The states of Karnataka and Telengana spend nearly 20 per cent of its revenue expenditure for wages and salaries, indicating a healthy fiscal situation.

Table 14.14: Revenue Expenditure of Southern States

Year	Andhra Pradesh	Karnataka	Kerala	Tamil Nadu	Telangana	All States
2009-10	63450 (13.3)	47540 (13.8)	31130 (13.5)	59380 (12.5)	–	799150 (12.4)
2010-11	78530 (13.3)	54030 (14.2)	34660 (12.5)	72920 (14.1)	–	932300 (12.1)
2011-12	90420 (13.8)	65120 (14.1)	46040 (14.6)	83840 (12.6)	–	1074570 (12.0)
2012-13	102700 (13.6)	76290 (14.7)	53490 (15.4)	97070 (13.0)	–	1231700 (12.3)
2013-14	110370 (12.9)	89190 (14.5)	60490 (15.3)	109820 (12.9)	–	1379750 (12.2)

(*Contd.*)

Year	Andhra Pradesh	Karnataka	Kerala	Tamil Nadu	Telangana	All States
2014-15	114870 (21.8)	103610 (11.2)	71750 (13.6)	128830 (11.8)	50670 (9.9)	1637290 (13.2)
2015-16	95950 (15.7)	117030 (11.6)	78690 (14.1)	140990 (12.1)	75900 (13.4)	1838270 (13.4)
2016-17	116180 (16.6)	131920 (11.6)	91100 (14.8)	153200 (11.8)	81430 (12.6)	2086890 (13.7)
2017-18	121213 (15.0)	142482 (10.6)	99948 (14.3)	167873 (11.5)	85364 (11.3)	2340080 (13.7)
2018-19	128570 (14.9)	164300 (10.6)	110316 (14.1)	197201 (12.1)	97083 (11.3)	2638122 (13.9)
2019-20 (RE)	137518 (14.1)	176970 (10.4)	116517 (13.4)	216933 (11.8)	110825 (11.4)	3076395 (13.9)

Figures in bracket represent Revenue Expenditure GSDP ratio.

Source: Same as Table 14.1.

Table 14.15: Expenditure on Wages and Salary

Year	Andhra Pradesh	Karnataka	Kerala	Tamil Nadu	Telangana	All States
Expenditure on Wages and Salary (Rs. Crores)						
2009-10	17410.0	10300.0	9930.0	19490.0	–	233770.0
2013-14	32350.0	17810.0	19620.0	31860.0	–	304850.0
2018-19	32743	31800	32698	52535	21301	690511
As Percentage of Revenue Expenditure						
2009-10	26.20	21.71	31.9	32.82	–	29.25
2013-14	29.31	19.97	32.44	29.01	–	22.09
2018-19	25.5	19.4	29.6	26.6	21.9	26.2

Source: Same as Table 14.1.

Another indicator of revenue expenditure is interest payment GSDP ratio (Table 14.16). We can infer that states such as Tamil Nadu, Andhra Pradesh and Kerala have higher interest payment GSDP ratio. This is due to higher debt servicing charges as a result of high volume of public debt. States like Karnataka and Telengana have relatively lower interest payment GSDP ratio. To combat the issue of increasing debt, the Telangana state plays an important role by elongating the duration of debts issued by state government more than 10 years up to a maximum limit of 30 years (Ghosh Anindita and Lekha Chakraborty, 2019). This has reduced the interest liability of Telangana. Pension Payment-GSDP ratio is yet another indicator of revenue expenditure (Table 14.16). The states of Kerala, Andhra Pradesh and Tamil Nadu have higher Pension Payment-GSDP ratio. The states of Karnataka and Telengana have relatively low pension payment-GSDP ratio.

Table 14.16: Interest Payment-GSDP ratio and Pension Payment-GSDP ratio of Southern States in India

Year	Andhra Pradesh	Karnataka	Kerala	Tamil Nadu	Telangana	All States
	Interest Payment-GSDP Ratio					
2009-10	1.9	1.5	2.3	1.4	–	1.7
2014-15	1.9	1.0	1.9	1.3	1.0	1.5
2019-20 (RE)	1.7	1.1	2.1	1.7	1.5	1.7
Pension Payment-GSDP Ratio						
2009-10	1.3	1.0	2.0	1.8	–	1.3
2014-15	1.9	1.1	2.1	1.6	0.8	1.5
2019-20 (RE)	1.8	1.2	2.3	1.7	1.1	1.7

Note: GSDP (Gross State Domestic Product).

Source: Same as Table 14.1.

Development Expenditure and Social Sector Expenditure

This section examines two major items of expenditure, viz. development expenditure and social sector expenditure. For this we have used the indicators, development expenditure-GSDP ratio and social sector expenditure-GSDP ratio.

The analysis of the expenditure data is disaggregated into development and non-development expenditure. All expenditures relating to revenue account, capital outlay and loans and services are categorised into social services, economic services and general services. While social and economic services constitute development expenditure, expenditure on general services is treated as non-development expenditure. Thus development expenditure includes the development components of revenue expenditure, capital outlay and loans and advances by state governments. Social sector expenditure includes expenditure on social services, rural development and food storage and warehousing (RBI, 2019).

For the state of Andhra Pradesh development expenditure-GSDP ratio has fallen from 18.7 per cent in 2014-15 to 11.1 per cent in 2019-20 which has adverse impact on social development. The state of Kerala recorded development expenditure-GSDP ratio of less than 8 per cent. Telangana and Karnataka have a higher development expenditure-GSDP ratio of more than 10 per cent (Table 14.17). The table also gives the social sector expenditure-GSDP ratio of the southern states. The state of Andhra Pradesh shows a reduction in social sector expenditure-GSDP ratio during the recent years. Though the state of Karnataka has a revenue surplus, its social sector expenditure-GSDP ratio is low. A study on Karnataka finances found that there was expenditure compression on social sector especially expenditure on education (Farida, Jacob Jannet and Lekha Chakraborthy, 2020). The state of Kerala also has lower social sector-GSDP ratio in the recent years indicating poor spending on critical services like health and education. The social sector expenditure-GSDP ratio of Tamil Nadu is also low. In the recent years, a shift is being projected from expenditure on education, health and family welfare to sectors like housing and urban development and expenditure on social security and welfare.

Table 14.17: Development Expenditure-GSDP ratio and Social Sector Expenditure-GSDP ratio of Southern States in India

Year	Andhra Pradesh	Karna-taka	Kerala	Tamil Nadu	Telangana	All States
Development Expenditure-GSDP Ratio						
2009-10	12.0	13.0	7.6	9.6	–	9.9
2014-15	18.7	9.6	7.4	9.0	9.0	10.7
2019-20 (RE)	11.1	9.3	6.6	8.3	10.3	12.2

(*Contd.*)

Year	Andhra Pradesh	Karna-taka	Kerala	Tamil Nadu	Telangana	All States
Social Sector Expenditure-GSDP Ratio						
2009-10	6.4	7.3	5.2	6.2	–	6.1
2014-15	10.4	5.6	5.4	5.7	4.8	6.7
2019-20 (RE)	8.3	5.4	4.7	5.0	5.4	7.0

Note: GSDP (Gross State Domestic Product).

Source: Same as Table 14.1.

Conclusion

The above analysis may be concluded as follows. In southern states, there is considerable difference in the fiscal situation in terms of fiscal indicators, revenue receipts, revenue expenditure, social sector expenditure and development expenditure.The factors influencing the growth rate of revenue receipts are issues related to implementation of GST, issues related to collection of non-tax revenue and devolution of taxes and grants according to recommendations of the UFCs. Persistent high level of revenue deficit forces the states such as Andhra Pradesh, Tamil Nadu and Kerala to rely on borrowings to meet revenue expenditure. This has weakened the fiscal capacity for spending on capital items, development and social sectors and has pushed these states to fiscal crisis. On the other hand, revenue surplus states such as Karnataka and Telangana can be rated as having sound fiscal management.

REFERENCES

Bharti Institute of Public Policy (2018). *Evaluation of state finances: A study of government of Telangana.* https://fincomindia.nic.in/writereaddata/html_en_files/fincom15/StudyReports/25.pdf (accessed on July 17, 2020)

Farida, Jacob Jannet & Lekha Chakraborthy (2020). Fiscal prudence for what? Analysing the state finances of Karnataka, *Working Paper* No. 293. New Delhi: National Institute of Public Finance and Policy (NIPFP).

Gayithri, K. (2014). *Evaluation of state finance of Karnataka, report submitted to the 14th Finance Commission.* Bangalore: Institute for Social and Economic Change.

Ghosh, Anindita and Lekha Chakraborty (2019). Analysing Telangana State Finances: Elongation of term to maturity of debt to sustain economic growth, *Working Paper* no. 288. New Delhi: NIPFP.

Government of Andhra Pradesh (2019). *White Paper on State Finances.* http://ipr.ap.nic.in/images/whitepapers/Finance-White%20Paper-English.pdf (accessed on July 17, 2020).

Government of Kerala (GoK) (2011). *White Paper on state finances.* Thiruvananthapuram: GoK.

Government of Kerala (GoK) (2016). *White Paper on state finances.* Thiruvananthapuram: GoK.

Issac Thomas & R. Mohan (2016). Sustainable fiscal consolidation: Suggesting the way ahead for Kerala, *Working Paper* series no. 469. Thiruvananthapuram: Centre for Development Studies (CDS).

Kerala Public Expenditure Review Committee (KPERC). (Third Committee) reports: First Report (2010-11). Second Report (2011-12), Third Report (2012-13), Fourth Report (2013-14). Thiruvananthapuram: GoK.

Kerala Public Expenditure Review Committee (KPERC) (fourth committee). Fourth report (2017-18). Thiruvananthapuram: GoK.

Kotasthane Pranay and Varun K. Ramachandra (2016). "Karnataka's changing fiscal landscape: Finances after FFC". *Economic and Political Weekly.* Vol. 51, No. 33, pp. 20-24.

Prakash, B.A. and Jerry Alwin (2018). "Kerala's Acute Fiscal Crisis: An analysis of causes" in B.A. Prakash and Jerry Alwin (ed.), *Kerala's Economic Development: Emerging Issues and Challenges,* pp. 331-357. New Delhi: Sage Publications.

Reserve Bank of India (RBI) (2009-10 to 2020-21), *State finances: A study of budgets.* Mumbai: RBI.

Sen, T.K. (2012). Recent development in Kerala state finances, *Working Paper* series no. 449. Thiruvananthapuram: CDS.

Shanmugan, K.R. (2018). *Tamil Nadu state government finances.* Chennai: Madras School of Economics.

Shanmugan, K.R., G.S. Ganesh Prasad and L. Venkitachalam (2014). *Tamil Nadu Finances: Report submitted to the 14th Finance Commission.* Chennai: Madras Institute of Development Studies.

Sreedevi, N. (2013). *Evaluation of Andhra Pradesh State Finances: 14th finance commissions study on evaluation of state finances.* Andhra Pradesh: Centre for Economic and Social Studies.

Sreedevi, N. (2019). *Evaluation of Andhra Pradesh State Finances: 15th Finance Commissions study on evaluation of state finances.* Andhra Pradesh: Centre for Economic and Social Studies.

15
In Pursuit of Financial Self-Reliance of Common People

Arindam Gupta

The Prologue

On 12th May, 2020, the Prime Minister raised a clarion call in the name of the *Atmanirbhar Bharat Abhiyaan* (Self-reliant India Campaign) announcing the special economic and comprehensive package of Rs. 20 lakh crore, which according to some estimate is equivalent to 10 per cent of India's GDP. Just before this monthly transfers of Rs. 500 were announced to women's *Jan Dhan* accounts on 26th March, 2020 for the next three months under the *Pradhan Mantri Garib Kalyan Yojana* (PMGKY). *Atmanirbhar* is no new term if introspected but it matters when and how a term is getting used. Moreover, in the backdrop of a gloomy environment particularly encompassing the economy and health during the peak of the COVID-19 wave the main objective of the Prime Minister must have been to deliver a vision for turning around the gloominess. It imbibes to a great extent the country's urgent need of self-reliance based on its own unused capacity and a little support from the fellow citizens who are capable of providing so. Later, in course of time, it turns into a concept which is extended to education with the announcement of National Education Policy, 2020 in July 2020 and also with announcements in the banking sector adding features to the existing schemes with attempts to make the people financially more stable. A country's self-reliance cannot be achieved if internally the people of the country suffer from poverty and if the common people remain financially excluded. The following sections of this chapter deal with two distinguished government schemes, *Pradhan Mantri Jan Dhan Yojana* (PMJDY) as announced on 15th August, 2014 and *Pradhan Mantri Mudra Yojana* (PMMY) as announced on 8th April, 2015, to examine to what extent those schemes help the people of the country to become financially "self-reliant". Also digital financial inclusion in the country and issue of entrepreneurship to promote self-employment is discussed.

Financial Inclusion: *Jan Dhan* as the Game Changer

Reserve Bank of India, the central bank and principal banking regulator in India has defined financial inclusion as "the process of ensuring access to appropriate financial products and services needed by vulnerable groups such as weaker sections and low income groups at an affordable cost in a fair and transparent manner by mainstream institutional players." If the term, financial inclusion is introspected into, it appears that so far the excluded people or places from any formal financial system are to be included with the help of a few measures. Financial exclusion remained a world-wide problem due to poverty and underdevelopment. Thus, to get rid of this menace, as a first step, providing a *no-frill* bank account, with minimum or no balance to be maintained in such account, has been largely experienced in many countries. Common and poor people suffer also from documentation required for opening such a bank account, if not a nominal balance to keep. Hence, relaxation in documentation like providing proper identity proof or address proof, at least initially, has been given.

Like the BSBDAs[1], the *Jan Dhan* accounts can also be zero-balance accounts. To promote financial inclusion, RBI has asked banks to drop the *no-frill* tag from the basic saving accounts as the nomenclature has become a stigma. Accounts could be opened only with photograph initially without any identity proof. But, to enable the account having transactions, the identity proof was to be submitted.

The only condition of the scheme for opening a bank account was that an individual should not have an existing bank account. The PMJDY accountholders got a *Rupay* debit card with in-built accident insurance cover of Rs. 1 lakh (Rs. 0.1 million), an overdraft facility up to Rs. 5,000 and a life insurance cover of Rs. 30,000 (to those who opened their accounts till 26th January, 2015). All BSBDAs have subsequently been converted into *Jan Dhan* accounts. The collateral-free overdraft option in the scheme was raised in August, 2018 to Rs. 10,000, the accidental insurance coverage to Rs. 2 lakh (Rs. 0.2 million).

World Bank's Global Findex Report, 2017, which had published adults holding bank accounts (%) of the total population of a particular country across the world, showed for India a 35per cent bank account ownership in 2011, which rose to 53 per cent in 2014, but literally jumped to 80 per cent in 2017.[2] World Bank's financial inclusion indicator is banking system-centric, measured by *access* (penetration of bank branches or point of sales devices in rural areas), *usage* (average balance in bank account, number of transactions per account), and *quality* (range of products on offer)[3]. But, in spite of attaining a high bank ownership rate, dormancy has been identified to be a problem for India as the 2017 report showed 48 per cent of the *Jan Dhan* accounts remaining inactive. Government enabled direct benefit transfer has brought the bank accounts technically out of the dormancy. 95.9 per cent of the bank accounts are now claimed by the government having been covered by at least one digital means of payment as on March 2021.

Further, *Jan Dhan* has been able to reduce the gender gap in bank account ownership. It has reduced from 20 per cent (2014) to 6.4 per cent (2017) in India (*Source:* Global Findex Database, 2017). About 84.4 per cent of the population of age 18 years and above had deposit account in rural India (88.1% male and 80.7% female), thus exhibiting a gap of 7.4 per cent. About 85.2 per cent of the population of age 18 years and above had deposit account in urban India (89.0% male and 81.3 per cent female), keeping a slightly lower gap of 7.3 per cent (*Source:* All India Debt & Investment Survey, January-December, 2019, NSSO, MOSPI).

The government wants to use bank account as the default channel for delivery of government payments, such as through the Direct

Benefit Transfer (DBT) system. DBT is a government-led initiative comprising multiple schemes for which benefits are directly transferred to beneficiaries channelled primarily through state institutions.

Financial Inclusion Indices in India

Financial inclusion refers to both the access and active use of financial products and services like savings, credit, insurance or even mobile money within the formal financial system for all groups of the population in pursuit of their holistic financial well-being. For individuals, financial inclusion can involve reduced transaction costs and increased safety provided by the formal system over cash or informal providers.

CRISIL (2013) measured the extent of financial inclusion in India in the form of an index using three dimensions, viz. (a) branch penetration, which signifies number of branches and ATMs, (b) credit penetration, which considers number of loan accounts, number of small borrower loan accounts and number of agriculture advances, and (c) deposit penetration, which signifies number of savings bank accounts, also judging the extent of the usage of formal credit. Among the three dimensions of financial inclusion, credit penetration is the key problem in the country. The index, as named *Inclusix* took into account the number of individuals having access to various financial services rather than focusing on the loan amount. *Inclusix* is India's first comprehensive measure of financial inclusion in the form of a relative index in a scale of 0 to 100.[4] The three parameters were updated annually based on the availability of data and additional services such as insurance and microfinance were added later. *Inclusix* as last published in 2018, shows that the *Jan-Dhan*, Aadhaar and mobile (JAM) trinity is slowly but surely making a seminal difference to financial inclusion. Although later the government's aim of achieving the JAM trinity suffered a setback due to the apex court ruling in September 2018. But, anyway a move in the value of *Inclusix* to 58.0 in 2018, even by revising the base, from 56.2 in 2015 and 50.1 in 2013 is depicting significant progress in financial inclusion.

Financial inclusion index (FI-Index) as unveiled on 17th August, 2021 by RBI is the second institutional effort in the country, after CRISIL's *Inclusix*. The FI-Index is similar to *Inclusix* as regards the scale of measurement, both ranging from 0 to 100. FI-Index covers financial services as a whole with a total of 97 indicators weighing three parameters, ease of access to services with 35 per cent, availability and usage of services with 45 per cent, and quality of services with 20 per cent. As per RBI's press release on the occasion of launch of the index, it captures the quality aspect of financial inclusion "as reflected by financial literacy, consumer protection, and inequalities and deficiencies in services". Its value is said to be 53.9 for the financial year ended March 2021, as compared to 43.4 for the year ended March 2017.The index value has improved to 56.4 as on March 31, 2022.

If the available financial inclusion indices are reviewed, it could be seen that financial inclusiveness of people of the country qualitatively is not as high as a quantitative assessment at the same point of time in terms of bank account ownership. So there cannot be any complacency, neither for the bankers nor for the policy-makers. Further, sustainability of banks has become a big issue. It should be so as to continue serving the people of the country in a friendly manner; they should be financially strong enough. The financial literacy issue is also of the concern for the government as it will help the people to be more financially included. People have to know more about the investment products and services.

Credit, Collateral and Entrepreneurship

The need of credit for entrepreneurship needs no explanation. Whatever may be the size of an enterprise, everyone needs fund to be established and more funds to be expanded. But generally, the enterprises which are related to self-employment of the poor people need fund more on priority basis. On the other hand, loan is not given ordinarily without security or collateral. But wherefrom the poor people will get that! So bridging the gap between the security requirement to obtain loan and available money or wealth to be furnished by the loanee as security is of utmost need. With that direction, the government of a developing country like India which nonetheless suffers from huge unemployment problem has started introducing schemes for lending poor people to start enterprises.

Bank credit remains the most crucial instrument of financial inclusion. An inclusive financial system can help in reducing the progress of informal sources of credit, namely the moneylenders that are often found to be exploitative.[5]

Collateral-free bank loan was made available in *Mudra Yojana*, a scheme as introduced by the present government just within one year of its previous tenure. Providing bank loan without security was, however, not new when *Mudra yojana* had the announcement. In the flagship financial inclusion scheme, PMJDY, a maximum Rs. 5,000 of bank overdraft was made available too to an accountholder initially on successful operation of the bank account for the preceding 6 months. While only the *Shishu* product of the *Mudra yojana* has the option of Rs. 50,000 for entrepreneurial borrowing, the *Kishore* and *Tarun* products have even a higher option of Rs. 5,00,000 and Rs. 10,00,000 loan respectively. Thus, the volume of collateral-free loan is much higher, throwing up a challenge to sustain the scheme because of higher probability of bad debts. But for generation of self-employment, government had to resort to even introducing such a scheme remaining fully aware of resistance from bank management.

Women owning SMEs in India widely point to the lack of access to capital as the biggest constraint in running their businesses. 90 per cent of women entrepreneurs in India have never applied for loans to formal financial institutions. They cited a hard constraint in the form of lack of collateral and softer constraints such as complicated application procedures and unfavourable terms of credit (IFC, 2016).

Microfinance is another form of credit more women-oriented which is generally routed through small groups commonly known as SHGs. These groups not only serve as a platform to supervise the activities of each other but also provide social collaterals. When poverty and patriarchy constraint women to badly paid wage-work or otherwise they remain more engaged in the poorly paid agriculture sector, credit can help them move into better paying self-employment.

As a sequel of announcement for *Atmanirbhar Bharat Abhiyaan*, enterprises now with the investment limit up to Rs. 1 crore (from Rs. 25 lakh) to be brought under micro enterprises, Rs. 10 crore (from Rs. 5 crore) under small enterprises, and Rs. 20 crore (from Rs. 10 crore) under medium enterprises. The turnover limit for micro, small and medium enterprises will be Rs. 5 crore, Rs. 50 crore and Rs. 100 crore respectively. Rs. 3 trillion collateral-free bank loan was provided to MSMEs with 100 per cent credit guarantee. Government investment of Rs. 100 billion is announced in May 2020 to be made available which in turn will invest Rs. 500 billion in the equity capital of MSMEs.

Mudra and Non-farm Self-employment

The rural economy contributes nearly 25-30 per cent to the GDP. Earlier, agriculture was the primary source of income and employment in rural India, but is now being displaced by the non-farm and non-agricultural sectors. Self-employment has become the option for many to earn their livelihood. Most of the individual entrepreneurs in the non-corporate small business (NCSB) segment operate as unregistered enterprises. The owners do not maintain proper books of accounts and suffer primarily from dearth of capital. Until the announcement of the *Mudra yojana*, non-agricultural collateral-free loan has not been so common. PMMY has exhibited an impressive performance of sanctioning loans of Rs. 3391.10 billion in 2021-22 continuously rising from Rs. 1374.49 billion in 2015-16 except for the last year which may be due to the effect of pandemic (*Source: PMMY* website). Union Minister of State for Finance, Bhagwat Kishanrao Karad in a written statement to Parliament on 26.11.2021 in response to some question stated that 68 per cent of *Mudra* accounts were held by women entrepreneurs, availing 44 per cent of sanctioned amount.

Mudra yojana too helped women a lot, by actually promoting women entrepreneurship in the country. The loan period for women may extend up to 7 years. According to the data produced by the Ministry of Finance on 26.11.2021, 68 per cent of *Mudra* accounts are held by women entrepreneurs, availing 44 per cent of sanctioned amount. However, 90 per cent of the loans are in the 'sishu' category providing loan up to Rs. 50,000.

Digital Financial Inclusion

Financial inclusion entails not just the availability of financial products —credit, deposit, insurance etc. but also the ability to transfer money around in an affordable manner. The mobile technology platforms came to the fore offering services like mobile wallet, mobile money etc. Over the past few years, India has seen a monumental development in digital and financial inclusion. Currently, there are nearly Rs. 500 million internet users all across the country, out of which those living in the rural areas make up for 200 million. Research shows that about 87 per cent of rural population uses mobile phones to access internet services. However, despite the growth, this platform has been vastly underutilized for monetary transactions. Currently, digitized banking has reached over 420 million people in India, making space for digital financial inclusion. Due to this inclusion, the country's digital payment value is expected to grow more than double to $135.2 billion by 2023, according to an ASSOCHAM—PwC, 2019 study.[6]

Unified Payment Interface (UPI) is created in April 2016 as an interoperable digital payments platform by the National Payments Council of India (NPCI). NPCI, an initiative of RBI and the Indian Banks Association as set-up way back in 2008, has provided the backbone and infrastructure to help the faster adoption of digital systems that has deepened financial inclusion. Before UPI, the NPCI launched other indigenous digital payment products like BHIM, Bharat Bill Pay, NACH, IMPS etc. among others. Fintech companies have been at the forefront of the growth in digital payments in India. To facilitate P2P and retail payments through mobile wallets along with UPI, other private initiatives some of which have foreign linkage too like *Paytm*, *PhonePe*, *PayU*, *MobiKwik*, *FreeCharge* etc. are now working in full swing. Mobile wallet transactions grew from 11.96 million transactions in April 2015 to 387.6 million transactions worth Rs. 154.08 billion in January 2020 (World Bank, 2018; RBI 2020).[7] During 2020-21, the total number of automated teller machines (ATMs) (on-site and off-site) operated by the scheduled commercial banks (SCBs) increased for the second consecutive year after declining in 2018-19. The number of public sector bank (PSB) ATMs, however, declined in their pursuit of greater cost efficiency.

Policy-makers say NPCI has emerged as a key institution supporting the digital form of financial inclusion. Mr. Amitabh Kant, the former CEO of *Niti Aayog* said, "It enabled large scale financial inclusion using DBT and Aadhaar Enabled Payment System (AEPS) which came extremely handy during Covid times for our poor and needy citizens, apart from eliminating leakages and duplicates on a large scale. Fourth, it acts as a public good, away from intentions of profiteering, stock market gyrations. It was created as a vehicle with the intention of driving innovation, bringing efficient, cost-effective, citizen-scale payment systems for a large country of 1.3 billion population. Fifth, because of the NPCI, India today is self-sufficient in payment systems."[8]

Women in the Centre of Financial Inclusion

For a long time, financial inclusion of Indian women was mainly led by the Self-help Group (SHG) movement which began in the 1980s. With the launch of the PMJDY too the focus was on women accountholders, although not women-only. Presently, under it 56 per cent are women accountholders. As zero-balance bank account was available for them, several other government programmes were floated with the objective to provide credit and other financial services. As a result, the share of women stands at 81 per cent in *Stand-Up India*, 71 per cent in *Mudra* loans, 37 per cent in *Pradhan Mantri Suraksha Bima Yojana* and 27 per cent in *Pradhan Mantri Jeevan Jyoti Bima Yojana*, which is encouraging. *Pradhan Mantri Awas Yojana* (PMAY) has enabled 68 per cent of over 2 crore *PMAY-Gramin* homes being either solely or jointly owned by women. *Pradhan Mantri Svanidhi Yojana* has provided more than 33 lakh loans to street vendors of which 41 per cent are women beneficiaries. A recent RBI report states that credit to women had a 22.5 per cent share in bank loans to individuals during 2021-22. TransUnion CIBIL further reports that the expansion in the footprint of women borrowers in the semi-urban and rural locations, with a compounded annual growth rate of 21 per cent between 2016 and 2021 exceeds the 16 per cent growth in metro and urban regions, both being remarkable. It has also accepted women to be better borrowers than men. According to the report, the delinquency rate for women borrowers was pegged at 5.2 per cent across retail credit products, compared to 6.9 per cent for their male counterparts. This indicates that giving more credit to women the country won't be financially loser as traditionally being perceived. This is also the reason, the micro finance institutions in the country have chosen the women to be the most preferred borrowers for their schemes.

Endnote

The financial literacy among the people has been exposed to be dismal among all categories of citizens, more acute in case of those with lower income and education. A survey by Standard & Poor's Financial Services estimates that only 24 per cent adults in India are financially literate (Klapper *et al.*, 2014).[9] Whenever a new government scheme for the common people either for bank account or insurance or credit has been launched, it has become the government's challenge first to let the target beneficiaries know about those schemes. A lot of expenses have been incurred on publicity yet the schemes remain largely unknown to the poorer people. To create awareness of government policies and schemes among the intended beneficiaries including the population living in far-flung and remote areas, through print, electronic and outdoor media, the government spent 1698.98 crore during the period 2018-19 to 2020-21. The government ultimately fixes target for these schemes for the executing officers or executives either within its own arms or through the banks to reduce the burden of publicity. This often jeopardizes the main objective behind introduction of a scheme.

The National Strategy for Financial Inclusion 2019-2024 (NSFI) and the National Strategy for Financial Education 2020-2025 (NSFE) were released by the RBI in January 2020 and August 2020 respectively, which provide a road map for accelerating the process of financial inclusion and promoting financial literacy and consumer protection. RBI issues NSFI with a focus on creating an outreach of financial services outlets to provide banking access to every household within 5 km radius. All eligible adults must have access to basic financial services such as bank account, line of credit, life and other insurance, pension scheme and suitable investment product. RBI's NSFE is focused towards inherent behavioural and practical aspects. Not undermining the importance of opening the brick and mortar branches, although in some areas those have proven to be not cost-effective, the public sector banks (PSBs) are targeting to open around 363 by December 2022 to scale up the financial inclusion drive by covering villages with a population over 3,000 and within 5 km radius. Thus, a road map is set in pursuit of financial self-reliance of common people.

NOTES

1. All the existing "No-Frill" accounts may be treated as Basic Savings Bank Deposit Accounts (BSBDAs) from August 17, 2012, the date of the RBI circular, and banks may issue ATM card to such accountholders. There is no minimum balance requirement but a maximum amount can only be maintained as its balance. There are periodical withdrawal restrictions.
2. https://globalfindex.worldbank.org/
3. http://www.worldbank.org/en/topic/financialinclusion/brief/how-to-measure-financial-inclusion (accessed on May 14, 2019).
4. https://www.crisil.com/en/home/what-we-do/financial-products/inclusix.html
5. Sarma, M. (2010). "Financial Inclusion and Development", *Journal of International Development*, published online in Wiley Interscience. available at www.interscience.wiley.com.
6. *Financial Express*, October 24, 2021.
7. RBI (2018), National strategy for financial inclusion 2019-2024. Reserve Bank of India: Executive Committee, India.
8. *Times of India*, Kolkata, July 18, 2022.
9. Klapper, Leora and Lusardi, Annamalai (2019). "Financial literacy and financial resilience: Evidence from around the world", *Financial Management*, Vol. 49, No. 3, pp. 589-614.

PART IV
Democracy and Governance in Practice

16

The Narendra Modi Government

The First Five Years

Sartik Bagh

Rise of Narendra Modi at the National Level

The Lok Sabha election 2014 was a landmark in the history of Indian politics. Bharatiya Janata Party (BJP) led by Narendra Modi got unprecedented mandate and for the first time a right wing and a non-Congress political party got absolute majority on its own. Thanks to India's electoral system of first-past—the post system and the fragmented opposition, with just 31 per cent of popular votes, it won a comfortable 282 Lok Sabha seats. This comfortable majority put to an end to the anxieties of coalition politics witnessed in the preceding years. The mandate of Lok Sabha elections 2014 also gave an impression that a true and popular leader has emerged with the support of cross-sections of people in the country. Exploiting on the failures of UPA government especially the corruption issue in its second tenure, Modi led the electoral campaign of the BJP and fought the elections as a normal right wing political party. The nationalistic agenda was not a prominent agenda during the Lok Sabha elections 2014. The major agenda was corruption and black money, employment, governance and so on—the issues which generated huge support for him including the electronic media. His speeches and slogans during electoral campaign captivated and caught the imagination of people at large and helped him to create a popular wave. Basically, he rode to power like a colossus winning hearts of young India across the country.[1] People believed his persona and commitment to deliver the public good immensely.

The electoral verdict of 2014 Lok Sabha elections was so huge and unprecedented that it came to be viewed as a political tsunami. As put by Rajdeep Sardesai (2014), with this election, the political earth of India shook, moving the centre of gravity of an Indian election from identity politics to aspirational politics. Modi has presented himself as India's first post-liberalisation politician, someone who has sought to combine a certain cultural rootedness with the vaulting desire of millions of Indians to get onto the superhighway to prosperity.[2] However, the euphoria and buzz attributed to Narendra Modi did fizzle out in the due course of time. In the course of its functioning, the Narendra Modi government has created an illusion in terms of its promises and slogans. People's high expectations from him did not materialise much rather plethora of new problems which are intimidating and dangerous have surfaced and haunt the people across. It has given rise to many consequences and implications for the people and nation at large.

Gap between Promises and Performance

After assuming power in 2014, initially Modi started giving some feelers to Indian voters. In this regard, the initiatives of Swatchh Bharat Abhiyan, Make in India, Start-up India etc. that spelt out the grand vision of Narendra Modi government for the country. Such ideas were new and innovative that impressed the Indian voters. This demonstrated his genuine leadership to address the problems that plagued the country—not merely a political gimmick to mislead the people. Undoubtedly, the Modi government has to its credit a slew of important reforms and welfare schemes, Ujjwala, Saubhagya, Mudra, bankruptcy and insolvency law, the Real Estate (Regulation and Development) Act, contract labour reforms etc.[3] But, it is believed that in due course of time, instead of pursuing constructive and much needed socio-economic agenda, the Narendra Modi government started deviating from the very hopes and dreams that he sold out to people of India during the 2014 Lok Sabha elections. Instead of a government responsive to the needs of the poor, resources have been squandered on pet projects.[4] The high pitch slogans of *sushasan* (good governance), *achhe din* (good times), *sabka saath sabka vikas* (together with all, development for all) so far proved to be elusive and mere political slogans for votes during elections.

Much was expected on the economic front of the government that promised everything to everyone in the run up to the elections. The problem here is not a lack of coherence but the emerging priorities of the government do not square up with its declared intent.[5] In this regard, the hiatus between the rhetoric of Modi and the reality on the ground was very much palpable. On the issue of employment which Modi promised to create 2 crore jobs every year was deplorable and disappointing. If we look at data from government sources (Labour Bureau), the unemployment rate was at 3.7 per cent in 2015-16. According to the National Sample Survey, the unemployment rate was at a four-decade high of 6.1 per cent in 2017-18. The data conclusively proves the Modi government's track record on employment generation is nothing but an abysmal failure. In urban and semi-urban India, where approximately 15 million young people are entering the job market every year, this has created an environment of frustration and disillusionment.[6] The Narendra Modi government suppressed the release of official job data cleared by National Statistical Commission which defy the very notion of accountability and transparency.

For power sake, Narendra Modi and his party is much adept at mixing economic and cultural religious issues with politics and politicises every single issue for its political gains. The party (BJP) and Narendra Modi have become extremely political in which they appropriate and politicise any events, symbols and historical personalities or freedom fighters. For instance, the Pulwama terrorist attack in Kashmir in February, 2019 and subsequent air strike in Balakot of PoK (Pakistan Occupied Kashmir) was used by Modi to enhance the electoral prospects of the party in 2019 Lok Sabha elections which diverted the people from the focus of joblessness and rural distress. Rather the issues of national security and nationalism which are mostly emotive issues raised ostensibly to influence the voters and hide the government's failures on many counts. Portraying Indian army as "*Modi ki Sena*" is another brazen instance of politicising Indian army for its political gains.

Perceived Image of Anti-Dalits and Minorities

It is a well-known fact that the BJP is associated with numbers of Hindutva organisations both at the national and state level. After the Lok Sabha elections, 2014, its affiliates, more so the fringes got emboldened with the BJP's coming to power and unleashed terror and atrocities on the most vulnerable sections of societies, i.e, Dalits and minorities. The incidence of atrocities is basically the accumulated and suppressed anger against Dalits and Muslims over a long period of time that has bust out when the BJP came to power with absolute majority. In the past few years, India has seen several instances of lynching in which frenzied mobs have targeted people mainly because of their religious or caste identity—for being Muslim or Dalit. This is part of a larger surge of hate crimes that is corroding social peace and trust across the country.[7] It is also reported that as many as 90 per cent of religious hate crimes since 2009 have occurred after Modi led the BJP to power at the Centre in 2014. This points compellingly to the conclusion that an environment has been created under Modi's watch in which people feel safe, enabled, even encouraged to act out their hate and attack religious minorities. As seen by Hate Crime Watch, around 66 per cent of the cases have occurred in BJP-ruled states.[8]

However, the long silence, the complicit and indifferent attitudes shown by party high command and Narendra Modi to condemn and rein in the hate crime and cow vigilantism over such matters speak volumes about how much it is committed to protecting the interest of vulnerable and marginalised groups in the country. In contrast to the ridicules heaped upon 'Manmohan' Singh for his many silences, Modi retreats into reticence when confronted by difficult events.[9] It is a matter of great concern that the foundational principles of modern state to secure security and preservation to its people is in jeopardy. It is utmost unfortunate that democracy which provides constitutional protections to its citizens is now a witness to violent attacks on hapless and vulnerable groups. Basically, it is a trailer of *Hindu Rashtra*—the agenda and motto which RSS wants to push through the BJP—its political front. Its full incarnation will be more deadly to the minorities and marginalised caste groups in future.

The cases of atrocities by the fringe elements against Dalits and Muslims overshadow whatever Modi government delivered on the ground. It was a grand opportunity for the BJP to accommodate and win over Minorities and Dalits into its fold. But the party did not take them seriously to address their basic issues and hardship. It is an irony that there is definite coincidence of BJP coming to power and some of the anti-reservation and anti-Muslim judgements being delivered by High Courts and Supreme Court in the country. With some grace when the Scheduled Castes and Scheduled Tribes (Atrocity Prevention) Act got restored by the parliament (which was diluted), the future of 200 points roster system in colleges and universities at this moment was uncertain following a Allahabad High Court judgement in 2017 which held that reservations in teaching posts in Universities are to be applied by taking subject/discipline/department as unit with 13-point roster system instead of university or institution as unit with 200-point roster system. The judgement was a result of a petition challenging the reservation policy for faculties in Banaras Hindu University and the High Court as mentioned above struck down a circular of UGC on filling of posts of teachers for SC/ST/OBC category and thereafter, the UGC without any advice or consultation with MHRD issued letter/ circular to universities to recruit faculty positions as per the 13-point roster. As per the judgement, the department as unit of reservations with 13 roster point system would have restricted further the entry of SCs and other marginalised groups into the institutions of higher learning which was already in place. The Bahujan community had a hard task to fight the case in the Apex Court and following the protests and resentment nationwide Modi government had to proclaim an Ordinance to restore the 200-point roster system little before the Lok Sabha elections, 2019. In this case intervention of the government came much latter. On the other hand, for providing the 10 per cent quota for Economically Weaker Sections (EWS) among the unreserved category, government took no time to pass it in the parliament. The day the decision was cleared by the cabinet, in next 48 hours, the 124th Amendment Bill was passed in both the houses of Parliament mandating 10 per cent quota for the EWS. It is amazing to see the seriousness and sincerity of the Narendra Modi government in this case. Similarly, the Constitutional Amendment Bill to ban *triple talaq* during his first tenure further reflects anti-Muslim sentiment (which was of course justified in the name of gender justice) may cause alienation of the community. Though party has expanded its reach to different castes, communities and regions, its operational practices suggest it continues to remain a *Brahmin-Bania* party in its core belief and ideology.

Attack on Diversity

The BJP government under Narendra Modi is embarking on a project of Hindu Rashtra based on a common culture, language and food habits. However, diversity is embedded in Indian society and its civilisation. It is a non-negotiable feature which can be infringed at our own peril. The working of government in the last five years reflects an attempt to homogenise the culture and practices of the people in some important domains of life. The implication is that this will lead to imposing over others the wishes, tastes and preference of majority Hindu community. Be it banning of *triple talaq* or banning of cow slaughter in some states will directly hit the culture of diversity and plurality in the country. The former relates to marriage and divorce and latter relates to food habits of the people. Decriminalising *triple talaq* would homogenise the personal law of the country which is justified in the name of gender justice for the Muslim women. This is a move towards Uniform Civil Code that Muslims have vociferously opposed. This is an initiative of party in power which of course identifies itself with the Hindu majority. The national laws on marriage and divorce are followed by Hindus whereas Muslims are allowed to have their own personal laws as prescribed by Islamic faith. This is an exemption which is based on the constitutional morality and also a matter of cultural diversity. As put by Bhikhu Parekh, partly out of respect for their religious and cultural identities and partly to assuage their fears of Hindu rule, the Constitution of India allowed its religious minorities to retain their personal laws and undertook not to change these without their consent. India has a common criminal but not civil law, and the Constitution hoped that the latter would develop over time. Among the conservative Hindus, it has led to a belief that state is privileging and pampering its minorities. However, when different communities have different needs and are not alike in relevant respects, it is unjust to insist on treating them alike.[10]A common civil code cannot be easily evolved out of their different systems of personal laws which runs the risk of enshrining the views of the powerful Hindu majority.[11]However, the state cannot remain indifferent to the iniquities of some personal laws and needs to insist on certain basic principles of justice.[12]

To go for a certain principles of justice to address such iniquities assumes importance. As the society evolves, it should lead to standardisation of religious practices. However, as there is an environment of animosity along the religious line between two large communities, the effort to ban the practice of *triple talaq* in this case has become a bone of contention. It carries the message that, '*They*' (Muslims) should also follow what *'We'* (Hindus) follow or what majority Hindus follow constitutes a standard for the rest. This sounds very erroneous and problematic argument. However, such matter requires dialogue and consensus across party line including the concerned communities. It is a dialogical subject which requires intercultural dialogue and discourse with the community rather than legislation in the first place to impose on them. As the dialogue was never pursued, the attempt to ban the practice of *triple talaq* demeans and does not show equal respect to the Muslim community no matter how much noble intention it might have. In this case, the government is following a group interest which pursued in the name of gender equality.

On the other hand, the banning of cow slaughter has added to another irritant. The message of banning of cow slaughter is loud and clear. The reason is cow is considered sacred in Hinduism. Therefore, cow slaughter is prohibited. But in day-to-day life it contrasts with those groups and communities whose food habit includes beef. Though it is a moral dilemma, the inherent message is to homogenise the food habits of the people as it is already happening under globalisation. But the decision on banning of cow slaughter in a state like Uttar Pradesh has become a serious concern for the farmers who are already in distress. The incidence of stray cattle menace is giving sleepless nights to farmers in Uttar Pradesh. On the one hand, the BJP government has levied 0.5 per cent 'Cow Welfare Cess' in the state, on the other hand, the growing population of abandoned cows are destroying crops and agricultural fields.[13] It has not only affected their economy but it has affected the very cows who the government want to protect. In the absence of proper and adequate shelter house for cows (*Gaushalas*), cows have become more vulnerable to smuggling and theft. This contrasts to the very purpose of banning of cow slaughter.

The Citizenship Bill which was initiated during its first tenure is another such a move to assault the very idea of diversity in the country. As rightly put by Mahesh Rangarajan (2019), "the new Citizenship Bill that makes religious identity the basis of refuge and fast-tracking to citizenship makes India akin to Israel (Jewish basis of nationhood) or paradoxically many Islamic Arab states. This is a far cry from the constitutional order that saw citizenship as equal and based on territory not a uniform culture".[14] The Bill mooted the idea that Hindu, Sikh, Buddhist, Jain or Christian illegal migrants would be considered for Indian citizenship but Muslims would not. It has added to the fears that their demographic balance would be further affected. Far from being a security measure, it has already provoked conflict and if imposed, would provoke more.[15] The Bill is already posing an existential threat to the North-East states but by excluding Muslims from the new Citizenship Bill, the Indian state under Modi regime is not shy of displaying its hate and malice against the community.

Tyranny of Majority

The representative democracy is inherent with the danger of tyranny of majority. India being a representative democracy, the coming of BJP to power with absolute majority on its own, there is a fear of tyranny of majority which looms large in the country, this was something very much observed in its style of functioning. In this regard, both Alex de Tocqueville and J.S. Mill apprehended the possibility of tyranny of majority under the liberal/representative democracy. The root cause of majority tyranny, Tocqueville argues, is the overweening desire on the part of democratic people for equality, which carried to its logical extreme, destroys liberty.... In the name of equality, the majority is willing to destroy the liberty of people to be different. What makes this ideal so extraordinarily dangerous de Tocqueville argues, is its pervasiveness. It is not simply political (for instance, "one man—one vote") but social, economic and cultural as well. The natural inclination of democratic people is to level all distinctions, not just political one. The majority expects others to think exactly like itself and will pressure minorities, and particularly intellectual minorities, to confirm to its opinion. Its danger resides in the fact that it possesses the power to tyrannize irrespective of constitutional protections guaranteeing liberty of thought and expression. Unless checked, says de Tocqueville, majority tyranny may become a form of despotism that extends beyond the majority itself.[16]

Similarly, for J.S. Mill, the tyranny may occur at the hands of racial, religious and national majorities where the average man tends not to look on his own interests as individual rather he identifies himself with groups and finds his interests in the common goals they set for their members. Over the period of time this group become active and develop class conscious which may inflict damage on the remaining interest in society. The greatest danger is the danger of class legislation of government intended for the immediate benefit of the dominant class to the lasting detriment of the whole which will always go against the minorities' views or minorities or less privileged sections of society itself.[17]In Indian context, certain instances of government or party in power that captures and resemblance the phenomenon of the tyranny of majority. Both, equality—to its extreme and group interest are pursued by the ruling dispensation to witness a phenomenon of majority tyranny in the country. The political party (BJP) supposedly represents the dominant and privileged groups who carry with them the massive resentment and anger against the previous government for its welfare agenda and pro-minority stance. It is this political party with huge majority is well placed to promote group interest, the group that the party identifies. Many of its legislations the Modi government tried to enact that reflect the inter-play of overweening desire for equality on one hand and promotion of group interest (of Hindu majority) on the other. The Bill or ordinance on *triple talaq*, and passage of 124th Constitutional Amendment Act, 2019 by the Parliament mandating 10 per cent quota for the Economically Weaker Sections (EWS) among the unreserved category, the idea to abolish Article 370 and Article 35A giving J&K a special status reflect pursuance of equality and group interest together. Why do Muslims not follow the personal laws as others? Why do the poor among the upper castes not have reservation benefits? Why Article 370 is there, why not Article 370 and 35A be abolished, why not people of J&K have same rights as others in the country? Such questions indicate both to the idea of equality and group interest which likely result into a situation of tyranny of majority. The banning of cow slaughter by some states is a case of promoting group interest of majority—the majority as defined by *Hindutva* politics. As per the argument put forth by J.S. Mill, the above instances of legislation may be interpreted as class legislation to benefit the dominant class/castes by the government.

The reflection of tyranny of majority was also seen in the sphere of civil society as well. The cases of atrocities on Dalits or lynching of Muslims in the name of cow protection also reflect the tyranny of majority because people who committed the crime know it very well that their party is in power to protect them. After all they are doing it to protect the group interest of Hindu majority. It is pertinent to mention here that people accused of lynching have actually been welcomed by union minister of the BJP government. The public display of loyalty and support to such accused legitimises the act of violence in the name of cow protection and Hindu right.

In any democracy the tyranny of majority is imminent, be it left or right. The parliamentary form of government without check and balance system of separation of power may prove disaster at some point of time. In a multicultural society like ours more danger it unfolds when a right wing party (BJP) captures power with overwhelming seats on its own. Being conservative and reactionary in its ideological orientation and known for its overt anti-minorities and anti-Dalit sentiment, it is more likely to pose a threat to minorities and disadvantaged sections of society and inhibits more secular and progressive policies and programmes in the country. The simple majority government or a coalition will scale down the intensity of aggression and rigidity of the party in power which will prevent any far right or far left agenda. In the present context, the BJP with its ideology of cultural nationalism and aggressive *Hindutva* politics will always pose a threat to secular progressive democracy in the country.

Majoritarianism and Consolidation of Core Support Base of BJP

Political parties and their leaders ceaselessly pursue power even it means dividing the entire community along a narrow and sectarian lines. Bharatiya Janata Party is no different from other political parties in its pursuit of political power. In its pursuit of power, it is moving ahead with the strategy of polarisation and is trying to create or consolidate a permanent vote bank among the Hindus particularly among the upper castes by harbouring to anti-minorities (particularly Muslims and Christians), anti-Dalit and anti-reservation sentiments. In fact, under Modi government, the ground beneath our feet as almost irrevocably shifted to accommodate the extreme right wing agenda of virulent masculinity, anti-minority and anti-Dalit hate.[18] In post-Independence India, various Hindu organisations always propagated this majoritarian view of democracy. They would argue that because Hindus are a majority in India, it is only natural that national identity and socio-cultural norms in India have to be based on *Hindutva*. This has led to majoritarian tendencies among the Hindus and constructed a narrative of how the Hindus are not getting their just due share in a Hindu majority India.[19] The BJP is in its full swing to benefit from the majoritarianism which itself is a part of that grand strategy of the party.

Besides, Narendra Modi has resorted to an unabated Congress bashing and attributing every single failure in the country to Congress rule in the last decades is another strategy to create deep aversion on the part of people against the Congress party in the country. There is also a call for '*Congress mukt Bharat*'. This reflects his deep aversion for political opponents. Speaking against the Congress and dynasty will possibly placate the upper castes and soothe the anti-reservationists. The party has succeeded this strategy in Gujarat (Gujarat model) and trying to replicate it at the national level as well. In the cultural sphere, the issue of cow protection, construction of Ram temple at Ayodhya and spread of Hindi as national language in other parts of the country that constitute a majoritarian agenda which the BJP thinks will help to build a permanent majority or a permanent vote bank for the party across the country. Once a permanent majority or permanent vote bank is in place, it will be easier for the BJP to come to power at successive elections. It appears true to some extent that the party has succeeded in creating a majoritarian impulses or right wing agenda based on religious and communal identity in Hindi heart land and Gujarat. This majoritarian impulse will not fade away so easily. That is the reason that the vote shares of the BJP in the state assembly elections, 2018 in Hindi heartland and Gujarat remains far formidable. The passage of the Constitutional Amendment Act mandating 10 per cent quota for economically weaker sections (EWS) among the general category will also help consolidation of upper castes in the country.

Apart from the majoritarianism and consolidation of its core support base, what is also seen is a trend of continuing dominance of upper castes in the power structure during Modi regime as well. It is well observed by Chibber and Verma (2018) that...of the twenty-seven cabinet minister in the Union Council of Minister (excluding the prime minister) five are OBCs, two Dalits, one Muslim, one Sikh and one ST Christian. So, two-thirds of the cabinet ministers belong to the upper castes, which is highly asymmetrical to the extent of support the party receives from these social sections. Moreover, almost half of the non-upper caste cabinet ministers belong to the BJP allies, and not the BJP. When we look at the situation in the states controlled by the BJP, we find that of the thirteen BJP chief ministers, eight are from the upper castes, two from the STs (but both states that are predominantly tribal—Assam and Arunachal Pradesh), only two belong to OBCs, and none from the SCs. The biggest challenge before the BJP, therefore, is the mismatch between the altered electoral support base of the party consisting largely of the OBCs, Dalits, and STs on the one hand, and the largely unchanging social character of its leadership on the other. This could become a major source of tension within the party in the coming years.[20]

Disruptive Style of Functioning

The functioning of Narendra Modi government over the last five years is found to be disruptive which is caused by the policy it makes and interference in various government and autonomous institutions. The decision on demonetisation and GST caused huge disruption to the normal course of life. Both the decisions were hurriedly planned and poorly executed causing hardship to the people. GST which was supposed to usher into "One nation, one tax", has complicated the process with multiple tax slabs. The current rate structure is too complicated. This would only perpetuate confusion, corruption, and litigation.[21] Further; it is prone to bureaucratic hassles which is likely to hurt the business prospects of MSME sector. There are several challenges that the GST is facing due to its premature implementation.[22] As the ground realities are reported, the GST is proving hard for small business and unorganised sector. Dalit ideologue Chandra Bhan Prasad says demonetisation and GST have impacted first-generation Dalit entrepreneurs who have neither capital nor bazar networks: "They only have labour skills and can compete on product quality. However, these inherent advantages are considerably offset in a regime where ease of doing business is only for Big Capital".[23] Regarding demonetisation it is reported that more than 105 people died in the post-demonetisation rush for cash across the country. Demonetisation also hit small-scale businesses and virtually destroyed India's informal and MSME sector, which provided 80 per cent of the jobs in the country.[24] According to the Centre for Monitoring Indian Economy (CMIE), demonetisation caused loss of about 15 lakh jobs. The CMIE compared the employment data for January-April 2017 with the figures for the September-December quarter of 2016, when demonetisation was implemented.[25] It had disastrous effect on the economy which Manmohan Singh, former UPA Prime Minister criticised as monumental mistake and has really pushed down GDP growth by more than two percentage points.[26]

Narendra Modi government has developed a tendency to interfere in the working of government institutions or autonomous bodies including university. The kind of role played by government in case of University of Hyderabad and JNU is well known. The way the government handled the case in these two universities that speaks poorly of Narendra Modi government. As rightly pointed out, the BJP government is wary of students who believe in interrogating, challenging and questioning authority and not letting the government be treated as sacrosanct. JNU and a couple of other universities where a fervent culture of political discourse has thrived have been at the receiving end of a lot of backlashes since Prime Minister Narendra Modi and his Bharatiya Janata Party-led government came to power in 2014. Left-leaning political students at these universities are an ideological threat to the saffron party at a hub where young minds are shaped and tempered.[27] In fact, both state and non-state institutions have come under pressure as the regime attempts to recalibrate and readjust the relationship between institutions of democracy and the popular mandate to consolidate its own authority and ideological control over institutions.[28]

In the similar fashion, the resignation of Dr. Urjit Patel as RBI governor in 2018 supposedly for alleged interference of government and shacking of CBI director Mr. Alok Verma in mid-night coup again supposedly to block the probe into the Rafale deal put government on back foot. Such interference affects their functional autonomy and it also reflects government's lack of professional approach to handle such institutions. Recently, CBI has become a tool of government at the centre to serve its political interest which the opposition allege it as political vendetta. Misuse of CBI, of course, has been a recurrent theme irrespective of whosoever party came to power at the centre in the past and Modi government has equally perfected the art of politics to use CBI for its political gains with ruthlessness. The extent of politicisation of CBI is so much that at one time, the Supreme Court called CBI a "caged parrot", which needs to be insulated from external interferences.

The Supreme Court also witnessed an unprecedented crisis during Modi regime in 2018 where four senior judges openly mounted a virtual revolt against the Chief Justice of Supreme Court. In a press conference, one of the judges Chelameswar said, sometimes administration of the Supreme Court is not in order and many things which are less than desirable have happened in the last few months. Unless this institution is preserved, "*democracy will not survive*" in this country.[29] The open dissension of Supreme Court judges is the first of its kind in independent India. One of the major reasons for the revolt is the manner in which cases having far reaching consequences for the nation and the institution have been assigned by the chief justice of this court selectively to the benches of their preference without any rational basis for such assignment.[30] One of the cases related to alleged mysterious death of special CBI judge B.H. Loya, who was hearing the sensitive Sohrabuddin Sheik encounter case where the BJP president

Amit Shah was an accused. Later on Supreme Court rejected review petition for a probe into Judge B.H. Loya's death.

Modi—The Leviathan

Modi appears to Indian people in various forms. His ascendance to power signifies a rise of populism in contemporary India which is also a great trend across the world. For many he is a *Hindu Hridaya Samrat* (Monarch of the Hindu Heart). He is also looked at as right-wing authoritarian leader who has the craving for command and control from a single point of authority based on *Hindutva* politics. Other thing we see in Modi is a mighty Leviathan which the English political philosopher Thomas Hobbes wrote long time ago and provided reasoning for an absolute Monarch for a state besieged with chaos and turbulence. People out of desire for security and preservation create a state and equip the Leviathan with absolute power. This absolute power is required to provide security and preservation to the people; otherwise it will relapse into earlier situation which is nasty, brutish and short. Narendra Midi's style of functioning also follows this dictum. Dealing dissent with iron hand supposedly to prevent and avoid chaos and conflict reflects a larger element of a Leviathan in Narendra Modi.

Over the period of time Modi has displayed his aversion for opposition political parties and their unity. The effort for a *Mahagathabandhan* (grand alliance) by opposition political parties before 2019 Lok Sabha elections was ridiculed and criticised as *gathabandhan* of corrupt leaders. It gives the message that, if elected to power, the Indian state will relapse into the era of Hobbes' state of nature which witnessed corruption and mis-governance; similar kind of argument which Hobbes justified for giving more and absolute power to the monarch. Narendra Modi has similar kind of trait to absolutize power. In fact, Modi has chosen to accommodate his friends and rivals in the Cabinet, but at the same time has given himself enormous authority by keeping 'all important policy issues' under his office. The PMO might not just be the driving force behind policies across ministries, but a super cabinet in itself.[31] It is well reflected in his actions and he has tendency to assume and concentrate more power in his hands in the guise of a strong leader or strong government.

To him the opposition coalition wants to form a *majboor* (helpless) government that would allow it to continue its *dukandaari* (transactional corruption), and the NDA want a *mazboot* (strong) government. He precisely said at a meeting of National Council of the party that "We want a strong government so that we can put an end to corruption. These days there is a failed experiment taking place in the country which is known as the grand alliance. They do not want a strong government which will lead to shutting down of their shops."[32] Narender Modi carries the capacity to easily dilute and divert the allegations and criticism of the multitude known as opposition parties which remains his strongest attribute as a politician in the country. In the process, he creates fear among the masses of unstable coalition government if united opposition comes to power.

In fact, ever since Indira Gandhi declared a state of emergency in 1975, no prime minister has been able to gain political momentum without triggering fears of creeping authoritarianism and inspiring the fragmented opposition to unite. This pattern brought down Indira in 1977, Rajiv in1989, and the first BJP prime minister, Vajpayee, in 2004. The same dynamics may repeat itself in this year's election... BJP knows this very well and will try to derail budding opposition alliance by casting them as cynical and unprincipled coalition whose only common interest is power.[33]

The Leviathan state under Modi regime has succeeded politically in drawing a line between true Indians and their enemies, and rallying a popular support for a crackdown on those enemies. It is here, in particular that the BJP regime creates the enemy within that it needs in order for the current incarnation of *Hindutva* to thrive. That enemy, of course, is the political dissident—the activist, the public intellectual, the student, the lawyer and the journalist who dares to question and challenge a government… The enemy within is accused of being "anti-national" and subjected to harassment, silencing and …. murderous violence. It is also crucial to acknowledge that this coercive dynamic does not only take the form of repression against social movement, activists and dissidents… it also takes aim at vulnerable groups and minorities, such as Muslims and Dalits, through the majoritarian cultural politics that has crystallised around issues such as cow protection, inter-religious love and religious reconversion.[34]

As succinctly put by Rudranshu Mukherjee (2018), ... A political party, and its various wings, because they enjoy a popular mandate are assuming that they have the right to impose their views on people who disagree with them. The first step is to label the dissenters with epithets that incite passion—'anti-nationals', 'Maoists', 'terrorists', 'perpetrator of sedition', 'beef eaters' are some of the common labels being used for anyone who dares to criticise. These epithets are then being used as an excuse for state action—arrests, humiliation, denial of bail.[35] The arrest of some prominent activists who participated the conference known as Elgar Parishad in 2018 at Shaniwar Wada near Bhima Koregaon was an example of intimidating role of the state.

The brutal manifestation of a Leviathan state under Modi regime in the last five years has witnessed severe misuse and abuse of sedition laws and National Security Act (NSA) which is unprecedented. As brought out by the *Outlook* magazine (a report by number of authors), the number of people booked under sedition laws and NSA is simply baffling. Even on flimsy ground people have been booked and arrested under many sedition laws and NSA. Those people often happen to be the poor, students and political activists. It has led to a scary situation. In fact, in cattle related cases people have been arrested under NSA. Students who assaulted an English TV channel crew in Aligarh Muslim University charged with sedition laws. People protesting against a contentious Bill have been charged with sedition in Assam. A journalist critical of a chief minister has been booked under the NSA in Manipur and left leaning activists have been slapped with the draconian Unlawful Activities (Prevention) Act (UAPA) in Maharashtra. Last year, Jharkhand police charged 20 Adivasi rights activists with sedition for Facebook posts criticising the BJP government and for allegedly inciting villagers to bar "outsiders". More bizarre was the case from Bihar's Rohtas district where eight people, including five children, were charged with sedition for dancing to a song carrying the word "mujahid" or holy warrior.... In December 2017, four women were charged with sedition in Uttar Pradesh after they blocked Adityanath's convoy. Chandrasekhar Azad, Umar Khalid, Kanhaiya Kumar and many others have been charged and arrested under NSA. For hundreds of people languishing in jails across the country for reasons as outlandish as dancing to a DJ's tune, the concept of human rights would appear a crude joke.[36]

While in office, Supreme Court Judge D.Y. Chandrachud laid down the guiding principle of a true democracy. "Dissent is the safety valve of democracy. If dissent is not allowed, the pressure cooker may burst", he said at a three-judge bench hearing on the Bhima-Koregaon violence. His caveat is hard to miss.[37] In fact, in most cases sedition charges invariably fail judicial scrutiny. But its misuse has put a great strain to the vitality of Indian democracy.

Conclusion

As the first tenure of Modi government has come to an end, it proved to be deceptive in terms of revealing the most inherent and hidden agenda of *Hindu Rashtra*. The huge mandate the party got in the Lok Sabha elections, 2014 was used to strengthening the *Hindutva* agenda of *Hindu Rashtra* thereby undermining the diversity in the country. In the guise of a strong and decisive leader, Narendra Modi has displayed typical authoritarian behaviour. In the last five years, the working of BJP government under Narendra Modi has reflected alarming democratic deficit. The most revered principles of democracy, liberty, equality, fraternity and dignity are under threat. The majoritarian agenda based on hatred towards others (minorities) is widening the rift and leading to huge resentment of people. This will erode the importance of solidarity, fraternity and unity among the people which we are missing every other day. To borrow a phrase from Peter Corning, human society is a '*collective survival enterprise*'. The virtue of sharing, cooperation and reciprocity displayed by everyone as a part of larger society have played immense role to sustain the human society to its present form.[38] We cannot afford conflict and war in the society. There is no substitute to human society as a collective survival enterprise. Therefore, the attempt to reverse the forward march of history in terms of assertion of marginalised sections, greater and progressive realisation of equality and liberty, relative peace and stability and economic prosperity will be met with stiff resistance in the time to come.

NOTES

1. Dayal, Raghu (2019). "Can Modi do a Virat Kohli?" *The Times of India*, 22 January.

2. Sardesai, Rajdeep (2014). *2014: The Election that changed India*, Penguin, pp. xi, xvii.
3. Dayal, Raghu (2019). "Can Modi do a Virat Kohli?" *The Times of India*, 22 January.
4. Thakur, Ramesh (2019). "Modi's Leadership Deficit". *The Times of India*, 19 January.
5. Yadav, Yogendra (2014). "At 100, More worries than hope". *The Hindu*, 3 September.
6. Ghatak Maitreesh and Mukherjee Udayan (2019). *Modi's five years prove that sustained economic growth is incompatible with toxic Hindutva politics,* Scroll.in, 25 March.
7. Mander Harsh (2018). *Hate Crimes,* Scroll.in. 13 November.
8. *Ibid.*
9. Thakur, Ramesh (2019). "Modi's Leadership Deficit". *The Times of India*,19 January.
10. Parekh, Bhikhu (2006), *Rethinking Multiculturalism: Cultural Diversity and Political Theory*, Palgrave, p. 192.
11. *Ibid.*, p. 193.
12. *Ibid.*
13. "Cattle Menace: Gaushalas Not a Solution, Lift Ban on Slaughter", 7 January, 2019, *News Click.*
14. Rangarajan, Mahesh (2019). "We the people at the cross road". *Outlook*, 23 January.
15. Kumar, Radha (2019), "A tale of two manifestos". *The Hindu*,16 April.
16. Nelson, Brian R. (1996). *Western Political Thought: From Socrates to the age of ideology*. Pearson, pp. 299-300.
17. Hacker Andrew (2006), *Political Theory: Philosophy, Ideology, Science*, Surjeet Publications, p. 586.
18. Mannathukkaren, Nissim (2019). "The ground beneath our feet has moved to the right", *The Hindu*, 25 January.
19. Palshikar, Suhas (2017). *Indian Democracy,* Oxford University, pp.148-49.
20. Chibber, Pradeep K. and Verma, Rahul (2018). *Ideology and Identity: The Changing Party System in India*, pp. 253-254. Oxford University Press.
21. Banerjee, Sudipto, Prasad, Sonia (2017). "Small Businesses in the GST Regime". *Economic and Political Weekly*, p. 21.
22. *Ibid.*
23. Damodaran, Harish (2019). "In Agra shoe bazar, lingering pinch of GST, note ban". *The Indian Express*, 17 April.
24. R.K. Sudhaman (2018). *Dailyhunt*, India Press Agency (IPA), 16 August.
25. Dutta, Prabhash K. (2018). "Demonetisation: What India gained, and lost". *India Today*, 30 August.
26. Sudhaman, R.K. (2018), *Dailyhunt*, India Press Agency, August 16.

27. Amin, Muntaha (2018). "Why the BJP wants to weaken an Indian University". *Asia Times*, 9 July.
28. Hasan, Zoya (2018). "Our institutions are at risk under Modi". *Business Standard*, 19 December.
29. PTI (2018). "Supreme Court Crisis: All not okay, democracy at stake". *Business Line, The Hindu*, 12 January.
30. *Ibid.*
31. Nathan, Sunder (2014). *Will Modi achieve—minimum government, maximum governance?* globalriskinsight.com/14
32. Hebbar, Nistula (2019), "Opposition coalition wants weak government to carry on corruption". *The Hindu*, 12 January.
33. Sharma, Ruchir (2019). *No Country for Strongmen: How India's Democracy Constrains Modi.* Foreign Affairs, March/April.
34. Alf Gunvald Nilsen (2018), *Authoritarian populism and popular struggles in Modi's India,* Open movements' series, Open Democracy, 22 November.
35. Mukherjee, Rudranshu (2018). *Twilight Falls on Liberalism,* Alpesh Spotlight, pp.113-14.
36. Bordoloi, Anupam, Nair, Preeetha, Ahmad, Saliketl (2019). *Outlook*, 14 February.
37. *Ibid.*
38. Corning, Peter (2011). *The Fair Society: The Science of Human Nature and the Pursuit of Social Justice,* The University of Chicago Press, p. 38.

17

Demystification of "Personalised" Foreign Policy of India

Vinod Khobragade

Introduction

The emergence of Narendra Modi as the powerful Prime Minister and his interests in foreign policy have significantly become the considerable subject of debates and discussions not only amongst the Indians but the International scholars and leaders as well. Mr. Modi grabbed the power with the dream of making 'New India' and the global ambition of pushing India in the elite club of the world's leading countries. The world also has been looking up to India's potentials with great expectations. So, with this perception, Mr. Modi began sending signals across the world that India, as self-confident and responsible power, has been intending to play strategically important and leading role in the world affairs, and as a result, he strategically triggered a robust paradigmatic shift in India's foreign policy by relinquishing, as believed by many, the traditional Nehruvian foreign policy framework or legacy. In this context, Harsh V. Pant opined, "Foreign Policies of nations do not alter radically with changes in governments, but with the backing of the Indian electorate's decisive mandate, the Narendra Modi government...underlined that it was keen to bring about a realignment of India's foreign policy priorities and goals."[1] Therefore, it will not be an exaggeration to refer the new approach of India's foreign policy as 'Modi's Policy'. For Tremblay and Kapur, "Modi has been able to bring about a shift in the global thinking from a perception of Indian foreign policy that lacks direction to one that is coherent, well-articulated and proactive."[2] The drastic transformations in India's foreign policy from the Nehruvian era includes 'the pragmatic decision making', 'unpredictability' and 'integrating defence into diplomacy', besides, 'the increasing business and building trade ties', and 'leveraging soft power'. Therefore, looking at the progress and transformation in India's foreign relations, India's Foreign Minister S. Jaishankar believed that under Modi, India's foreign policy underwent paradigm shift. Furthermore, Pant observed that the foreign policy of India has been slowly becoming 'personality driven', and India's outreach has also been increased, as it has been engaging more with others.[3] Sreeram Chaulia called Mr. Modi as 'a force of nature', who has been "changing India's strategic culture and the DNA of India's foreign policy."[4]

Looking at India's mounting prestige across the globe, Mr. Modi demonstrated a vision of making India a $5 Trillion economy by 2024. The main goal of the Indian diplomacy has been set to create an enabling environment for economic development, which has been one of the main mottos of India's foreign policy since Independence. To achieve this, Mr. Modi has consistently made untiring visits across the world to engage with major countries in terms of trade, commerce, investment, and also for defence and military procurements, and besides, to attract the world towards India and its great heritage and culture. Therefore, looking at the major transformation in foreign policy, Happymon Jacob stated:

> New India's foreign policy has not only given up the Nehruvian normative angst but has even shunned the pretences of normative behaviour. Economic and military power today are seen as tools to gain advantage *vis-à-vis* others, be it neighbours or the larger international system. To that extent, there is a strong link between internal and external posturing, unlike in the case of most previous governments which made a deliberate attempt to be internally liberal and externally realist.[5]

Offensive and Risk Taking Approach

The military action taken by any government demonstrates that that state is led by a strong leader with the deterministic approach and strong conviction for the security of the state and its people. On Mr. Modi's deterministic actions, it has stated that:

> Narendra Modi came to office as a decisive populist promising a more virile foreign policy. We have seen this machismo in action in India's willingness to retaliate against military and militant violence with cross-border strikes. The stand-off on the Sino-Bhutanese border at Doklam was a sign that India was willing to draw red lines for China and back them up with military resolve...Modi's air strikes on Pakistan in the wake of the Pulwama atrocity were seen as a departure from the unwillingness of Congress-led governments to risk cross-border reprisals. The reprisals ...symbolized the government's determination to call Pakistan's bluff.... The willingness to talk up military retaliation is a departure for Indian foreign policy.[6]

However, in 1971, the then Prime Minister Indira Gandhi, keeping the national security in mind, had also followed the offensive and risk taking approach against Pakistan and created Bangladesh. Besides, Indira Gandhi could also be successful in incorporating Sikkim in India in 1975. Subsequently, since 2014, India's Foreign policy shifted from idealistic to pragmatic approach. With this transformation, it has ecstatically argued that Mr. Modi has joined the club of world leaders who are firmed and dare to take military actions against the enemies of the nation. Mr. Modi's robust actions against the militancy have apparently displayed his strong militarily diplomatic approach. India's air strike on terrorist's training centres in Pakistan occupied territory has occupied the space in India's foreign policy which appearing to be impacting and staggering the world and moving forward to reshape the global narratives. His action has obviously shaken not only Pakistan's leadership and military establishments, but bewildered Pakistan's friends also. This exhibited that Indian Prime Minister has potentials to apply military power, though limited, in its foreign policy means if it requires. So, Mr. Modi is believed to be a 'Risk Taker', and his military action is held as "a massive diplomatic gamble."[7] He believed that one must plan for the future, and everything cannot be seen from a political point of view. This rightly reflects in his readiness to military options. In fact, to accomplish his strategic vision, Mr. Modi focused on his personal equations, and he also believed to be disruptive and unpredictable, and if required unhesitatingly forceful.[8] Furthermore, Modi government's robust decision to abrogate Article 370 and division of Jammu & Kashmir into Union Territories of J&K and Ladakh further shook the neighbours, especially Pakistan and its all-weather friend China, and the world community as well. This division is held as "Modi's largest foreign policy gamble."[9] Mr. Modi has been branded as "a decisive prime minister unwilling to be constrained by political correctness or external censure."[10] In fact, the "Foreign policy choices, or political choices with foreign policy implications, are, in fact, shaped by ideological positions."[11]

However, despite Modi's action in Jammu & Kashmir has been convincingly justified by India in the UN, but, it could not be abstained from criticism from around the world. The United States Senate Committee on Foreign Relations has called the situation in Jammu & Kashmir as 'humanitarian crisis' and also called the Indian government to normalise the situation there. Moreover, the US House Foreign Affairs Committee stated, "India's communication blackout in Kashmir is having a devastating impact on the lives and welfare of everyday Kashmiris. It's time for India to lift these restrictions and afford Kashmiris the same rights and privileges as any other Indian citizen."[12] However, some countries maintained silence believing the matter as an internal issue of India. Contrarily, China supporting Pakistan called the official bifurcation of J&K as 'unlawful' and 'void'. However, India discarded this by stating its action as internal matter. By and large, however, "the internationalization of the Kashmir issue points to troubling diversions from India's traditional foreign policy."[13]

Neighbourhood First and its Complications

As Stanly Johny argued, "Realistically, an emerging power should stay focused on building capacities while maintaining good ties with the neighbours, deep engagement with the extended neighbours and balancing between great powers."[14] By learning this, Mr. Modi has been strategically and adroitly moved forward in the realm of diplomacy. India's 'Neighbourhood First' policy, as held, appeared to be refining further. Except Pakistan, as believed, India's neighbouring countries seemed to be nurturing better approach towards India without making major grudges, and even Modi's India has also demonstrated equal gesture towards them. Some analysts joyfully upheld that India and its neighbours today seem to be enjoying one of the best periods of their bilateral relationship with the positively pervasive developments in the areas of diplomatic, political, economic, cultural and security affairs.

Since Mr. Modi occupied power, the Bangladesh government led by Prime Minister Sheikh Hasina has "uprooted security threats and acts of insurgency against India, and today, India-Bangladesh border is one of India's most secured."[15] In 2015, both the countries showing mutual goodwill and positive approach signed the Land Boundary Agreement, which led to the relations between India and Bangladesh, and "the two border guarding forces at their best right now."[16] As a result, India's foreign policy under Mr. Modi can claim great success in terms of India's relations with Bangladesh today. In fact, as has been rightly observed, the regular and frequent diplomatic meetings between the leaders of the neighbouring countries have always been the hallmarks of strong friendship. The visit of Sheikh Hasina to India in October 2019 further strengthened bilateral relations. Both the countries now have developed proximity by improving their engagement in the strategic sphere, alignment on regional and global issues, connectivity and trade, and also, both the countries committed to upgrade port facilities, implementation of India's underutilised Lines of Credit, a coastal surveillance system, and agreements on education, culture and youth. Besides, they have also committed to coordinate better border management and counter terror cooperation. They are also working on a regional trilateral energy sharing agreement with Bhutan. Moreover, Mr. Modi and Ms. Hasina have assured each other to cooperate and resolve the bilateral issues of concerns amicably. It has believed that "Bangladesh has emerged as the good news story for India among its neighbours, and an anti-thesis of India's western neighbour, Pakistan. Bangladesh's growth engine promises prospects of mutual benefits."[17] However, it has stated that "India's abiding regional strategic objective ought to be one which ensures that Bangladesh does not morph into a Pakistan, either by way of being compelled into choosing Beijing over Delhi; or nurturing radical Islamic ideologies domestically."[18] Above all, however, despite improved Indo-Bangladesh relations, with the help of its economic diplomacy, China has embraced Bangladesh in terms of trade. This has further added in India's concerns.

Furthermore, India's relations with Maldives, today, also appear to be friendly and cordial which rightly justifies by the supportive argument of Maldives former president and Maldivian Parliamentary Speaker Mohamed Nasheed. He supported India's stand on Article 370 and distanced Maldives from the statement issued by the 57-member Organisation for Islamic Cooperation (OIC) criticising India on the Kashmir episode. Mr. Nasheed held Kashmir as India's internal issue, and argued, "The Maldives cannot be with the OIC on this issue. None or very few OIC countries are democracies and we don't think they should be commenting on human rights in India, which is a democracy."[19] Moreover, given improvement in bilateral ties, both India and the Maldives are said to be promoting defence cooperation very shortly, and they have also finalised the agreement for lease of a Dornier aircraft aiming at bringing the Maldives under India's coastal radar network (maritime surveillance). But, the question remains that how long these states would maintain cordiality with India as with the change in regimes and leaders in the states like the Maldives have always brought differently sour flavour in bilateral relations with India. Therefore, India's foreign policy with these states should be designed according to the volatile situations in these countries and also should understand the nature of major leaders, both in power and off the power, there.

Further, Mr. Modi's visit to Nepal in 2019 has been held more crucial and positive and both the countries signed various agreements of mutual benefits. However, Nepal has always nurtured grudges against India for myriad reasons, and Nepal also has exhibited its negative perception on various occasions blaming India's interference in Nepal's domestic politics. Recently in May-June of 2020, the tensions between two countries resurfaced. And this time, Nepal dared India hinting, perhaps, that Nepal has been ready to wage war against

India. The tensions between two took place after Nepal's move of redrawing its political map that claiming India's territory as its own. In fact, it seems that a small Nepal following the steps of expansionist China. The tensions reached at the height when the Nepalese Security Forces opened fire on Indian nationals. Arguably, Nepal seems to be joining gradually India's 'enemy club of China and Pakistan' in the neighbourhood. This has unfortunately raised major question on India's approach towards Nepal. In fact, it explicitly appears that Nepal has come under huge influence of China, which has been providing indomitable spirit to Nepal's leadership against India's posture and its leadership.

Moreover, as it's 'Neighbourhood First' policy, Modi-led India positively enjoyed better relations with Sri Lanka under President Sirisena who was pro-India against former pro-Chinese President Mahinda Rajapaksa. However, now, Sirisena is out and Mahinda Rajapaksa is back in the Sri Lankan politics which has unequivocally heightened India's concerns in its neighbourhood. The on-going developments in South Asia exhibit that India's opposite group led by China appearing to be gaining more vigour against India's interests in the region. Besides, with the major political developments in Afghanistan after withdrawal of the US, the Taliban could gain more strength that challenging India's interests there. Since 2001, India has huge investment there, but due to the changing political equations, India's interest in Afghanistan seems to be vanishing and India may probably face huge loss. In other words, India seems to be losing ground in Afghanistan too. The anti-India states China and Pakistan have greater proximity with the Taliban. But, India failed to understand the significance of the Taliban, consequently, failed to reach and engage with the Taliban. Contrarily, by understanding the reality of geopolitics there, all the major powers have engaged with the Taliban. India's stand further proved to be moralistic rather realistic on Afghanistan.

By and large, given India's foreign policy interests, Mr. Modi and his team have tried their optimum efforts to bring success in India's neighbourhood first policy. According to Pant, "Modi has tried to redefine India's strategic periphery, reimagining the country's neighbourhood on more favourable terms."[20] However, India's foreign policy fails at many fronts and even in resulting in countering/breaking the China-Pakistan dyad. Because, they together seem to be proactive at every front to rise against India's interests in and beyond the region. By and large, India has tensions with almost every bordering state because of which India's neighbourhood diplomacy, which premised on unrealistic multiple efforts, could not add regional leverage in its credit. The analysts are thinking and looking at the situation as if India is isolated in South Asia? Despite its regional superpower stature and all other fall under China's influence. This has obviously mounted India's concerns in its hinterland. India failed to extend needed priority to these countries. It is believed that India promises and China delivers.

India's Multilateralism

India was criticised earlier for being a 'rule taker' or even a 'rule breaker' rather than a rule maker or rule shaper in global governance. Besides "India's selective behaviour in the international negotiations have contributed to a reputation of being reluctant to fully engage in global cooperation and act as a responsible rule maker."[21] However, the US has observed India as rising power that could help to shape the balance of power in Asia.[22] India also looking at its strategic interests in the Indo-Pacific region became the part of Quadrilateral Initiative with the US, Japan and Australia. Significantly, India's engagement with the multilateral platforms, such as the UNO, the WTO and others, which also became a part of its diplomacy as they offer opportunities to gain and protect its interests in the world politics. This has honestly learnt by Mr. Modi. During his scintillating speech in United Nation's General Assembly (UNGA) in September 2019, Mr. Modi smartly demonstrated a distinctive nature of 'India's multilateralism.' He garnered and mobilised support of the world community and leaders against the cross-border terrorism or violent extremism especially spotting Pakistan, and he could succeed pushing Pakistan under the cudgel of the FATF (Financial Action Task Force) also. He gave the message to the world focusing across the contemporary global issues such as the dangers of violent extremism and the exigency for combating the problem of climate change rather focusing or responding futilely to the Pakistan Prime Minister Imran Khan's frustrated drum beating on the Kashmir problem and trying to invite the world community's sight against India. Mr. Modi made his brilliant efforts to convince the world on India's stand of changing the constitutional status of Jammu & Kashmir. Except China and Turkey that had overtly extended support to Pakistan, most of the member countries at UNGA remained silent and exhibited no opposition to India. By and large, India's diplomacy in UNGA has won the valuable political breathing space for India on the Kashmir issue.[23] Significantly, it has observed that "If the PMs' campaign on terrorism was about aligning India's concerns with those of the world, Modi's commitment on combating climate change is about accepting national responsibility and demonstrating international leadership."[24] And Mr. Modi "invited the UN member states to join coalition to promote resilient infrastructure that can cope with climate change and disaster," and Mr. Modi has reversed India's earlier stand on climate change as it was caused by the industrial countries and reluctance to address it.[25] Moreover, giving more importance to the environmental security and climate change, Mr. Modi (Champions of the Earth award) earned prestige for pioneering work in championing the International Solar Alliance and promoting new areas of levels of cooperation on environmental action. Since the withdrawal of the United States by President Trump from the Paris Agreement in 2017, India has been emerged as a responsible nation in front of the other developing nations of "how stronger [environment and] climate actions could be successfully aligned with development imperatives."[26] Besides, India has shown more interests to work for the maritime security. More significantly, India along with the other potential states (G4-Brazil, Germany, Japan and India) has been pushing forward to enter the UN's Security Council as permanent members. During his September 2019 UNGA speech, Mr. Modi said, "In this new era, we have to give new energy and direction to multilateralism and the United Nations." However, the idea of multilateralism has been facing multiple problems because of the great power rivalries and geopolitical competitions especially between the US and China today. It has stated that though multipolarity is strengthened, but multilateralism is weakened.

India at the High Table of Global Politics

Since long, India witnessed a special tilt towards Russia, given the

American proactive support to Pakistan, and its long-standing hostility with Pakistan and China. In fact, India's leadership due to lack of self-confidence and meagre power leverages at the global level, never dared to come out of the stereotyped thinking approach for its calculative foreign affairs, and strictly appeared sticking to it by virtue of securing the Russian support. However, gradually, with the changing leaderships that contributed towards the maximization of its multiple power that making India's entry in the circle of the globally recognised emerging powers, global community started thinking of the potentials of India to play major and crucial role in the making of new world order. Focusing more, Mr. Modi's foreign policy furthered India's relations with the U.S. which have, today, attained new heights, and relations with Russia also have gained new and fresh colour that covering economics and longstanding military engagement. In this section, India's foreign policy engagement with Russia, the US and China, during Modi period, has been taken for analysis.

Keeping the Legacy of Relations with Russia

In the presence of Russian President Vladimir Putin, in Vladivostok, Prime Minister Narendra Modi, on 5 September, 2019, unveiled 'The Act Far East Policy' (Russian edition of India's Look East, Act East Policy) to re-invigorate India's proactive engagement with the Russian Region and also announced unprecedented $1 billion line of credit for the development of Russia's Far East. During the plenary session of the fifth Eastern Economic Forum (EEF), which was set up by President Putin to attract investment in the farthest outlying East Siberian and Arctic-pole areas of Russia, Mr. Modi stated, "Let us deepen the bond between India and Russia even further...India is proud of the achievements of the Indian Diaspora. I am sure here in the Russian Far East, too, the Indian Diaspora will make an active contribution towards the region's progress."[27] In this EEF, India believed to be concluded 50 agreements worth of $5 billion especially on energy exploration and procurement, that including a specific MoU on cooperation on LNG supplies to India and more importantly, a maritime route from Vladivostok to Chennai, which would be used for energy trade also. Moreover, both the countries also agreed on a five year roadmap for cooperation on prospecting for hydrocarbons and

LNG in the Far East and the Arctic, building on a history of Indian investment in oilfields in the region. In fact, aiming at India to become a $5 Trillion economy by 2024, Mr. Modi believed that that region would provide major investment opportunities for India. He also extended India's assurance that India would walk shoulder-to-shoulder with Russia in its quest for the development of the resource-rich region, Vladivostok. In fact, India's lending to Russia has been held unique and Mr. Modi held Russia's Far East region as India's launching pad. According to Mr. Modi, the line of credit would help finance Indian business projects there and the region would also be 'take-off point for Act Far East.' This will, as Mr. Modi believes, further strengthen bilateral relations between two traditional partners. Moreover, it has believed that Mr. Modi's visit to Vladivostok was held special as "several initiatives being launched towards increasing the value of economic ties between the two countries, which, at approximately $10 billion in terms of bilateral trade, lags far behind their strategic partnership and defence relationship."[28] In the year of 2018 alone, India has contracted defence deals worth of about $14.5 billion from Russia.[29] Given Modi's strategic inclination towards Russia's Far East, it has upheld that:

> The emphasis on energy from this region is as much a bid to benefit from explorations and trade routes in the Arctic that are becoming accessible due to global warming, as it is reflective of India's desire to diversify its energy sources away from an unstable West Asia. The investment in the Far East, which is often neglected given that Russia is seen as a European power in the post-Soviet era, also underlines India's desire to draw Russia into its strategic forays in the Indo-Pacific.[30]

The Indian government also exhibited its willingness to welcome cooperation from Japan also for the investment in Russia's Far East Region, despite their territorial disputes in the region. Significantly, India looks at this as its "attempt to not only keep a traditional friend close, but to ensure some space in the current clinch between Russia and China."[31] Moreover, it has believed that "the push to Act Far East allows India to demonstrate its commitment to an area of concern for Moscow, thus reassuring its traditional partner that in an increasingly polarised world, India is confident of working with multiple alignments, even if they are at cross purposes with each other.[32] Russia also offered a joint design and development of conventional submarines through an inter-governmental agreement at the delegation level dialogue between Mr. Modi and Mr. Putin in Vladivostok.[33]

However, while dealing with the old and reliable friend Russia, India should also be more alert and understand strategically while making its more reliable foreign policy towards Russia. In fact, given the strategic changes in the world politics and accordingly the foreign policy dimensions and thereafter priorities, the states also keep changing their approaches towards the other countries. It should be kept in mind that Russia shocked India by establishing strategic military/defence partnership with India's traditional enemy Pakistan in 2015, which India never had imagined of. Moreover, today Russia and China, the rivals of the past, have developed strategic bilateral proximity given their common hostility with the US. Despite, however, being the part of 'Quadrilateral Initiative', India may face probably a new challenge, the Russia-China Dyad/Russia-Pakistan-China Triad, besides, the China-Pakistan Dyad. Indian leadership needs to take the cognizance of such newly emerging partnership equations and keep India's strategy intact given the possible inevitable critical developments in the future. Therefore, with the consolidation of Indo-US relations and increasing Russia's proximity with China and so with Pakistan, the heydays of India-Russia friendship inclined to be declined. When Russia and China had antagonistic relations, Pakistan was also nowhere in Russia's good book. However, Russia maintained *status quo* in military trades with India and gratifying India's almost all military needs and requirements.

India-US Unprecedented Partnership

Arguably, India's foreign policy of the day led by Mr. Modi has been apparently appears as pro-American, and, however, also simultaneously maintaining its traditional links with Russia though with some diversions. From 2014 to September 2019, Mr. Modi made six visits to the US. During his visit to the US in 2016, then US President Obama had elevated India to the status of 'Major Defense Partner', which as believed, a status which no other country could gain. As a result, India's External Affairs Minister S. Jaishankar convincingly believed that Indo-US relations have been on an upward trajectory and in a very good health. The US President Donald Trump has also extended very warm hands towards Mr. Modi making India convincingly as a 'global strategic partner'. In fact, it will not be an exaggeration to make an argument that India-US proximity today has been depicted best ever and stronger. Mr. Modi and Mr. Jaishankar brought major transformations in Indo-US relations. However, Mr. Trump has extended his disagreements with India over 'trades, climate change and H-1B visas'. However, by side-lining the issues of disagreement, both the countries made steps forward in Defence Partnership by means of 'Two-plus-Two Dialogue' in September 2018. The two countries signed an agreement "the Communications Compatibility and Security Agreement (COMCASA)" which provided India access to advanced communication technology used in US defence equipment and allows real-time information sharing between the two countries' militaries. Yet, on 5 June, 2019, the Trump Administration terminated India's preferential trade status on the plea that India has not provided equitable and reasonable status to the US in its own markets.

However, despite some grudges, during Mr. Modi's visit to the US, the mesmeric 'Howdy Modi' event of a gathering of 50,000 Indian Diaspora, at Houston took place on 22 September, 2019 in the presence of President Trump. During his Houston speech, Mr. Modi won the hearts of the Diaspora by asking the audience there to offer 'Standing Ovations' to the Indian law-makers who had helped pass the legislation to abrogate Article 370.[34] Earlier, Mr. Modi advancing partnership with the Indian Diaspora had addressed the Diasporean events in New York in 2014 and San Jose in 2015. Subsequently, during Mr. Trump's first India's visit, 'Trump Event' in Ahmedabad in February 2020 was organised that showcased that India and the US have shed Cold War baggage. Indo-US new partnership has been seen in terms of "what was ignited by P.V. Narasimha Rao, carried forward by Atal Bihari Vajpayee, solidified by Manmohan Singh and had now been given new wings by Modi."[35] In fact, both the events believed to be as a greater achievement for the Indo-US community. Mr. Modi was depicted as in the words of what Theodore Roosevelt had described, "It is not the critics who counts; not the man who points out how the strong man stumbles, or where the doer of deeds could have done them better. The credit belongs to the man who is actually in the arena, whose face is marred by dust and sweat and blood; who strives valiantly."[36]

Additionally, both India and the US have developed a global strategic partnership based on democratic values. The frequent and regular high level meetings between the leaders of both the countries have further provided sustainable bilateral cooperation. In fact, Mr. Trump's intensive affection for India and its Diaspora has its own reasons given the Presidential elections in 2020. By and large, however, the Indo-US relations today reached to the highest level of proximity. As stated by Happymon Jacob, "the two are unprecedently close and despite its nativist leanings, the present regime seems to offer no excuses or qualifiers for getting so close to a superpower, for it knows that hardly any challenges are posed to its foreign policy pursuits in the domestic sphere. Consequently, there is little talk of strategic autonomy."[37] However, despite concretization of bilateral relationship, India should learn the mind of the US's leadership and should take optimum care that India would not be trapped in the US's game of conspiracies for self-interests and cunning global politics given the US's hegemonic standing. The general opinion is that 'the American always tries to fool the world.'

In fact, India cannot afford loosing Russia which has, in recent years, strategically aligned with China and Pakistan, though India demonstrating its balancing policy towards the US and Russia. Further, it is need to understand that both India and Pakistan are the clients for the US's and Russia's arms business. The US is selling sophisticated weapons to Pakistan, and Russia to India, and may be both US and Russia to both the neighbours. In fact, both the US and Russia doing their business, and also demonstrating their traditional rivalry. Even China is not behind in context of arms trade with the South Asian countries barring India. India's defence system has been aiming against the security threat emerging from both Pakistan and China, and Pakistan's especially against India. In other words, the great powers strategically and deliberately helping the India-Pakistan hostility to be alive keeping them under the eternal shadow of mutual fear and strain and provocating the neighbouring countries to fight against each other by using their weapons. So, India as a big and responsible country in the region needs to try and make optimum efforts to create an ambience of peace by developing the confidence amongst the neighbouring countries especially Pakistan and must discourage arms race in the region that initiated by the great powers. However, time will tell how long the Indo-US relations are maintained strongly.

India-China Engagement and Estrangement

The period from 2014 to 2017 has been uncertain between India and China. Both the state's policies and intensions were observed with full of tensions, mistrust and competition that leading to instability of bilateral ties between them. However, after Doklam (Bhutan) dispute of 2017, both India and China pondered on improving the bilateral relations. And in this direction, the first Informal Summit (Wuhan Summit) took place in April 2018 that brought the leaders of both the countries across the table. In fact, at Doklam, Mr. Modi's robust stand compelled the Chinese leadership to move in for Wuhan Summit. In this summit both the leaders decided to "arrest the deterioration in the relationship and attempt to chart a fresh course," and it was "an attempt to articulate some norms that could serve as a renewed set of guidelines to policy-makers and bureaucracies in both countries."[38] But, after abrogation of Article 370 by the Modi government, China grappled with uncomfortedness, and showing its frustration and anguish by supporting Pakistan's logic of opposition to India's domestic action. Further, however, looking at the future relationship, in October 2019, Mr. Modi and Mr. Xi again met at the second informal summit in Mamallapuram in Tamil Nadu further aiming to stabilise and normalize the bilateral ties. In fact, the fundamental motives of both the informal summits aimed at as an initiative to enhance mutual cooperation and furthering the positive relationship for the resolution of bilateral issues. And Mr. Modi's colourful diplomacy of events has been held as unique way of meetings with the world leaders. Mr. Modi met Mr. Xi in India always out of Delhi; for example, in Ahmedabad in 2014, Goa in 2015 and Mamallapuram in 2019. By meeting with Xi, Modi aimed at to successfully normalise the trust deficit and misunderstanding between two countries, but failed. Foreign Affairs, analysts, Zorawar Daulet Singh opined, "India's China policy should be guided by three grand strategic goals: an inclusive security architecture in Asia that facilitates a non-violent transition to multi-polarity without disrupting economic interdependence, a fair and rules-based open international order to better reflect Indian and developing economy interests; and geopolitical peace and sustainable economic development in the neighbourhood. China is important to the successful pursuit of each of these goals..."[39] However, despite everything that appeared to be colourful and enthusiastically positive, the former secretary of India Shyam Saran cautiously stated that the Mamallapuram summit, while a useful and positive development, should not be over-interpreted."[40] Therefore, given China's overall power and leverages, "India needs to engage in careful and nuanced balancing, seeking closer partnerships with other major powers which share India's concerns over the Chinese penchant for unilateral assertion of its new found power."[41] In fact, Saran's four guiding principles for India-China relations are needed to be understood adroitly. Saran hopefully believed that:

> ...India is not a threat to China and China is not a threat to India... there is enough room in Asia and the world for both a resurgent India and China...India-China relations have now acquired a strategic and global dimension and their cooperation is critical to tackling a host of global challenges such as climate change; and... India and China should seek an early settlement of the border issue within this larger perspective so as to better work together on the strategic dimension of their relations.[42]

However, despite multiple efforts by the Modi government to strengthen bilateral relations with China, it often evidenced that China would not render its aggressive posture against India as it has observed that China trespasses into Indian territory more than 300 times every year that further heightening the India-China tensions at the borders. In June 2020, the soldiers of both the countries faced skirmishes at the border near Ladakh region that causing the deaths of about 20 Indian soldiers. The killings of soldiers perhaps took first time in last few decades. During these decades, India followed a balanced diplomacy with China. However, analysts believed that Modi's 'Appeasement Policy' towards China further led the later for trespassing Indian land.

In fact, since the outbreak of COVID-19 crisis, China has become the centre of global criticism and huge international pressure and since then China has been trying to put pressure on India also. Besides, India's pro-US policy also made China more aggressive against India. The Quad group also collectively poses major challenge to China's influence in the Asia-Pacific region as perceived by Beijing also. And China has taken this very seriously. The fact is that China's June 2020 aggression was not a coincidence, but it was pre-planned. When India adopts appeasement policy towards China, whilst Beijing hatches conspiracy. This is evident in the bilateral history of India and China. While looking at India's post-Independence past, J.N. Nehru as the first Prime Minister of India had also followed appeasement policy towards China, and both the countries signed Panchsheel Agreement in 1954, but, behind this agreement China had very serious hidden plan which was resulted into China's war on India in 1962. Similarly, after Modi's Informal Summits with Jinping, China trespassed Indian Territory and killed the Indian soldiers. Looking at the Indo-China bilateral past, the future of bilateral relations may be storming. Therefore, analysts see Mr. Modi also followed appeasement policy towards China.[43] Mr. Modi made about 18 personal meetings with the Chinese President Jinping and visited China for five times. Mr. Modi's Informal Summits with Mr. Xi could take place as an ingredient of Modi's appeasement policy. Therefore, on failures, it has critically argued that "Modi's foreign policy puts Modi First, India Second."[44] In fact, analysts believe that India's foreign policy led by the Modi government has been seen in terms of earning the credits and points in domestic electoral politics. When war or war like situation develops, it is the result of bad diplomacy and its debacle further worsens the bilateral tensions. China does not see India in terms of friend. This is crystal clear reality.

Conclusion

Unfortunately, because of the miscalculated diplomacy, India's neighbourhood are slipping away from India's influence. The Modi government's overinclination towards the US, has further distanced

India from Russia and optimized rivalry with China. China's surging over India in all respects is apparent. The Indian government could not maintain *status quo* of stability with China that causing severe tensions between two countries. India's leadership could not read the mind of China's leader instead followed appeasement policy towards Beijing. Arguably, India's foreign policy making capacity seems to be declining or confused. India cannot afford regular military clashes at the borders with both Pakistan and China. This situation would put heavy blot on India. Therefore, to normalise relations with both China and Pakistan will be major challenge for the government and policy-makers in New Delhi. India should think of standing up to China so that to retain the Beijing from crossing the line. Given its global strategic ambitions, Mr. Modi and his government must focus on advancing India's capabilities and bargaining power at every front. The sustainability of the balanced engagement with the major/great powers in the world need to be maintained for the present and future long term benefits. Suggestively, the politics of the great game rivalry of the US, Russia and China should be learnt and observed adroitly. India should learn and play crucial role in reshaping the equations of international politics aiming India's national interests to be achieved and safeguarded in and beyond the region. The situation in post-COVID-19 will further create and pose major challenges before the government in New Delhi in terms of both domestically and internationally. Therefore, the mechanism should be made ready before the worst situation occurs.

NOTES

1. Pant, Harsh V. (2019). *New Directions in India's Foreign Policy: Theory and Praxis.* New Delhi: Cambridge University Press, p.1.
2. Tremblay, Reeta Chowdhari, and Ashok Kapur (2017). *Modi's Foreign Policy.* New Delhi: Sage Publications.
3. Pant, Harsh V. (2019). *Indian Foreign Policy: The Modi Era*. New Delhi: Har Anand Publications.
4. Chaulia, Sreeram (2016). *Modi Doctrine: The Foreign Policy of India's Prime Minister*. New Delhi: Bloomsbury.
5. Jacob, Happymon (2019). "India's Big Foreign Policy Shake-up." *The Hindu,* October 26, 2019.

6. Kesavan, Mukul (2019). "Modi's Biggest Foreign Policy Gamble: Abolition of Jammu & Kashmir as a State." *The Telegraph,* September 29, 2019.
7. Gokhale, Nitin (2017). *Securing India The Modi Way: Pathankot, Surgical Strikes and More*. New Delhi: Bloomsbury.
8. *Ibid.*
9. Kesavan, 2019.
10. *Ibid.*
11. *Ibid.*
12. Lakshman, Sriram (2019). "Kashmir Curbs Devastating". *The Hindu,* October 9, 2019: 11.
13. Haider, Suhasini (2019). "The Perils of Post-370 Diplomacy". *The Hindu,* November 2, 2019: 8.
14. Johny, Stanly (2019). "Making a Friend of the Neighbour". *The Hindu,* October 12, 2019: 8.
15. Khasru, Syed Munir (2019). "Furthering This Neighbourhood Friendship." *The Hindu,* October 3, 2019, 8.
16. *Ibid.*
17. Roy, Shubhajit (2019). "Hasina in India". *The Indian Express,* October 6, 2019: 3.
18. Bhaskar, C. Uday (2019). "A Triangular Affair". *The Indian Express,* October 9, 2019: 6.
19. Haidar, Suhasini (2019). "Kashmir is India's Internal Issue: Maldives ex-President Mohammed Nasheed". *The Hindu,* October 5, 2019.
20. Pant, Harsh V. (2019). "Modi Reimagines India's Role in the World". *Foreign Policy,* June 4, 2019. https://foreignpolicy.com/2019/06/04/modi-reimagines-indias-role-in-the-world/
21. Debiel, Tobias and Herbert Wulf (2019). "More Than a Rule Taker: The Indian Way of Multilateralism". In *Theorizing Indian Foreign Policy*, edited by Mischa Hansel *et al.,* New York: Routledge, p. 49.
22. *Ibid.*
23. Editorial (2019). "A Win For Diplomacy". *The Indian Express,* September 30, 2019.
24. *Ibid.*
25. *Ibid.*
26. Roy, Aparna (2019). "India and Multilateralism: Climate Change Agenda". *Observer Research Foundation,* August 22, 2019.
27. Press Trust of India (2019). "PM Unveils Act Far East Policy". *The Hindu,* September 6, 2019: 11.
28. Editorial (2019). "Bear Hug". *The Hindu,* September 7, 2019: 8.
29. *Ibid.*
30. *Ibid.*
31. *Ibid.*

32. *Ibid.*
33. "Russia for Joint Submarine Development". *The Hindu*, 6 September, 2019, p. 11.
34. Vashisht, Sunanda (2019). "Man in the Arena". *The Indian Express,* October 1, 2019: 7.
35. *Ibid.*
36. *Ibid.*
37. Jacob, Happymon (2019). "India's Big Foreign Policy Shake-up". *The Hindu,* October 26, 2019.
38. Singh, Zorawar Daulet (2019). "Maintaining the India-China Stride Length". *The Hindu,* October 10, 2019: 8.
39. *Ibid.*
40. Shyam Saran (2019). "After Mamallapuram, the Reality of Asymmetry". *The Hindu*, 21 October, 2019, p. 8.
41. *Ibid.*
42. *Ibid.*
43. Chellaney, Brahma (2020). "India's Appeasement Policy Toward China Unravels". *The Japan Times,* June 8, 2020.
44. Vij, Shivam (2020). "Modi's foreign policy puts Modi First, India Second". *The Print,* June 19, 2020.

18
India's Maritime Security
Issues and Challenges

Ramesh Kumar

Introduction

The Indo-Pacific area runs from the east coast of the Indian Ocean to the west coast of the Pacific Ocean, with the Strait of Malacca connecting the two. The Indo-Pacific region has emerged as a focal point for security, maritime geopolitics, economic, and environmental issues. The Indo-Pacific area is also a crossroad for world trade, with 32.2 million barrels of crude oil passing through each year as well as the region accounting for 40 per cent of global exports. Because of its significance, the region has been challenged by major countries like China, Australia, India, Southeast Asia, Japan, and even the United States. The Indo-Pacific security dynamics have been driven by the power struggle between Beijing and Washington. China has increased its military budget over the years in order to update its military technology and disowning approach capabilities. China's aggression in the South China Sea has resulted in boundary conflicts with Southeast Asian countries, attracting the attention of the US. Meanwhile, as part of the Rebalance strategy, the US has expanded the occurrence of provincial support with Japan, Australia, the Republic of Korea, New Zealand, India, and Southeast Asian countries. In contrast, the

US uses a deterrence strategy to deal with the DPRK's armaments of mass destruction (WMD) operations and China's growing soldierly capacity. In addition to growing seaborne activities, the area now faces additional maritime security problems. The security concerns of protecting sea lines of communication (SLOCs) are growing as a result of the consequential naval conflicts in the East and South China Seas. China and India are stretching their naval troops in the Indian Ocean, escalating tensions between the two countries. Simultaneously, the Rebalance strategy has allowed the US to execute a variety of naval security missions in the Indo-Pacific. Meanwhile, other nations in the area, including Japan, Indonesia, Australia, the Philippines, and Pakistan, are expanding their maritime scope in order to shelter SLOCs and get additional assets. Not to mention unconventional marine concerns like piracy, maritime radicalism, illicit trade, and environmental deprivation. The Indo-Pacific region's security dynamics have been affected by the numerous concerns of maritime security.[1]

What do you mean by Maritime Security?

Maritime security, the newest phrase in international affairs, lacks a widely accepted meaning. National security, economic development, the marine environment, and human security are all classified as concerns in the maritime sector. It also agreements with provincial seas, territorial waterways, ports and rivers in addition to the world's oceans.

Why it is so Important?

Marine security is of paramount importance to the international public, as there are several maritime challenges extending from at-sea piracy to illegitimate immigration and weapon trafficking. Threats of terrorism and environmental disasters are also addressed. A recent incident in the north Arabian Sea off the coast of Oman relating an alleged drone assault on an Israeli-controlled tanker, which killed two crew members, is a case in point. Because India has a coastline of over 7,000 kilometres, marine security is a crucial part of national security for the country. Physical risks in the marine region have been surpassed by technical threats as technology advances. India's imports and exports have mostly persisted inside the Indian Ocean's maritime channels. As a result, safeguarding Sea Lanes of Communication (SLOCs) has become a priority for India in the twenty-first century.[2]

The Indian Ocean

In the north, the Indian Ocean is bordered by the Asian landmass, while in the west; the African continent separates it from the Atlantic. The Indonesian archipelago and Australia to the east limit its access to the Pacific, while Antarctica offers a frigid base to the south. The Indian Ocean's seaborne shipping channels link to the Pacific by small rivers in its eastern and southern reaches, whereas the Atlantic is connected through a challenging path around Africa's southern point. Through the Red Sea's small channels, the Mediterranean and Europe's continental hinterland are likewise allied to the Indian Ocean.[3]

India in the Indian Ocean

India enjoys an advantageous geographic position at the head of the Indian Ocean, halfway between both routes, agreeing it to dominate these tactics and, as a result, its commerce. This peculiarity

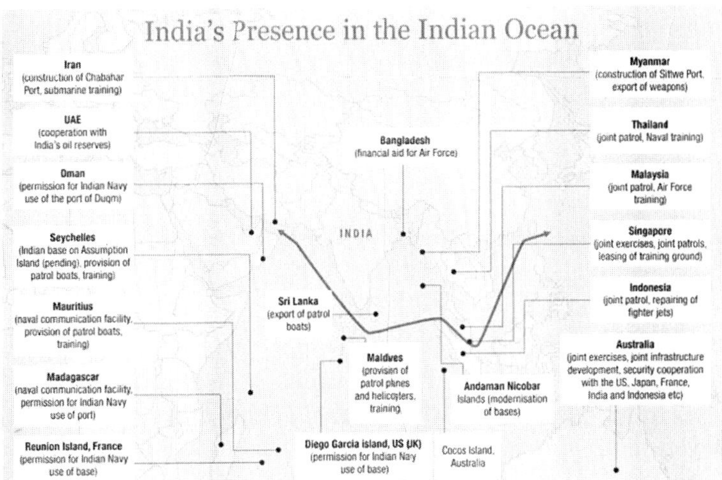

Source: Editor, I. (2021). Insights into Editorial: An opportunity for India to pitch for holistic maritime security [English]. In https://www.insightsonindia.com/2021/08/09/insights-into-editorial-an-opportunity-for-india-to-pitch-for-holistic-maritime-security/

of geological development, along with monsoon and trade wind climatic phenomena, has assumed India an exclusive place in the antiquity of Indian Ocean commerce and occupation. The history of the Indian Ocean is littered with tales of Indian and Arabian nautical traders using these winds to trade to and from India. Because of its geographic location, India served as a platform for European colonial development in the Far East throughout the 16th and 17th centuries. The Portuguese economic kingdom in the Indian Ocean was aided by their base at Goa, which served as a trigger for the conquest of Malacca that followed. This set the precedent for British control of the Indian Ocean from Aden to India, and eventually to Southeast Asia.[4]

Issues and Challenges before India's Maritime Security

The geo-strategic and geo-economic interface is related not just too conventional maritime struggles between nation-states, but also to non-traditional dangers including environmental hazards and non-state actors (maritime piracy and terrorism). Bangladesh acknowledged the need of safe and secure territorial water when the maritime boundaries were delineated. The BIMSTEC, IORA, and ASEAN are now focusing on modern-day maritime piracy, learning from Somalia's coast. Despite the presence of piracy in the waterways between India and Bangladesh, the Indo-Pacific is quickly fetching a hub for maritime crime. In the Bay of Bengal, for example, a criminal nexus has been discovered to be involved in coercion, armed robbery, and maritime abductions. The Straits of Malacca have seen robberies, while the Sulu Sea has seen a wave of piracy related to extremist groups like Abu Sayyaf. Illicit marine commerce and trafficking are on the rise, in addition to maritime piracy and terrorism.[5]

China, India's rich northern neighbour, poses the most serious strategic challenge. Without delving into the specifics of their capabilities and intents, it is safe to say that China and India will be unhappy neighbours. It will take either deft diplomacy or a miracle, may be both, for the two nuclear-armed states to emerge practically concurrently without confrontation. With its strong anti-Indian bent, the all-weather Sino-Pakistan partnership complicates our security challenges even more. The marine component is a relatively recent aspect in the Sino-Indian strategic equation. Both countries' fast expansion has resulted in a greater reliance on energy and raw resources carried by sea. This has drawn attention to the need of uninterrupted sea-lane use for trade and energy transit for both economies. As a result, the IN has additional obligations in the South China Sea, while the PLA Navy undertakes ventures into the Indian Ocean.[6]

The navy's largest issue will be replacing obsolete platforms and equipment in a timely manner. The proposed combat order of 150-170 ships and submarines, as well as may be 250-300 aircraft, anticipates particular supply rates from shipyards and aircraft manufacturers, which they appear to be unable to match. At the same time, our other main source of hardware, the Russians, have blatantly breached solemn commitments on pricing and delivery deadlines. One of the most difficult tasks facing the navy's command will be persuading Russian and Indian DPSUs to deliver on time and on budget. India has become the world's largest importer of weaponry as a result of the DRDO and DPSUs' failure to achieve even a fair degree of self-reliance in major weapon systems during the last 66 years. This must be considered a failure of the DRDO and DPSUs. Another important task for the IN will be to establish a credible and time-bound plan that will persuade the DRDO to develop, reverse-engineer, or import technologies for armaments and sensors for our indigenously constructed warships. Because of its high-profile economic overtones, China's pursuit of a so-called "string of pearls" strategy attracts a lot of attention in strategic circles. While India's navy may not be able to match China's financial prowess, its 'foreign cooperation' programmes have guaranteed the region's maritime environment remains favourable. Aside from training, joint patrols, port visits, and flag-showing deployments, the navy's outreach also involves providing maritime protection on request from neighbours.[7]

Some more challenges are before India's maritime security. These are some of the followings:

Piracy

Commercial shipping, particularly those travelling through some of the IOR's pirate hotspots, has been severely impacted by this international crime. Modern piracy is a complicated issue that is frequently the result of underlying socio-political issues. As a result, piracy in a given place is frequently dissimilar in its approach from piracy in other parts of the world. The solution to removing this plague does not rest just at sea, and it necessitates a multi-pronged effort to address the core of the problem rather than relying solely on naval use to suppress it. While the pirate problem in Somalia in the Horn of Africa has significantly improved as a result of tremendous international pressure, multi-pronged operations, and several navy patrols and task groups—the situation of Indonesia and the Straits of Malacca appears to be deteriorating. Unless adequately addressed (as previously dealt with by MALSINDO, Eyes in the Sky I and II, and others), the intense flow of maritime traffic through the region will be significantly hampered.

Maritime Terrorism

The worldwide fight against terrorism has taken on new meaning in the post-9/11 period, with the Mumbai terrorist strikes of 26/11 emphasizing its maritime component. The latter event ushered in a new era of marine terror, demonstrating the use of the waters as part of the supply chain dynamics for onshore occurrences, as assaults at sea do not generate the appropriate amount of media attention and devastation. Previously, just 2-3 per cent of all terrorist strikes were directly related to the waters, thus governments and security organizations alike overlooked maritime terrorism. However, the present focus has refocused attention, leading to the implementation of a number of effective programmes such as CSI, the overall MDA effort, and the development of coastal security apparatus.[8]

The Rise of Narco-Terrorism/Terror Crime Nexus

Drug trafficking, with profit margins in the hundreds of per cent, has often been used to fund maritime terrorism, insurgencies, and piracy. This is most likely what prompted SAARC Secretary Fathimath Dhiyana Saeed to say in her first statement at the Timphu conference of Interior/Home Secretaries, "Ample evidence points to possible ties between piracy and terrorism, drug trafficking, human smuggling, and other forms of crime", says the report. She went on to say that because the threat was transnational in nature, regional collaboration was the best way to deal with it.

Maritime Pollution and Environmental Disasters

At sea, oil spills and related environmental disasters are a severe concern for maritime traders, environmentalists, and security experts alike. They have the potential to disrupt the free movement of trade and shipping, in addition to wreaking havoc on the maritime environment. Ships must avoid ports and areas affected by such calamities, resulting in financial losses for shipping corporations.[9]

Political Conflict at Indian Ocean Region

Extra-regional powers including the United States, the European Union, Japan, and China have historically exploited the geopolitical situation in a variety of ways. Non-State players and regional states are increasingly influencing global politics. In the last five decades, the IOR has seen at least 160 political confrontations, as well as 12 notable wars, including the two World Wars. Throughout history, the IOR has mostly served as an international thoroughfare. It is quickly establishing itself as a key global crossroads for geostrategic, economic, natural resource, and environmental concerns. Multiple security, maritime policy, and governance concerns are prompting regional and extra-regional parties to pay more attention to Indian Ocean issues in a complex geopolitical context where foreign countries' interests and aspirations are intricately linked.[10]

Mechanisms Existing against Maritime Challenges

UNCLOS

It is also identified as the Law of the Sea Treaty or the UN Convention on the Law of the Sea. It establishes states' rights and obligations in relation to the usage of the world's seas. It protects the awareness that all matters regarding ocean space are entangled and must be handled as a whole.

SAGAR

In 2015, the Indian Prime Minister proposed the SAGAR (Security and Growth for All in the Region) initiative. Its goal is to strengthen security and economic connections with its maritime neighbours while also assisting in the development of their maritime security abilities.

IPOI

The Indo-Pacific Oceans Initiative helped to flesh out SAGAR's concept (IPOI). Marine Ecology, Capacity Building, Maritime Resources, and Reserve Sharing, Disaster Risk Reduction and Management, Academic Cooperation, and Science, Technology, and Trade Connectivity and Maritime Transport were the seven pillars of maritime security that the programme focused on.

QUAD

It is a deliberate conversation between India, the United States, Australia and Japan. The goal is to ensuring that the Indo-Pacific area is "free, open, and wealthy".

Contact Group on Piracy off the Coast of Somalia (CGPCS)

It is a worldwide governance system that was founded on January 14, 2009 in New York. Its goal is to make it easier for nations and organizations to discuss and coordinate steps to combat Somali piracy.[11]

India's Position as an International Maritime Supremacy

India's marine strategy efforts are growing in popularity and are well-received. In 2013, India inked a trilateral maritime security agreement with the Maldives and Sri Lanka, which is expected to develop a five-power alliance that includes Mauritius and Seychelles in the future. For the meantime, China has launched a slew of programmes, including the Belt and Road Plan (BRI), a multi-billion-dollar initiative involving 80 nations across Africa, Asia, and Europe. India has declined to become a member. The China-Pakistan Economic Corridor (CPEC), which is fragment of the Belt and Road Endeavour, is one such Chinese ingenuity to increase its economic dominance with Pakistan, which might have influx consequences on Indian governance. In light of these concerns, India's participation in the BRI might be beneficial if the country portrays itself as a strategic partner. The Asia Africa Growth Corridor (AAGC), a maritime corridor connecting Africa with India and other nations in Southeast Asia and the Pacific, has brought India and Japan together. India has been gradually increasing its strategic reach beyond the oceans, although ties with other littoral governments in the area may yet be improved. It is improbable that India would be able to sustain two beneficial bilateral relationships with the United States and China at the same time in order to extend and improve its maritime profile. However, if India is competent to strike stability, it will be able to cement its position as one of the region's two great powers. Rather of focused on maritime dominance, India would gain from improved coastal government, prosperity and peace in the Indian Ocean region. As a result, Indo-Pacific governance should be built on collaboration rather than domination in order to maintain shared opulence in a free and open Indo-Pacific. India is also expanding its marine policy beyond the Indian Ocean, shifting its focus away from the Indo-Pacific. Beyond IOR, India has bolstered its ties with ASEAN and is observing to the future of the region. China's goal, on the other hand, is to invest in tiny islands and economically strengthen them, as seen by the recent defence cooperation pact with Peru. This is a geopolitical worry since China is fundamentally altering the tactical stability in the Pacific islands, which are still occupied by numerous western nations. "We look forward to goodwill visits by the Indian Navy to Pacific Islands, and the ships might also give help in areas like healthcare through medical camps on the islands", Indian Prime Minister Narendra Modi said at one of the sessions. The Indo-Pacific is one of the world's principal oceanic and land regions, with enormous available mineral assets in some of the world's major fiscal sectors, and Indo-Pacific countries frequently search for assistance from other nations (such as Russia and the United States) in order to guard their marine assets. India, like Russia and China, has set-up satellite surveillance stations to keep an eye on the Indo-Pacific area. As a result, India should increase its investment in Indo-Pacific initiatives, as China has recently done.[12]

Conclusion

India's perspective on maritime security in the Indian Ocean has been shaped and influenced by colonial and Cold War influences and strategic thought processes. Extra-regional states' presence, inter-state interactions, and the lingering, unsolved border concerns have all influenced India's marine strategic vision. India's stance has shifted as a result of the post-Cold War period, China's encroachment, and the US's current posture in the area. Any rise in US involvement and policy shifts to engage places where both an established Indian presence and rising Chinese interest exist might stifle India's image as a net security supplier. The plethora of challenges might turn the Indian Ocean from a relatively "calm" region into one of fierce competitiveness and hostility. As a result, resolving border disputes and establishing a cooperative security system incorporating both regional and extra regional entities is a viable alternative for keeping the 'peaceful' element of the Indian Ocean security discussion alive.

NOTES

1. Tertia, J. & Perwita, A.A.B. (2018b). "Maritime Security in Indo-Pacific: Issues, Challenges, and Prospects". *Journal Ilmiah Hubungan Internasional, 14*(1), 77. https://doi.org/10.26593/jihi.v14i1.2795.77-95
2. August 9, T. C./U., 2021, & Ist, 16:23. (2021, August 9). *Explained: What's maritime security | India News-Times of India.* The Times of India. https://timesofindia.indiatimes.com/india/explained-whats-maritime-security/articleshow/85175697.cms
3. Suri, G. (2016). "India's Maritime Security Concerns and the Indian Ocean Region". *Indian Foreign Affairs Journal, 11*(3), 238-252. http://associationdiplomats.org/Publications/ifaj/Vol.11/11.3/11.3-ARTICLE%202.pdf
4. *Ibid.*
5. Enam Khan, S. (2021, May 3). *New Maritime Security Challenges in the Indian Ocean: Shared Concerns and Opportunities from Bangladesh Perspective/Near East South Asia Center.* Nesa-Center.org. https://nesa-center.org/new-maritime-security-challenges-in-the-indian-ocean-shared-concerns-and-opportunities-from-bangladesh-perspective/
6. Parkash, A. (2013, November 26). *Maritime Security of India: Future Challenges* [English]. Speech, IDSA, New Delhi, India.
7. *Ibid.*
8. Ghosh, P. (2016, January 12). *Maritime Challenges in Indian Ocean Region – Indian Response Strategies and Cooperative Approaches.* Papers.ssrn.com. https://papers.ssrn.com/sol3/papers.cfm?abstract_id=2725267
9. *Ibid.*

10. J. Devakumar (2017). Littoral States Maritme Security: Issues and Challenges. *IOSR Journal of Humanities and Social Science, 22*(05), 47-58. https://doi.org/10.9790/0837-2205014758
11. Khureja, K. (2021, August 12). *Maritime Security Challenges—Explained, Pointwise*. ForumIAS Blog. https://blog.forumias.com/maritime-security-issues-explained-pointwise/
12. Juneja, M. & Ganeshan, S. (2019). *TERI-KAS RESOURCE DIALOGUE V on The Emerging Global Maritime Order—India's Strategy CONFERENCE SUMMARY.* https://www.teriin.org/sites/default/files/2019-08/maritime-strategy.pdf

19
Exploring India's Maritime Connectivity through Bay of Bengal
A Critical Assessment

Dipankar Dey

Introduction

The importance of maritime connectivity is increasingly growing in the 21st century to boost economic transit, strategic interdependency, and logistic support across the Bay of Bengal maritime surface. In recent decades, Ocean has occupied an important place in the contestation of power. If we analyse land power *versus* sea power, traditional geopolitics refers to how to land space has played an important factor in international politics. In a later phase, maritime power did not consider an important factor in enhancing the national interest in terms of economic, political, and socio-cultural interactions. In this period, land power got more attention rather than maritime power. This segmental process has changed rapidly in the 21st century because of the rising multipolar world order. Both land and sea consider as equal power domination in international relations. In contrast, maritime power has seemed as a suitable trading route for many countries to accumulate strategic interest and natural resources.

Hence, it has also been critically reviewed that sea power is crucial for multipolar world order because it has been estimated that 75 per cent of the earth surface is covered by water. Whereas, approximately 40 per cent of the world population living within the 100 kilometres of coastline (The Ocean Conference, 2017). Apart from that, Ocean and Sea have also played an important role in influencing power politics by the blue economic, marine ecology and environment, maritime strategy and international engagement. There have also been certain challenges faced by the maritime environment in the 21st century, namely sea-level rise due to climate change, reducing marine ecosystem, lack of common governance system, increasing reliance on satellites and data sharing, increasing cyber security exposure and risks, ocean acidification etc.

In the present context of maritime connectivity, the Indian and Pacific oceans have emerged with new opportunities to establish power competition and cooperation among the Nation-States. It has accounted that the Indian Ocean and the Pacific Ocean share approximately 60 per cent of World GDP (Gross Domestic Product), and many populations live in this region. In 2007, former Japanese Prime Minister Shinzo Abe addressed the Indian parliament with the title "Confluence of the Two Seas" that he said, the Indian Ocean and the Pacific Ocean has brought "dynamic coupling as seas of freedom and prosperity across the region" (Abe, 2007). Hence, importance of the Ocean has proliferated throughout the Indo-Pacific region in general, and Bay of Bengal in particular in the 21st century.

The Bay of Bengal has a total area of 26,00,000 sq. km and spans a maximum length of 2,090 kilometres and a maximum width of 1,610 kilometres (Indianetzone, 2016). Although, it has a maximum depth of 4,694 metres and an average depth of 2,600 metres (Misachi, 2021). The Bay of Bengal is often known for its richest resources and also refers to the world's biggest bay. However, the Bay of Bengal has located in a very strategic position and trades route which connects from Sri Lanka to the Eastern Indian coast, curving beneath Myanmar and Bangladesh before expanding South through Thailand, Malaysia, and Singapore to the Northern Shore of Sumatra in Indonesia (Chaudhury & Chatterji, 2019). From the account of history, the Bay of Bengal has been a major commercial zone for South and Southeast Asia.

In the context of the current scenario, it has critically reviewed the two main aspects of maritime connectivity—First, need to analyse local level, regional level, and global level; Second, to understand the major threats for implementing free and open maritime domain and long-term maritime resource development. It has been argued that the Bay of Bengal needs to revive its old age sea linkages throughout the littoral coastal region in multiple ways in the 21st century. Currently, the process of maritime connectivity among the region's rim states varies, and these ties are frequently susceptible to political developments that disrupt smooth operations. Improved connectedness would allow for more efficient economic transactions and stronger cultural and political bonds. Furthermore, greater maritime connectivity would open the path for increased security and better management of Ocean resources (Chaudhury & Chatterji, 2019: 241).

In the influx of European colonial powers, the Bay of Bengal was largely used for the colonial power competition, in which British colonial power played an important role to connect this Bay through Southeast Asia. At this point, not only British power, France and Dutch have also developed their strong influence on the Bay of Bengal. Thus, this colonial era had further developed the inter-sea connectivity for transiting agricultural goods, penal settlement, voyage for labour from South Asia to Southeast Asia etc. However, post-World War II, many countries got independence, and the decolonisation movement started across the African and Asian Continent. These newly independent States try to protect their sovereign territory and prioritise their economic interest in a way to self-sufficient to reduce overdependency on trade. As a result, the Bay of Bengal has been marked as one of the significant water bodies in the Indian Ocean region to fulfil the developing countries' economic and strategic desires, such as India, Bangladesh, Sri Lanka and Myanmar.

Maritime connectivity has been re-explored to strengthen economic and strategic domination in the maritime zone despite this historical background. The regional institution has also contributed mainly towards the development of maritime connectivity; the Association of Southeast Asian Nations (ASEAN) and South Asian Association for Regional Cooperation (SAARC) reintegrate the littoral states in the Indo-Pacific region. In 1997, the formation of the Bay of Bengal Initiative for Multi-Sectoral Technical and Economic

Cooperation (BIMSTEC) marked the new era of connectivity has begun with a new opportunity in the Bay of Bengal (Basu & Ghosh, 2020).

Objectives of the Study

- To examine the importance of maritime connectivity in the growing influence of the Indo-Pacific region;
- To examine the significance of the Bay of Bengal and the role of India's engagement in the Indian Ocean Region; and
- To critically examine the cost and benefit analysis of trading and socio-culture engagement through the Bay of Bengal.

Research Methodology

This chapter has focused on the contemporary issue of exploring advanced trading routes in the maritime domain, especially in the Bay of Bengal. This chapter has based on the exploratory research method to explore the insight of maritime connectivity in the Bay of Bengal. The sources of material were collected from various books, articles, newspapers, magazines, reports, government documents etc.

India's Maritime Boundary and its Influence to the Neighbour Countries: Historical Perspectives

India's maritime outreach has huge and oldest to connect the Indian subcontinent to Southeast Asia *via* the Bay of Bengal. Historically, the Chola dynasty had developed its trading routes and involved various maritime connectivity, which extended from the Western to Eastern part of the Indian peninsula to the Southeast Asian Nations. In the 3rd century BCE, Chola rulers prominently used the maritime domain for trading purposes and also used ships for better logistic support and naval warfare (Sagarmala, n.d). The Chola dynasty had got enormous gain in the maritime affairs in order to increased trade, and commerce throughout the Indian Ocean region. It has been argued that the Chola dynasty expanded their economic interest rather than following land expansionism. However, during the era of the Chola dynasty, it has marked that shipbuilding, ports infrastructure development, roads, the establishment of overseas markets, and lighthouses had prioritized by Chola rulers. For instance, there were major ports developed by

Chola rulers across the inland rivers and coastal belt of the Bay of Bengal such as Mamallapuram (Now it is called Mahabalipuram) was the main port for the Chola Dynasty, and other ports had evidence at the various sources that includes Kaveripattinam port located at the junction of Cauvery where meet the Bay of Bengal. There were another couple of ports developed by Chola dynasty such as Kancheepuram, Thootukudi, Kulachal, etc. to promote trade and commerce and enhance their naval capabilities across the maritime region of the Indian Ocean.

This long historical legacy of India's maritime domination through connectivity, trade and security providers across the Bay of Bengal. It is also significant for India to build modern maritime engagement in terms of naval activities, connectivity, trades, and logistics. In colonial times, India's approaches towards the maritime domain greatly influenced the Indian National Army (INA) to fight against the British Raj. Notably, in the account of Netaji Subhash Chandra Bose visit to Andaman in 1943, maritime routes had played an important role.

In 1945, K.M. Panikkar, an Indian historian, diplomat, and statesman wrote a seminal work on tittle '*India and the Indian Ocean: An Essay on the Influence of Sea Power on Indian History*', where he said,

> "...Indian Ocean is only one of the important oceanic area, to India it is very vital sea. Her life line are concentrated in that area. Her future is dependent on the freedom of that vast water surface. No industrial development, no commercial growth, no stable political structure is possible for her unless the Indian Ocean is free and her shore fully protected" (Panikkar, 1945).

Despite this historical legacy, India has shared the largest coastline in the Bay of Bengal, with additional Andaman Sea. In terms of India's immediate neighbours in the Bay of Bengal region are Bangladesh, Sri Lanka and Myanmar. India and Bangladesh have both land and maritime connectives opportunities for the better movements of people and mercantile across the border. It has provided better movement of goods and people and improved sub-regional connectivity.

India and Sri Lanka have shared only maritime boundaries in the Gulf of Mannar and the Bay of Bengal (Bureau of Intelligence and

Research, 1978). However, Myanmar has a special case for India's long-term interest to connect with the North East States. India and Myanmar have very critical maritime boundary spanning through the Coco channel, the Andaman Sea, and the Bay of Bengal.

Whereas, India's extended neighbourhoods, this chapter considers three countries such as Thailand, Indonesia and Singapore. All these extended neighbour countries are very important for India's maritime interest in the Southeast Asia, in order to strengthen its strategic relations, economic partnerships, and people to people contact.

India's Maritime Connectivity: Assessment of Immediate Neighbours and Extended Neighbours Initiatives

India's relations with immediate neighbours have a long historical legacy and played a central position or 'big brother' role in the South Asia region, whether it has connected through land or maritime boundary. This present chapter is only considered Bangladesh, Sri Lanka and Myanmar as a study of immediate neighbours for India.

The Coastal Shipping Agreement (CSA) has been discussed between India and Bangladesh to enhance maritime connectivity. From 2012 onwards, India and Bangladesh are working towards the development of the Coastal Shipping Agreement. However, in 2015, both countries have finally signed the Coastal Shipping Agreement, which aims to enhance bilateral trades directly through ports and launched the new mooring container terminal at Chittagong Port. It has also possible for Indian commodities to transport to the Northeast *via* the Chittagong Port. For instance, finished goods and raw materials can be transported from Kolkata to India's Northeast States *via* Chittagong port or Mongla port in Bangladesh by using multimodal transportation (rail, road, or inland waterways). In this regard, Bangladesh has provided such route to allow India's goods to transport Northeast *via* this possible route through Bangladesh; such routes are: First, Chittagong port or Mongla port to Agartala (Tripura); Second, Chittagong port or Mongla port to Dawki (Meghalaya) and; Thirdly, Chittagong port or Mongla port to Sutarkandi (Assam) (Chaudhury, 2020: 219-227). Although, India and Bangladesh have signed several agreements to promote the blue economy and security through the collaboration of joint working groups, training, capacity building in the Bay of Bengal. Many Bangladeshi vessels have registered in India as a category of river-sea vessels. This kind of relaxation has promoted the trade and commerce.

Bangladesh has two major ports for international transits and the biggest container-handling port is Chittagong Port, located in the riverbank of Karnaphuli, and another is Mongla port, located on the Pussur River in Khulna.

Whereas, the Maritime connectivity between India and Sri Lanka are inextricably linked. For example, approximately 30 per cent of outgoing containers from India have anticipated passing through Sri Lanka, while 70 per cent of containers heading for India pass through Sri Lanka.

Moreover, Sri Lanka has several ports, which are most important for India's maritime trading purpose. Colombo port has played a vital role in handling 87 per cent of containers and transhipment. Whereas, Myanmar has one-third of the total surface of territory covered by the three major coastlines such as the Rakhine coastline (northwest area, 713 km), the Delta coastline (lower delta area, 437 km) and the Tanintharyi coastline (southern area, 1078 km) respectively, along the Bay of Bengal and the Andaman Sea (Myoe, 2016). The major ports are responsible for international seaborne; such ports are Yangon, Sittwe, Pathein, Mawlamyine, and Myeik in Myanmar (Chaudhury *et al.*, 2018).

India's Policy Initiative for Maritime Connectivity

The Bay of Bengal Initiatives for Multi-sectoral Technical and Economic Cooperation (BIMSTEC)

The Bay of Bengal Initiatives for Multi-sectoral Technical and Economic Cooperation (BIMSTEC), which was founded in 1997, includes the seven-member States in the Bay of Bengal. This initiative has played a significant role in accelerating mutual cooperation in different areas such as transport, technology, energy, security, people to people contact etc. Scholars have argued that BIMSTEC must be taken as a priority for India's consideration, if India is to really expand its strategic orientation and approaches in the Bay of Bengal.

Since the inception of BIMSTEC, there have been fourteen major areas being identified to address with mutual cooperation and collaboration in the Bay of Bengal. In this regard, India played an important role in being the leading country to address these issues. In the context of maritime connectivity, BIMSTEC Member States constantly discussed the improvement of shipping transits, container-handling capacity, security etc. However, India and Bangladesh had already initiated Coastal Shipping Agreement (CSA) and such type of agreement being simultaneously discussed with other Member States. This agreement basically applied to the coastal shipping and dealing with ports. It has applied to shipping facilities within 20 nautical miles of the coastal Member States. It has referred that coastal shipping is considered the cost-effective way to promote cross-border trading because it has provided small vessels through lesser draft or even expense lowest cost to implement.

Although, there has been another project which is going on to improve the infrastructure development, that is, the Dawei project plan in Myanmar. This construction has mainly deep-water seaports, which provide an industrial zone in the Bay of Bengal. Moreover, it would have become Asia's largest special economic zone in this region. This project has been planned at the location of near the Andaman Sea and the Gulf of Thailand, which can help India's multimodal linkage with South Asia to Southeast Asia. Not only that, but this project will also highly help integrate the BIMSTEC Member States, especially Thailand.

Security and Growth for All in the Region (SAGAR)

India has the largest coastal area in the South Asia region, including Mainland India and Islands, approximately 7,500 kilometres (Kanodia, 2020). With this huge coastal area, the Government of India has taken various policies and initiatives that impact the entire Bay of Bengal, including its approaches playing an important role in extending further maritime connectivity and prosperity. In 2015, Indian Prime Minister Shri Narendra Modi launched a proactive initiative with the vision of maritime cooperation in the Indian Ocean region, the SAGAR (Security and Growth for all in the Region) initiative. The main objectives of the SAGAR initiative are divided into five major areas: security, capacity building, collective action, sustainable development, and maritime engagement (Sarangi, 2019). This initiative was taken after the Prime Minister's diplomatic visit to three countries, namely Seychelles, Mauritius, and Sri Lanka, in 2015. It has argued that India's action plan on the maritime connectivity has dramatically improved in the entire Indian Ocean region in general and the Bay of Bengal in particular. Because, within SAGAR initiatives, another project has been incorporated to strengthen the maritime connectivity, such as Sagarmala initiatives which refer to port-led development and robust port infrastructure which modernised them for better trade and economic development (Schöttli, 2020: 568-581).

The SAGAR programme advocates that the Indian Occan Rim Association (IORA) facilitated trade and fisheries management. It will help shape the concept of the Blue Economy by promoting tourism and cultural exchanges. Though India has already initiated and working towards the Humanitarian Assistance and Disaster Relief (HADR) in the entire region. For instance, HADR has one of the significant objectives of the Indian Navy to conduct rescue operations and naval support missions and always post the first responder in the region.

India's Act East Policy

India's Act East Policy focuses on the Asia-Pacific region's expanded neighbourhood. The strategy, which began as an economic effort, has grown to include political, strategic, and cultural components, as well as the creation of institutional frameworks for conversation and cooperation. India has upgraded its partnership up to a strategic level with the ASEAN Member States, and others in the East Asia region. The main objectives of "Act East Policy"—is to promote economic ties, cultural cooperation, and strategic relationships throughout the bilateral, as well multilateral levels in the Asia-Pacific region. It has also emphasised to enhance India's North-Eastern region connectivity with immediate neighbour countries in the Bay of Bengal.

In the narrow sense, India's Act East Policy has aimed to improve trading partnership, cultural connection and develop a strategic tie with countries in the Indo-Pacific region with a pragmatic approach.

It has also indirectly enhanced India's North Eastern Region (NER) in order to economic development and connectivity have played an important role by access of gateway to Southeast Asia. The prime focus is economic integration, maritime connectivity and strategic partnership with India's immediate and extended neighbourhood. There is another argument on security issues in the Maritime domain, India's Act East policy has provided a concrete action plan to block the assertive Chinese policy in the Indian Ocean region.

Indo-Pacific Oceans Initiative (IPOI)

The growing impact of the Indian Ocean and the Pacific Ocean—global power domination has concentrated in this oceanic region. Both oceans have merged with new opportunities by the construct of the Indo-Pacific region. This new region has been explored by various actors according to their interests, but the question remains unsolved about how to resolve security challenges, strengthen the maritime concavity, improve international trading partnerships, cultural exchanges etc. At this point, Indian Prime Minister Shri Narendra Modi announced the Indo-Pacific Ocean Initiative (IPOI) during the 14th East Asia Summit to overcome these issues and integrate them into an institutional framework in the Indo-Pacific region (Mishra, 2021). This initiative has largely expanded and facilitated the SAGAR programme.

It has a broader scope in terms of jurisdiction, policy framework, and area specification to deal with security, trade, culture, governance, rule-based order, and so on and so forth. Although, Indo-Pacific Ocean initiatives have been identified as seven pillars; such as maritime security; marine ecology; maritime resources; capacity building and resource sharing; disaster risk reduction and management; science, technology and academic cooperation; and trade connectivity and maritime transport (Ministry of External Affairs, 2020). In the last pillar of IPOI, trade connectivity and maritime transport have significantly impacted the littoral States in this region. It has aims that all the littoral States have integrated and share their mutual interest from African Coast to the Pacific Ocean region.

Potential for Trade and Commerce in the Bay of Bengal

The Bay of Bengal has surrounded by potential locations for utilising its port constructions and transhipment facilities throughout the region. Eventually, the Bay of Bengal has centrally located in the Indian Ocean region, and it has connected South Asia to Southeast Asian countries through the maritime domain. India, Sri Lanka, Bangladesh, Myanmar, Indonesia, Thailand, Malaysia and Singapore are interconnected through the Bay of Bengal. One of the prominent integration factors between the littoral State in the Bay of Bengal is trading and commerce. Contrary, it has been argued that the Bay of Bengal was isolated from major trading capabilities for so long. Because all the countries are placed at the developing Nations. Bangladesh and Myanmar are excellent examples of the crucial infrastructural demands that economic expansion is causing in the Bay of Bengal, the increasing likelihood that they will be met, and the risks that obtaining essential capital investment can entail.

However, if we look into the cost and benefit analysis of trading parameter and its future opportunities, it can generally be argued that China has major economic partner in this region. China tried to involve with their economic investment in this region. In detail, Bangladesh has the second largest exporter of clothes and apparel in the world, but they do not have enough deep-water ports for transhipment facilities. Although, Bangladesh has two major ports, one is in Chittagong, and another is in Mongla.

Meanwhile, China gives to offer to build infrastructure development in Bangladesh, particularly in the sector of ports development. This has a major drawback for Bangladesh to analyse its cost and benefit factors of foreign investment in their soil. Because it has also been highlighted that Bangladesh has focused on the development of a Special Economic Zone (SEZ).

Whereas, Myanmar has isolated itself from the major international engagement during the military rule over the decades. But in the recent era, Myanmar tried to develop its new industrial park, Special Economic Zone (SEZ), to facilitate the international supply chain. For instance, Myanmar Government has a plan to develop the Dawei project in southern Myanmar. This project will play an important role for Myanmar to facilitate international supply chain and transhipment activities. On the other hand, Myanmar has to face with major infrastructure like rail and road to support these Special Economic Zones (SEZs).

In the case of India, most of the part of the Bay of Bengal is covered by the Indian territory, and it was largely impacted on the regional economic activities. In recent years, India's maritime trading has increased. It has been estimated by the Ministry of Shipping, Government of India, out of total 95 per cent of trading volume 70 per cent of trading volume was done through maritime transport (IBEF 2021). Similarly, India has increased its maritime trading partnership in the Bay of Bengal region. BIMSTEC has prominently placed at the centre of maritime trading platform for India.

Concluding Remarks

In the 21st century, the good maritime connectivity has decided that how country's foreign policy position at the both regional levels as well global platform. If the country has more and modern equips/ technology-based developed shipping ports across the chessboard of the maritime domain, then country's geopolitical power has obtained as maximum level to dominate the world order. In this regard, India has already initiated several policies to enhance its maritime connectivity across the Indian Ocean region.

It has argued that India needs to collaborate BIMSTEC with ASEAN Member States, that is, Myanmar and Thailand through Andaman and Nicobar Islands, because ANIs have geographical proximity with these countries. Although, it has also been concluded that India can utilise the Andaman and Nicobar Islands in terms of shipping, security as well disaster relief response.

And also, it has been argued that Bay of Bengal has the potential of the Sea Lines of Communication to extend the economic interconnection among the littoral States of this region. It was found that two-dimensional factors of maritime connectivity stretch through the Bay of Bengal. First, historical trading routes have played an important role in integrating the present scenario of maritime connectivity. Second, newly constructed ports and exploring the new trade route through various policies like Act East Policy, identifying

Special Economic Zone (SEZ), BIMSTEC-Free Trade Agreement (FTA), Bangladesh, China, India and Myanmar Economic Corridor (BCIM), Project Sagarmala and so on gives the new potential to extend the maritime connectivity in this region. Therefore, the historical account of maritime connectivity through the Bay of Bengal had glorious trading capabilities and socio-cultural engagement. But extensive rate of progress of maritime connectivity development lack behind the recent scenario.

REFERENCES

Basu, P. & Ghosh, N. (2020). *Breathing New Life into BIMSTEC: Challenges and Imperatives*. New Delhi: ORF Occasional Paper, 243.

Bureau of Intelligence and Research (1978). *Limits in the Seas, No. 77 Maritime Boundary: India and Sri Lanka*. US Department of States, Retrieved from https://www.state.gov/wp-content/uploads/2019/11/LIS-77.pdf

Chaudhury, A.B.R. (2020). "Re-Connecting Neighbours: India-Bangladesh Relations @ 50". *New Delhi: Indian Foreign Affairs Journal, 15*(3): 219-227.

Chaudhury, A.B.R. & Chatterjee, R. (2019). "Maritime Order and Connectivity in the Indian Ocean: The Renewed Significance of the Bay of Bengal". *Journal of the Indian Ocean Region, 15*(3): 241-244.

Chaudhury, A.B.R., *et al.* (2018). *India's Maritime Connectivity: Importance of the Bay of Bengal*. Observer Research Foundation.

IBEF (2021). *Indian Ports Industry Report*. New Delhi: India Brand Equity Foundation. Retrieved from https://www.ibef.org/industry/ports-india-shipping.aspx

Indianetzone. (2016). *Islands of Bay of Bengal*. Indianetzone. Retrieved from https://www.indianetzone.com/78/islands_bay_bengal.htm

Kanodia, H. (2020, December 25). "India's SAGAR Policy in the Indian Ocean Region". *Diplomatist*.

MEA. (2020, February 07). *Indo-Pacific Division Briefs*. New Delhi: Ministry of External Affairs, Government of India. Retrieved from https://mea.gov.in/Portal/ForeignRelation/Indo_Feb_07_2020.pdf

Misachi, J. (2021, February 4). Bay of Bengal. *World Atlas*. Retrieved from https://www.worldatlas.com/bays/bay-of-bengal.html

Mishra, R. (2021, August). 'Indo-Pacific Oceans' Initiative: Providing Institutional Framework to the Indo-Pacific Region. *New Delhi: ASEAN-India Centre*. Retrieved from http://aic.ris.org.in/sites/default/files/AIC%20commentary%20No%2020%20August%202021%20final.pdf

Myoe, M. (2016). The Maritime Frontier of Myanmar: Challenges in the Early 21st Century. In. Su-Ann, *Myanmar's Mountain and Maritime Borderscapes: Local Practices, Boundary-Making and Figured Worlds*. Singapore: ISEAS.

Panikkar, K. (1945). *India and The Indian Ocean: An Essay of Influence of Sea Power on Indian History*. London.

Sagarmala (n.d). A Peek into India's Maritime History under the Chola Rulers. Maritime Glory. Retrieved from http://sagarmala.gov.in/sites/default/files/A%20peek%20into%20India%27s%20maritime%20history%20under%20the%20Chola%20rulers%20%282%29.pdf

Sarangi, S. (2019). *Unpacking SAGAR (Security and Growth for All in the Region)*. USI Occasional Paper.

Schöttli, J. (2020). "Security and Growth for all in the Indian Ocean: Maritime Governance and India's Foreign Policy". *India Review, 18*(5): 568-581. https://doi.org/10.1080/14736489.2019.1703366

United Nations (2017). *The Ocean Conference proceeding: Factsheet: People and Oceans*. New York. Retrieved from https://www.un.org/sustainabledevelopment/wp-content/uploads/2017/05/Ocean-fact-sheet-package.pdf

20

Emerging Shifts in India's Nuclear Policy

Strategic Implications for Regional Security in South Asia

K.S. Pavithran

Nuclear weapons are the most crucial factor which influenced the course of international politics and diplomacy in the last few decades. Since the advent of nuclear weapons, they have become a symbol of power and prestige among the nations of the world. Nuclear power gives the nation that has it, prestige in world politics and psychological leverage in dealing with both friends and foes. However, India's attitude to nuclear weapons has been marked by ambivalence. There was a gap of 24 years in between India's first test of nuclear weapons at Pokhran in 1974 and the second set of tests in 1998. Pakistan also conducted nuclear detonations in 1998. The nuclear capabilities of both India and Pakistan are factors of importance in determining the regional security in South Asia.

Evolution of India's Nuclear Policy

Regarding the Nuclear Policy of India, Jawaharlal Nehru foresaw the utility of nuclear energy in augmenting power generation and wanted the atom to be harnessed for developmental purposes. India's approach to the problem was, therefore, a question of economic freedom of the Third World. Thus as early as 1947, the late Homi J. Bhabha, the physicist entrusted with running the country's atomic energy programme, envisioned India employing nuclear energy for the development of its economy. A year later, researches in the nuclear field commence when "Tata Institute of Fundamental Research" was established. In 1948, the "Indian Atomic Energy Commission" was set up by an Act of Parliament. The nuclear policy of India was changed to a certain extent by both Lal Bahadhur Shastri and Indira Gandhi. The changes were made as a result of the changed environment. Before and after the war with China, there were those who argued that nuclear weapons were vital in the competition and conflict with China. Thus Shastri, upon assuming office of the Prime Minister, ordered India's nuclear scientists to work on a subterranean nuclear explosion (SNEP) (Mohan, 2003:10). However, in September 1965 India went to war with Pakistan over Kashmir and the great powers especially the Soviet Union arranged a ceasefire with Pakistan (Bajpai, 2015). After the Tashkent Declaration and death of Shastri, Indira Gandhi assumed power and she directed to stop the SNEP. However, in 1972, after India-Pak war on the liberation of Bangladesh (1971), Mrs. Gandhi ordered India's nuclear scientists to go ahead with a nuclear test. Thus in May 18, 1974, India carried out its first nuclear explosion at Pokhran (Pokhran-I) in Rajasthan.

The explosion was a culmination of India's nuclear energy efforts and it opened up the possibilities of deriving the economic benefits out of peaceful nuclear explosions. The Indian approach under Mrs. Gandhi sought only to redefine the concept of nuclear proliferation. It demanded a control over on the race for nuclear arms among the nuclear weapon powers (vertical proliferation) and on the spread of nuclear weapons (horizontal proliferation). It continued to endorse the concept of nuclear arms control in principle and had kept open the possibility of further tests when the 'need for a peaceful experiment is established'.

The Indian nuclear explosion revised the hypothesis that, for some, it is desirable to have a nuclear weapons option without a policy of converting it into weapons. Thus, while rejecting the Nuclear Non-Proliferation Treaty (NPT), India always emphasized that a non-proliferation treaty, if it was to be effective, viable, and generally acceptable, should prevent both the nuclear weapon and non-nuclear weapon powers from proliferation. It should be a real and meaningful step towards disarmament without in any way hampering the utilization of nuclear energy for peaceful purposes.

Later, the Nuclear policy of India changed significantly when the Janata Party came to power in March 1977. The nuclear policy of Janata Party government had four strands:

1. India would utilize atomic energy for peaceful purpose only and would not manufacture nuclear weapons under any circumstances;
2. India would not sign the Nuclear Non-Proliferation Treaty (NPT), unless the Nuclear Weapon Powers denounce these weapons;
3. Inspection of autonomously controlled or domestically established nuclear facilities would not be permitted; and
4. Peaceful nuclear explosions would not be conducted.

The fourth aspect was a distinct feature of the Janata government's Nuclear Policy as outlined by Prime Minister Morarji Desai. But after assuming power in 1980, Indira Gandhi as Prime Minister reaffirmed India's commitment to the peaceful uses of atomic energy and added that, India would not hesitate to carry out nuclear explosion or implosion, whatever is necessary in the national interests. The succeeding governments in India followed this policy.

NPT and South Asia

The fact is that the five nuclear weapon powers also happened to be five permanent members of the United Nation's Security Council. Now that nuclear weapons have come to symbolize the hierarchical status in the international power system, the real purpose of the NPT was and is to freeze the '*status quo*' and perpetuate the international power system as it exists. Another objective of the NPT was to keep tight control over the new technology so that the industrialized world of North America and Europe would continue its dominance over the rest of the world. In short, the NPT was an exercise in disarming the unarmed and it was calculated to prevent decentralization of international power.

South Asia consists of eight countries (Afghanistan, Bangladesh, Bhutan, India, Maldives, Nepal, Pakistan and Sri Lanka) share common geographical boundaries, historical ties, religious and cultural traditions and linguistic affinities. The region suffers from various kinds of problems such as poverty, underdevelopment, deprivation, terrorism, environmental issues and so on. India can be considered as the main power in the South Asian Region. Pakistan comes next to India and there is a power conflict between these two countries which shapes the security patterns of the region. Since conducting its second nuclear tests in 1998, during the Vajpayee regime India has adhered to a self-imposed commitment to 'No first use' (NFU) of nuclear weapons on another country (*The Hindu*, 2019).

It is to be noted that the idea of a multilateral conference for non-proliferation in South Asia mooted by George Bush Sr. administration was not acceptable to India.[1] The American proposal was similar to one earlier put forward by Nawaz Sharif, former Prime Minister of Pakistan, for a five nation conference involving India, Pakistan, China, Russia and the United States to discuss nuclear non-proliferation in South Asia. The sinister part of Pakistan's proposal is that, by repeating the call for a nuclear free zone in South Asia, Islamabad hopes to gain international support for its position and provide an excuse for itself going nuclear, as it did, but laying the blame for this development at India's doors.

Having failed to denuclearize the South Asian region through a bilateral process, the United States embarked on a multilateral process. The first move was the Nawaz Sharif proposal in 1991. The Clinton Administration has modified the proposal to 5 + 2 + 2 conference[2] on arms control and regional security in South Asia. The United States has adopted a one-to-one approach with India and Pakistan separately. The US has been peddling with the idea of capping the nuclear capabilities of India and Pakistan. This means getting India and Pakistan to end production of nuclear material such as highly enriched uranium or plutonium that can be used in nuclear weapons. In the wider context of the tactical approach to South Asia, the Clinton Administration was not ready to throw away the zero-sum game tactics that until now marked the approach of successive US Administrations to the region.

Pakistan seeks to expedite her nuclear efforts to catch up with India and is simultaneously mobilizing international opinion to bear pressure on India to place her nuclear facilities under international control. However, the move was resisted by India.[3] The traditional position of Indian foreign policy that placed emphasis on the non-discriminatory and global framework for nuclear non-proliferation is favoured by India.

Regarding the nuclear weapon free-zone in South Asia, the Indian attitude is that a nuclear weapon-free-zone in South Asia can only be developed and matured from within the region concerned. For this purpose, South Asia cannot be treated in isolation. It is a sub-region and an integral part of the region of Asia and the Pacific. A genuine nuclear weapon-free-zone in that region can only follow the total absence of nuclear weapons. The attitude of western powers in voting for the South Asian peace zone, having rejected a similar plan for Central Europe, is in line with their proclaimed view that they have special security needs, implying that the non-white nations do not have any.

Pakistan and Kashmir

As far as India is concerned, Pakistan's thrust in the Kashmir 'problem' is to disturb the *status quo* to its own advantage with the help of the United States and China. There is, no doubt that Pakistan, having nuclear weapons, may have reasons for again raising the Kashmir Question on grounds of human rights violations[4] by using its acquired nuclear capability as a tactical, if not military ploy. Pakistan has more effectively leveraged its advantages in the employment of terrorism under the atomic umbrella. India has had few answers to Pakistan's resort to sub-conventional violence under the cover of nuclear weapons. The most it has been able to militarily launch limited attacks on Pakistan's side of LOC.

However, despite more than two decades of international pressure that followed to make India abandon its pursuit of nuclear weapons, India again carried out a test in May 1998, Pokhran-II, involving a fission device and a thermo nuclear device. A fortnight after the Pokhran-II tests, Pakistan also carried out similar tests. Thus, in 1999 India came out with an explicit nuclear doctrine[5] that committed, 'No first Use'—that is, it would never carry out a nuclear first strike. This doctrine emphasised "minimal deterrence, no first use and non-use against non-nuclear weapon states." Indian attitude is a Credible Minimum Deterrence (CMD) built on an assured second strike capability. This implies that in the event of another nation carrying out a first nuclear strike of any magnitude against India, India's nuclear forces shall be so deployed as to ensure survivability of the attack and the capability to carry out a massive, punitive nuclear retaliation aimed at inflicting damage that the aggressor will find unacceptable. "In respose to a nuclear attack in any form, India must respond with 'massive retaliation' by undertaking multiple nuclear attacks in keeping with the tenets of our nuclear policy" (Compose, 2016), puts in Philip Compose in another way.

The historical trajectory of India's nuclear policy shows that there are two main reasons for India to develop its nuclear capability. They are security prospects and energy prospects. The most important reason behind India's nuclear policy related to security, particularly border security. Both Pakistan and China are nuclear powers. India's relation with Pakistan is hostile. China's nuclear arsenals and its assistance to Pakistan nuclear power programme with missile technology exacerbates India's concern.[6] Further, India's security policies are driven by its desire to be recognized as the dominant power in the region. Thus, Pakistan's nuclear capability and China's expanding nuclear weapons create a greater concern in India.

India also seeks energy security through nuclear power plants. Thus, by undertaking new co-operation on Civil nuclear energy, India expects to be able to count on a reliable fuel supply for its civilian reactors. However, Indo-US Civil Nuclear Co-operation Agreement, if implemented without initiating sufficient confidence and security building measures could lead to arms competition in the South Asian region involving India, Pakistan and China, thus destabilizing the entire region. It could force major stakeholders to re-evaluate their security interests in the face of the emerging Indo-US strategic partnership, thus triggering the transformation of regional alliance structures, where India is seen decisively shifting towards the United States and Pakistan exploring defence and nuclear power from China.

The Balakot strikes that followed the Pulwama attack (both in February 2019) demonstrate that the Narendra Modi government is not shy of taking cross-border military action. Further, there are rethinking in official circles to revoke the policy of 'no first use'. In 2016, then Defence Minister Manohar Parrikar raised doubts on

India's adherence to the policy of 'no-first-use'. Then in August 16, 2019, while visiting Pokhran, Defence Minister Rajnath Singh said that in the future, India's NFU promise "depends on circumstances". Yet revoking the NFU would have its own costs. India's image as a responsible nuclear power is central to its nuclear diplomacy. Nuclear restraint has allowed New Delhi to get accepted in the global mainstream. From being a nuclear pariah for most of the Cold War, within a decade of Pokhran-II, it has been accepted in the global nuclear order. Revoking the NFU pledge would harm India's nuclear image world-wide.

In the emerging scenario, nuclearisation of South Asia following the Indian and Pakistan nuclear tests in 1998 held out the prospect that nuclear weapons might induce caution and push both states towards the cooperative management of their nuclear relationship if only to avoid the shared danger of nuclear war. The evidence thus far of the 1999 Kargil conflict, the 2001-02 border escalation crisis, the post-26/11, 2008 incidents and indeed the recent developments including the Phulwama and Balakot incidents and of course the Kashmir issue does not appear to support this.

Conclusion

India faces a very challenging strategic environment in South Asia, with its immediate opponents possessing significant military and nuclear capabilities that are modernizing rapidly. The challenge facing New Delhi has been how to leverage its conventional advantages in the shadow of nuclear weapons. The proliferation dynamics in South Asia are driven by a need to establish some measure of relative parity against their principal adversaries—India against China and Pakistan against India. The regional nuclear development was also influenced by the continued global hegemonic nuclear order and the flawed non-proliferation regimes. Therefore, India must decide by this decade what her role in South Asia must be, if nuclear weapons are to be accommodated. At the foreign policy level, the possibilities of the signature of 'no first use' pledge between India and Pakistan or the codification of a peaceful intent may be considered as one of the options that is with their merits and demerits. At the international level, India must project the view that the only alternative to nuclear proliferation is that, there should be international safeguards in all countries to ensure that nuclear power is used only for peaceful purpose. National security demands restraint from all the stakeholders in the region. In this context, the US must realize that India cannot be a party to any multilateral arrangement, unless it includes all states which have South Asia within their nuclear reach. This includes Israel and Kazakhstan, apart from Big Five. In this respect, India's call for global abolition of nuclear weapons and non-discriminatory interim steps are quite relevant.

NOTES

1. The U.S. in November 1991, first mooted the idea of multilateral conference for non-proliferation in South Asia when Regional Bartholomew, the Under Secretary of State, visited India. In January 1992, the then President, George Bush, pressed the Prime Minister, P.V. Narasimha Rao, to join the conference.
2. Five permanent members of the Security Council + India and Pakistan + Germany and Japan.
3. The Foreign Assistance Act, drafted by Larry Pressler in 1985 and invoked in October 1990, bars military and economic assistance to Pakistan, unless the President certifies that it does not possess a nuclear weapon devise. Now, with the firm pro-Pakistan tilt in the American South Asian Policy, the Clinton Administration is seeking a one-time exception to the U.S. non-proliferation law, giving it legal sanction to proceed with the sale of The F-16 fighter aircraft to Pakistan.
4. In recent months, U.S. and the Western Powers have made the issue of human rights, one of the central concerns in their dealings with India. The issues of human rights and Kashmir is being raised as a lever to make India sign the NPT.
5. Under the chairmanship of the doyen of its strategic community, K. Subrahmanyam, India published a Draft Nuclear Doctrine, which was written by the National Security Advisory Board (NSAB) on August 17, 1999.
6. The latest estimates of India's nuclear weapons by the *Bulletin of Atomic Scientists* points to a small arsenal of 130-150 nuclear war heads, eventhough it has enough military grade plutonium to produce 200 warheads.

REFERENCES

Bajpai, Kanti (2015). "India and Nuclear Weapons", in Atul Kohli and Prerna Singh, eds. Routledge *Handbook of Indian Politics*, London: Routledge.

Cohen, Stephen, P. (1993). "India's Regional Impact", *Seminar,* No. 401, January.

Compose, Philip, (2016). "India's National Security Strategy: Imperative of Integrating Defence Policy", *CLAWS Journal.* Winter, pp.15-32.

Ganegoda, Anuja (2017). "Characteristics and Dynamics of South Asia as a Sub-regional Security Complex". *South Asian Journal of Socio-Political Studies,* Vol. XVII(2), January-July, pp. 24-28.

Kapur, Asok (1979). *India's Nuclear Option: Atomic Diplomacy and Decision Making,* New York: Praeger Publishers Inc.

Kumari, Ruby, (2009). "India's Nuclear Weapon Programmes: Present Capabilities". *The Indian Journal of Political Science,* Vol. XX(1), January-March, pp. 227-238.

Lakshman, Narayanan (2019). "Will India Change its 'No First Use' Policy?" *The Hindu,* August 25.

Misra, K.P. (ed.) (1979). *Janata's Foreign Policy,* New Delhi: Vikas Publications.

Mohan, Raja, C. (2003), *Crossing the Rubicon: The Shaping of India's New Foreign Policy,* New Delhi: Viking/Penguin India.

O'Donnel, Frank and Debalina Ghoshal (2019). *Managing Indian Deterence : Pressures on Credible Minimum Deterrence and Nuclear Policy Options,* https://doi.org/10.1080/10736700.2019.1565187-Accessd 8 September, 2019.

Pant, Harsh V. and Kartik Bommakanti (2019). "India's National Security: Challenges and Dilemmas", *International Affairs,* Vol. 95(4), July, pp. 835-857.

Pathak, K.K. (1980). *Nuclear Policy of India,* New Delhi: Gitanjali Prakasan.

Pavithran, K.S. (2013). "Indo-US Nuclear Deal: Implications for India's Foreign Policy and National Security". In K.S. Pavithran ed., *Foreign Policy and Maritime Security of India,* New Delhi: New Century Publications, pp. 255-268.

Prasad, Bimal (ed.) (1977). *India's Foreign Policy: Studies in Continuity and Change,* New Delhi: Vikas Publications.

Rose, Leo E., and Noor A. Hussain (ed.) (1987). *United States – Pakistan Forum: Relations with the Major Powers,* Lahore, Vanguard Institute of Asian Studies.

Sinha, P.B. and R.R. Subramaniam (1980). *Nuclear Pakistan: Atomic Threat to South Asia,* New Delhi: Vision Books.

Vinodan, C. (2008), "Indo-US Nuclear Deal and South Asian Regional Security", *International Journal of South Asian Studies,* Vol. 1(2), July-December, pp. 269-283.

The Hindu, August 17, 2019, Kochi.

21

India's Strategic Interest in SAARC Countries

Soft Power Approach

Lawrence Prabhakar Williams, Pooja Raghav and *Trishna Rai*

Introduction

South Asia is an eccentric region defaced by inter-state provocation, various disputes and several absurdities. India, despite being a dominant nation in South Asia in every possible parameter from territory to population, economy to the military, has paradoxically not got the privileged position in the region. Indian strategists are still admiring how to get genuinely acceptable leadership. SAARC activities have always remained frustratingly sluggish ever since its existence. Despite signing numerous agreements, SAARC has hardly produced any remarkable outcome. During the decade of establishment of SAARC, the use of hard power was a common approach in India's foreign policy towards South Asian nations. During 1970s India's military build-up because of East Pakistan crises, in 1983-1990 India's intervention in Sri Lanka and economic pressure imposed on Nepal in 1989 are the separate instances of hard power imposed by India. The changes in India's foreign policy since the 1990s have intensified the debate about her future status in the international system (Cohen, 2001, Mohan, 2003). From the beginning of the 21st century, India is using more soft power strategies towards SAARC nations to improve its stand. This chapter examines transition in India's foreign policy from hard power to soft power strategies towards the South Asian Association of Regional Cooperation (SAARC) nations to improve its stand in the prosperous region. The greater cohesion can be achieved among the SAARC nations through the possibility of soft power. The most crucial determinant in this era is science and technology, which can change the multilateral relations amongst the SAARC nations. India being the primary centre for IT developments can foster this as a profession in the region.

India is the heart of the South Asian nations, sharing its permeable borders with Nepal, Bhutan, Pakistan, Afghanistan, Bangladesh and water boundaries with Sri Lanka and the Maldives. Therefore, it is strategically vital for India to maintain balance with all of these nations in case a military confrontation. It has been noticed over the past decades that India's foreign policy had focused on the country's cultural and political values. Liberal institutions and welfare-oriented policies are essential instruments of its soft power. India's soft power is aimed at fostering regional cooperation and solidarity achieved through a holistic approach encompassing a benign foreign policy, promotion of economic interdependence, strong cultural cooperation and foreign assistance (Kugiel, 2012). Amidst the above-given parameters, the counter efforts of China to Indian attempts cannot be ignored. The analysis is done on how to achieve a multilateral approach from bilateral strategies.

This chapter is based on the multidimensional approach by collecting data and analysing it from various viewpoints. Both print and online sources were consulted during the research process. This includes primary sources such as bilateral treaties, official reports, letters and speech of political leaders. For the secondary source research papers, reports, peer-reviewed journal articles and books were also consulted. The later part of the chapter is organised as follows: Section two will give an overview of the conceptual framework of the soft power and transition of power in India's foreign policy towards other South Asian countries. Section three will assess India's foreign policy towards other South Asian countries before the establishment of SAARC. Part four focuses on India's stand after the establishment of SAARC. Further, the future aspects of SAARC are discussed, followed by the Conclusion.

Conceptual Framework of Soft Power in India's Foreign Policy

Neo-realist school of thought defines the importance of regional powers in analysing various approaches of international relations. The idea of Neo-realists who emphasised on military and economic factors might have been unsuccessful in the post-Cold War era. The Neo-realist approaches focus on the *hard power* on the position of the state, especially in terms of their military capabilities and economic strength. Those enable regional powers to influence their neighbours and to protect themselves from disagreeable outside interference (Waltz 1979: 191/192). On disparity, liberal institutional approaches have emphasised *soft* power aspects with cultural attraction, ideology, and international institutions as the primary resources (Nye, 1990: 167). The soft power concept of a neo-liberal scholar, Joseph Nye (1990), shaped the foreign policy of the majority of nations. Soft power depends on the capability of manipulation, to prioritise and convince on your reality. Initially, the concept of soft power was mainly based on the sources as given by (Nye, 2004: 11): "its culture (in places where it is attractive to others), its political values (when it lives up to them at home and abroad) and its foreign policies (when they are seen as legitimate and having moral authority)." 'Soft Power', as defined by Joseph Nye, rests on the ability of a country to represent its foreign policy motives, attractively enough for its counterparts to accept them and thus eliminates the use of coercion. After some time, the concept of soft power has increased its horizon.

According to American Journalist, Joshua Kurlantzick (2007) soft power is not only limited to military and security realm, including not only popular culture and public diplomacy but also more coercive economic and diplomatic levers, like aid and investment and participation in multilateral organisations. The best example of this is when India in the 1960s provided technical assistance and training to developing nations during the critical famine and widespread starvation. The Indian Technical and Economic Cooperation (ITEC) programme were offered to civil servants from developing countries to get training in India. This programme indeed has strengthened India's relations with recipient nations. Subsequently, Afghanistan's former President Hamid Karzai enjoyed warmer relations with

India after attending the programme. Globalisation and economic liberalisation after 1991 added another component in Indian foreign policy both at the International and the regional level. It leads to cross-connections, non-state actors' influence, democratic regimes, accentuation of diplomacy, the most conspicuous form of soft power was displayed with immense significance in the international system. A country like India, having a considerate amount of soft power can be seen as more legitimate. Other South Asian nations can comply with their objectives. From Nehruvian idealism to real politik to soft power transition in Indian policy can be seen. After the post-Cold War epoch, the question of military power became unrealistic in International affairs.

In 2010, India had signed an agreement of 1 billion credit deal with Bangladesh for the advancement of 14 infrastructure projects primarily in the communication services. This deal was signed between Exim Bank of India and the Economic Relations Department of Bangladesh. India has altered its concept of foreign policy by making a "coherent effort…to raise India's image and brand value in foreign countries." The evolution was highly classified, but it was known to all that power was being redefined. Harsh Pant remarks on it that "under Prime Minister Modi, India is taking a strategic approach towards using its soft-power resources to enhance the nation's image abroad." The conduct of soft power is intricately linked to the practice of public diplomacy. The basic idea of public diplomacy is when the government tries for the promotion of national interest generally by public sentiments of both the host and the target country. Public diplomacy gained its momentum in protecting a nation's foreign policy with the increase in global interdependence and integration. Traditionally public diplomacy meant diplomatic relations amongst the government officials, but this definition has evolved with time. Today public diplomacy incorporates ideas and interaction of both governmental and non-governmental organisations that include inter and intrastate diplomacy to incorporate variations of cultures and enhance relationships which further influence ideas for the advancement of their values. By appealing to the public, encouraging outcomes *via* soft power could undeniably be included through the arena of new public diplomacy.

The conduct of soft power is also intrinsically linked to Information technology. Information technology has become inalienable art of every country in foreign policy formulation. Countries' trajectory can be developed with science and technology. As compared to the developed nations, South Asian countries are still lagging in science and technology. However, from the second half of the 20th century successive amount of programmes in the IT sector has been instigated. Information technology in general terms is all about creation, manipulation, using a different kind of software and hardware system. Computers and communication technology can be significantly used to improve multilateral relations in the South Asian region. In the age of information and advancement of technology, with free movement of people, capital and ideas, it is claimed that communication strategies become more critical, and outcomes are shaped not merely by whose army wins, but also by whose story wins (Nye, 201: 18).

India's Foreign Policy Towards SAARC Nations: Before the Existence of SAARC

In 1600, the royal charter to the East India Company was given by Queen Elizabeth-I for trade purposes. For the next hundred years, the East India Company became the most persuasive power in South Asia as the successors after the Aurangzeb was weak. In 1768, Maharajadhiraja Prithvi Narayan Shah, the last ruler of the Gorkha Kingdom conquered Kathmandu and became the first ruler of the Kingdom of Nepal. In the southern part of the South Asian region, Ceylon (Sri Lanka) became a British Colony in 1802. Then the first Anglo-Afghan War between the British East India Company and the Emirates of Afghanistan between 1838-1842 and led to the withdrawal of British forces from Afghanistan. Straight after the Indian Sepoy Mutiny, India came under the direct rule of the Britishers in 1858. The power of the East India Company was being transferred to the British Crown. In the second Anglo-Afghan war, British gained control of Afghan foreign affairs and in the Third Anglo-Afghan war happened in 1919, Afghanistan being recognised as an independent country by the British. Even before Independence, there was a desire to 'self' amidst the now Independent nations. Indian leadership back then also had a vision of world peace and Afro-Asian unity. The then government, the Indian National Congress (INC) inclined towards the formation of a congregation by assimilating the anti-imperial feelings. Therefore, in its Bombay session of 1921 resolved on the resolution, "to promote feelings of amity and concord with neighbouring states to establish goodwill and sympathy to formulate a clear and definite foreign policy of India" (A.M. Zaidi, 1987). For Congress, anti-imperialism was the standing pillar of its foreign policy and expected nations throughout Asia to partake on its theory. According to the INC, any nation in bondage would always question the sovereignty of all the other nations (The Encyclopaedia of the Indian National Congress, 1981). Pursuing the idea of an Eastern-Federation Congress discussed political ideas that scaled the ramparts of the Himalayas and most of the surrounding seas to recognise that the freedom of Asiatic nations would contemplate the organisation of an Eastern-Federation (Mohamad Ali, 1923). The agenda of regional cooperation and unity in Asia aggravated when INC nursed a sense of grievance for India not securing a position as a member of the Security Council of the United Nations. In July 1945, Congress Working Committee (CWC) adopted a firm resolution to express their resentment to allotment of position to the smaller nations in UN Organisation. The Great Power not only wholly controlled and dominated the new organisation but was placed above the law they had framed themselves. Henceforth, India realised to attain the status of a sovereign state and an independent position to contribute to the maintenance of peace, security and freedom. In 1947, British India was partitioned into two countries as India and Pakistan with the sparkling communal clashes which continue even now over the status of Jammu & Kashmir. Sri Lanka gained independence in 1948. Following the adoption of the new Indian Constitution in 1950, India signed the Treaty of Peace and Friendship drawing the framework of future bilateral relations. After Indian independence, Indian foreign policy generally had three phases and approaches: The Nehru period, the Indira-doctrine and the Gujral-doctrine (Christan Wagner, 2005). Although Nehru formulated the concept of the five principles of peaceful coexistence, it was not automatically used in the relations with the neighbours (Maxwell, 1970: 78-80).

Nehru had a very deferential approach in India's bilateral relations not necessarily in the regional respective. Jawaharlal Nehru mentioned that small states do not have any future, and they will be reduced to the status of the satellite states only. Hereafter, he advocated the creation of a South Asian Federation of India, Iraq, Afghanistan and Burma (J.S. Bright, 1950). However, the primary reason for the regional cooperation for India was the issue of 'trade'. Still, it not clearly defined whether a trade is to be considered as an element of *hard power* or *soft powers*. However, in the initial process, trade was not considered due to the fear that a liberal trade regime would work for the benefits of India. India suggested a carefully balanced interdependence in the regional cooperation in South Asia with an equal division of labour in order to strengthen economic base and infrastructure.

Indira Gandhi used a more coherent concept of regional policies. Domestic conflicts should only be solved with the help of India and not by the interference of outside powers or international organisations (Hagerty, 1991). Furthermore, India intervened, for instance, in Sri Lanka in 1971 and 1987 to 1990 and the Maldives in 1988. During Indira Gandhi era, Indian foreign policy was shaped more by hard power strategies than by soft power approaches. Amidst the India Gandhi era and Gujral doctrine, the entire structure came into being to coordinate and monitor the implementation of SAARC activities in 1987. The third era of foreign policy under Prime Minister Gujral and establishment of SAARC is explained in the next section of the chapter.

India's Foreign Policy Towards SAARC Nations: the Modern Context

Bangladesh then-president Zia-Ur Rahman first initiated the idea of closer regional cooperation in the late 1970s. In 1985, despite all the bilateral tensions, SAARC came into existence. SAARC established with a goal of collaboration in the social, economic, cultural, scientific and technical fields. Their main objective was socio-economic welfare and cultural development. It also included the provisions that the decisions had to be taken unanimously and contentious issues were to be kept out of the organisation. The Secretariat with Security General, seven Directors and General Services Staff was mentioned in the Charter. Until the 1990s, the progress of SAARC was just decent. An essential part of SAARC was the annual summits as they could be considered as a mode of confidence-building measure for the Member States. After the advent of liberalisation in 1991 SAARC got momentum through economic cooperation. The policy of economic reforms, exports promotion was also followed by all South Asian countries. SAARC Preferential Trading Arrangement (SAPTA) was established in 1995 to look into the prospects of regional economic collaboration. However, due to the lack of complementarity and structural constraints, the intra-regional trade remained only two to three per cent. In order to further improve the trade in the South Asian region, SAARC Free Trade Arrangement (SAFTA) was signed in Islamabad in January 2004. SAFTA aimed to have free intra-regional trade in South Asia from 2006 in order to bring the economic, like alternation in less developed economies, like Bangladesh, Bhutan and Nepal.

It seems that the idea of Gujral doctrine of the 1990s and economic cooperation produced an outright gain for all players was circumstantial. The foreign policy under the doctrine of the then Prime Minister Gujral was the principle of no reciprocity, emphasising that India not only had a more significant responsibility but also should give more to the smaller neighbours than she would receive. He reflected the domestic changes, especially liberalisation after 1991. South Asia did not figure very prominently in the BJP's concept of the extended neighbourhood after 1998 (Singh, 2001). BJP with the South Asian region mainly followed the policies of its predecessors of focusing on the West, Central and Southeast Asia. However, the focus on SAARC nations was back in 2004 after the electoral victory of the United Progressive Alliance (UPA) under the leadership of the Congress Party. In February 2005, foreign secretary Shyam Saran and Prime Minister Manmohan Singh tied up more explicitly to the Gujral doctrine and stressed the need for increased economic relations and promoted the idea of partnership with the neighbours. They also underlined that the promotion of democracy would not be a tool in India's relations with her neighbours (Mohan, 2005). India's South Asian overview shows the fundamental conceptual shifts in certainly curtailed and compressed way. The debate about the interference in other nations and threats which are still in existence is taken in the next section.

During the formative years (1985-1990) progress was comparatively slow with five meetings. India's chasing dream of a larger role beyond the geographical border manifested it with the policy of non-alignment. India became the most significant features of SAARC because of centrality, size and potential of power. Nevertheless, India also faced deep uncertainties to the small countries particularly Pakistan, Bangladesh, Nepal and Sri Lanka about her objectives because of a yearning global role after a vast industrial infrastructure, a strong military, massive technological and scientific human resources and stable democracy relatively. With the Indo-centrality 'baggage' SAARC had a meek start by adopting a Charter in 1985 Dhaka Summit. During this period, India pursued her objective on trade and cultural cooperation in SAARC and continuously excommunicated contentious and divisive politics in SAARC. India, in the Fourth Summit, demonstrated its frustration over the crawling speed of cooperation and coordination in aspects of the economy. Then-Prime Minister of India clearly said in his statement:

> "We also need to strengthen linkages between ourselves to give us strength, individually and as a region. This call for increased economic exchanges within our region, covering the gamut of economic activities from agriculture to industry infrastructure technology and human resource development. Economic cooperation must lie at the heart of regional cooperation. There has to be a degree of harmonisation to ensure that complementarities in our economics are matched to give strength to our respective economies and strength to our voice and influence in world forums.

However, we shy away from trade and economic cooperation (Gandhi, R., 1988). Still, Pakistan and Bangladesh opposed the inclusion of 'trade' in the cooperation areas. In 1989, due to India's withdrawal of Indian Peace Keeping Force (IPKF), Sri Lanka refused to host SAARC Summit. That was the first test for the Indian approach of encasing SAARC from disputed bilateral issues. The SAARC process pulled through crossroad, and the Summit congregation was hosted in Male in the Maldives in 1990 after the pullout of IPKF from Sri Lanka as stated by (Muralidharan, S., 1999) that the new focus on economic cooperation became evident in the everyday activities of both countries within the SAARC and in the bilateral Free Trade Agreement that was signed in 1998. The disintegration of USSR and the end of the Cold War led to a paradigm shift in international relations. Economist and political scientist pointed out that with the Cold-War coming to an end the 'geo-politics' primarily got transformed into 'geo-economics' or aggressive areas of non-interference and free trade (Indra Nath Mukerji, 2000).

With the advent of globalisation, India in 1991 declared an alteration in her economic policy allotment to coincide her approach with international marketisation. Other SAARC member countries also undertook the process of policy alteration to establish their markets for the entire world. During this epoch, remarkable political changes were witnessed in South Asia too. Like the re-establishment of representative democracy in Pakistan (1988), democratic movements in Nepal (1990), and Bangladesh (1991). It truly did bring significant constructive aspirations for regional cooperation. Since mid-1990s, India's public diplomacy was primarily determined by the Gujral Doctrine. The doctrine firmly adhered to sovereign equality, non-reciprocal and non-interference magnanimity. Due to its strategic locations and national concerns, India has been more acceptable to adopt the policy of soft power approach, especially towards its immediate neighbours. Its diplomatic arrangement is more highlighted with the incorporation of soft power. If we examine India's strategic association in past relations in the last ten years, two events get highlighted. One, Narendra Modi's becoming of Prime Minister in 2014 and the Uri attack that took place in Kashmir on 18 September, 2016, which altered power dynamics and also the switch of strategy in dealing with the SAARC nations altogether. Henceforth it is essential to understand India's strategic interest. However, South Asian Region has always been in a conflictual relationship between India and its neighbours. Other South Asian countries always had that suspecting mindset towards India's objectives in the region.

On the other hand, India feels genuine security concerns, particularly with Pakistan. The most significant negative factor which retards the SAARC process is the asymmetry between India and other SAARC nations. India's relation with Pakistan deteriorated even further after the Kargil war because of escalation in cross-border terrorism in Jammu & Kashmir. During the same time, an Indian Airplane to Kandhar (Afghanistan) through Lahore was hijacked in Pakistan. India's foreign policy towards Pakistan and Afghanistan is mainly dependent on its national security and counter-terrorism. India and Pakistan relations primarily involves national security in terms of Kashmir dispute and secondly, on hydro-diplomacy. By focusing on the various political, socio-cultural and economic factors, the link between the national interest and policy formulation can be understood. Hydro-Diplomacy has become a global phenomenon due to the increasing instance of water scarcity. Turkey decreasing the outflow of water in the Euphrates and also with Palestine's water supply being snipped off by Israel is some of the few examples of how countries are using water as a weapon to facilitate personal tactical affairs and political ultimatum. Likewise, is the Indus Water Treaty signed by Pakistan and India in 1960 significantly pointed out the necessity of collaboration among the two nations on water allocations for the well-being of their agricultural economies. Indus Valley Treaty assimilated the national governments, experts and also conflict resolution bodies for obvious reasons. However, again in 1971, Bangladesh seceded from Islamabad; relations became a cause for concern for five decades. "Nuclear crises", 2002 and the daring insurgent strike in Mumbai, December of 2008 only to add fuel to the fire.

India always quests to boost its capacity building and economic growth through greater regional cooperation in SAARC countries. If we take the case of Afghanistan, its geostrategic position connects South Asia and mineral and abundant oil parts of Central and West Asia. This consciousness ushered India to firmly stand up for Afghanistan's permanent membership in SAARC in 2007. India shares strong cultural and historical links with Afghanistan ever since Agreement on Cultural Relations in 1963 to the Strategic Partnership Agreement signed in 2011. India's diplomatic advancement in attaining these goals focuses on the belief of the principles of peaceful co-existence and regional accord.

Future Aspects of it in India's Foreign Policy Towards SAARC Nations: Scope and Organisation

Some critics think that the relevance of SAARC is almost negligible when it comes to reducing tensions, advancing regional reliability and encouraging economic prosperity. India is persistent in its efforts to appease the strategic branching amid the SAARC countries *via* social, cultural and economic cooperation. To tackle problems between SAARC nations, India can rely on soft power capabilities. Indian policy should be framed to smooth the political and strategic factors in the region. The bilateral tension between India and Pakistan has subsequently reduced in the post-Cold War. Nevertheless, we can also raise a question of whether soft power can bring silver lining on the horizon for India-Pakistan relations. There is enormous potential energy for changing the *status quo*. The idea of regionalism can only be, India being a prime-mover in convincing her neighbours. India, as SAARC nations, cannot rely on plans to concentrate on bilateral relations alone. Indian foreign policy has not shown any significant shift in its policy to change the issue of bilateral disputes. Most of the studies do not discuss the impact of recent developments of the economic rise of India and democratic transitions in many SAARC nations. A gradual change in India's relationship with other SAARC nations has been seen after India's economic growth. A trade which is one debatable topic whether it should be considered in soft or hard power. The liberalisation of trade at the regional level would significantly contribute to economic growth and development at the national level. Trade not only facilitates lower prices and an increase in consumer choice but also promotes civil liberties and political rights. New ideas, science and technology and tools can be transmitted through trade. Regional trade liberalisation can foster twin goals of development and democratic consolidation of SAARC countries. Many experts have noted that India's advancing alliance with the United States has made it more assertive and less susceptible in the use of the coercive technique to address regional issues (Cartwright, 2009; Jain, 2010; Kapur and Ganguly, 2007; Mitra, 2009). India is cautiously welcoming the presence of the US in the South Asian region because of growing Chinese influence in the region. Both India and China strive to influence their neighbours in terms of strategic importance.

Conclusion

This chapter traces the evolution of India's foreign policy primarily on the SAARC nations and has concluded with these observations. First, the practice of *hard power* strategy from the 1970s to 1980s created a deep mistrust towards India. Secondly, India's relation with neighbouring nations was perceived primarily of security and foreign focus, political and economic was considered secondary. However, it declares that in the last 20 years, India probably has initiated a large number of soft power tactics, and has brought some constructive results in its regional policy. Therefore, if it carries on with this strategy in the nearing future and addresses the flaws in its policy, it can retrieve the identity of a well-founded and commendable regional leader. One cannot deny that India has also faced significant criticism in the practice of soft power. As India's sabotaged, the summit conference of SAARC, which was planned in Pakistan in November 2016 was considered as an apparent deviation from its path of peace, prosperity and stability in the region. South Asian counties are perhaps practising soft diplomacy. They have to prevent future crises *via* upbeat and forthcoming attitudes. The new political imperative may be the first step. It remains to be seen in how far India's 'positive unilateralism' will create a better regional framework or in how far the growing outside interference will bring about a shift towards multilateralism in India's regional policy.

REFERENCES

Bright, J.S. (1950). "Before and After Independence: A Collection of the Most Important and Soul-Stirring Speeches Delivered by Jawaharlal Nehru". Vol. I: *India's Struggle for Independence*, 1922-1946.

Goel, O.P. (Ed.). (2004). *India and SAARC Engagements* (Vol. 2). New Delhi: Gyan Publishing House.

Gujral, I.K., *A Foreign Policy for India*, 1998.

Gupta, S. (1964). *India and regional integration in Asia*. Asia Publishing House.

Hagerty, Devin T., "India's Regional Security Doctrine", in: *Asian Survey*, 31 (April 1991) 4, pp. 351-363.

Indian National Congress & Zaidi, A.M. (1987). "INC, the Glorious Tradition: Texts of the Resolutions Passed by the INC, the AICC, and the CWC". *Indian Institute of Applied Political Research*.

Kurlantzick, J. (2007). *Charm offensive: How China's soft power is transforming the world*. Yale University Press.

Kraska, J. (2009). "Sharing water, preventing war—hydrodiplomacy in South Asia". *International Journal of Phytoremediation, 20*(3), 515–530. https://doi.org/10.1080/09592290903293852

Kugiel, P. (2012). "India's soft power in South Asia". *International Studies, 49* (3-4), 351-376.

Larson, D.W. (2018). "New perspectives on rising powers and global governance: Status and clubs". *International Studies Review, 20* (2), 247-254.

Maxwell, Neville (1970). *India's China War*, New York.

Mazumdar, A. (2014). *Indian foreign policy in transition: relations with South Asia*. Routledge.

Mohan, C. Raja (2003). "India's positive unilateralism", in: *The Hindu*, 27. October.

Mohan, Raja C. (28 February, 2005). "The Manmohan Doctrine", in: *Daily Times*.

Morgenthau, H.J., Thompson, K.W. & Clinton, W.D. (1985). *Politics among nations: The struggle for power and peace*.

Mukherji, I.N. (2000). "Indo-Sri Lankan Trade and Investment Linkages: With Special Reference to SAPTA and Free Trade Agreement". *South Asia Economic Journal, 1*(1), 53-77.

Muni, S.D. (1985). "SAARC: Building Regionalism from below". *Asian Survey, 25*(4), 391-404.

Muralidharan, S. (January 16-29, 1999). "Towards free trade", in: *Frontline*, Vol. 16, No. 02 (accessed 13 February, 1999).

Nye, Joseph S. (1990). "Soft Power." *Foreign Policy No. 80*, 153-71. doi:10.2307/1148580.

Nye, Joseph S. (2004). *Soft Power: The Means to Success in World Politics*. New York: Public Affairs.

Nye, Joseph S. (23 February, 2006). "Think Again: Soft Power", *Foreign Policy*. https://foreignpolicy.com/2006/02/23/think-again-soft-power/

Pant, Harsh (2011). "India's changing role: The Afghanistan conflict." *Middle East Quarterly*, 18, No. 2, pp. 31-39.

Patryk Kugiel (2012). "India's Soft Power in South Asia", *International Studies, 49* (3&4), 363 doi: 10.1177/0020881714534033

Prime Minister's Address at Fourth SAARC Summit at Islamabad on 29 December, 1988, Foreign Affairs Record, Vol. XXXIV, No. 12 December 1988, p. 426.

Prasad, B. (1960). *Origins of India's Foreign Policy*, Calcutta: Bookland Pvt. Ltd.

Rajagopalan, R. (2018). "India's Post-Policy Agenda". *Carnegie Endowment for Intern, 2017*.

Sharma, S. (2001). "India and SAARC". *India Quarterly, 57*(2), 99-120.

Sikri, R. (2009). *Challenge and strategy: rethinking India's foreign policy.* Sage Publications, India.

Singh, Jaswant, India's Perspective on International and Regional Security Issues, Lecture, 17 January, 2001, Berlin, manuscript.

Sridharan, E. (2017). "Where is India headed? Possible future directions in Indian foreign policy". *International Affairs, 93*(1), 51-68.

Thussu, D. (2013). *Communicating India's soft power: Buddha to Bollywood.* Springer.

Wagner, C. (2005). From hard power to soft power? Ideas, interaction, institutions, and images in India's South Asia policy.

Waltz, Kenneth, *Theory of International Politics,* Reading 1979.

Yousaf, N., Ahmad, M., & Shah, Z. (2017). "SAARC Summit and Pakistan's Foreign Policy: An Analysis". *Journal of the Research Society of Pakistan, 54*(2).

22

BJP's Return to Power

An Analysis of Assam's 2021 State Election

Phulmoni Das and *Robin Hazarika*

Introduction

Electoral Politics of Assam has been witnessing different dimensions since its Independence. It was the Congress which dominated the electoral politics of late British and the early post-Independence period. Till 1996, the party had suffered defeat only in 1978 and 1985 assembly elections. But the electoral politics of the state since 1985 became a turning point in Assam politics. It was the period which seen the debacle of Congress and it also coincided with the emergence of community based smaller parties often called regional parties. The one party dominant system was giving way to a multi-party system in which political parties of various ethnic groups or smaller cultural communities began to play a significant role. This period also showed the emergence of Bharatiya Janata Party (BJP) and the party has been gradually playing a significant electoral force in the politics of the state. Electoral politics in Assam is also reflecting the political significance of its multi-ethnic reality and which has consequently played a predominant role in the electorate politics of the state. Rise of regional political party as well as rise of BJP in the state politics has not only challenged decade old dominance of Congress but also added new dimension to political scenario of the state. Despite having regional political party and the presence of Congress as the dominant political party, BJP has been continuously rising and able to make its stronghold in the state politics by winning both parliamentary and state assembly election of Assam. It is in this context the rise of BJP in the politics of the state can be contextualised. Since general elections 2014, the Bharatiya Janata Party (BJP) has successfully challenged the dominance of Congress, particularly in the state of Assam. Similarly, since 2016 and subsequently followed by 2019 as well as recently conducted assembly election of 2021 in the state, has also given mandate in favour of BJP. Rise of BJP not only can be contextualized in terms of Assam, in fact the Indian party politics has also experienced ascendency of BJP in the Centre too. With its landslide win in 2014, the BJP made a far-reaching recalibration of the social coalitions that confer political influence in India (Palshikar and Suri, 2014). Following the 2014 general election, the BJP steadily expanded its electoral footprint across India, especially in states where the party was not previously considered a viable option; along the way, the party extended its reach across great swaths of the country. The BJP's electoral powerful force has prompted many observers of Indian politics to suggest that Indian politics is once more witnessing a dominant-party phase, but this time with the BJP rather than the Congress as the central pillar (Palshikar, 2017). Therefore in this context this chapter seeks to understand the return of BJP in the state of Assam consecutively for the second term by focusing on three key questions. First, How far BJP's win in Assam can be socio-historically contextualized? Second, How far the decline of Congress and AGP helped BJP to ascendance in the politics of the state? Third, Despite facing stiff criticism for its Citizenship (Amendment) Bill (2016), what factors helped BJP to retain its position in 2021state assembly election? State has witnessed massive protests against the Citizenship (Amendment) Bill (2016) and which later on further paved the way for the emergence of the two regional political parties in Assam. Here in this context, the BJP's winning the election is interesting in the state. The above mentioned questions are discussed in different sections of this chapter. First section describes the socio-historical contextualization of electoral politics of Assam. Second segment deals with the decline of Congress and AJP which correspondingly led to the emergence of BJP in the state politics. Third section of this chapter describes the rise of BJP followed by the factors which helped BJP to win the election in 2021.

Contextualizing Electoral Politics of Assam

Electoral politics in Assam cannot be understood without taking in to account the history of the composite state of Assam. Present state of Assam includes territories inhabited by a large number of ethnic groups and communities who migrated to the area at various point of time. Ever since the advent of the British in 1826, the colonial power followed a policy of expansion. Through the Yandaboo Treaty, it initially legitimised its occupation. The process of colonisation in Assam was aimed towards the fulfilling of the imperial interests. The whole process of administration, land revenue, taxation measures, the process of territorial adjustments and re-adjustments had its impact on the economic, socio-cultural and demographic aspects of Assam. Here in this context noted political scientist Sanjib Baruah has called the North East as 'Settlement Frontier' and 'Resource Frontier' region. Settlement frontiers are relatively sparsely populated regions that attract repeated waves of immigration and settlement, while resource frontiers are associated with economic activities such as mineral extraction, timber harvesting, plantation agriculture, or hydro-power generation (Baruah, 2021). Therefore, Assam which was a sparsely populated area has turned to settlement frontier with the massive immigration process which was initiated primarily by the colonial administration for their own benefits. The colonial administration in Assam opened the floodgates of migration and in that process; it transformed the social composition of Assam's population. Therefore, Assam has been constructed as both settlement frontier and resource frontier region and it has consequently a major cause of contentions among the natives and the outsiders. This process of massive immigration into Assam has also added a different dimension to the politics of the state. It adds a historical and comparative dimension to one understand the region's politics. It is expected to witness the controversy around the issue of immigration and the rights of the indigenous people in the politics of the settlement frontier. Indeed this has also been the case with Assam since the earliest days of electoral politics in British colonial times as well as in post-Independence period where immigration has been playing a decisive political effects in the state.

Even without the immigration, Assam's indigenous population is extremely diverse in cultural, linguistic and religious terms. Therefore, the social composition of Assam is strongly influenced by two inseparable historical facts—the extraordinary role of immigrants in the state's population and the ethnic cultural diversity of the immigrants (Goswami, 2003). The issue of immigration and identity politics in the state has been associated with the notion of 'Resource frontier' as referred by Sanjib Baruah. Because the sparsely populated territory has become the target of resources extraction which has not only impacted the lives of the indigenous ethnic groups but gradually it has also raised tension and conflict over resources in the region. This has subsequently paved the growth of serious issues such as indigenous *versus* settler, insider *versus* outsider or tribal *versus* non-tribal. Hence, the phenomenon of ethno nationalism and the rise of different ethnic assertion and its significant impact in the politics of the state can be viewed from this perspective. Apart from these social economic and political conflicts between the immigrants and natives, state has also witnessed number of movements such as movement for state language (1960), the movement for instruction of Assamese medium in educational institutions up to the graduate level and also in Assam's two universities, this movement is also called as medium movement of 1972, the most particularly the movement against foreign nationals 1979 to 1985 (historic Assam Movement) which has led to the growth of regionalization in the politics of the state. Assam movement of 1979-85 on the foreign-national issue has brought considerable changes in the support structure and issue articulation of political parties in Assam (Baruah and Goswami, 1999). Assam movement gave expression to Assamese nationalism and at the same time it raised various subregional and ethnic aspirations. The regional aspirations of the Assamese people culminated in the formation of a regional party called the Asom Gana Parishad (AGP) in 1985. The party came to power in the same year and thus managed to consolidate its presence in Assam politics. Emergence of State's regional political party definitely impacted in Congress position. However, both Congress and AGP have seen erosion of their support in succeeding elections and this has given BJP a space to enter into state's politics. Therefore, following section of the chapter gives an analysis on the decline of Congress and AGP in state politics.

Debacle of Congress and AGP in State Politics of Assam

The rise of BJP in the state politics of Assam is also simultaneously associated with the debacle of Congress. Like at the national level, Congress dominated the electoral politics of the late British and the early post-British period. So it is in this context the decline of Congress is one of the main causes for the winning BJP for the second term in the state. Setback to Congress does not come suddenly with the winning of BJP in 2016, 2019 or 2021 election's results. During the pre-Independence period, the Congress championed the cause of the 'Assamese national identity' in terms of safeguarding Assamese language and culture. Congress can be considered as the 'catch all parties' with its mass support base. This historical fact was in some way responsible for the uninterrupted dominance of the Congress Party in the electoral history of Assam for three decades from 1952 to 1978. The Congress never lost more than three to four parliamentary seats out of the 12 or 14 Lok Sabha constituencies in the first six general elections to the Lok Sabha. Even in 1977 when the voters in most parts of India had rejected the Congress Party of Indira Gandhi for the emergency aspects, the electorate in Assam gave the party 10 out of14 seats in the Parliament with 50.6 per cent vote share. Its share of votes in the parliamentary elections, up to that period, remained above 45 per cent; in the assembly elections its lowest vote share during this period was 43.5 per cent (Goswami, 2003). The first major setback for the Congress was when Janata Party came to power at the centre. Indira Gandhi's defeat was followed by a split in the Congress Party, into two sections: Congress (U) and Congress (I). The first trial of strength took place in the assembly elections of 1978 in which the Congress(I) was reduced to a single digit both in terms of votes and seat. The Congress (U), on the other hand, turned in a more respectable performance with 26 seats and 24 per cent votes. The split of votes among both the parties benefited the non-Congress parties. The Janata Party that largely drew upon the socialist parties emerged as the single largest party with 53 seats and 27 per cent votes. The change of government in the centre, leading to corresponding changes in the political alignment in the state, had affected the results of these elections. Though the same issue of Emergency which remained central to the campaigns of both the 1977 parliamentary and the 1978 Assembly elections, yet the results were very different. The years following this election were full of political instability and upheaval (Goswami, 2003).

During this period the Congress Party was gradually losing its widespread support base. The six-year long Assam agitation was a political watershed in this respect. It was only after this agitation that the regional forces in the Asomiya areas could become significant in the electoral arena. The 1985 Assam Accord paved the way for the dissolution of the Assembly that was hold through 1983 election. 1983 assembly election was political disaster. The officially reported turnout was 32.3 per cent; the media reported the real turnout, especially in the Asomiya areas, to be much lower. The Congress came to power led by Hiteshwar Saikia, but the government lacked popular legitimacy. The 1985 election was a 'critical' election for Assam. This 1985 election led to a reconfiguration of the party system and a durable realignment of social groups with political parties. It is the AGP which came out as the manifestation of regional forces in Assam and also won the election. This regional party derived its strength from the perception of a threat to the Asomiya identity as a result of large scale immigration. In the assembly elections of 1985, the AGP rode on a wave to power, on the foreigner's issue. Part of the reason behind the AGP's victory was that during this election the pro-Asomiya nationalist votes remained solidly behind the AGP, but the votes of the forces inimical to the movement got divided, with the United Minority Front (UMF) capturing 17 seats and securing about 12 per cent votes. The weakening of the Congress coincided with the emergence of community based smaller parties often called the regional parties. The one-party dominant system was giving way to a multi-party system in which political parties of various ethnic groups or smaller cultural communities began to play significant roles. The support base, the Congress Party showed a steady decline while regional parties which have started coming to the electoral scenario. Regional parties consolidate their support either on regional issues or ethnic aspirations of smaller communities. Electoral politics in Assam was gradually reflecting the political significance of its multi-ethnic reality, with the respective educated elites of various communities consolidating their hold over the politics of their own communities.

Table 22.1: Party-wise Assam Assembly Election Results, 1985

Party Name	Percentage of Votes
AGP	35.0
Congress	23.2
UMFA	12.1
ICS	3.2
Left Parties	5.7
PCTA	3.6
Other Parties	2.8
Independent	14.4

Source: CSDS, Data Unit.

1985 election was significant in terms of ending of Congress, decade long dominance, but the close look at the verdict shows a different result in terms of vote shared by two political parties—AGP and Congress. Put together, the two big parties did not command even 60 per cent of the popular vote. The Congress' rainbow coalition had begun to come apart and each slice was headed in a different direction. What the 1985 election had instituted was a system of high mobilisation and intense competition among different social groups, a competition that was bound to introduce and sustain party fragmentation. The subsequent elections were to demonstrate this (Goswami, 2003).

But in 1991 election verdict shows that there is the decline of AGP votes and gradual entry of BJP in state politics is also observed. Although 1991 election gave favours to Congress again, but it does not directly proved that Congress won all the massive supports. It was primarily because of the division of the pro-Assamese nationalist votes between the AGP and Natun Asom Gana Parishad (NAGP), a breakaway faction of the AGP, and the unprecedented performance of the BJP. The BJP took a significant slice of the anti-migrant voters in the migrant dominated areas and thus made things difficult for the

AGP. For the first time, the BJP registered its presence in the state in the Asomiya and the immigrant dominated areas.

The Congress came back to power in 1991, as it would later in 2001, but not in its traditional role as a party representing a rainbow social coalition of all the major communities of Assam. It did not enjoy the confidence and the electoral support of the largest and the dominant Asomiya community. Therefore, the Congress was gradually forced to forge a coalition of the various 'minority' groups that put together constitute a majority in the state. It was a precarious strategy, for even when it succeeded it could barely give Congress the kind of majority it had enjoyed in the past. In that sense, the decline that started in 1977 continued despite the party being able to form a government in the state (Mahanta, 2014). In the parliamentary elections as well, the Congress fared better in the areas dominated by tea garden labour and the Muslim immigrants. The Muslim immigrants have been insecure particularly in view of the aggressive posture of the Asomiya middle class. Moreover, because of the Assam movement and the aggressive posture taken by AGP against the minorities have eventually shifted the votes towards the Congress.

Therefore, from the above analyses Congress' performance can be summarized. It is as such in 1991 parliamentary elections, the Congress won eight seats with a vote share of 28.5 per cent. In 1996, the Congress and AGP won five seats each. In 1999, Congress won 10 seats and its vote share rose to 38.4 per cent. Congress won nine and seven seats in the 2004 and 2009 elections respectively. In the 2014 elections, the party's seat share and vote share both came drastically down (Sultana, 2019).

Another factor for the reduction of Congress votes is the emergence of AIUDF as primarily a Muslim minority oriented party. The AIUDF emerged into the electoral politics of Assam due to various socio-economic and political reasons. In their first attempt in the 2006 Assembly election they made their presence felt in the electoral politics of Assam by winning 10 seats out of the 69 seats they contested (Karmakar, 2014). Their emergence in the electoral politics of Assam has disturbed the traditional Muslim support base of the Congress. The party became stronger in the Assembly election 2011 by winning 18 seats and emerged as the second largest party ahead of the AGP. In the 2014 general election also, the AIUDF shook up the politics of Assam as they won three seats (Mahanta, 2013). Though the Assamese Muslims are spread out in Assam, the Muslims of East Bengal origin are generally concentrated in the middle and lower parts of Brahmaputra valley as well as in the Barak valley districts. The Assamese Muslims who have traditionally been supporters of the Congress and the AGP are more assimilated with Assamese culture and identity. Gradual emergence of AIUDF in the electoral politics of Assam and its role in successfully playing a pivotal role in mobilising Sylhetia and the Mymensingia Muslims in favour of the AIUDF is the significant cause of the rise of AIUDF and decline of Congress in the state politics.

It is important to mention here that it is not only Congress which have seen its gradual erosion of its support but also the AGP, a significant regional political party which is the product of the historic Assam movement has also faced stiff decline in due course of time. Despite its success in 1985 election it has only managed to polled only 33 per cent of the votes. In a diverse multi-ethnic state like Assam, movements prioritizing a dominant Assamese identity, later on gave birth to different ethnic aspirations. Further, it has given birth to number of sub-regional parties and organizations such as Autonomous State Demand Committee (ASDC), United Minority Front (UMF) and All Bodo Students' Union (ABSU). These different parties and organizations began to dot the political landscape in the state. Disgruntled with the nature and the outcomes of the Assam agitation, the leadership among different ethnic groups, who had participated in the movement, began reviving earlier demands for autonomy. Thus, it has not only made fragmentation of different political parties and groups but also added a new dimension to the state's politics. AGP has begun to lose its popularity since its first term in government due to its lackadaisical attempt in implementing the Assam Accord. The detection, deletion and deportation of 'illegal' immigrants from Assam seemed politically less viable for the AGP, the promise with which it had come to power in the first place. Moreover, AGP's inability to form government at the state level in subsequent elections was also because of the result of rampant factionalism, lack of leadership and its ambiguity in dealing with the separatist group of ULFA. The rapidly diminished political capital of the AGP, once considered an indomitable regional force, demonstrated the limits of aggressive ethno-nationalist politics in a state with complex ethnic diversity and the presence of cross-cutting cleavage (Saikia, 2020).

Therefore, with the gradual erosion of support of AGP as well as the decline of Congress as the rainbow social coalition of all major communities have made the space open for BJP and its saffron politics to enter into the electoral scenario of the state. Therefore, next section of the chapter analyses the rise of the BJP in the socio-political context of Assam.

Rise of BJP

The political dominance that the Bharatiya Janata Party (BJP) has enjoyed since 2014 General Election in Assam remains a significant factor in giving the National Democratic Alliance (NDA) an better opportunity over other parties in the Lok Sabha elections. The Lok Sabha elections to Assam held in 2019, as well as the recent assembly election of 2021 and its results seemed to represent continuity with the political consolidation of the BJP that was witnessed during the assembly elections held in 2016.

Table 22.2: Parliamentary Election in Assam (1991-2019) (Total Seats for Assam 14)

Year	Voters %	Party	Seats	Voters %
1991	75.3	INC	8	28.5
		AGP	1	17.6
		BJP	2	09.6
1996	78.5	INC	5	31.6
		AGP	5	27.2
		BJP	1	15.9
1998	61.1	INC	10	38.97
		AGP	0	12.7
		BJP	1	24.47
1999	71.30	INC	10	38.42
	69.08	AGP	0	11.92
		BJP	2	29.84
2004	69.08	INC	9	35.07
		AGP	2	19.95
		BJP	2	22.94

(*Contd.*)

Year	Voters %	Party	Seats	Voters %
2009	69.53	INC AGP BJP AIUDF	7 1 4 1	34.9 14.6 16.62 16.1
2014	80.13	INC AGP BJP AIUDF	3 0 7 3	29.6 03.8 36.5 14.8
2019	81.60	INC BJP (alliance with AGPAIUDF) AIUDF Independent	3 9 1 1	35.44 46.76 7.80 7.80

Source: CSDS Data Unit.

As Table 22.2 shows that in Assam the BJP has seen a steady growth of vote share since 1991, with a slump in 2004 and 2009 (in the latter year it was in an alliance with the AGP which got 14.6 per cent vote share). BJP has benefited from its alliance with the AGP in the 2006 assembly and 2009 parliamentary elections. The traditional support base of AGP—the Assamese Hindus, the Assamese Muslims and tribals—has gradually shifted their allegiance to other political parties. Factors such as the detection, deletion and deportation of foreigners were the principal electoral agenda of the AGP, but in the last two decades it has been observed as some of the important election agenda of BJP.

Despite losing in 2011 assembly election, BJP has able to won the maximum number of seats in 2014 parliamentary election by gaining support from all social, ethnic and tribal groups of Assam. 2014 election results in Assam can said to be an anti-Congress mandate rather than a pro-BJP one, as the former has failed to tackle all the major issues of the state. People disgruntled with Congress has voted BJP for change, perhaps the most dissatisfying performance of Congress in terms of solving unemployment, corruption and inability to contain ethnic and group clashes in areas like NC Hills, Karbi Anglong and Bodoland, Darrang and Udalguri are some of the reasons for people's dissatisfaction with Congress. One of the important feature that has been observed in the 2014 Lok Sabha and the 2016 Assembly elections is that the BJP's performance had been extraordinary in upper Assam, it is primarily due to the swing of tea garden communities towards the BJP, which used to be a solid vote bank of the Congress in the past (Pisharoty, 2019). Since 2014, BJP has managed to retain its success in Assam primarily for its in-depth strategy to mobilize different communities of people. BJP involved itself unprecedentedly in local politics to imbalance the local dominance enjoyed by the Congress. The BJP made entry into the Autonomous Councils as well as the Sixth Schedule Councils which enabled it to reach out to the tribal communities and forge social alliances with the tribal leaderships (Tripathi, Das and Goswami, 2019). Moreover, BJP has also made its entry into BTAD area as well as North Cachar Hills, as both these areas come under Sixth Schedule domain. Another major factor which help in proliferation of saffroinisation in the state is the role of Rashtriya Swayamsevak Sangh (RSS), the movement wing of BJP. The organization's real contribution towards the BJP's victory in the state since 2014 has been the outcome of its decades-long work in the state, particularly among the tea tribe communities and the tribal communities (Dutta, 2019). Moreover, BJP in succeeding elections has been successfully portraying localization of Hinduism. Similarly, in 2016 Assembly election too BJP concentrated mainly on regional issues and localized symbols. This worked well for the party as issues of illegal immigration, education, good governance, economic and cultural development resonated with the electorate which results BJP to successfully win the election. Another noticeable incident in the politics of the state is the winning of BJP in the Parliamentary election of 2019, despite a huge protest made by the people of Assam against the Citizenship (Amendment) Bill, 2016. Citizenship (Amendment) Bill, 2016 seeks to bestow citizenship upon certain categories of non-Muslim migrants escaping religious persecution in neighbouring Muslim-majority country such as Pakistan, Afghanistan and Bangladesh. But BJP has successfully retained its support by raising threat perception against the increasing infiltrate Muslim immigrants among the different ethnic groups of Assam. Thus, BJP has made religious consolidation by making illegal Muslim immigration as crucial issue. It marked successful inroads in Assam election 2019, by raising the issue of protection of *jati, mati, bheti* (community, land and homestead) from "illegal Bangladeshi Muslim migrants", and drawing support from the Assamese Hindu as well as diverse ethnic communities with its promise of freeing the land from the foreigners' control (Sharma and Tripathi, 2019). Following 2019 Parliamentary election and 2016 Assembly election, BJP has successfully continuing its second term by winning 2021 State Legislative Assembly election in Assam. Therefore, following section of the chapter analyses the BJP's return to the state's power for the second term.

Understanding BJP's Victory in Assam State's Election, 2021

BJP, not surprisingly, has retained the state of Assam with a comfortable majority of seats (75) in the 126-seat House in 2021 election.

Table 22.3: Performance of Political Parties—Assam Assembly Elections (2011, 2016, 2021)

Number of Constituencies: 126

Party	2011	2016	2021
	Seat Share	Seat Share	Seat Share
BJP	5	60	60
UPPL	–	–	6
AGP	10	14	9
BPF	12	12	4
Congress	12	26	29
AIUDF	18	13	16
Others	3	1	2

Source: Election Commission of India.

Table 22.3 show how BJP has been able to retain its dominance in the state power. Therefore, it is in this context the understanding BJP's return to power is significant. There are different factors which have played crucial role in helping BJP's return to power and which can be analysed under following sub-headings.

Political Alignments

Ahead of election 2021, state politics has seen the major political alignments among different political parties. There are two significant alliances seen this time as Mahajot *versus* Mitrajot. Though the Congress forged *Mahajot,* a grand pre-election alliance with the All India United Democratic Front (AIUDF), the Bodoland People's Front (BPF) and Left parties, the ruling alliance managed to defeat it. Whereas BJP fought this election with its ally AGP and new partner the United People's Party Liberal (UPPL) formed by ex-president of the All Bodo Students' Union (ABSU) Pramod Bodo and this alliance has been termed as *Mitrajot*. In fact, the Congress' tie-up with the 'Muslim party' AIUDF seems to have helped the BJP and it helped them keep Hindu voters firmly on their side and wean away a small but sizeable chunk of Assamese Muslim voters (*The Hindu*, 2021).

However, one of the significant development that has been observed ahead of 2021 election was the formation of two new regional political parties in the state—Assam Jatiya Parishad and Raijor Dal. AJP formed by former All Assam Students' Union Leader Lurinjyoti Gogoi and Raijor Dal formed by KMSS leader Akhil Gogoi. Both these two political parties were formed against the backdrop of an anti-CAA [Citizenship (Amendment) Act] agitation 2019-20. The two local parties, AJP and the Raijor Dal (RD), had a limited impact, and the RD could win just one seat in Upper Assam. Their influence remained confined to Upper Assam.

CAA and NRC Evokes Mixed Sentiments

In 2019, the BJP had faced violent protests in Assam, leading to five deaths in police firing, after the Centre passed the Citizenship Amendment Act (CAA) in Parliament. But the BJP's campaign in Assam carefully avoided playing up the CAA. The Congress as well as new regional parties tried their best to keep the CAA issue alive, but it does not make any influence over the election result. BJP while formulating CAA, it very strategically exempting the three Sixth Schedule Council areas—the Bodo Territorial Council (BTC), the Karbi Autonomous Council and the Dima Hasao from the purview of the CAA—the BJP government succeeded in keeping away many ethnic nationalist organizations from the anti-CAA movement. It has subsequently helped BJP to get the support from different ethnic groups. Though CAA remains a contentious issue, but according to the Lokniti-CSDS post-poll survey mentioned that study shows that just 3 per cent of respondents mentioned CAA/NRC as the most important issue in the election. Almost one-third (30%) of respondents mentioned 'development' as the key issue. Moreover, study also shows that, even though opposition to CAA was high across both Hindus and Muslims, the latter were more likely to be against it, with 61 per cent reporting opposition as against 47 per cent of Hindu voters. Across ethnicities, Assamese Muslims recorded the highest opposition, with three-fourths (73%) against it, followed by Bengali Muslims (59%), Assamese Hindus (51%) and Bengali Hindus (40%) (*The Hindu*, 2021). Therefore, it can be said that BJP has been able to make the sense of the voter by not making CAA as main plank during election campaign, even though rejection of CAA was the main issue for the entire opposition.

Co-opting different Communities

One of the striking feature of 2021 election was that, BJP has successfully consolidated different ethnic groups and communities including tea garden communities of Assam. BJP has strategically maintained alliance with almost all the mainstream political outfits of tribal ethnic groups and the AGP. The Bodoland People's Front (BPF) was replaced by the United People's Party Liberal (UPPL) as the key NDA ally in the Bodoland Territorial Area Districts (BTAD). Moreover, people of BTAD are highly dissatisfied with BPF and have given their votes for UPPL and rejection of BPF was primarily for the cause of development and the protection of Bodo identity (Saikia, 2021). Iconic figure of UPPL president Promod Bodo has also helped UPPL to win over this time. Promod Bodo is considered as to be an architect of recent BTR agreement of 2020 signed with the Central Government. This recently signed agreement was done among students outfit as well as several splinter groups of the National Democratic Front of Bodoland (militant group) and the Centre. This has been described as 'final and comprehensive solution' to the Bodo demands and this can be said as significant reason for the victory of UPPL, the major ally of BJP in BTAD.

BJP also sustained its alliance with the mainstream Rabha and the Tiwa ethno-political outfits and also co-opted the mainstream leadership of the Mising community. To mitigate the discontent of the six OBC communities (Ahom, Moran, Motok, Koch, Chutiya, Koch Rajbongshi and Tea tribes) over the failure of the Union government to grant them ST status, the state government awarded three of those communities—Motoks, Morans and the Koch Rajbongshis—non-territorial ethnic councils through legislations in December 2020. All these factors contributed to the BJP's success in 2021 election.

Apart from the BJP's consolidation among different ethnic communities, it has very positively managed in co-opting tea garden communities of Assam. These communities constitute around 17 per cent of Assam's total population and have a 35-40 per cent vote share in the Brahmaputra Valley. In the 2014 Lok Sabha and the 2016 Assembly elections, the BJP's performance had been extraordinary in upper Assam primarily due to the shifting of these communities towards the BJP, which used to be a solid vote bank of the Congress in the past (Pisharoty, 2019). In the past five years, BJP has introduced financial, educational and health schemes for tea garden workers of Assam , including the hike of wages from Rs. 137 to Rs. 217 are some of the important contributory factors for shifting their support to BJP. BJP government's ambitious move to ensure financial inclusion of tea garden workers of Assam under 'Cha Bagichar Dhan Purasakar Mela' (fair for gifting wealth to tea garden workers) through which Rs. 2,500 were credited to tea garden workers who hold bank account can be referred as one of the important step of BJP's inroads to tea garden workers of Assam.

Populist Policies

BJP government's hyper-populism based on welfare and development is one of the reasons behind the BJP's success in the state election 2021. BJP has launched number of welfare policies targeting various section of the society. For instance, the Orunodoi scheme gives a monthly assistance of Rs. 830 given to accounts of women members of marginalised families through a Direct Benefit Transfer procedure.

The government has said the scene benefits around 22 lakh women. BJP consolidated its base among the different sections of the masses by foregrounding developmentalism, accompanied by hyper populism. post-poll study conducted by Lokniti-CSDS has mentioned that the only schemes that had a fair amount of beneficiaries were the 'Orunodoi' and the 'Chah bagichar dhan puraskar mela' (financial aid to tea garden workers). About a quarter of voters (23%) claimed that the Orunodoi scheme was helpful to them; of those, 59 per cent voted for the NDA, 27 per cent more than Mahajot. Among non-beneficiaries of Orunodoi, NDA lagged by 9 per cent. Notably, the respondents were more likely to have benefited from the Central Government's schemes, such as the Pradhan Mantri Ujjwala Yojana (43%) and the Mahatma Gandhi National Rural Employment Guarantee Act (31%). Moreover distribution of two wheeler to meritorious girl students who have passed the higher secondary examination and announcement made by the government that it would provide "one tolä of gold" (1 tola = 11.664 g) to brides belonging to all communities of the state provided the marriage is formally registered under 'Arundhati Gold Scheme" are some of the major policies through which BJP gained prominent attention in the state. Offering gold to the brides under the government scheme has come under criticism; however, the government has remained steadfast on it. Admission fee waiver and free textbooks up to the degree levels to the students of economically backward families are some of the other welfarist policies which have attracted the electorates towards BJP. BJP through these hyper populist policies has successfully generated a good number of beneficiaries and subsequently it became a major cause for retaining power in the state.

Social and Religious Polarisation

BJP has benefited from social and religious polarization in the 2021 election. This polarization reduced the Congress to a party dependent on the electoral base of the East Bengal-origin Muslims. In this election, Congress tied up for the first time with MP Badruddin Ajmal's All India United Democratic Front (AIUDF), which enjoys a large support base among Bengali-origin Muslims. This alliance has been constantly targeted and criticized by BJP. Moreover, during the campaign, BJP has created the allegation against AIUDF which is the most important political outfit of the East Bengal Origin Muslim as a threat to the interests of indigenous communities of Assam. This polarized the votes to the BJP's favour in most regions, while the alliance consolidated votes in the Muslim-dominated districts of Lower Assam. Religious polarization is one of the factors that have worked for BJP's victory in 2021 election. Popularising 'civilisational threat' emanating from AIUDF and targeting Badruddin Azmal as the leader of the communal party has surely impacted the electorates of Upper Assam. As per the Lokniti-CSDS post-poll survey it shows that religious polarisation, particularly Hindu consolidation, is one factor that helps in making sense of the election verdict. Over two-thirds of Hindus (67%) rallied behind the BJP whereas Congress alliance, on the other hand, managed to secure only two of every ten (19%) Hindu votes. Further the support for the BJP among Hindus cut across linguistic-ethnic differences and came both from the Assamese-and Bengali-speaking communities— 67 per cent of Assamese Hindus and 74 per cent of Bengali Hindus favoured the BJP this time. According to Lokniti's post-poll survey, the major reason for the curtailment of Hindu votes for the Congress lead alliance is that most Hindus were found to consider the AIUDF as communal. Given the religious profile of Assam, where the Hindu share in the State's population is around 62 per cent, this consolidation proved to be a decisive point once again for BJP (*The Hindu*, 2021). Apart from consolidating Hindu votes on religious ground, BJP has also focused on adapting local cults and symbols such as those associated with Kamakhya and Sankardev-Sattra traditions. Moreover, it is also seen that BJP has also valorized greatest military hero of Assam, Lachit Borphukan, who was a general during 17th century period of Ahom dynasty. He is best known for the Battle of Saraighat on Brahmaputra, where he beat the Mughals. While the BJP has been valorizing Lachit Borphukan as a 'Hindu' warrior who fought against Mughals and they equate Mughals with Muslim. This is primarily done for the purpose of mobilizing Assamese sentiment for electoral gain and it helps BJP to enhance their Hindutva Narrative through the valorizing of local legends and their associated history.

Conclusion

This chapter was an attempt to understand the return of BJP's state power. Through the above discussions and arguments it has been observed that 2021 election was fought primarily on the basis of hyper populism, politics of development and consent manufactured on the ground of religion. Despite having a massive anti–CAA protests in the state and civil-political alliance against BJP, it failed to impact on the behaviour of the electorates. Electorates' choice was guided by the factor of the politics of indigeneity *vis-à-vis* immigrant Muslims. However, despite having absolute majority in the state, the challenge for the newly conducted government is to deal with the rising unemployment issue, increasing discrimination and intolerance in the society. Therefore, it is in this perspective the duty of the present government to protect interest of not only the Assamese identity but also the smaller nationality who are the integral part of the Assamese society as a whole.

REFERENCES

Baruah, Apurba and Sandhya Goswami, (1999). "Fractured Identities and Politics in a Multi-ethnic State", *Economic & Political Weekly*, Vol. 34, September 3.

Goswami, Sandhya (2003). "Assam Multiple Realignments and Fragmentation of Party System", *Journal of Indian School of Political Economy*, January-June.

Karmakar, Rahul (2014). "Assam Polls: Badruddin Ajmal's AIUDF Emerging as a New Alternative". *Hindustan Times*, Guwahati, 9 March.

Sultana Parvin (2019). "General Elections in Assam: Persistent Issues and Shifting Alignments". *Economic & Political Weekly*, Vol. VII, No. 16, April 20.

Sharma, Dhruba Pratim and Vikas Tripathi (2019). "Assam 2019: NDA Deepens Its Dominance," *Economic & Political Weekly*, Vol. 54, No. 34.

Saikia Smitana (2020). "Saffronizing the periphery: Explaining the rise of the Bharatiya Janata Party in Contemporary Assam". *Studies in Indian Politics 8*(1), 69-84.

Suhas Palshikar and K.C. Suri, (2014). "India's 2014 Elections: Critical Shifts in the Long Term, Caution in the Short Term". *Economic and Political Weekly,* 49, No. 39-49.

Suhas Palshikar, (2017). "India's Second Dominant Party System". *Economic and Political Weekly,* 52, No. 11.

Tripathi, Vikas, Tamasa Das and Sandhya Goswami (2018). "National Narrative and Regional Subtext: Understanding the Rise of BJP in Assam". *Studies in*

Indian Politics, Vol. 6, No. 1, pp. 60-70. https://journals.sagepub.com/doi/full/10.1177/2321023018762676

The Hindu (2021). "Assam Assembly Elections Hindu consolidation pays off for BJP". 7 May. https://www.thehindu.com/elections/assam-assembly/hindu-consolidation-pays-off-for-bjp/article34509288.ece

The Hindu (2021). "Assam Assembly elections CAA, NRC evoke mixed sentiments". 7 May. https://www.thehindu.com/elections/assam-assembly/assam-assembly-elections-caa-nrc-evoke-mixed-sentiments/article34509427.ece

The Hindu (2021). "Tale of two Congress guarantees: one clicked, another did not". 8 May. https://www.thehindu.com/elections/assam-assembly/a-tale-of-two-congress-guarantees-one-clicked-another-did-not/article34508315.ece

The Hindu (2021). "Assam Assembly elections | Welfare measures not a decisive factor". 8 May. https://www.thehindu.com/elections/assam-assembly/assam-assembly-elections-welfare-measures-not-a-decisive-factor/article34509481.ece

23
The Assembly Elections (2021) in Kerala
Success of Political Pragmatism and Social Engineering

M.R. Biju and *M.R.B. Anantha Padmanabha*

Prelude

The Election Commission of India (ECI) made the formal announcement for the assembly elections in the state of Kerala on 26th February, 2021, along with the states of Tamil Nadu, West Bengal, Assam and the Union Territory of Puducherry. The assembly polls to Kerala has generally treated as an indicative of a new social compact that is taking place in the state. It could also mark as a realignment of Kerala's political landscape. The Congress-led United Democratic Front (UDF), the CPI(M)-led Left Democratic Front (LDF) and the BJP-led National Democratic Alliance (NDA) were all betting on an outsize impact by putting their respective political ideals and agendas. The BJP, long seen as a North Indian Political Party has made significant inroads in Kerala in the recent past and hoping to emerge as a Third Alternative through social engineering that includes wooing a section of the Christians. But the CPI(M)-led LDF is experimenting with daring political moves to win a second term which is quite unusual in the state.

The CPI(M) decision to deny seats to several of its veterans has not been taken positively by its cadres, who have taken to the streets and social media to challenge it. The party wooed Kerala Congress

(Mani) from the UDF into the LDF, which was embarrassing to the party to explain before the cadres. Charges of corruption and nepotism, including a multi-agency investigation into the links between the former principle secretary to the Chief Minister and a smuggling racket have taken the shine off the governance record of the left government. The Chief Minister, however, was trying to turn in his favour by claiming to be at the receiving end of the political conspiracy by the Central Investigating Agencies at the behest of the BJP. On the other hand, the Congress was trying to keep the leadership squabbles within by, not formally announcing a leader, but signalling the former Chief Minister Oommen Chandy could get another term. It is also struggling hard to hold on to traditional basis. Over and above, the BJP in Kerala had never imagined itself as a serious contender of power, and the opportunity in sight has intensified internal factional rivalries. No doubt, the Assembly elections will be an indicative of a new social compact that is taking place in Kerala and in that sense it is not merely electing a new government.

In this context, it has to be added that in the previous assembly election of 2016, the LDF led by CPI(M) secured the majority by capturing 91 seats and 43.1 per cent votes, defeating the Congress-led UDF which won 47 seats and 38.6 per cent votes. The BJP-led NDA won 1 seat and secured 14.9 per cent of the votes. In the polls, the CPI(M) with 26.5 per cent votes followed by the Congress with 23.7 per cent votes. In this context it has to be added that in the 2019 Lok Sabha Polls, the Congress secured 37.3 per cent of the votes followed by the CPI(M) which won 26 per cent. In the seat-wise, the UDF captured 19 out of the total 20 seats. The remaining seat went in favour of the LDF. In the 2021 Assembly elections, unlike the previous elections NDA posed a potential threat to the bipolar political order of the state in several places.

Voters and Candidates

As per the electoral statistics of the Election Commission of India, 2,74,46,039 voters figure in the integrated electoral rolls published for the 2021 Assembly elections. Of it 1,41,62,025 are women, 1,32,83,724 are men and 290 are transgenders. Non-resident Indian voters number in 93,415 in the state. Among them 6,086 are women,

87,318 are men and 11 are transgender voters. Malappuram has the highest number of voters, 33,21,038. The district has 16,64,017 women voters, 16,56,996 male voters and 25 transgender voters. Wayanad with 6,16,110 voters has the lowest number of electors. It has 3,12,870 female voters, 3,03,239 male voters and 1 transgender voter. The electorate in other districts are Kasargode (10,58,337), Kannur (20,61,041), Kozhikode (25,58,679), Palakkad (22,94,739), Thrissur (26,12,032), Ernakulam (26,49,340), Idukki (8,88,608), Kottayam (15,93,575), Alappuzha (17,82,900), Pathanamthitta (10,54,100), Kollam (21,35,830), Thiruvanthapuram (28,19,710). Of the total voters, 5.18 lakh voters are in the age group of 18-19. There are 6,22,064 voters in the age group of 80 plus. More than 4 lakh voters are eligible for postal ballots.

With regard to the candidates are concerned in all 957 candidates were left in the fray for the Assembly elections. A total number of 2180 nominations were filled across the state. The number had plunged to 1061 after the primary scrutiny. Malappuram had the highest number of candidates at 111 while Wayanad has the lowest at 18. The filling of nominations had opened on 12th March in the state with the issue of notification by the Election Commission of India. The number of candidates is much lower this time compared to 2016 elections. This time 1119 nominations were rejected on various grounds during the scrutiny.

Keeping this in background, an attempt has been made in this study to examine the facets of Assembly elections 2021 in Kerala. This study has been categorised under four parts. Part one examines the significance of poll manifestos presented by the major players in the state politics—UDF, LDF and the NDA. Part two unfolds the major electoral issues confronted by the state politics in the recent past. The central theme of discussion of Part three is on the polling statistics and the concluding part makes a critical enquiry on people's verdict.

PART I: POLL MANIFESTOS

United Democratic Front (UDF)

1. The United Democratic Front election manifesto guaranteed a minimum monthly income of Rs. 6,000 to Kerala's most

impoverished families. The unconditional cash transfer under NYAY (*Nyuntam Aay Yojana*) would reduce income inequalities, mitigate starvation and help indigent households escape the worst deprivations of daily life. The scheme would increase spending, spur demand and catalyse the economy. The other promises include:

(a) Welfarism seemed to take centre stage in the UDF manifesto. The opposition attempted to outdo the ruling front by promising a monthly welfare pension of Rs. 3,000 instead of the 2,500 guaranteed by the LDF.

(b) The UDF also appeared to cast its net far and wide to draw voters of various income brackets, social background, employment status, age and gender. IT seemed social welfare and subsidies trumped economic constrains in the UDF manifesto. The UDF's 2016 election promise to prohibit liquor found no mention in the 2021 manifesto.

(c) The UDF targeted home makers aged between 40 and 60 by vowing to transfer them 2,000 monthly if not already covered by the minimum scheme: income guarantee scheme.

(d) The UDF fixed the minimum daily wage at Rs. 700. It also proposed a law to recover 5.5 lakh acres from illegal owners and accord the land to landless tribal people and Dalits. At a stroke, the UDF had sought to eclipse the free ration and food kits supplied by the LDF government during the COVID-19 pandemic.

(e) The UDF manifesto put immense stock in subsidised health care. It would underwrite the medical expenses of cancer, heart, kidney, organ transplant and haemophilia patients and promised 'no bill hospitals' in the public health sector.

(f) One lakh unemployed youth would get two-wheelers at half the market price. An *ex gratia* one-time payment of Rs. 5,000 is on the cards for auto-rickshaw and taxi drivers. Free housing for five lakh low-income families and maternity allowance for Scheduled Caste/Tribe mothers are other highlights. The UDF matched the LDF by promising Rs. 250 minimum price for rubber. It would write off agriculture loans up to Rs. 2 lakh. It vowed to subsidise public transport and self-owned auto-rickshaw and taxi fuel to make travel more affordable.

(g) On the political front, the UDF promised a law to defend the Sabarimala faith. It promised to stop back-door appointments, make it mandatory for government departments to report vacancies to the Public Service Commission and preserve the high seas for traditional fishers.

Left Democratic Front (LDF)

The Left Democratic Front (LDF) election manifesto released on Friday promised increased spending on social welfare, health and education. It pledged modernised transport and urban infrastructure, industrial corridors, high-speed rail connectivity, free housing for the poor, enhanced social welfare pensions, improved public services, better child and elderly care, rapid re-skilling of unemployed youth and creation of a knowledge-based world class economy.

According to the LDF reversing in equality, protecting secular and progressive values, defending federalism, raising the standard of living, and building a welfare state were the overarching political imperatives of the front. The front would increase monthly welfare pension from Rs. 1,600 to Rs. 2,500. An estimated 60 lakh persons would be benefited. It would include homemakers in the expanded pension net.

The Scheduled Castes and Scheduled Tribes would get free and modern housing. The LDF announced special schemes to rehabilitate Gulf returnees and further bolster the public distribution system. It promised 40 lakh new employment opportunities, a 5,000 crore coastal development package, welfare schemes for taxi and autorickshaw drivers, coir and agriculture workers, traditional seafaring fishers, toddy tappers and cashew workers. A 50 per cent hike in farm wages is a key election promise.

The manifesto emphasised the State's tourism potential. It projected future Kerala as a Mecca of liberal arts, a magnet for creative persons and an oasis of secular and progressive values. The LDF manifesto strived to shore up its core base while attempting to woo fence-voters as it approached a tight three-cornered electoral contest on April 6. The open-handed blend of increased social welfare benefits with stress on infrastructure development, reservation for economically disadvantaged forward community persons, resistance to majoritarian politics and strident opposition to the Centre's "trespasses" on to federalism lie at the heart of the LDF's election pitch.

National Democratic Alliance (NDA)

The Bharatiya Janata Party (BJP)-led NDA manifesto released on Wednesday leaned heavily on populist measures targeted at low-income families. It reaffirmed the alliance's core commitment to nationalistic politics. Union Minister of Environment, Forest and Climate Change Prakash Javadekar unveiled the declaration. The manifesto promised employment for at least one member in each family. An increased social welfare pension of Rs. 3,500 a month, free housing, piped drinking water and power for the poor are on the cards.

Five acres of land to deprived SC/ST families, free laptop for high school students, the promise of a hunger-free Kerala, six free cooking gas cylinders for BPL families, a monthly medical grant of Rs. 5,000 to in-patients from BPL households, travel concession for senior citizens and fair wages are the other highlights. The BPL families would receive medical assistance up to Rs. 5 lakh under the *Ayushman Bharat* scheme. The NDA would open *Jana Oushadhi* centres in all panchayats. It also promised an AIIMS centre in Kerala and upgrading district hospitals and medical colleges in the State to speciality and super-speciality centres.The NDA promised to be a bulwark against the global Islamist threat and terrorism. It pledged a State law against *Love Jihad.* It vowed to free temple administration from political control and hand the institutions over to collectives of devotees. The coalition promised to target terrorism, anti-national organisations and end political violence in Kerala for good.

The manifesto seemed to hark back to the principles of "integral humanism" propounded by the Hindu right wing ideologue

Deenadayal Upadhyay. The manifesto promised to transform panchayats to *gram swaraj* mooted to self-sufficiency in food production, housing, drinking water supply and hygiene. Namo food joints would serve breakfast (10), lunch (20) and dinner (10) in all panchayats.

The NDA vowed enhanced rural road, internet and power connectivity, electric crematoria and garbage disposal units in villages and rapid re-skilling of rural youth to meet the demand of the global economy. A six-lane highway linking Kaliyikkavila in the south to Manjeswaram in the north would open up the State's hinterlands for development. Motels would dot the freeway. New airports in Idukki, Wayanad and Sabarimala, development of minor ports, a new road parallel to the Thamarassery Ghat in Wayanad are other election pledges.

Profesor Pulapre Balakrishnan has made a detailed investigation on the three political manifestos presented by the UDF, LDF and the NDA (*The Hindu*, March 24, 2021). It would be quite appropriate to reproduce his comments and findings which can be summed up as under:

- The manifestos have been received with scepticism by the public, for they could not but have wondered how the fresh expenditures will be funded. Kerala today has one of the highest levels of public debt per capita among India's states. Without fresh resource mobilisation of which intent there is no indication in either party's manifesto—enhanced public expenditure assures higher levels of public debt in the future.
- Individual well-being enabled by public action is a perfectly legitimate aspiration in a democracy. However, what distinguishes the decades' long practice in Kerala is that it is a form of welfarism far from what is generally understood when we speak of a welfare state.
- What distinguishes a genuine welfare state from the Kerala Model is that in a genuine welfare state, benefits are financed by taxes. There were two considerations underlying this design in the original. The first was the crucial issue of financial viability. The second was to give citizens a sense of ownership

of the programmes, signifying that the welfare state is not some sort of munificence extended to them by the political class but something they had contributed to themselves.

- It is difficult to imagine that Kerala will be able to permanently fund its welfare schemes through borrowing. At least, that would only be possible at ever rising interest rates, leading to a higher fiscal burden, if not actually a debt trap. At that stage, the welfare schemes would have to end, or a Herculean effort to raise revenues would have to be initiated.

PART II: ELECTIONEERING

The LDF's perceived advantage was its high powered campaign projecting Pinarayi Vijayan as its brand icon. That advantage got zoomed in against the backdrop of the initial disarray in the UDF over the candidate selection. The UDF led by former Chief Minister Oomen Chandi and the leader of Opposition, Ramesh Chennithala conveniently chose to leave unanswered the question of who would lead the government if it came to power. The UDF relied on road shows by Rahul Gandhi and Priyanka Gandhi for its campaign. As for the BJP, its election rallies were addressed by its top national leaders including Narendra Modi, Amit Shah, Rajnath Singh, Yogi Adityanath which gave a boost to its electoral ambition in the state. However, hard the LDF tried to restrict the electioneering discourse to its development track record and social welfare initiatives such as pensions and distribution of ration kits etc. The sparring between the LDF and the UDF over Chennithala's disclosure of over 4 lakh multiple entries on the electoral rolls across the state further augmented the campaign's decibel levels.

Electoral Issues

Out of a series of electoral issues, Sabarimala tops the list. It was to a large extent championed by the BJP which won the lone Nemom Assembly seat in 2016. Further, the candidature of Metroman E. Sreedharan in Palakkad and the party's top state leaders in constituencies, viz. Nemom, Kazhakootam, Thiruvananthapuram Central, Konni, Thrissur, Manjeshwaram etc. could create an atmosphere and impression that the party is serious in its mission to change the bipolar politics of the state. The LDF on the other hand amplified its hopes for the continuity of the Pinarayi Vijayan dispensation, with poll surveys lending support to its claim that there were no anti-incumbency sentiments among the electorate. The LDF Government's handling of crisis including floods, NIPAH virus outbreaks and the COVID-19 pandemic is used to vindicate that perception. The LDF sort to neutralise its vulnerability *vis-a-vis* the investigations by Central agencies into various scams by projecting them as the BJP-led Central Government efforts to destabilise the left government.

As a routine process a mix of caste and religious interest is present to spice up to electoral scene. The UDF's efforts to capitalise on the resentment among the fishermen over the LDF government's pact with a US based company on deep sea fishing are pegged on the hope of wresting coastal constituencies in the Southern and Central Kerala. Further, the electoral significance of a pastoral letter issued by the Kollam Diocese of Latin Catholic Church flaying the left government for devising policies detrimental to fishermen. The three fronts are kept guessing by caste organisations like NSS, SNDP representing Nair and Ezhava communities respectively. The stand of the NSS against the left government on the Sabarimala issue may turn harmful to the LDF but the SNDP leadership has decided to keep neutrality. However, BDJS headed by the son of SNDP General Secretary is continuing as an ally of the NDA. Further, the election will put to the test the LDF's hope of gaining entry into the Christian belt (Central Kerala) that has traditionally supported the UDF. The inclusion of Jose K. Mani in the LDF has raised the expectations of the Front. The LDF's sweep of Thrissur and the inroads it made in Ernakulum in 2016 showed that the UDF's strongholds in Central Kerala are not invincible. The LDF has also fielded more dissident UDF leaders as independents in UDF stronghold, hoping a repeat of its experiments which succeeded in the earlier polls.

Battle of the Kerala Congress Factions

The 2021 poll also witnessed the direct fight between two factions of the Kerala Congress, one led by Jose K. Mani and the other by

P.J. Joseph. Apart from these two major factions, other small groups led by Anup Jacob, K.B. Ganesh Kumar, Antony Raju, Dr. K.C. Joseph, P.C. Thomas, Scaria Thomas, Kuruvila Mathews, P.C. George and Prakash Kuriakose. For most of them it was a do or die battle. This was the first poll after the death of Kerala Congress stalwarts like K.M. Mani and C.F. Thomas. Another founder of the Kerala Congress Party R. Balakrishna Pillai could not participate in the electioneering due to his critical health condition.

In the poll Jose K. Mani's Kerala Congress(M) and P.J. Joseph's Kerala Congress contested in 12 and 10 seats respectively. The Kerala Congress Party is locking horns in five constituencies, with the Jose-Joseph fight on show in four-constituencies—Changanassery, Kaduthuruthi, Idukki and Thodupuzha. In Piravom, Jose faction takes on KC (Jacob). Though KC(M) has gained an upper hand in Kerala Congress politics by way of a significant position in the LDF, the party leader, Jose, is facing a tough fight in his home turf of Pala. Jose takes on Mani C. Kappen of the Nationalist Congress Kerala (NCK), a new constituent of the UDF. Going by the ground situation, Kappen appeared to have gained an edge in the final stage of campaigning. Realising the trend, the CPM state leadership sent special squads to Pala to ensure that its entire cadre votes are polled on Tuesday. The battle between Jose and Joseph faction is tight in Changanassery, Kaduthuruthi and Idukki as well. Of all the Kerala Congress candidates in the fray, only P.J. Joseph, who is contesting from Thodupuzha, is on a strong footing. While the Jose faction's Sindhumol Jacob is putting up a strong fight against K.C.(Jacob)'s Anoop Jacob in Piravom, Pathanapuram is witnessing a fierce battle between KC(B)'s Ganesh Kumar and Jyothikumar Chamakkala of the Congress. In the UDF bastion of Idukki, Roshy Augustine of KC(M)—representing the constituency since 2001 faces one of the toughest contests of his career after switching to the LDF. Francis George of the UDF is his rival there. The Janadhipathya Kerala Congress, which had contested three seats in the previous assembly elections, was allotted only the Thiruvananthapuram seat this time. Its candidate Antony Raju is facing a tough battle there against UDF's V.S. Sivakumar and BJP's Krishnakumar.

Minority Votes as the Deciding Factor

As per the 2011 Census, 45 per cent of the state's population is minorities—26.6 per cent Muslims and 18.4 per cent Christians. Historically, Christians and Muslims in the state have taken a political view which is against that of the CPM-led fronts over the years. The front comprising CPM and CPI enjoyed minority support in between when Muslim League and strong Kerala Congress factions aligned with them like in the seven-member alliance government led by EMS in 1967 and the Left Front government led by E.K. Nayanar in 1980. On other occasions, Congress had benefited from the support of minorities. It was Congress leader and former Chief Minister K. Karunakaran who first identified the power of a Muslim-Christian alliance that would serve as a fixed deposit for the Congress. The idea led him to constitute the United Democratic Front (UDF) which scored an impressive win in the 1982 assembly polls. The Indian Union Muslim League and Kerala Congress became an integral part of the front since then. By then, the Muslim population in the state had overtaken Christians and Karunakaran foresaw that minorities would form half of Kerala's population in another 50 years. In fact, the identity politics played by Kerala Congress and Muslim League in the early 1980s was so strong that even a section of CPM leaders feared that Left parties would not be able to come back to power if League and Kerala Congress remained as strong allies of Congress.

The alternative document presented by senior CPM leader M.V. Raghavan which was believed to have the blessings of stalwart leaders like E.K. Nayanar argued for cooperating with parties like Muslim League. This eventually led to the ouster of Raghavan from the party in 1985. CPM ideologue and then General Secretary EMS Namboodiripad could very well turn the debate and present the Left Democratic Front as a true secular alternative for UDF, which he alleged was a den of communal forces of all hues. The victory of Left Front in 1987 was the fruit of EMS's 'secular strategy' that indirectly led to the consolidation of Hindu voters behind the CPM-led front. Three decades later, when the same LDF is facing another important electoral battle, one of the key constituents is Kerala Congress (M) led by Jose K. Mani, son of the late K.M. Mani who had founded the

UDF along with K. Karunakaran. Though Muslim League is still in the UDF camp, the Left Front has Indian National League (INL), another Muslim party, as its constituent. INL was formed by former Muslim League national president Ibrahim Sulaiman Sait after the demolition of Babri Masjid. Though the party had collaborated with the LDF since then, the formalisation of their relationship was only done in 2018 when INL was inducted as a constituent of the LDF. The fight by both fronts this year is spiced up with several issues that concern minorities. The target of LDF is to poll at least 40 per cent of Christian and Muslim votes which will ensure a win in several fiercely fought constituencies. The calculation of UDF leadership is that a win is possible only if the front gets at least 65 per cent of minority votes.

Political and Social Re-Alignment in Central Kerala

There has been a political and social realignment of influential forces in areas in Pathanamthitta, Kottayam and parts of Alappuzha, Ernakulam and Idukki districts considered to be a stronghold of the Congress-led United Democratic Front (UDF) in the past few years. The split in the Kerala Congress (Mani) and the subsequent alignment of the official faction led by Jose K. Mani with the Left Democrat Front (LDF), in which CPI(M) is the lead partner, yielded rich dividends for the grouping in Kottayam and Ernakulam districts in the local body polls held in December last year. The KC(M) is the Front's trump card as it seeks to return to power. The CPI(M) went to the extent of annoying its own cadres by allocating the new entrant 13 seats, including some sitting CPI(M) seats where the KC(M) is not numerically strong. When protests erupted in Kuttiady in the north, for instance, Mr. Mani leveraged it to prove his worth as an 'accommodative partner' by returning the seat to the CPI(M). But the partnership came at a cost, though minor, as per the LDF's assessment, as it caused a split in the Nationalist Congress Party (NCP), an ally. The decision to allow the KC(M) to field its candidate from Pala, a seat held by the late K.M. Mani for half-a-century, disenchanted the NCP's Mani C. Kappan, who had created history by wresting the seat from the KC(M) for the Left Front in the by-election held in 2019. In a reversal of roles, Mr. Kappan, now with the UDF, is taking on the Left's Jose K. Mani in Pala. The ongoing strife between the Jacobite and Orthodox factions of the Malankara Syrian Church is also expected to have its echoes in the poll outcome.

Dispute between Jacobites and Orthodox

The Christians form 18.4 per cent of Kerala's population. Jacobites/Orthodox sect is the second largest Christian denomination after Catholics. While Catholics form 61 per cent of the total Christians, Jacobites/Orthodox sect 16 per cent. As per the 2011 Census, total Christian population in the state of Kerala is 61.4 lakh. Of them Catholics are 37.4 lakh followed by 9.8 lakh Jacobite/Orthodox believers. Among them 4,93,858 are Orthodox Syrian Christians and 4,82,762 are Jacobite Syrian Christians. Pathanamthitta, Kozhikode, Ernakulum and Thiruvananthapuram districts have strong presence of Orthodox population. Whereas Ernakulam, Kollam, Pathanamthitta and Kottayam districts have a strong Jacobite presence. Ernakulam accounts for more than 25 per cent of the Jacobite population in the state.

The long standing dispute between Jacobites and Orthodox Church factions was a hot political debate in the strongholds of both factions in the 2021 polls. The issues between these two factions is connected with the ownership of assets spread over 1100 parishes of the Church by two splinter groups was closed by the Supreme Court in 2017, when it ordered to handover all the churches and related assets to the parental factions, i.e. Malankara Syrian Orthodox Church. However, emotional fights by Jacobites in the grassroots for protecting their churches and denial of ritualistic funerals of believers by the other factions had delayed full execution of the Supreme Court order. In 2020, the LDF government brought in an Act to make burial in accordance with religious rituals, the fundamental right of a Christian believer. In this context it has to be added that the origin of the dispute between the Jacobites and the Orthodox can be traced back from a case filed in a court in Kottayam in the year 1974 regarding the ownership of church property. A special court was formed in Ernakulam to deal with this case, popularly known as Malankara Case. Though the court, had ruled in favour of the Jacobite Church, appeals were sent to higher courts and finally in 1995, the Suprreme Court passed a judgment of the Orthodox Church. The next round of legal battle concluded with the ruling of the Supreme Court in favour of Orthodox Church in 2017. As the state government did not initiate takeover of Jacobite faction's churches, the Supreme Court threatened Contempt of Court Actions and imprisonment of Chief Secretary in 2019 forcing the State Government to start acting finally.

Splits and reunions between Orthodox and Jacobite factions had been a regular feature ever since the establishment of the Catholic Malankara Orthodox Church in 1912. Jacobite Syrian Christian Church consists of believers who consider patriarch of Antioch (Head of Syrian Orthodox Church of the entire East) as the Supreme Head of the Church while Malankara Orthodox Syrian Church consists of believers who consider the Catholics of the East residing in Kottayam who is also the Metropolitan of the Malankara Orthodox Church as the Head. In the 2021 Assembly Polls, this Church dispute came as an active issue debated in the strongholds of both factions. UDF's chief ministerial candidate Oommen Chandy is a member of Orthodox Faction. With the Jacobite/Orthodox sect forming the second largest Christian denomination, it is only natural that major political parties including the Left seek their support and patronage.

SDPI and Welfare Party of India (WPI)—Spoiling the Prospects of Major Fronts

The Socialist Democratic Party of India (SDPI) and Welfare Party of India (WPI) fielded 41 and 19 candidates respectively in the 2021 polls. Though both the parties are not major political players or forces in the state politics but they can definitely spoil the electoral prospects of both the LDF and UDF in a number of constituencies where both have strong mass base. The SDPI had contested in 89 Assembly seats in the 2016 elections. In 2021, it has fielded 41 candidates to focus on those seats where it can show its strength to both UDF and LDF. In the 2016 elections, SDPI secured over 1.2 lakh votes from 89 seats which was 0.61 per cent of the total votes polled. Similarly, the Welfare Party of India which contested in 41 assembly segments garnered over 60,000 votes in 2016. Both UDF and LDF had the taste of the damage inflected by SDPI and WPI when there candidates lost by a thin margin in a few seats. In Koduvally where WPI and SDPI secured 1566 and 1466 votes respectively in 2016. M.A. Razak of the IUML lost to the LDF candidate Karatt Razak by 573 votes. In Perunthalmanna where SDPI and WPI secured 698 and 1757 votes respectively, LDF's V. Sasikumar lost to IUML's Manjalamkuzhi Ali by 579 votes. Kannur is a classical example of how SDPI and WPI can through a spanner in the works of a main political front. UDF's Sadeesan Pacheni lost to Ramachandran Kadannappally by 1196 votes after SDPI and WPI together managed to secure 3685 votes. These parties know there actual votes strength in each pocket and such votes can prove crucial in the electoral battle.

Massive Shifting of Nair and Ezhava Votes to BJP

The poll analysis done by Centre for the Study of Developing Societies (CSDS) and the Centre for Public Policy Research (CPPR) reveals that there is a massive increase in the vote share of the BJP in state of Kerala. It is ranged from 6 per cent in 2011 to 15 per cent in 2015. It was largely due to the massive shifting of two major communities in the state of Kerala—Nairs and Ezhavas. The survey categorically shows that from the year 2006 to 2019, a significant number of voters from both the communities shifted their political interest from their earlier faiths. The study reveals that there was a sudden surge in the Ezhava vote base of the BJP in 2016 which can be partly attributed to the work of its ally Bharath Dharma Jana Sena (BDJS) which was formed in the year 2015. Further 11 per cent of Nair community members voted for BJP in 2006 and 2011. The study further shows a three-fold increase in 2016 when BJP polled 33 per cent of the Nair votes. The gain of BJP was the loss of the UDF whose Nair vote share decreased from 43 per cent in 2011 to 20 per cent in 2016. UDF had polled 38 per cent Nair votes in 2006. Interestingly, LDF gained marginally among Nair voters in 2016 as its vote share was 45 per cent in 2016 against 44 per cent in 2011.

The shift of Nair votes was more visible in the 2019 Lok Sabha Election when the Sabarimala issue was in its peak. BJP polled 43 per cent of Nair votes in the elections. The UDF's share was 35 per cent slightly higher than 34 per cent, it polled in the 2014 Lok Sabha elections. The real loss was that of LDF's as it could poll only 22 per cent of the Nair votes against 30 per cent in 2014. Almost similar is the case of Ezhava votes. BJP's vote share among the Ezhava community was only 6 per cent in 2006 and 7 per cent in 2011. However, it touched 17 per cent in 2016. The loss here was that of LDF. Ezhava community member have been a traditional vote bank of the Left which got 64 per cent and 65 per cent of votes of the community in 2006 and 2011 prospectively.

Crusade of the Leader of Oppostion Against Bogus Voters (Operation Twins)

In an appreciable initiative, the leader of opposition Ramesh Chennithala approached the High Court of Kerala seeking a directive the Election Commission and the CEO to take urgent steps either to delete or freeze the fake and multiple entries of names on the final electoral roll. The KPCC just after the Lok Sabha polls of 2019 constituted and expert team following large scale complaints of bogus voters. The study found that the final electoral roll published contained duplication of names, fake entries and enrolment of a single voter in many booths either in one Assembly segment or other segments. In his petition he pinpointed 3,24,441 cases of duplication and 1,09,601 cases of bogus votes spread across 131 Assembly constituencies. In a state like Kerala where the change of a government usually take place in a negligible votes, therefore, the manipulation of 4,34,042 votes will have significant consequences in the electoral front. In fact he had given a complaint regarding the gross irregularities on the electoral rolls to the CEO in this regard. But he had not taken any action on it. In the landmark judgment, the High Court of Kerala observed that free and fair elections are part and parcel of the democratic rights of the citizens. The Court made clear it that all the safeguards provided in the Representation of People's Act (RPA) be scrupulously followed to avoid multiple and bogus voting. Later Chennithala released the entire list on the website www.operationtwins.com.

PART III: POLLING

The state went to the poll on 6th April, 2021 in a single face to elect its 15th Legislative Assembly. As per the data provided by the Election Commission of India, the overall turnout figure for the state was 74.06 per cent. The highest polling was recorded in Kunamangalam constituency (81.52%) in Kozhikode district and the least was in Thiruvananthapuram constituency (61.85%). Out of the 2,74,46,039 eligible voters in the state 2,03,27,893 exercised their franchise. The district-wise polling percentages are: Thiruvananthapuram (70.04%), Kollam (73.11%), Pathanamthitta (67.22%), Alappuzha (74.71%), Kottayam (72.21%), Idukki (70.41%), Ernakulam (74.13%), Thrissur (73.77%), Palakkad (76.25%), Malapurram (74.31%), Kozhikode (78.34%), Wayanad (74.98%), Kannur (77.70%), Kasargod (74.92%).

As cited earlier, the average voter turnout stood at a creditable 74.06 per cent, though it was lower than the 2016 turnout of 77.35. The ruling Left Front expressed confidence of retaining power with a comfortable majority. The UDF camp also expressed satisfaction over the voter turnout. According to the leader of the opposition, the people of Kerala expected a change and stated that the LDF government destroyed the state during the five year rule. The Left leaders and top officials are immersed in corruption. UDF wave is visible. The UDF should win anywhere between 75-85 seats. The BJP-led NDA hopes to make its presence felt with authoritative victories in 5-7 seats in addition to finishing second in about 10 seats. Significantly, the Sabarimala issue dominated the political discourse on the polling day. Chief Minister Pinarayi Vijayan claimed Lord Ayyappa and all other gods would stand with the Left for being there for the people to which Congress leader A.K. Antony retorted the CM should first apologize to the Lord for the Sabarimala issue.

The state also witnessed isolated incidents of violence in some districts like Thiruvananthapuram where CPI(M) and BJP workers clashed with each other. Violence was also reported in Haripad where CPI(M) and Congress workers fought each other. In Kannur, an IUML worker was hacked. In many closely fought constituencies, the voting percentage remained relatively low with BJP's lone sitting seat Nemom recording 69.80 per cent compared to 74.11 per cent in 2016.

Table 23.1: Polling Percentage in Kerala from 2011 to 2021

Assembly Constituency	**Legislative Assembly 2011**	**Lok Sabha 2014**	**Legislative Assembly 2016**	**Lok Sabha 2019**	**Legislative Assembly 2021**
Manjeswaram	75.21	71.70	76.33	75.88	76.81
Kasargod	73.50	73.04	76.62	76.32	70.87
Uduma	74.17	77.30	80.45	79.33	75.56
Kanhangadu	78.54	79.82	78.66	81.25	74.35
Thrikkaripure	80.81	82.11	81.88	83.46	76.77
Payyanur	82.42	84.67	81.76	85.86	78.95

(Contd.)

Assembly Constituency	Legislative Assembly 2011	Lok Sabha 2014	Legislative Assembly 2016	Lok Sabha 2019	Legislative Assembly 2021
Kalliyaseri	79.36	81.67	78.33	82.93	76.41
Thaliparamba	82.63	85.03	80.97	86.18	80.94
Irikkure	77.26	78.97	78.59	80.99	75.63
Azhikkodu	82.45	80.10	81.91	81.04	77.89
Kannur	78.82	77.44	77.34	79.21	74.94
Dharmadam	83.31	83.90	83.30	85.21	80.22
Thalassery	78.68	78.72	79.43	80.33	73.93
Koothuparambu	79.80	79.61	81.03	81.44	78.14
Mattanoor	82.73	84.47	83.57	86.26	79.54
Peravoor	80.03	78.40	81.03	81.46	78.07
Mananthavadi	74.25	72.13	77.54	81.55	76.44
Betheri	73.27	71.32	78.81	81.93	74.29
Kalppatta	74.36	72.53	79.03	80.94	74.31
Vadakkara	80.76	81.56	81.54	83.03	79.33
Kuttiyadi	87.73	84.15	85.48	83.13	81.27
Nathapuram	82.28	80.04	80.77	82.59	78.80
Koilandy	81.87	79.84	81.53	81.05	77.50
Perambra	84.76	84.83	85.45	84.61	79.74
Baluserry	81.59	82.41	83.26	82.50	78.18
Elathur	82.27	83.44	83.28	83.31	78.07
Kozhikode North	77.32	76.60	78.12	78.25	73.85
Kozhikode South	78.08	75.93	77.57	78.54	74.24

(*Contd.*)

Assembly Constituency	Legislative Assembly 2011	Lok Sabha 2014	Legislative Assembly 2016	Lok Sabha 2019	Legislative Assembly 2021
Bepur	78.88	77.39	81.46	80.34	77.97
Kunnama-ngalam	84.35	83.06	85.85	84.40	81.55
Koduvalli	79.96	77.83	81.88	81.39	80.03
Thiruvambadi	79.42	75.33	80.57	81.26	77.09
Kondotti	75.76	74.37	79.40	78.11	78.21
Eranadu	80.69	78.08	81.82	81.35	77.68
Nilamboor	77.96	72.83	78.83	77.55	75.23
Vandoor	73.40	72.30	74.16	77.89	73.65
Manjerri	70.01	73.13	73.02	76.50	74.30
Perunthal-manna	71.58	71.99	77.66	73.56	74.66
Mangada	73.91	69.30	77.17	73.55	75.17
Malappuram	72.91	73.35	73.20	76.87	74.78
Vengara	68.97	95.26	70.90	71.88	69.87
Vallikunnu	72.49	70.35	74.86	77.16	74.46
Thirurangadi	65.62	70.81	73.97	74.89	74.03
Thanoor	78.12	75.00	79.99	77.00	76.59
Thiroor	75.98	75.56	76.36	74.93	73.23
Kottakkal	70.65	73.95	74.66	75.74	72.38
Thavanoor	78.15	74.51	76.88	74.54	74.38
Ponnani	76.36	71.16	74.31	71.85	69.58
Thrithala	78.46	75.84	78.8	5.64	77.30
Pattambi	76.66	77.20	77.90	77.09	76.50

(*Contd.*)

Assembly Constituency	Legislative Assembly 2011	Lok Sabha 2014	Legislative Assembly 2016	Lok Sabha 2019	Legislative Assembly 2021
Shornur	73.39	76.04	76.33	78.22	76.64
Ottappalam	75.09	76.41	76.00	77.23	75.76
Kongadu	72.85	75.82	77.14	78.80	75.15
Mannarkadu	72.90	73.95	78.38	78.22	75.46
Malampuzha	75.47	75.95	78.74	78.71	75.04
Palakkad	72.80	72.39	77.25	75.42	73.71
Thiroor	75.17	76.43	78.13	80.18	75.90
Chittur	81.18	79.13	82.95	82.37	79.03
Nenmara	77.94	76.39	81.03	81.45	76.78
Aalathoor	75.95	77.20	79.21	81.12	77.54
Chelakkara	76.52	77.34	79.21	79.12	75.75
Kunamkulam	75.42	74.33	78.91	78.94	76.37
Guruvayur	72.01	68.35	73.17	74.34	68.40
Manalur	73.44	72.44	76.73	77.98	73.14
Vadakkanjerry	79.08	77.23	80.91	79.37	76.07
Ollur	74.47	74.19	77.93	79.76	73.84
Thrissur	69.70	68.79	73.79	74.43	68.90
Nattika	71.62	72.81	76.49	77.46	71.30
Kayppaman-galam	77.39	74.53	79.29	80.21	76.62
Irrinjalakkuda	75.99	72.97	77.80	78.86	74.73
Puthukkadu	78.53	75.42	81.28	81.78	75.55
Challakkudi	76.48	73.76	78.87	77.70	72.62

(*Contd.*)

Assembly Constituency	Legislative Assembly 2011	Lok Sabha 2014	Legislative Assembly 2016	Lok Sabha 2019	Legislative Assembly 2021
Kodungalur	76.15	73.88	79.52	78.78	74.94
Perumpavur	81.42	78.04	84.25	81.71	76.32
Angamaly	81.44	78.65	83.18	79.93	76.08
Aluva	80.52	78.58	83.17	80.44	75.39
Kalamassery	79.77	76.05	81.29	80.14	75.83
Paravoor	84.20	79.14	83.94	81.70	77.15
Vyppin	79.41	74.94	79.87	78.37	74.72
Kochi	66.61	68.60	72.33	75.21	69.81
Thrippunithura	76.35	73.91	78.03	77.14	73.11
Ernakulam	71.16	68.86	71.72	73.29	65.91
Thirkkakara	73.66	72.31	74.46	76.06	69.27
Kunnathunadu	83.63	81.67	85.93	84.40	80.99
Piravam	79.37	73.03	80.58	75.13	72.46
Muvattupuzha	75.29	72.81	80.15	77.87	73.53
Kothaman-galam	74.48	74.01	80.50	79.84	76.77
Devikulam	72.42	70.55	71.23	70.88	67.32
Udambanchola	72.00	71.77	75.56	79.24	73.33
Thodupuzha	71.97	68.83	72.24	75.63	70.16
Idukki	70.50	70.16	76.69	74.09	68.94
Perumedu	69.67	67.94	73.36	76.67	72.27
Pala	73.66	68.71	77.61	72.68	72.54
Kaduthuruthi	77.17	67.01	69.59	71.11	68.02
Vayikkam	79.15	77.35	81.19	79.85	75.51

(Contd.)

Assembly Constituency	Legislative Assembly 2011	Lok Sabha 2014	Legislative Assembly 2016	Lok Sabha 2019	Legislative Assembly 2021
Ettumanur	78.51	73.59	79.96	77.25	72.88
Kottayam	77.54	72.84	78.37	76.54	72.57
Puthuppally	76.44	70.13	77.36	75.45	73.22
Changanassery	72.56	69.55	75.24	72.62	70.29
Kanjirappally	70.01	68.52	76.39	77.96	72.12
Punjar	70.16	65.23	79.39	77.27	72.47
Aroor	84.23	81.86	85.82	83.67	80.02
Cherthala	75.08	84.22	86.73	84.98	80.52
Alappuzha	81.20	79.40	80.68	80.44	76.16
Ambalappuzha	79.68	77.04	78.90	78.43	74.60
Kuttannad	78.64	74.34	78.76	76.28	72.21
Harippadu	78.42	77.04	78.89	78.16	74.06
Kayamkulam	76.73	76.01	73.13	76.55	73.02
Mavelikkara	75.21	73.58	75.45	74.53	71.09
Chenganoor	70.88	67.73	73.73	70.19	68.98
Thiruvalla	65.33	63.38	69.23	71.43	63.34
Ranni	68.54	64.12	70.42	70.65	63.82
Arannmula	65.63	64.91	70.82	72.00	65.45
Konni	71.86	68.12	72.9	74.24	71.42
Adoor	69.61	68.14	74.37	76.64	72.04
Karunagappally	75.51	75.95	79.37	78.23	78.51
Chavara	79.59	76.47	78.55	77.21	76.09
Kunnathur	74.09	74.49	76.63	77.78	75.22

(*Contd.*)

Assembly Constituency	Legislative Assembly 2011	Lok Sabha 2014	Legislative Assembly 2016	Lok Sabha 2019	Legislative Assembly 2021
Kottarakkara	74.34	71.78	75.04	73.81	72.23
Pathanapuram	74.23	68.96	74.83	73.69	72.05
Punalur	70.14	70.38	70.60	72.43	69.28
Chadayaman-galam	71.78	70.91	73.78	73.81	70.72
Kundara	71.48	73.70	76.22	75.79	73.92
Kollam	71.06	72.86	74.92	75.05	72.12
Eravipuram	68.16	70.11	73.40	73.52	70.57
Chathnoor	73.13	70.44	74.03	72.98	72.24
Varkkala	72.55	67.83	71.54	70.30	70.23
Attingal	66.78	69.82	69.53	74.59	70.61
Chirayinkeezhu	66.25	68.62	70.22	73.86	70.79
Nedumgadu	71.07	68.51	74.11	75.38	71.54
Vamanapuram	70.75	69.06	71.70	73.59	70.90
Kazhakkuttam	67.11	67.58	73.70	73.19	69.63
Vattiyurkkavu	64.24	65.06	70.23	69.34	64.16
Thiruvanantha-puram	60.39	63.04	65.36	67.41	61.92
Nemam	67.60	68.17	74.24	73.31	69.80
Aruvikkara	70.29	69.25	75.86	75.97	73.27
Parasala	71.80	73.12	75.17	76.91	72.41
Kattakkada	70.57	67.75	76.65	75.58	72.21
Kovalam	68.09	71.07	74.23	76.00	70.76
Neyyattinkara	70.77	72.40	75.25	77.27	72.23

Source: The Malayala Manorama Daily, Kollam, 7th April, 2021.

Table 23.2: Legislative Assembly Polling Percentage in Kerala—1957-2016

Year of Poll	Polling Percentage
1957	65.49
1960	85.72
1965	75.12
1967	75.67
1970	75.29
1977	79.19
1980	72.23
1982	73.51
1987	80.54
1991	73.42
1996	71.16
2001	72.47
2006	72.38
2011	74.92
2016	77.10
2021	74.06

Source: The Malayala Manorama Daily, Kollam, 7th April, 2021.

PART IV: PEOPLE'S VERDICT 2021

The Left Democratic Front (LDF) won the assembly election with an impressive tally of 99 out of 140 seats, which matches the victory of A.K. Antony-led UDF in 2001 and V.S. Achuthanandan-led LDF in 2006. In 2001, A.K. Antony emerged winner by bagging 99 seats and in 2006 V.S. Achuthanandan won by bagging 98 seats. Yet another example too can be traced back from the political history of Kerala. In 1977, the United Front-led by the Congress, CPI and the Muslim League returned to power by capturing 111 seats out of 146. Further, the state of Kerala has a unique political record of alternating between the two Fronts in every five years. This record of four decades has been broken now and the LDF government has been voted to power with a two-third majority. It becomes a landmark as it is rare for an incumbent government to retain power by capturing more seats than the previous time. A mix of policies in which development and welfare measures were added in the right proportion and executed over the last 60 months paved the way for the spectacular victory of the LDF. It is a new experience in the state politics after 1977. In other words, the present victory of the LDF can be described as a well thought out political strategy coupled with political pragmatism and social engineering which helped the LDF to capture power. Certainly, the entry of Loktantrik Janata Dal (LJD) and Kerala Congress (Mani), the formal induction of Indian National League (INL), the popularity of Pinarayi Vijayan in handling the governance in times of crisis and calamities and the goodwill generated through social security measures especially welfare pension scheme, distribution of food kits through ration shops have helped the Left in an enormous way. Further right from the implementation of Nava Kerala Mission projects to bring remarkable changes in the education and health sectors and to provide housing for the poor under Life Mission Project which also paid rich dividends for the Left over and above Pinarayi also made some daring moves in social engineering.

Yet another reason for the spectacular return of the LDF was that after the humiliating defeat in the Lok Sabha Polls of 2019, the LDF took a strategic retreat by the front in the Sabarimala Women's Entry issue. The civic polls held in November 2020 was the testing ground for this strategy and the Left made huge gains out of it. The more accommodative stand cured the hurt feeling of majority communities and the reading of the Assembly Poll Results makes it clear that the LDF could win the sizeable number of Hindu votes along with minority votes that had mobilized through strong stands taken during issues such as beef ban and Citizen's Amendment Act etc. On the other hand, the strategy of UDF was to put up strong fight with young, new faces did not fetch the desired results as voters seemed to have made their choices based on policies.

Further, the voting pattern in the poll showed that the party-wise vote share of the CPI(M) stood at 25.38 per cent, the Congress 25.12 per cent and the BJP-led NDA 12.47 per cent. Incidentally, the vote share of the CPI(M) was 26.70 per cent, Congress 23.80 per cent, and the BJP-led NDA 10.60 per cent in the 2016 Assembly polls. Moreover, the voting pattern of the LDF further reveals that party heavy weights though secured huge margins, many sitting legislators and fresh faces failed to either maintain the lead in the previous polls or managed to scrape through. The overall poll strategies further reveals that both the LDF and UDF secured more votes in 2021 polls compared to the earlier assembly elections of 2016 and Lok Sabha Elections of 2019. The LDF scored 2.67 per cent more votes this time than the earlier assembly polls and 10.73 per cent more votes compared with the Lok Sabha Polls of 2019. For the UDF, it was a marginal increase of 0.78 per cent in 2021 with the earlier assembly polls 2016. But in the 2019 Lok Sabha Polls, UDF won 19 out of 20 seats. Compared to Lok Sabha Polls its vote share went down to 7.87 per cent this time. In contrast to it, the NDA recorded a less vote share (minus 4,29,834 votes) this time compared to 2016 assembly polls.

Regarding the total votes secured by various fronts are concerned, the LDF secured a total number of 87,28,934 votes (43.10%) in 2016 assembly polls. In 2019, it came down to 71,40,120 (35.08%) and in 2021 it went up to 94,36,990 (45.33%), an increase of 7,08,056 compared to 2016 assembly polls. The UDF on the other hand got 78,08,743 (38.63%) votes in 2016. It gone to 96,16,265 (47.24%) in 2019. But it came down to 81,94,991 (39.37%) in 2021. Though the vote share of the UDF came down from 96,16,265 in Lok Sabha polls 2019 to 81,94,991 in 2021, but compared to the 2016 assembly polls it depicted an increase of 3,86,248 votes. In contrast to the performance of both LDF and UDF, the BJP-led NDA presented a downward picture in 2021. In 2016, the NDA secured a total number of 30,20,830 votes and in 2019 it increased its tally slightly by securing 31,61,922. But in 2021 it came down to 25,90,966, a steady decline of 5,70,956 votes in 2021. In short, the vote variation of the LDF and UDF in 2016 was 4.55 per cent. In 2019, the difference between both the fronts was 12.16 per cent and in 2021 it came down to 6.14 per cent.

The following tables further illustrate the details of poll outcome, both party-wise and region-wise in a detailed manner.

Table 23.3: Election Results 2021 in Nutshell

LDF	
CPI(M)	68
CPI	17
KCM	5
JD(S)	2
NCP	2
LJD	1
INL	1
CONGRESS(S)	1
RSP(L)	1
KC(B)	1
UDF	
INC	22
IUML	14
KC	2
NCK	1
KC(J)	1
RMP	1

Table 23.4: Women Representation in Kerala Legislature—2006-2021

Year	**Seats contested and won**			**Percentage**
	LDF	**UDF**	**NDA**	
2006	11/7	7/0	11/0	5
2011	13/7	8/1	14/0	5.7
2016	17/7	9/0	12/0	5
2021	15/10	12/1	18/0	7.8

Table 23.5: Assembly Segments won/lead*

		Assembly segments won/lead*			**Strike Rate %^**		
	Party	**2021**	**2016 (c)**	**2019 (c)**	**2021**	**2016 (c)**	**2019 (c)**
LDF	CPI(M)	62	4	46	81	11	68
	CPI	17	-2	17	74	-2	74
	KEC(M)	5	-1	-1	42	2	-44
	JD(S)	2	-1	2	50	-25	50
UDF	INC	21	-1	-75	23	-3	-63
	IUML	17	-1	3	68	-10	-32
	Kerala Congress	2	2	2	20	20	20
	RSP	0	0	-7	0	0	-100
	AIADMK	0	0	0	0	0	0
	BDJS	0	0	0	0	0	0

^ (wins/contested seats) *leads in 2019 c* Change (increase or decrease).

Source: The Hindu, 3rd May, 2021, Thiruvananthapuram.

Table 23.6: Vote share in Percentage—2016-2021

		Vote share %			**Contested vote (%, points)**		
	Party	**2021**	**2016 (c)**	**2019 (c)**	**2021**	**2016(c)**	**2019 (c)**
LDF	CPI(M)	24.9	-1.9	-1.0	46.9	2.7	18.5
	CPI	7.2	-1.1	1.1	46.1	1.3	16.1
	KEC(M)	3.8	-0.3	1.7	41.3	2.6	-5.0
	JD(S)	1.5	0.3	1.5	45.2	3.4	45.2
UDF	INC	23.9	0.5	-13.6	37.5	-0.4	-8.7
	IUML	8.6	1.0	3.1	45.0	-0.4	-9.1
	Kerala Congress	2.8	2.6	2.0	40.5	31.4	23.5
	RSP	1.3	0.3	-1.1	33.9	2.9	-17.8
	BJP	11.6	1.4	-1.4	13.8	-1.1	-3.2
NDA	AIADMK	0.1	-0.1	0.1	6.8	3.4	6.8
	BDJS	1.0	-2.8	-0.8	7.8	-7.3	-1.7

Source: The Hindu, 3rd May, 2021, Thiruvananthapuram.

Table 23.7: Vote Percentage of LDF, UDF and NDA—2016-2021

	LDF			UDF			NDA		
Year	**2016**	**2019**	**2021**	**2016**	**2019**	**2021**	**2016**	**2019**	**2021**
% of votes	43.10	35.08	45.33	38.63	47.24	39.37	14.93	15.53	12.47
Total No. of votes secured	87,28,934	71,40,120	94,36,990	78,08,743	96,16,265	81,94,991	30,20,830	31,61,922	25,90,966

Note: (a) In 2021, the LDF secured 7,08,056 more votes compared to 2016 assembly polls. (b) The UDF on the other hand scored less than 3,86,248 votes compared to 2016 assembly polls. (c) Compared to 2016 assembly polls the NDA got 4,29,834 votes less than 2016 assembly polls.

Source: The Malayala Manorama, 4th May, 2021, Kollam.

Table 23.8: Difference of Votes in Percentage—Front-wise 1982-2021

Elections	UDF		LDF		BJP		Difference of votes
	Seats won	%	Seats won	%	Seats won	%	
1982 Assembly	77	42.28	63	47.24	0	2.75	1.04
1984 Lok Sabha	17	50.38	3	41.86	0	4.83	8.52
1987 Assembly	78	44.40	61	45.07	0	6.48	0.67
1989 Lok Sabha	17	48.99	3	44.14	0	4.82	4.85
1991 Lok Sabha	16	48.59	4	44.28	0	3.85	4.31
1991 Assembly	92	48.18	48	45.97	0	4.76	2.21
1996 Lok Sabha	10	44.75	10	44.00	0	6.09	0.75
1996 Assembly	59	44.84	80	46.03	0	4.76	1.19
1998 Lok Sabha	11	46.08	9	44.06	0	8.02	2.02
1999 Lok Sabha	11	46.63	9	43.36	0	8.05	3.27
2001 Assembly	99	48.90	40	43.70	0	5.02	5.20
2004 Lok Sabha	1	38.38	18	46.15	0	12.08	7.77
2006 Assembly	42	42.99	98	48.58	0	4.84	5.59
2009 Lok Sabha	16	47.83	4	41.98	0	6.45	5.85
2011 Assembly	72	46.03	68	45.13	0	6.04	0.90

(Contd.)

Elections	UDF		LDF		BJP		Difference of votes
	Seats won	**%**	**Seats won**	**%**	**Seats won**	**%**	
2014 Lok Sabha	12	41.96	8	40.09	0	10.81	1.87
2016 Assembly	47	38.59	91	43.14	1	14.93	4.55
2019 Lok Sabha	12	47.24	8	35.08	0	15.53	12.16
2021 Assembly	41	32.23	99	38.37	0	12.4	6.14

Note: Table has been compiled by the authors based on the data provided by the Election Commission of India. Here the details of National and State Level Parties alone are taken into account.

Table 23.9: Region-wise Vote Percentage—2016 & 2021

	LDF		NDA		UDF	
Region	**2021**	**2016 (c)**	**2021**	**2016 (c)**	**2021**	**2016 (c)**
Cochin	45.8	3.5	13.7	-1.8	35.8	-2.0
Malabar	37.7	0.3	10.3	-0.8	39.4	-0.6
Travancore	41.5	1.5	14.7	-2.4	36.3	0.2

Source: The Hindu, 3rd May, 2021, Thiruvananthapuram.

Region-wise Poll Analysis—2021

(a) *Southern Kerala*

Systematic campaigning, government's pro-welfare measures, electorates' hesitation to change guard mid-pandemic, motivated voting and an optimistic election manifesto had aided the LDF in South Kerala. The BJP had emerged as a decisive third force during the early phase of the Election Campaign. However, the last minute consolidation minority votes favouring the ruling front had blended the party's edge hustings. So had intra party feuding between the leaders. The BJP did not lack campaign funds, crowd pullers, the National Leaders and party workers. However, it failed to make an impact in the southern region of the state despite being resource rich. Emotional issues like Sabarimala had a low impact on voters. South Kerala was also swept up in the pro-LDF wave that swamped the state. Most ruling front legislators retained their seats. LDF dominated Thiruvananthapuram bagging 13 out of 14 seats. In Kollam, the LDF retained 9 out of 11 seats.

(b) *Central Kerala*

In spite of the impressive victory of the LDF, Jose K. Mani's unexpected setback in Pala to UDF candidate Mani C. Kappen by a margin of 15,378 votes was a shocking one not only for Central Kerala but for the entire state. A shift in about 10,000 votes from the BJP's kitty from 2016 was sighted by Jose K. Mani as the key reason for his defeat. Jose's loss has also created a confusion within his party whether the victory of LDF has to be celebrated or to mourn the defeat of the party chief. The party boss will have to lead Kerala Congress(M) without any parliamentary position at a time when the Political front of his party going to be part of the New Government. Certainly it will be a testing time or Jose's capability to control his own senior colleagues with more experience and political wisdom than him. But, it is a fact that the victory of Kerala Congress(M) in 5 seats out of 12 contested, it has opened a lot of opportunities for Jose in the LDF. Like the previous local body elections, LDF's association with the KC(M) helped it make inroads into the Christian vote banks in Central Travancore. Taking advantage of the situation, he can act as a link between LDF and the Church. Similar to the position of Jose K. Mani, the other faction of the Kerala Congress led by P.J. Joseph and P.C. Thomas too was not comfortable, in the electoral battle. The party contested in 10 seats and won in two constituencies—Thodupuzha and Kaduthuruthy.

(c) *Northern Kerala*

In Northern Kerala this time incumbency wave seems to have helped the LDF to win almost the same number of seats it bagged in 2016 polls. By sweeping the election, the LDF gained from the positive attitude of voters towards the Chief Minister. Out of the 60 seats in Kasargod, Kannur, Wayanad, Kozhikode, Malappuram and Palakkad districts, the LDF emerged victorious in 36 seats. The Front has lost a few seats but it also captured others. The LDF not only retained the 3 seats in Kasargode but gained an additional seat of Azhikode in Kannur district. Palakkad which saw some exciting photo finish moments in some constituencies and also gave upper hand to the LDF. The BJP saw its major defeats in Manjeswaram and Palakkad. In Wayanad, the LDF lost its sitting Kalpetta seat. Similarly in Kozhikode, the front lost Vadakara seat to RMP nominee K.K. Rema who was backed by the UDF.

Exit Poll Surveys

A detailed analysis of the exit poll survey and its results showed that absence of anti-incumbency was the major reason behind their prediction of LDF's big victory. Exit Poll by Chanakya found that 63 per cent of voters were satisfied and did not want a change in government against 28 per cent who preferred a change. The poll also noted that all major communities favoured LDF in the poll.

LDF has support of 43 per cent of Nairs and 57 per cent of Ezhavas. Among Christians 44 per cent supported LDF against 45 per cent who supported UDF which also won support of 53 per cent Muslims. LDF would fetch 36 per cent of Mulsim votes and 68 per cent of SC/ST votes predicted the survey. The agency predicted a sweep winning from 93 to 111 seats. The survey conducted by VMR for Manorama News preferred LDF and respondents from all age groups except above 65 years preferred LDF. The exit poll conducted by C Voter found that vote share of BJP would reduce by 1.2 per cent and also hinted that BJP's loss would be gain for the UDF. In reality, the vote share of BJP dipped by over 2.5 per cent.

Erosion in NDA and Sharp Decline in Ezhava Votes

The vote share of the BJP and its allies, which was 6.03 per cent in 2011 Assembly Election, jumped to 10.81 per cent in 2014 Lok Sabha polls. It then saw a considerable rise to 14.96 per cent in 2016 Assembly polls and then to 15.54 per cent in the 2019 Lok Sabha polls. In the local body polls of 2020, the figure dipped slightly to 15.02 per cent. In the present Assembly polls BJP alone had recorded a voted share of 11.33 per cent. If the votes of BJP's allies are also taken into consideration, the NDA has provisional vote share of 12.4 per cent denoting a decline of over 2.5 per cent compared to the 2016 Assembly Election. What worried the BJP more was the 12 per cent erosion of votes in its stronghold Nemom constituency which the Saffron Party proudly calls it as Gujarat in Kerala. The Congress national leadership deployed its senior leader and parliament member K. Muraleedharan to the battlefield to close the loan account in the state. Muraleedharan's mission was successful in ensuring the defeat of BJP but it indirectly helped LDF candidate V. Sivankutty. In fact Muraleedharan turned out to the biggest spoiler for the BJP. The erosion of BJP votes in Nemom was unbelievable. While BJP's O. Rajagopal polled 47.46 per cent votes in 2016 in 2021 Kummanam could garner only 35.56 per cent of votes. It is clear that a major share of Hindu votes came for the rescue of Muraleedharan son of Late K. Karunakaran. Moreover, NSS too extened its support to him. Muraleedharan polled nearly 23,000 more votes than the UDF candidate who contested in 2016.

UDF's vote share which was below 10 per cent in 2016 increased to 25 per cent this time.

The state-wide performance of BJP further shows that the party managed to emerge as runner-up in nine constituencies this time. Interestingly, the party had emerged as runner-up in seven seats in the 2016 Assembly Election. Among the seats where the BJP emerged runner-up in 2021, the party was able to increase its vote share only in Palakkad (6.26%), Attingal (5.94%), Chathannur (5.69%) and Malambuzha (1.78%), when compared to the 2016 Assembly Election. However, it has also to be noted that the Saffron Party suffered vote erosion in Kasargod (-3.89%), Vattiyoorkkavu (-3.1%), Kazhakkuttom (-2.84%), Manjeswaram (-1.96%) compared to 2016 Assembly Election. Moreover with regard to the Ezhava votes are concerned, it depicted a graph of decline. Certainly, it is highly damaging to the NDA in general and BJP in particular. The NDA's vote share in the state had climbed from 6.6 per cent in 2011 Assembly polls to 14.96 per cent in 2016 after BDJS joined its fold. However, its vote share declined to 12.04 per cent in 2021. The vote share of BDJS declined from 3.93 per cent in 2016 to 1 per cent in 2021. It seems that a sizeable section of Ezhava voters who were with the Left parties before the formation of BDJS have now returned to their mother fold.

Concluding Observations

1. The overall poll analysis undoubtedly shows that a mix of policies in which development and welfare measures were added in the right proportion and executed over the last 60 months paved the way for the spectacular victory of the LDF. It is a new experience in the state politics after 1977. In other words the present victory of the LDF can be described as a well thought out political strategy coupled with political pragmatism and social engineering which helped the LDF to capture power. Certainly the entry of Loktantrik Janata Dal (LJD) and Kerala Congress (Mani), the formal induction of Indian National League (INL), the popularity of Pinarayi Vijayan in handling the governance in times of crisis and calamities and the goodwill generated through social security measures especially welfare pension scheme, distribution of food kits through ration shops

have helped the Left in an enormous way. Further right from the implementation of Nava Kerala Mission projects to bring remarkable changes in the education and health sectors and to provide housing for the poor under Life Mission Project which also paid rich dividends for the Left. Over and above Pinarayi also made some daring moves in social engineering.

2. Yet another reason for the spectacular return of the LDF was that, after the humiliating defeat in the Lok Sabha Poll 2019, the LDF took a strategic retreat in the Sabarimala Women's Entry issue. The civic polls held in November 2020 was the testing ground for this strategy and the Left made huge gains out of it. The more accommodative stand cured the hurt feeling of majority communities and the reading of the assembly poll results makes it clear that the LDF could win the sizeable number of Hindu votes along with minority votes that had mobilized through strong stands taken during issues such as beef ban and Citizen's Amendment Act etc.
3. Though the BJP projected themselves as a challenge to the state's bipolar polity, the party miserably failed even to retain its lone seat. Despite working out a Nair-Ezhava binary and securing confidence of a section of Christian community, the party could not hold on. Multiple factors led to poor performance of the party. Generally, the BJP or NDA was unable to match the social base of either the CPI (M) or the Congress. The poll results was nothing but a total washout of the BJP and NDA from the state of Kerala.
4. The NDA's vote share in the state had climbed from 6.6 per cent in 2011 Assembly polls to 14.96 per cent in 2016 after BDJS joined its fold. However, its vote share declined to 12.04 per cent in 2021. The vote share of BDJS declined from 3.93 per cent in 2016 to 1 per cent in 2021. It seems that a sizeable section of Ezhava voters who were with the Left parties before the formation of BDJS have now returned to their mother fold.
5. This electoral predict can also be treated as a reply to the critics of the CM within the party and Left Front who were baiting for his blood after the 2019 Lok Sabha poll setback. It has come as a major morale booster from both CPM and CPI which have

been reduced to a mere patch in the national political scenario, but also gives hope of a re-emergence.

6. In conclusion it can be stated that Pinarayi Vijayan broke a long term jinx that prevented any incumbent from retaining power beyond a single term in the state. The state-wise picture shows that the LDF was triumphant in both southern and central regions of the state but came a bit short in the northern region. Before conclude it can be added that no doubt the second Pinarayi government will have to deal with a series of challenges from the day of its entry. The worsening COVID situation, the unpleasant fiscal position of the state and above all the group rivalry within the CPI (M) will certainly pose threat to the Chief Minister.

REFERENCES

Abhilash Chandran, "Make-or-break battle for Kerala Congress factions", *The New Indian Express*, Kollam, 6th April, 2021.

Abhilash, C., "Captain's Defeat Dampens KC (M) Triumph", *The New Indian Express*, 3rd May, 2021.

Ajay Kanth, "SDPI and welfare party may dent vote share of LDF, UDF this time too". *The New Indian Express*, Kollam, 3rd April, 2021.

Ajith Kumar, P.K., "Silver screen stardust in focus this poll season", *The Hindu*, 19th March, 2021.

Amiya Methal, "For polls, women not in men's League", *The New Indian Express*, Kollam, 2nd March, 2021.

Anandan, S., "Central Kerala takes center stage in polls", *The Hindu*, 28th March, 2021.

Anandan, S., "Warhorses Forced to Face New Equations", *The Hindu*, 3rd May, 2021.

Anand, G., "BJP hopes to unsettle LDF, UDF Calculations", *The Hindu*, 8th April, 2021.

Anand, G, "Stormy campaign season ends, now it's for the people to decide", *The Hindu*, 5th April, 2021.

Anand, G., "Surprise Wins, Unexpected Losses in South Kerala", *The Hindu*, 3rd May, 2021.

Anand Kochukudi, "In Kerala, the Church is a crucial political player", *The Hindu*, 6th April, 2021.

Anil Radhakrishnan, S., "80.53 per cent turnout of 1987 Assembly election, Yet to be surpassed", *The Hindu*, 7th April, 2021.

Anil, S., "Joy Heartbreak and Soul Searching", *The New Indian Express*, 3rd May, 2021.

Biju, Govind, "A Repeat of the Familiar Pattern for the LDF", *The Hindu*, 3rd May, 2021.

Biju, Govind, "A young blood up against battle-hardened veterans", *The Hindu*, 19th March, 2021.

Biju, Govind, "Change or continuity? Kerala plays it close", *The Hindu*, 3rd April, 2021.

Biju, Govind, "Good Strategy, Rainbow Coalition Helped LDF", *The Hindu*, 3rd May, 2021.

Biju, Govind, "Rising BJP vote share to mar UDF prospects", *The Hindu*, 5th April, 2021.

Chandran, C., "Sabarimala, back in focus, UDF sharpens attack on left front", *The New Indian Express*, Kollam, 19th March, 2021.

Express News Service, "Alleging pact with Welfare Party, CPM keen to deal UDF a blow", *The New Indian Express*, Kollam, 24th March, 2021.

Express News Service, "Massive shift of Nair, Ezhava votes base fuels saffron surge in state", *The New Indian Express*, Kollam, 23rd March, 2021.

Jayakumar, K., "Alarming notes from electoral battle ground", *The New Indian Express*, Kollam, 9th April, 2021.

Jayanth, A.S., "When parties bank on serving and former MPs", *The Hindu*, 17th March, 2021.

Meera, K.R., "Victory for a CM Who Redefined Governance", *The New Indian Express*, 3rd May, 2021.

Mohamed Nazeer, "In Kerala, A Battle Over the Elusive Fruit of Continuity", *The Hindu*, 4th April, 2021.

Navamy, Sudheesh, "Glass ceiling limits women's political foray", *The Hindu*, 18th March, 2021.

Oomman, M.A., "Still no recognition of the third tier", *The Hindu*, 1st April, 2021.

Prabhash, J., "Throw away politics or end of politics", *The New Indian Express*, Kollam, 18th March, 2021.

Pulapre, Balakrishnan, "The absent programme at the Kerala hustings", *The Hindu*, 24th March, 2021.

Raj Kaleeswaram, "Elections as a Constitutional Reminder", *The New Indian Express*, Kollam, 20th March, 2021.

Rajan Gurukkal, "Politics apart, troubles aplenty for Kerala", *The Hindu*, 12th March, 2021.

Shelley Walia, "Reinventing radical politics, by looking left", *The Hindu*, 16th March, 2021.

Shibu, B.S., "Social media wings keep fight alive in cyberspace", *The New Indian Express*, Kollam, 19th March, 2021.

Sovi Vidyadharan, "BJP Out for a Duck", *The New Indian Express*, 3rd May, 2021.

Sovi Vidyadharan, "Muraleedharan BJP's Nemesis in Nemom, *The New Indian Express*, 4th May, 2021.

Sovi Vidyadharan, "Vote Erosion Leaves Saffron Camp Worried", *The New Indian Express,* 4th May, 2021.

Sreejan, "For LDF, A Win Cutting Across Barriers", *The New Indian Express,* 5th May, 2021.

Sreejan, "Keep Left, Stay Safe", *The New Indian Express*, 3rd May, 2021.

Sudhi, K.S., "LDF confident of 1977 repeat; UDF faces leadership hitch", *The Hindu,* 13th March, 2021.

The Editorial, *The Hindu*, "Clear and Distinct", 3rd May, 2021.

The Hindu, "Kerala Assembly poll on April 6", 27th February, 2021.

The Hindu, "LDF Manifesto balances growth, social welfare", 20th March, 2021.

The Hindu, "LDF Manifesto targets low income families", 25th March, 2021.

The Hindu, Thiruvananthapuram, "Kerala Triangle", Editorial, 16th March, 2021.

The Hindu, "UDF promises Rs. 6,000 a month for the poor", 21st March, 2021.

The New Indian Express, Kollam, "Good score, Kerala!", 7th April, 2021.

The New Indian Express, Kollam, "Minority votes hold key in deciding majority", 23rd March, 2021.

The New Indian Express, Kollam, "Stand of between Left front & NSS deepens over Sabarimala issue", 25th March, 2021.

The New Indian Express, Kollam, "UDF does an encore: welfare paramount", 21st March, 2021.

"The Return of the Left", *The Hindu*, 3rd May, 2021.

24

Determinants of Voting Behaviour of People in Indian Political System

A Literature Review

K. V. Manjunatha

Introduction

Elections are an essential component of any democratic society and are the conventional means by which a population selects individuals to represent them politically (Guo, Q., 2020; N. Ismail, 2018). Generally, citizens participate in the election process to express their voice as well as their right to elect officials to represent them in a government (He, B., 2006). In addition, through election, citizens as voters can choose their representatives in conditions of openness, equality and transparency that simulate political competition (Kleinen Von Königslöw, K., 2016). Voting as means for expression his/ her approval or disapproval of governmental decision, policies and programmes of various political parties and the candidates who are engaged in the struggle to get the status of being the representatives of people (Antunes, R., 2010). In other way voting refers to the function of election representatives by casting votes in elections (Singh, S., 2020). According to Samuel S. Elderveld voting behaviour is not new term. It is not confined to the examination of voting statics, records and computation of electoral shifts and swing. It also involves an analysis of individual psychological process like perception, emotion, and motivation and their relation to political action as well as of institutional patterns, such as the communication process and their impact on election (Abdullah, M., 2020).

The choices of voters in election are affected by various factors, especially social-group identity, which helps to forge enduring partisan identification (Khan, M.S., 2015). In addition, voters are influenced more by short-term factors such as issues, campaign events and candidate's appeal (Nizah *et al.,* 2016). Voting is the main form of political participation in liberal democratic societies and the study of voting behaviour is a highly specialized sub-field within political science (Hossain, 2017). The analysis of voting patterns invariably focuses on the determinants of why people vote as they do and how they arrive at the decisions they make (Noor Hamid Khan Mahsud, 2020). Sociologists tend to look to the socio-economic determinants of support for political parties, observing the correlations between class, ethnicity, sex, and age and vote; political scientists have concentrated on the influence of political factors such as issues, political programmes, electoral campaigns, and the popularity of party leaders on voting behaviour (Amila, S.E., 2020). However, both disciplines share much the same terrain, and increasingly tend to overlap in their analytical approaches. Voters have a special significance in electing their representatives (Hazarika, B., 2015). There are more than 90 crore voters in India's democratic structure. They have a right to cast their votes in election. About voters and their voting, Rojanthal says, "When India votes, the whole world votes." There are more voters in India than voters in America, England, France, Japan, Brazil, Canada, Germany, Denmark, Sweden and Bangladesh. Moreover, voters belong to different castes, communities and creeds in India. This diversity has great impact on the political system, political culture and political developments in the vast democracy of India (Adams, 2015). The election process exhibits voting behaviour of Indian voters (Ashok Kumar, 2015). This chapter is descriptive in nature. The information used in it have collected from secondary sources. Necessary secondary data is collected through literature review from journals, reference books and research articles.

Literature Review

Determinants of Voting Behaviour

Voting pattern in India is the greatest democracy compared to other countries. Every citizen of 18 years or more than that age have the right to vote in Indian elections (Onder, M., 2017). Most of them are or half of them are illiterates, they have in the past acted wisely and in a mature way to elect their representatives. They have already participated in several elections to Lok Sabha, state legislative assemblies and a large number of bi-elections. At the first general elections in India in 1952, some election studies were conducted. In the beginning, these studies lack methodological rigour and sophistication. However, with the increased use of the survey method and observation technique has improved the quality of election studies in India. Indian electoral studies are mainly inspired by Western research on voting behaviour, particularly in the United States, Colombia, and Michigan. Scholars at Columbia University in New York highlighted the impact of social and environmental forces on voter choice.

Voting Behaviour in India and its Determinants

In India following are main political and socio-economic factors which act as determinants of voting behaviours in our Democratic system.

Local Issues

Local issues always influence the choice of the voters. A regional or a local party always tries to identify itself with local issues and thereby secures for itself popular local support (Porta, B., 2015). The success of the Jharkhand Mukti Morcha in Jharkhand region of Bihar is a classic example which highlights the role of local issues as determinants of voting behaviour. The spectacular success of the Telugu Desam Party in Andhra Pradesh in the 1999 Lok Sabha and Andhra Vidhan Sabha elections was largely determined by its image as a local party identified with the local interests of the state and having a good support with the Centre. All regional parties try to win elections on local issues. In fact, all agencies of public opinion always act as determinants of voting behaviour (Seran, G.G., 2018).

Election Campaigns

Each party launches a vigorous campaign for influencing the voters in its favour. Use of such means as mass meetings, street meetings, personal contacts, posters, poster war, speeches by film stars, T.V and radio broadcasts, Newspaper advertisements, hand bills, processions and propaganda are made to win votes, particularly the floating votes during the election campaigns (Ojekwe, G.I., 2016). The election campaigns are designed to make a voter believe that his interest can be best served by the party/the candidate of the party contesting from his constituency. Thus acts as an important determinant of voting behaviour (Beyer, A., 2014).

Current Events

The current problems and difficulties faced by the people as well as recent political developments or the poll eve developments also act as determinants of voting behaviour (Pradesh, M., Gwalior, 2017). The political and economic events of the election year also act as determining factors (Nasser, A.N., 2013). The price rise, shortages and other economic hardships faced by the people during 1966-67 helped several Political parties in considerably reducing the popularity of the Congress with the masses. In 1967, the Congress, though it retained its majority at the Centre, suffered a loss of popularity which was reflected in its poor performance in the elections to the Legislative Assemblies. However, the victory in the 1971 Indo-Pak war turned the tide in favour of the Congress in the elections that followed. In 1984, the assassination of Mrs. Gandhi created a huge sympathy wave in favour of the Congress(I) and its leader Mr. Rajiv Gandhi in1991, the assassination of Mr. Rajiv Gandhi on 21st May, stemmed the swing away to a low swing in favour of the Congress(I).

Money Factor

The role of money cannot be ignored in the study of electoral behaviour. Though India is a poor country, crores of rupees are spent in election (Muhtadi, B., 2019). In the present political and economic context, the conduct of election and the electioneering campaign led by candidates and political parties have tended to be costly (King, G.,

Rosen, O., 2008). While the 1952 elections to parliament and the state legislatures cost Rs. 10.50 crore, the 1980 elections to the Lok Sabha alone cost about Rs. 52 crore, notwithstanding all the economic measures taken to keep the costs down. It must be stressed here that this is a conservative estimate based perhaps on the returns filed by the candidates to the Election Commission. These incurred certainly with the present system of conducting elections, the costs will escalate at least in proportion to the rise in the cost of living. Moreover, in spite of specifying a ceiling on expenditure that a candidate can make in his election, the amendment in the Representation of the People Act of 1974 has laid down that the amount spent by a party shall not be taken as an expenditure made by the candidate. The role of money in the politics of our country should, however, be discovered in the politics of political funding. It finds place in the world of big industrialists and capitalists to various political parties, particularly the Congress Party.

Religion

The establishment of a secular state in India by guaranteeing the right to freedom of religion to everyone, treating every religion as equal and non-recognition of any religion as a state religion—has not been successful in preventing the role of the religion as a determinant of political behaviour in general and voting behaviour in particular (Gul Said, 2021). The existence of such political parties and non-political groups as stand linked with a particular religion, for example, the Muslim League, the Akali Dal, the Hindu Maha Sabha, the Shiv Sena etc. has been one of the reasons behind the continued role of religion as a determinant of voting behaviour (Iyer, S., 2018). Religious pluralism of the Indian society is a major feature of the environment of the Indian political system and it greatly influences the struggle for power among political parties. The selection of candidates is done with an eye upon the presence of a religious majority in a particular constituency. In Karnataka, there is a demand that Kannada alone should be the medium of instructions in schools, but it is being opposed by other ethnic groups. Such problems are presenting in almost all the states since people have emotional attachment with their languages, they easily get influenced whenever there comes up any issue relating to language. Linguistic interest always influences voting behaviour.

Social Group

When members of a particular social group (e.g. racial, economic, gender, or age) identify especially strongly with that group, those people develop a group consciousness that appears to increase turnout (Ben-Bassat, A., 2012). People who say that their lives are intrinsically tied to other members of their social group (especially if that group is disadvantaged) appear to change their political behaviour accordingly and increase their turnout. People with high solidarity could have higher motivation to vote because they are concerned with issues affecting their group, or their strong connection to members of that group could give them skills that better enable them to vote (Kopiva, R. & Varvažovská, P., 2011). The social and psychological forces that inspired voting the first time may have enhanced impact directing future voting decisions. After being successfully mobilized to vote once, a citizen may attract repeated mobilization efforts at the times of subsequent elections. Voting may be self-reinforcing, meaning that the social and psychic rewards one enjoys after voting once may be memorable and motivating at the times of subsequent elections. And the act could change a person's self-perception into one of an active, civically engaged individual, and by voting once, a voter might realize the ease of doing it and may, therefore, be less inhibited from doing it again.

High-profile Events

High-profile events might impact elections, but personal tragedies and investments also impact voter decision (Healy, A.J., 2010). Because traumatic events and natural disaster certainly leads to strong emotional reactions is fear (Suna, J.M., 2013). People tend to vote for the candidates who they feel best protect their freedoms. Appeals to voter fear are, therefore, common method of swinging voter's opinion during election. Some researches shows that fear might be the most effective way of cultivating electorates.

Social Pressure

Social pressure has been found to be a major influence on people's decision to vote. Voting is sign of our membership in larger group.

People are often motivated to vote because they want to suitable in. This social pressure comes from many sources, most notably parents, friends, and romantic partners (Panagopoulos, C., 2010). Our social environment and events indirectly influence voting behaviour by heightening emotion and drawing attention to specific issues (Rogers, T., 2017).

Trust and Belief

Trust and Belief also influence behaviours of voters because people who are especially trusting of others are more likely to vote. Perhaps distrustful people think of the political system as corrupt, which might sap their motivation to participate (Turska Kawa, A., 2013). But low levels of interpersonal trust might also sometimes inspire higher turnout if lack of trust motivates people to take action to minimize the damage they might fear others might inflict. People who feel a personal sense of civic duty believe they have a moral obligation to participate in politics and are especially likely to vote in elections. Similarly, people who believe that all citizens have the obligation to vote go to the polls more than those who do not hold this belief (Oostveen, A.M., 2015). Presumably, civic duty is a source of motivation to turnout. Citizens who have a great sense of political efficacy turnout more. This is true for both internal efficacy, the belief in one's capability to understand and participate in politics) and external efficacy, the belief in the responsiveness of political institutions to citizen involvement; The higher an individual's efficacy, the more motivated he or she presumably is to cast a ballot.

Motivational Factors

The behaviour of voters is influenced by motivational factors. The more motivation or ability a person has to vote, the more likely he or she is to turnout on a given election day (Glasford, Demis, 2008). Thus, a citizen's turnout behaviour is likely to be a joint, multiplicative function of these three classes of causes, so pointing to a single factor as causing a person's turnout or lack of turnout would be a vast oversimplification. The multiplicative feature of this equation means that high motivation or high ability or low difficulty is not sufficient to ensure turnout deficit in any area may be sufficient to undermine a person's turnout.

Motivation to vote could come from a strong preference for one candidate over his or her competitor. But motivation can also come from the belief that being a responsible citizen requires that a person votes from pressure from one's friends or family to vote, or from other sources that we outline below (Gerber, A.S., 2009).

Public Esteem of the Candidate

A candidate's report with the people with a constituency or his known qualities or contribution in any value spread of activity always acts as a factor of voting behaviour (Guo, Q., 2020). In addition to his party loyalty or opinion on various issues and problems, the voter, while making his choice, always takes into account the nature and level of his association with the candidate (Spenkuch, J.L., 2018). A positive image of a party's candidate is a source of popular support for the party. A voter prefers to vote for a candidate who is approachable and who can help him anyway (Hultman, M., 2019).

Factionalism

The Indian political life from the village level to the national level is characterized by factionalism. Neither political party nor even the cadre-based BJP and the two communist parties is free from factionalism (Hazarika, B., 2015). It is at work, as Rajni Kothari points out, at all level of the Congress. It has adversely affected the strength of the Congress is a political party with a glorious past, a weak present and not a bright future. Other parties are also suffering from factionalism. The voters are getting disappointed with some of the political parties because of their inability to overcome factionalism (Basedau, M., 2011). They are moving to regional parties which, because of their small organizational network and limited operational base are relatively less affected by factionalism.

Mass Literacy

Mass Literacy has been another determinant of voting behaviours in India (Rozenas, A., 2018). Due to this weakness of the people that political parties, communal groups, and militant outfits, are in a position to exploit the sentiments of the people in the name of caste, religion, region and another such factor (Bhavnani, R.R., 2019). The votes of the illiterate constitute a big proportion of the votes polled and hence it plays a big role in determining the outcomes of elections (Agomor, K., 2014). However, despite this fact, the common sense and maturity borne out of the past experience have also been playing a big role in influencing the voters' mind and actions.

Performance of the Party in Power

Each political party contests elections on the basis of an election manifesto, and after coming to power, it is expected to fulfil the promises made therein. Good or bad performance of the ruling party, just on the basis of the election promises made and promises actually fulfilled influence the basic behaviour of the people in a big way (Singh, A.K., 2020). The main reason for this is a corresponding increase in the number of "floating voter" or "switchers" who are mostly young citizens from an educated upper middle class and are ready to transfer their support from one to another party on the basis of their performance (Carney, K., 2022).

Influence of Money

India is a poor country with a large number of people living below the poverty line. Money as such plays a crucial role in determining the behaviour of voters in India (Cruz, C., 2015). A rich candidate or party has more chances of winning the elections always. At the time of elections, the poor are allured by the glitter of the money and their votes are purchased (Mitra, A., 2021). In this way, the process of 'give a note and take vote' goes on in India.

Language

India is a multi-lingual state. The language also serves as a factor in voting behaviour. The organization of states on a linguistic basis fully reflects the importance of language as a factor of politics in India (Cáceres Miranda, 2020). There have been problems in states like that of the status of one particular language in that state, or relating to the quality of the status of a language of a state (Akhter, Z., 2018). Since people have an emotional attachment with their languages, they easily get influenced whenever there comes up any issue relating to language.

Party Loyalty

In India, many of the people are attached to their different political parties and they always cast their vote in favour of the party rather than the candidate (Young, D.J., 2007). We cannot change their party loyalty even when they know that their candidate would not be going to win, such voters are known as committed voters (Biswas, A., 2014).

Personal Contacts

Personal contacts of the candidate and voters also affect the voting behaviour of the voters. Most of the voters get influenced by personal visits of the candidate and they cast their vote in their favour. Besides this, the relatives and friends of the candidate also cast their votes in favour of them because of their personal relationship (Ohman, M., 2015).

Populist Slogans

Sometimes different political parties raise the populist slogans according to the need of the time and affect the thinking of the voters (Rahul, V., 2017). For example, Congress raised the slogan of, 'Garibi Hatao' in 1971. During the 16th Lok Sabha election the slogans like 'Aabki bar Modi sarkar'.

Ideological Commitment

The ideological commitment of the voters also affects the voting behaviour, most of the voters are crazy about particular ideology and they keep in view the ideology of the candidate and the political party at the time of casting their votes (Mader, M., 2017). This fact is applicable to the voters who are the supporter of the Leftist parties.

Caste

Caste continues to be a determining factor in voting behaviour in India. It has deep roots in society and constitutes an important basis for social relations at all levels (Akhter, Z., 2018). Despite the adoption of various provisions that prohibit action and discrimination on the basis, the caste continues to be a determining factor in political behaviour. The politicization of caste and casteism in politics has been a well-known reality of the Indian political system (Usman, A., 2017). The political parties in India, without exception, in formulating their policies, programmes and electoral strategies always keep the caste factor in mind. Rural voters pay special attention to the caste of the candidate. Despite the adoption of democratic values that conceive a society free from casteism, the caste continues to characterize politics in India (Devi, Y.S., 2021).

Charisma

One important factor of voting behaviour is Charisma. It means the exceptional quality of a factor and overrides group elements leader that becomes a source of attraction and reverence for the people in large numbers in an opposite sense. It also means a source of fear to many people because they do not speak or dare to speak against the wishes of a powerful leader (Takens, J., 2015). Fortunately, in our country, the constructive aspect of charisma has had its role at the time of the election. The enormous participation in the meetings faced by imposing personalities such as Nehru, Indira, Vajpayee, Modi and a sudden change in the minds of the voters in response to the appeals launched by such great figures can be considered concrete proofs of the role of the charisma in the electoral behaviour of our people (Williams, E.A., 2009). The slogan of "Garibi Hatao" performed miracles in the 1971 elections, the personality of Mrs. Gandhi after India's miraculous victory in the Bangladesh war had the same wonderful impact on the mind of the electorate in the State Assembly elections of 1972. The image of Jayaprakash Narayan had the same effect in the elections of 1977. Due to personality of Modi, BJP won the election of 2014.

Education

It is often seen that the educated people take more interest in casting their vote as compared to the illiterates because they know the importance of their right to vote and consider the use of this right a national duty (Hansen, E.R., 2021). They know that they can elect the government of their choice by executing their right to vote. Thus, education affects the voting behaviour of person and with the spread of education the ratio of the use of franchise is also increasing and during the election of the 16th Lok Sabha, the percentage of voting had gone up to 66.38 per cent which was quite high in comparison to previous elections.

Conclusion

These are thus the important determinants of voting behaviour in India. The continuity in the operation of India's political system as a developing democratic political system is gradually training the Indian voters. The process of emergence of an issue based political struggle in place of a caste or religion or personality dominated struggle for power is very slowly but gradually taking shape. Elections occupy a prominent place in the democratic government. It is a means through which people express and enforce their political opinion and regulate political organization of the society. However, the behaviour of a voter is influence by several factors such as religion, caste, community, language, money, policy or ideology, purpose of the polls, extent of franchise and the like political parties and groups make use of these variables for the sake of winning the battle of the ballot box. It is therefore, imperative that the use of these determinants should be avoided and elections should be conducted in a very free and fair manner. It also depends upon whether the system allows freedom of thought, expression and association to the people. Mere presence of an electoral system does not make a political system democratic. The will of people is expressed through voting in elections and therefore, all undemocratic and unfair means like manipulating and rigging need to be avoided in the elections. No such action is taken which would in any way undermine the popular will expressed through elections.

REFERENCES

Abdullah, M., Hakam, K.A., Wilodati, W., & Ratnafitria, R. (2020). *Analysis of Vote Behavior in Election (Psychological Study of Election Behavior on the Young Generation).* 400 (Icream 2019), 147-150. https//doi.org/10.2991/assehr.k.200130.158

Adams, S. & Agomor, K.S. (2015). "Democratic politics and voting behaviour in Ghana". *International Area Studies Review, 18*(4), 365-381. https//doi.org/10.1177/2233865915587865

Agomor, K. & Adams, S. (2014). "Determinants of Voting Behaviour in Ghana". *Global Awareness Society International 23rd Annual Conference, 4*(May), 1-12. http//organizations.bloomu.edu/gasi/

Akhter, Z. & Ah., S.Y. (2018). "Theoretical Perspective of Voting Behaviour in India/Approaches and Determinants". *Public Policy and Administration Research*, 5(12), 104-109.

Amila, S.E. (2020). *A Study of Factors that Influenced Voters' Behaviour A Case of Billiri Local Government (2019 General Elections).* November 2019.

Antunes, R. (2010). "Theoretical models of voting behaviour". *Exedra, 4* (January 2010), 145-170.

Basedau, M. & Köllner, P. (2011). "Factionalism in Political Parties: An Analytical Framework for Comparative Studies". *SSRN Electronic Journal*, January 2018. https//doi.org/10.2139/ssrn.909172

Ben-Bassat, A. & Dahan, M. (2012). "Social identity and voting behaviour". *Public Choice, 151*(1-2), 193-214. https//doi.org/10.1007/s11127-010-9742-2

Beyer, A., Knutsen, C.H. & Rasch, B.E. (2014). "Election campaigns, issue focus and voting intentions: Survey experiments of Norwegian voters". *Scandinavian Political Studies, 37*(4), 406-427. https//doi.org/10.1111/1467-9477.12029

Bhavnani, R.R. & Jensenius, F.R. (2019). "Voting for development? Ruling coalitions and literacy in India". *Electoral Studies, 62* (August 2019), 102069. https//doi.org/10.1016/j.electstud.2019.102069

Biswas, A., Ingle, N., & Roy, M. (2014). Influence of social media on voting behaviour. *Journal of Power, Politics & Governance, 2*(2), 127-155.

Cáceres Miranda, A. & Florez niño, Y. (2020). View metadata, citation and similar papers at core.ac.uk. *Pengaruh Penggunaan Pasta Labu Kuning (Cucurbita Moschata) Untuk Substitusi Tepung Terigu Dengan Penambahan Tepung Angkak Dalam Pembuatan Mie Kering*, 274-282.

Carney, K. (2022). *The Effect of Social Media on Voters' Experimental Evidence from an Indian Election.* 1-44.

Cruz, C., Keefer, P. & Labonne, J. (2015). *Incumbent Advantage, Voter Information and Vote Buying*. July.

Devi, Y.S. (2021). "A Study on Voting Behaviour Among Voters of Thongju Assembly Constituency in Manipur", *International Journal of Multidisciplinary Management Studies. 11*(02), 24-36.

Gerber, A.S. & Rogers, T. (2009). "Descriptive social norms and motivation to vote Everybody's voting and so should you". *Journal of Politics, 71*(1), 178-191. https//doi.org/10.1017/S0022381608090117

Glasford, Demis. (2008). "Predicting Voting Behavior of Young Adults: The Importance of Information, Motivation, and Behavioral Skills". *Journal of Applied Social Psychology. 38.* 2648-2672. 10.1111/j.1559-1816.2008.00408.x.

Gul Said, M., Ur Rahman, A. & Yousufi, M. (2021). "The Impact of Religion on Voting Behavior". *Humanities & Social Sciences Reviews, 9*(2), 14-24. https//doi.org/10.18510/hssr.2021.922

Guo, Q. (2020). "The Relationship between Voting Behavior and Election Commitment: A Literature Review". *Open Journal of Social Sciences, 8,* 201-210. doi 10.4236/jss.2020.82016.

Hansen, E.R. & Tyner, A. (2021). "Educational Attainment and Social Norms of Voting". *Political Behavior, 43*(2), 711-735. https//doi.org/10.1007/s11109-019-09571-8

Hazarika, B. (2015). "Voting Behaviour in India and Its Determinants". IOSR *Journal of Humanities and Social Science,* Ver. IV, *20*(10), 22-25. www.iosrjournals.org

Healy, A.J., Malhotra, N. & Mo, C.H. (2010). "Irrelevant events affect voters' evaluations of government performance". *Proceedings of the National Academy of Sciences of the United States of America, 107*(29), 12804-12809. https//doi.org/10.1073/pnas.1007420107

Hultman, M., Ulusoy, S. & Oghazi, P. (2019). "Drivers and outcomes of political candidate image creation: The role of social media marketing". *Psychology and Marketing, 36*(12), 1226-1236. https//doi.org/10.1002/mar.21271

Iyer, S. & Shrivastava, A. (2018). "Religious riots and electoral politics in India". *Journal of Development Economics, 131*(9522), 104-122. https//doi.org/10.1016/j.jdeveco.2017.11.003

Khan, M.S., Phil, F.J.M., Khan, R. & Phil, R.A.M. (2015). *The Impact of Violence on the Voting Behavior: A Critical View. 5*(1).

King, G., Rosen, O., Tanner, M. & Wagner, A.F. (2008). "Ordinary economic voting behavior in the extraordinary election of Adolf Hitler". *Journal of Economic History, 68*(4), 951-996. https//doi.org/10.1017/S0022050708000788

Kleinen Von Königslöw, K. (2016). "Voting Behavior and Communication". *The International Encyclopedia of Political Communication,* January, 1-12. https//doi.org/10.1002/9781118541555.wbiepc228

Kopiva, R. & Varvažovská, P. (2011). "Social structural model and voting behaviour under the conditions of Czech rural areas". *Agris On-Line Papers in Economics and Informatics, 3*(3), 45-52.

Law, W. & Flavin, P. (2019). *Issue Importance and Voting Behavior.* October. https//orcid.org/0000-0001-9408-7001

Mader, M. & Schoen, H. (2017). "Ideological voting in context: The case of Germany during the Merkel era". *Voters and Voting in Context Multiple*

Contexts and the Heterogeneous German Electorate, September, 209-229. https//doi.org/10.1093/oso/9780198792130.003.0011

Mitra, A. & Mitra, S. (2021). "Cash for Votes Evidence from India". *SSRN Electronic Journal, 2016*(June). https//doi.org/10.2139/ssrn.3987965

Muhtadi, B. (2019). "Vote Buying in Indonesia". In *Vote Buying in Indonesia* (Issue May 2019). https//doi.org/10.1007/978-981-13-6779-3

Nasser, A.N. (2013). "Media effects on voting behaviour". *European Scientific Journal, 9*(20), 1-11.

Noor Hamid Khan Mahsud & Husnul Amin. (2020). "Theoretical Approaches to the Study of Voting Behaviour: A Comparative Analysis". *SJESR, 3*(3), 65-73. https//doi.org/10.36902/sjesr-vol3-iss3-2020(65-73)

Ohman, M. (2015). "Entendendo o sistema de financiamento político". In *Financiamento de partidos políticos e campanhas eleitorais um manual sobre financiamento político*. http//www.idea.int/publications/funding-of-political-parties-and-election-campaigns/loader.cfm?csModule=security/getfile&pageID=64347

Ojekwe, G.I. (2016). "Political advert campaigns and voting behaviour Akinwunmi Ambode's 2015 Election Campaign in Lagos State". *Journal of African Elections, 15*(2), 13-27. https//doi.org/10.20940/jae/2016/v15i2a1

Onder, M. & Karabulut, N. (2017). "A Research About the Youngs" Voting Behavior in Local Elections: The Case of 2009, Ankara Metropolitan Municipality Election". *Republic of Turkey Ministry of Youth and Sport, 5*(12), 69-88.

Oostveen, A.M. & Van Den Besselaar, P. (2005). "Trust, identity, and the effects of voting technologies on voting behaviour". *Social Science Computer Review, 23*(3), 304-311. https//doi.org/10.1177/0894439305275852

Panagopoulos, C. (2010). "Affect, Social Pressure and Prosocial Motivation Field: Experimental Evidence of the Mobilizing Effects of Pride, Shame and Publicizing Voting Behaviour". *Political Behavior, 32*(3), 369-386. https//doi.org/10.1007/s11109-010-9114-0

Porta, B. (2015). *Issues, party strategies and voter behaviour: A Dynamic Approach.*

Pradesh, M. Gwalior, O.F. (2017). *Impact of Social Media on Voter's Behaviour—A Descriptive Study of Gwalior, Impact of Social Media on Voter's Behaviour—A Descriptive Study of Gwalior, Madhya Pradesh [5-8] Impact of Social Media on Voter's Behaviour—A Descriptive Study*. December 2016. https//doi.org/10.13140/RG.2.2.29416.26880

Rahul, V. & Shreyas, S. (2014). "Does Media Exposure Affect Voting Behaviour and Political Preferences in India?" *Economic and Political Weekly, 49*(39), 82-88. http//www.epw.in/national-election-study-2014/does-media-exposure-affect-voting-behaviour-and-political-preferences-i

Rogers, T., Green, D.P., Ternovski, J. & Ferrerosa Young, C. (2017). "Social pressure and voting: A field experiment conducted in a high-salience election". *Electoral Studies, 46*, 87-100. https//doi.org/10.1016/j.electstud.2017.02.004

Rozenas, A., & Sadanandan, A. (2018). "Literacy, Information, and Party System Fragmentation in India". *Comparative Political Studies*, *51*(5), 555-586. https//doi.org/10.1177/0010414017710262

Seran, G.G. (2018). *Identifying the Voting Behavior and Its Determinants: A Case of the 2015 Local Executive Election in Malaka Regency, East Nusa Tenggara, Indonesia*. *4531*(3), 12-22.

Singh, S. (2020). *The role of psychological factors on Voting behavior*, *9*(8), 1-2. https//doi.org/10.35629/7722-0908010102

Spenkuch, J.L. (2018). "Expressive *versus* strategic voters: An empirical assessment". *Journal of Public Economics*, *165*, 73-81. https//doi.org/10.1016/j.jpubeco.2018.06.008

Suna, J.M. (2013). *The Effect of Exercise Training on*. *0*(May), 1-9.

Takens, J., Kleinnijenhuis, J., Van Hoof, A. & Van Atteveldt, W. (2015). "Party Leaders in the Media and Voting Behavior Priming rather than Learning or Projection". *Political Communication*, *32*(2), 249-267. https//doi.org/10.1080/10584609.2014.944319

Turska-Kawa, A. (2013)."Political Trust and Electoral Behaviour". *Polish Political Science Yearbook*, *42*(1), 9-1. https//doi.org/10.15804/ppsy2013007

Usman, A., Hussain, S. & Usman, M. (2017). "Caste and Character of Candidates, Political Patronage and Voting Behaviour in India". *Journal of Indian Studies*, *3*(2), 89-94.

Williams, E.A., Pillai, R., Lowe, K.B., Jung, D. & Herst, D. (2009). "Crisis, charisma, values, and voting behavior in the 2004 presidential election". *Leadership Quarterly*, *20*(2), 70-86. https//doi.org/10.1016/j.leaqua.2009.01.002

Young, D.J. (2007). *Politics without Positions: Party Loyalty and Voting Behaviour in Malawi*, *UCLA*, 1-37.

Index